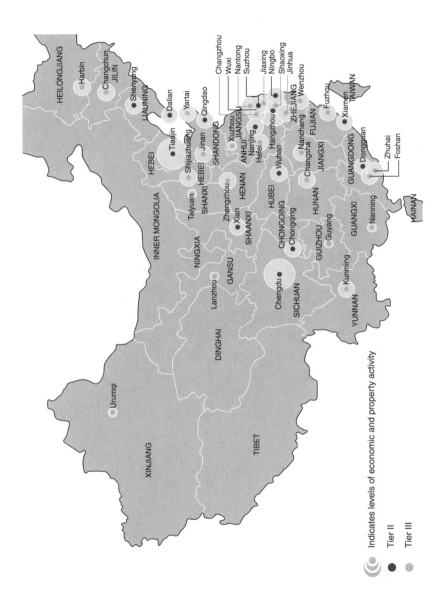

Indicates levels of economic and property activity

Tier II

Tier III

China and Globalization

"There are few books on China that are this coherent."—**Hong Zhang, East Asian Studies, Colby College**

". . . an exceptional accomplishment that will set the standard for works on China for years to come."—**Lisa Keister, Sociology, Ohio State University**

"*China and Globalization* provides a lot of information in a theoretically informed way. The writing style is conversational and argumentative, so it is very good to spur discussion."—**Thomas Gold, Sociology, University of California, Berkeley**

In its quarter-century-long shift from communism to capitalism, China has transformed itself from a desperately poor nation into a country with one of the fastest-growing and largest economies in the world. Doug Guthrie examines the reforms driving the economic genesis in this compact and highly readable introduction to contemporary China. He highlights the social, cultural, and political factors fostering this revolutionary change and interweaves a broad structural analysis with a consideration of social changes at the micro and macro levels.

Cited by *Choice* in April, 2009 as "essential" and as "easily one of the most comprehensive, incisive, and readily intelligible introductions" on post-Mao China for undergraduate students and the general reader, this new edition is completely updated to reflect new developments in China from 2010 and beyond, and many new case studies have been included. The book has also been reformatted with a new and larger page design to make the book even more accessible for undergraduates.

Doug Guthrie is Dean of the School of Business at The George Washington University, USA.

China and Globalization

The Social, Economic, and Political
Transformation of Chinese Society

Third Edition

Doug Guthrie
Dean of the School of Business
The George Washington University

NEW YORK AND LONDON

Third edition published 2012
by Routledge
711 Third Avenue, New York, NY 10017

Simultaneously published in the UK
by Routledge
2 Park Square, Milton Park, Abingdon, Oxon OX14 4RN

Routledge is an imprint of the Taylor & Francis Group, an informa business

First edition published by Routledge 2006
Revised edition published by Routledge 2009

Library of Congress Cataloging in Publication Data
Guthrie, Doug, 1969–
China and globalization / by Doug Guthrie. – Rev. ed.
   p. cm.
Includes bibliographical references and index.
1. China—Economic conditions—2000–   2. China—Economic
conditions—1976–2000.   3. China—Social conditions—2000–
4. China—Social conditions—1976–2000.   5. China—Politics and
government—2002–   6. China—Politics and government—1976–2002.
I. Title.
HC427.95.G87 2008
337.51—dc22

                                                              2008012998

ISBN: 978–0–415–50400–3 (hbk)
ISBN: 978–0–415–50401–0 (pbk)
ISBN: 978–0–203–12145–0 (ebk)

Typeset in Adobe Caslon and Copperplate
by RefineCatch Limited, Bungay, Suffolk, UK

To view full-color versions of the images in this book, please go to the website
www. routledge.com/9780415504010

Printed and bound in the United States of America
by Edwards Brothers, Inc.

DEDICATION

For Mira, Paloma, and Jules

TABLE OF CONTENTS

PREFACE

One of the great ironies of our time is this: today, the largest communist society in the world is also the world's most dynamic and business-friendly capitalist economy. To examine this seemingly paradoxical circumstance, this book analyzes the economic reforms that have been sweeping across China for over three decades. As we view the changes in China through the prism of media representations, political rhetoric, and the many other distortions that have shaped perceptions of the reform process in China, the picture is murky at best. In the chapters that follow, I examine the changes that have actually occurred in China and the forces that have brought about this process of change. As it turns out, China's course of building a market economy can teach the world's capitalist powers a great deal about healthy market economies.

The book is organized around four central points. First, the changes in China have been more dramatic than most people (especially in the United States) realize. The lack of a sudden shift in political structure and economic policy—and the lack of a symbolic moment in which the Chinese government has suddenly broken from the past and embraced western systems and values (like the fall of the Berlin Wall in 1989 or Yeltsin's tank speech in 1991)—has often led observers to underestimate the significance of the social and political reforms that have occurred in China. The reality is that changes in China have been radical and deep, and the view that significant social *and* political reforms have not been pushed forward in China is simply wrong. Second, reforms have been successful in China precisely *because* of state involvement. Contrary to the economic assumptions that have guided many reform prescriptions—that rapid privatization is a necessary ingredient of successful reform—gradualism and state involvement not only works, but it is a superior policy. China has built the world's most dynamic economy through direct state involvement. This argument also extends to current political wrangling in the United States: state involvement in markets is a positive thing, and China is surging ahead in several key sectors precisely because of a healthy balance between state and market.

Third, democracy in China is inevitable. Despite the Chinese leadership's apparent goal of holding political reforms at bay, the process of economic reforms has fundamentally altered the structure of the political system. Reforming the economic realm has radically shaken the foundations of the one-party system. However, the thesis I advance here is not that there is an inevitable link between capitalism and democracy. Rather, it is through the purposive transformation of certain institutions that a gradual process of democratization has been set in motion in China, and although they do not advertise it, many key leaders of the economic reforms have been transforming China politically from within. Finally, the economic reforms in China have been political, cultural, and above all, global processes. Understanding these processes of economic reform tells us much about the role of governments, culture, and globalization in the transition from socialism to capitalism, a transition that many countries across the globe are undergoing in one way or another. It also tells us a great deal about China's future role in the international community of nations. The social consequences of the transition to a market economy in China have been dramatic for the citizens of the most populous nation on Earth, and these changes have implications for how we think about capitalism and the trade-offs between socialism and a market-based economic system. It is also the case, as China emerges as a global leader in the geopolitical system, that we might have much to learn from the ways in which China is using economic interdependence to create leverage in thorny political situations.

This book has two points of departure. First, years ago, as I was finishing *Dragon in a Three-Piece Suit: The Emergence of Capitalism in China* (Guthrie 1999), I was determined to write something that was more accessible to a wider audience. Like many academic books, *Dragon* dealt in a technical way with specific theoretical debates that are central to a field of scholarship—in this case, the field of scholars studying economic reform in China and economic transitions more generally. It seemed to me at the time that, while there are many highly readable firsthand accounts of life in China—Nicholas Kristof and Sheryl Wudun's books, for example, are excellent windows onto the issues individuals face in this rapidly transforming society—we still lacked an account that brought that firsthand experience together with a readable version of the staid academic debates. The field of scholars studying economic and social change in China still lacks a corpus of work that translates the scholarship in this field in the way that Jonathan Spence had made Chinese history readable for a wider audience.

Around the time that I was finishing *Dragon*, I was also developing a course at New York University on the economic reforms in China. That course would eventually draw nearly 400 students per semester—testament, I think, not to my skills as a teacher but to the fervent interest of today's young students in the emergence of China as a global economic superpower. Once again, over years of teaching this course, I was struck with the fact that while the academic literature on Chinese society has dealt in rigorous detail with many of the ideas presented in this book, we lacked a comprehensive overview that rendered the key ideas portrayed in the scholarship on China's economic reforms understandable for a non-specialist audience. My goal in this book is to draw on the academic research, including my own, as well as my own experiences in China, to give a clear and accessible sense of the forces that have reshaped Chinese society over the last thirty years. I would like to thank the roughly 2,000 undergraduate students at NYU who served as the sounding board for the ideas presented in these pages and the hundreds of Chinese executives who shaped the ideas presented here.

In the short time since the first edition of this book was published (2006), the world has changed in dramatic ways. While it used to be somewhat of an extreme position that China was doing a brilliant job in building a robust market economy, today that view is a little less controversial. China's economic decision makers still have their detractors, but there is increasingly a groundswell of interest in understanding deeply what is going on there economically and politically, and that is the primary objective of this book. However, the United States has been seriously humbled in the last three years and, more generally, over the last decade. This began, perhaps, with the accounting crisis of 2000–2001, but even during that crisis, it was believed that, at least in the area of global finance, we were untouchable. The financial crisis of 2008–2009 changed many things. Not only did it shake our confidence in our most hallowed industry; it also contributed to the loss of trillions of dollars of value in the global economy. This third edition of *China and Globalization* also engages the ways in which the world has changed in the last decade and China's changing role within it; it looks at what we might learn from China as a new model of global capitalism.

Parts of this manuscript have emerged from work that has been published previously in various venues, and I would like to acknowledge those publications for the use of copyrighted material. Parts of the book originally appeared in various forms in the following publications: "Information Technology and State Capacity in China," in *Digital Formations: Cooperation and Conflict in a Connected World*, edited by Robert Latham and Saskia Sassen (© Princeton University Press, 2005); "The Quiet Revolution: The Emergence of Capitalism in China," *Harvard International Review* 25(2) (2003): 48–53 (© Harvard University Press, 2003); "Organizational Learning and Productivity: State Structure and Foreign Investment in the Rise of the Chinese Corporation," *Management and Organization Review* 1, no. 2 (2005): 165–95 (© Plenum, 2005); "The Transformation of Labor Relations in China's Emerging Market Economy," *Research in Social Stratification and Mobility* 19 (2002): 137–68 (© Plenum, 2002); "Entrepreneurial Action in the State Sector: The Economic Decisions of Chinese Managers," in *The New Entrepreneurs of Europe and Asia: Patterns of Business Development in Russia, Eastern Europe and China*, edited by Vicki Bonnell and Thomas Gold (© M. E. Sharpe, 2002); "The Great Helmsman's Cultural Death," *Contexts Magazine* 7(2) (© American Sociological Association); "Work and Productivity in Reform-Era China," *Research in the Sociology of Work* 19: 35–73 (©Emerald); "Messy Details: Ownership Networks and New Institutional Forms in Transitions from Plan to Market," in *Small Worlds in Comparative Context*, edited by Bruce Kogut (Cambridge, MA: © MIT Press), "Innovation in the Chinese Mode," *Science* (vol. 333: July 22, 2011); "Multiple Principals, Ownership Concentration and Profitability in China's Publicly Traded Companies," *Management and Organization Review* (© Wiley); and "Inefficient Deregulation and the Global Economic Crisis: The United States and China Compared," *Research in the Sociology of Organizations* 30B: 283–312 (© Emerald).

For help in completing this project, many friends, colleagues, and family members read portions of the manuscript and offered helpful advice along the way; indeed, as this book is the culmination of many years of work research, writing, and talks, I have benefited from more colleagues than I can thank here. However, I would like to offer special thanks to a few people who went above and beyond. My editors at Routledge, David McBride and later Steve Rutter (Revised and Third editions), have been very helpful in shaping the project over the years. Indeed, this book probably would never have been finished without the editorial patience and encouragement it has received along the way. Junmin Wang and John McKiel provided invaluable research support. Niobe Way and Gerald Frug offered extensive comments on early versions of the completed manuscript at a time when I most needed outside perspectives. The Revised and Third editions also benefited from reviews from a number of educators and scholars like Thomas Gold, Zouhair Ghazzal, Jiping Zuo, and several anonymous reviewers. Finally, I would like to thank my family: my parents Kathy, Tim, Joe, and Wanda for all their support throughout my formative years; and Mira, Paloma, and Jules to whom all my work is dedicated. You all support me way more than I deserve and I love you all way more than you know.

Doug Guthrie
Washington, DC, 2011

1

GLOBALIZATION AND THE
ECONOMICS OF RADICAL
CHANGE IN CHINA

A Place of Radical Change

Shanghai, 2011—standing on Shanghai's Bund, overlooking the Huangpu River, one cannot help but see how dramatic the changes have been in China in the last two decades. Especially in the evening. Neon signs light up the night sky; strobe lights dance across the river, as if to announce the arrival of the new city. Nouveau riche couples dining at the swanky restaurants, like M on the Bund, overlook this panorama and enjoy a nightlife scene that might place them in London, New York City, or Paris. Across the river, an entirely new skyline has emerged from virtually nothing: In the early 1990s, when I started doing research on China, Pudong (the area east of the Huangpu River) was an area of fields and old housing projects; today it is a high-tech urban landscape with immaculate and gaudy buildings that touch the sky, including one of the tallest buildings in the world. The scene is eerily reminiscent of a futuristic science fiction movie. These days, when I give talks about China's emergence as a global economic superpower, I often invoke the contrast between what the skyline looks like today and what it looked like eighteen years ago. Those stories seem more and more distant today, but it is still less than two decades ago that Pudong was not even on the map in terms of infrastructure or economic development; today it is emerging as a financial center of Asia if not the world.

Other places in China also show the signs of extreme change. The Beijing skyline lacks the panache of Shanghai's "Bund" (the area along the western side of the Huangpu River), but the changes occurring there are no less dramatic. In Beijing, cranes dot the skyline of the city's sprawling urban landscape; the immaculate architectural feats constructed for the 2008 Olympics are always around the next corner; fast food restaurants and Starbucks stores buttress up against the borders of the Forbidden City and Tiananmen Square; skyscrapers have been built upon the wreckage of Beijing's old urban neighborhood blocks. In western Chinese cities like Chengdu and Chongqing, China's most populous city, signs of urban development are everywhere as well. And in smaller towns in rural areas, new buildings run up against small houses made of straw-and-mud bricks.

The scenes are breathtaking, even to those unfamiliar with urban development and architectural planning. They are also clearly—even to the untrained eye—tied to foreign investment, economic reform, and the complex processes of globalization. Across the Shanghai skyline, for every neon sign advertising a Chinese company, you will also see the logo of a foreign multinational. The Motorola name is as well known as that of the famous Chinese telecommunications company, Huawei; DuPont is among the most well-known names in areas ranging from chemicals to renewable energy; most cabs are made by a joint venture corporation backed by Volkswagen; most luxury cars made by Audi, GM (Buick), and BMW; brands like Coca-Cola, McDonald's, Kentucky Fried Chicken, Pizza Hut, and Starbucks are ubiquitous. At the same time, powerful Chinese domestic multinationals such as Geely, Haier, Lenovo, PetroChina, Huawei and SinoPec are shaking the world with their own economic power.

All of these facts and images are, by now, well known. Indeed, the headlines announcing "China's Century," "The China Challenge," "The China Syndrome," "Buying up the World," "America's Fear of China," "China Goes Shopping," "Can China be Fixed?" and many others, have thundered across the covers of such magazines as *BusinessWeek*, the *Economist*, *Forbes*, *Newsweek*, *U.S. News and World Report*, and many other major publications. However, if the fact of China's emergence as an economic and political superpower today is widely recognized, the processes by which we have arrived at this moment in time are less clear. What global and local processes lie beneath the dramatic transformation we have witnessed over the last quarter century in China? What are the political, economic, and social forces that have shaped the Shanghai, Beijing, and Chengdu skylines? And what impact do competing foreign and Chinese national interests have on the citizens of China and on the rest of the world? The story that lies beneath is one of deep-seated national interests of the world's most populous nation as it *gradually* edges its way down the path of economic reform toward the hallowed land of capitalism; and of foreign investors that seek access to the world's largest single-nation marketplace. It is a story of the forces of globalization, played out locally; a story of the complex political situation that saw a dying Communist regime transform itself, in part, by allowing foreign multinationals to set up shop in China for the first time since the Communist Revolution. Uncovering these forces and trends is the purpose of this book.

The Emergence of China as a World Economic Power

There are many reasons why we should develop an informed understanding of the state of affairs in Chinese society. Not only is China the most populous nation on earth, but it has also, in recent years, stormed onto the world political and economic stages. The country has accomplished in three decades what many developing nations have taken half a century or more to achieve. For the better part of the last 30 years, China has had the fastest growing economy in the world, sustaining impressive double-digit growth for much of the 1980s and 1990s and high single-digit growth for the 2000s. Throughout the 1980s, China's real gross domestic product (GDP) grew at an average annual rate of 10.2 percent, a level that was only equaled by the growth rate in Botswana (and it is much more common for small countries like Botswana to achieve such high growth rates). From 1990 to 1996, the average annual rate of growth for real GDP was 12.3 percent, the highest rate of any country in the world for that period. It has also had the highest industrial growth rate (an amazing 17.3 percent average annual growth from 1990 to 1996) and the second-highest growth in services (9.6 percent per annum, 1990–1996) in the world (World in Figures 1999, 2010). It is an understatement to say that China's economic reforms have been a remarkable and dramatic success. Table 1.1 shows how China compares with the countries that are generally considered to be the top ten economies in the world, according to various economic indicators. Where China was a third-world developing economy three short

Table 1.1 Largest Economies in the World According to Various Economic Indicators

	GDP, $bn (rank)	GDP PPP, $bn (rank)	Largest Industrial output, $bn (rank)	Largest Services output, $bn (rank)	Largest market capitalization, $bn (rank)	Population, mm (rank)
United States	14,093 (1)	14,093 (1)	3,073[a] (1)	10,562[a] (1)	15,077 (1)	309 (3)
Japan	4,911 (2)	4,358 (3)	1,282[a] (3)	3,036[a] (2)	3,378 (3)	128 (10)
Germany	3,649 (4)	2,905 (5)	1,101 (4)	2,517 (3)	1,298 (8)	83 (15)
China	4,327 (3)	7,909 (2)	2,104 (2)	1,734 (6)	5,008 (2)	1,336 (1)
United Kingdom	2,647 (6)	2,178 (7)	634 (5)	2,022 (5)	2,796 (4)	61 (22)
France	2,857[a] (5)	2,122 (8)	584 (8)	2,215 (4)	1,972 (6)	62 (21)
Italy	2,303 (7)	1,872 (10)	622 (7)	1,635 (7)	317 (22)	59 (23)
Spain	1,604 (9)	1,443 (12)	463 (9)	1,096 (8)	1,297 (9)	45 (29)
Russia	1,679 (8)	2,260 (6)	625 (6)	970 (10)	861 (14)	142 (9)
Brazil	1,575 (10)	1,978 (9)	440 (10)	1,029 (9)	1,167 (12)	194 (5)
Canada	1,501 (11)	1,302 (14)	–	–	1,681 (7)	33 (36)
India	1,159 (12)	3,359 (4)	334 (13)	622 (14)	1,179 (11)	1,186 (2)

Source: *Pocket World in Figures* (2011, 14, 24, 46, 47, 68)
[a] Includes overseas departments.

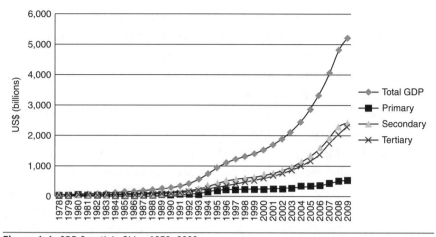

Figure 1.1 GDP Growth in China 1978–2009.

Source: National Statistical Bureau of China (2010, 38).

decades ago, today it has the second-largest economy in the world overall in terms of GDP, and it is second to the United States when GDP is adjusted for purchasing power within the country.[1] To the extent that economic and political power are intimately intertwined, China's sizable role as a political force on the world stage is all but guaranteed. It is no longer a question of whether China is going to play a major role in world economic and political arenas; it is only a question of what role China will play.

The emergence of China as a world economic and political power has serious consequences for the structure of relations in Asia and for the global economy in general. If the twenty-first century will be Asia's century, as many scholars and pundits have predicted, then China is certain to be *the* major player in a region that is sure to play a definitive role in the current century. And this lumbering giant has only begun to flex its political and economic muscle. However, because of its size, China's role in the coming years is almost certain to have greater gravity than would be suggested by simply acknowledging its position as a leader in a pivotal region. Take, for example, food: because of the loss of crop land that comes with rapid industrialization and a still-growing population in China (despite austere family-planning measures), some estimates suggest that China currently cannot produce enough food to feed its citizens. These same estimates suggest that, at current rates of growth, all the excess in the world's grain markets will not meet China's needs by the year 2030.[2] So here we have a country that rose in three decades to be the second-largest economy in the world—a country that could very well cripple international grain markets and have a large starving population before the middle of the twenty-first century. As another example, consider information technology: based on the size of China's population and recent developments in the country's telecommunications sector, China is now the single largest market for Internet and telecommunications use in the entire world. Here again, we have the strange paradox of development in China: as the country struggles with the basic developmental tasks of laying phone lines and building roads, it threatens to be the crucial market in driving the evolution of one of the most important industries in the global economy. Then there is the issue of oil and energy: China's rapid economic development has led to an insatiable thirst for energy and, more specifically, fossil fuels. With its consumption more than doubling over the last five years, China sits behind only the United States as the second-largest consumer of oil in the world.[3] The high demand for oil has contributed to rising rates of oil prices, which have hit record highs in cost per barrel in recent years, a fact that affects American consumers with higher gas prices. Another important, though less understood, issue involves China's influence over the U.S. bond market. China is now the largest foreign holder of U.S. Treasury bonds. People frequently point to the oft-decried trade deficit between the United States and China, but China's rapid purchase of U.S. Treasury bonds in recent years is a much more significant factor in U.S.–China economic interdependence. If the People's Bank of China decided to begin dumping U.S. Treasury bonds, the effects could have a devastating impact on the already weakening U.S. economy. In all of these issues and many others, the simple fact is that understanding China's role in the world economy and how this country has arrived at its current position is imperative to an understanding of global economic and political trends as well as the interrelated nature of political, economic, and social change in developing economies.

Yet, while China's rise in power over the last three decades has been meteoric—and we are only beginning to feel the impact of that rise in power—our understanding of the changes that have occurred there lags far behind the reality. Many current views of China fail to grasp the depth and magnitude of the reforms, and we have even less understanding of the

only a gradual rate. More than this, the state has experimented with, and gradually introduced, the policies and laws through which the new markets that increasingly govern economic processes in China have been constructed. Even beyond methodical involvement of the state in shaping China's transition path, the political nature of economic change runs even deeper, as the legacies of the former institutions of the state-run economy shape the country's development path in important ways.

The critical point here is that China's successful path through three decades of economic reform has been gradual, experimental, and fundamentally political. Politics and economics have been so closely intertwined that we cannot understand one part without the other. Advocates of the rapid privatization approach claim that China's reforms have been successful *despite* the state's close relationship with the economy. For example, Sachs and Woo (1994a, 1997) argue that the economic structure of China—a largely peasant-based agricultural economy with a large supply of surplus labor and a tight monetary policy—explains China's success relative to Eastern Europe. They argue that, even with the dramatic growth in China's economy over the last three decades, the reform effort there would have been much more successful if a program of rapid privatization had been adopted. It is difficult to see, at this point, how one could argue that gradualism was not a dramatic success in the China case.[6] But these claims ring hollow, especially when one compares the undeniable success of economic reform in China with the serious problems experienced in countries such as the Czech Republic and Russia. As we examine China's successful path and trajectory through the economic reforms, the heavy hand of the state lurks everywhere, and we must understand this reform process through this lens. Other authors have argued that because of the state's role as a continuing agent in the economy, corruption is endemic (e.g., Kwong 1997; Gong 1994) and the collapse of this national economy is inevitable (e.g., Chang 2001). This position is also not credible, as it is simply not supported by the empirical reality of what is occurring in China. A third position on China's progress is that the authoritarian government has held onto power and not allowed a democratic transition to occur there. However, here again, the reality is very different: although China remains an authoritarian political system, over the last three decades of reform, the government has gone a great distance in gradually making the transition to democracy. Though many in the

West—particularly among U.S. politicians—do not want to acknowledge it, China is gradually but steadily building the institutions of a democratic society.

Culture and Capitalism

In the most general sense, culture refers to the norms, values, and systems that shape social action and behavior. It is that part of political, economic, and social systems that produce deeply ingrained understandings of the world. Many scholars have written on the nature of economic behavior in Asia and the ways that the economic decisions of Chinese people are shaped as much by culture as by the changing economic and political systems in which individuals are embedded (Hamilton 1996; Hamilton and Biggart 1988; Bian 1994a; Yang 1994). They have argued that there is something distinctive about Asian and, specifically, Chinese business practices. Despite the fact that some of these writings border on essentialism in their understandings of Chinese culture, it is important to take some of the notions depicted in these scholarly works seriously.[7] There are two ways that culture plays an important role in China's transforming economy. First, Chinese society is different in undeniable ways. Its institutional and cultural history is unique, and this history has an impact on the type of capitalism that is emerging in China. This becomes important as China enters the global market because, in the global marketplace, negotiations often hinge on common understandings, expectations, and norms of behavior, all of which can be heavily influenced and shaped by different cultural traditions.

Second, and perhaps more important, contrary to the economic assumptions that link capitalism and human nature, I argue here that capitalism itself is a system that requires deeply ingrained practices that must be learned over time. In this book, I am interested in the extent to which economic systems are shaped by political institutions and norms of behavior. The process of building a new global economic system in China is not only about a clash of cultures in the marketplace. It is also about the ways that economic systems are themselves cultural systems, where learned practices and behaviors become embedded in the norms and rules by which individuals operate over time. As Chinese managers make the transition from the old economic system to the new, they must unlearn the practices, norms, rules, and meanings through which the old system operated and learn the practices, norms, rules, and meanings of the new system.

Both of these elements of culture can be observed in the experiences of economic actors in China's emerging markets. With the passage of the Joint Venture Law in 1979, companies from around the world have flocked to China, enticed by the idea of a captive market of over a billion consumers (the first two being Boeing and Coca-Cola), but many have been deeply troubled by the extent to which investment in China is a more complicated process than company executives anticipated. Entire fields that are integral to an advanced capitalist economy have struggled in the China market, and they have struggled because the baseline conditions are simply not met in the early phases of the transition from a planned to market economy. Take, for example, the issue of the flow of information: information flow is critical to an advanced market economy if only because economic actors need to be able to make informed decisions about potential economic transactions. However, information has a very specific history in China—a history shaped by the preexisting institutions of China's economy and society. In the command economy, the system under which the managers of China's transforming economy learned economic decision-making, information was a source of power hoarded by bureaucrats and managers alike. Under the command economy, managers learned to coax information from bureaucrats and peers by spending social capital and calling in favors; similarly, they learned to closely guard the information they had. The idea that information could be generated, bought and sold as it is routinely in the fields of consulting, investment banking, and other advisory services was simply antithetical to Chinese economic practices in the 1980s. Goldman Sachs, McKinsey, PricewaterhouseCoopers, and AIG were all successful in China because they took a long-term view about teaching potential future clients about how and why the types of information and security they could provide might be useful sometime in the future.[8] All of these companies patiently invested in the relationships and partnerships, gave free advice, and worked with local governments to teach what "appropriate" behaviors in their respective industries were. The success of these companies in China has been based on a clear realization that China's culture and recent institutional history have shaped the ways that individuals there understand capitalism and that these understandings will change slowly over time. Each of them shifted to marketing strategies that emphasized education as much as salesmanship. Chinese managers needed to be taught the norms and behaviors associated with a capitalist economy; they needed to learn why information was important in a market economy before they could be convinced to pay for it. And, for each of these companies, those investments paid off in significant ways down the line.

But the issues are even more basic than this. We tend to assume that given the right institutional circumstances—for example, a deregulated market environment where the state has minimal involvement—that individuals will know how to make profit-maximizing economic decisions. Indeed, this is the triumph of neoclassical economic theory: we all seem to accept that "homo economicus" is the main star of all economic plays, meaning that, by default, we all assume that individuals are rational, profit-maximizing actors and that, for the most part, politics, culture, and social context do not matter all that much—just give these individuals the right institutional conditions and they will rationally pursue profit. This idea, which is pretty close to the core assumptions of neoclassical economic theory of the 1970s–1990s, makes no sense when one is attempting to traverse the turbulent economic waters of the transition from planned to market economy. When individuals have grown up in the system of state socialism, they often do not know how to act in a free market system. In the early 1990s, I had many conversations with managers who were simply baffled by the idea that "the market would set the price" as they were repeatedly told. "Who sets the price?" they would ask. "How will we know what to do?" "Who will tell us what to do?" "How does the market economy really work?" I would often reply with some type of calming rejoinder, "Over time you'll learn. It just takes practice to learn the rhythms of a market economy." The point here is, what seems to us like a natural set of actions in one system may take a generation or more to learn in the context of another system. Whether this is culture or institutional learning, the main point is that the practices of an economic system are learned slowly over time. This is what is happening in China today.

The Social Consequences of Economic Reform

Markets allocate resources in ways that are fundamentally different from socialist command economies. This change in the allocation of resources has important consequences for individuals in Chinese society and around the world. One of my central concerns in this book, in addition to examining the economics and politics of the transition from a command to market economy in China, is to illuminate the impact this transition has on the lives of Chinese citizens. Changes in the economic system have consequences for the life chances of individuals in Chinese society, and it is critical that we come to terms with the social consequences of the transition to a market economic system. These changes have fundamental implications for the stratification order of society.

Moreover, markets themselves are social systems. Rather than the abstract mechanistic structures that are often portrayed in theoretical economic models, markets are embedded in complex social worlds, and they are shaped by the social institutions, norms, and customs that define a given society. The social embeddedness of markets is a basic feature of capitalist systems, but it is particularly important for understanding the emergence of markets in China in two ways. First, the transition from a command to market economic system requires the destruction (or, in the Chinese case, the gradual erosion) of existing institutions and the construction of new institutions. In the period of transition between systems, institutional instability pervades, and the reliance on social networks and social institutions becomes exaggerated. This is exactly what occurred in Chinese society in the 1980s during the first decade of economic reform. However, that is a situation that has eroded as the new institutions of China's emerging market economy have become more stable. Second, in the case of Chinese society, there is a long tradition of emphasizing the importance of personal networks, and the cultural prominence of social networks in Chinese society has important implications for the emergence of markets there. This history makes an examination of the growing reliance on legal institutions all the more interesting. Throughout the chapters that follow, we will look extensively at both the extent to which markets are socially embedded in China and the ways the emergence of markets has shaped the lives of Chinese citizens.

The Outline of the Book

This book begins by examining the process of economic reform in China. It then examines a number of the social consequences the economic reforms in China have wrought and, finally, concludes with a consideration of China's place within the world economic system. Before outlining the content of the book, it is useful to provide a few notes on data and evidence. The evidence upon which this book is based comes from two sources. First,

I rely heavily on my own firsthand experiences with research on the Chinese economy over the last twenty years. Since 1994, I have conducted well over five hundred in-depth interviews with Chinese managers, Chinese officials, managers of Western multinationals investing in China, and American politicians.[9] In China, the vast majority of interviews were conducted on-site, in Chinese, and they were unaccompanied (i.e., no state officials or other "chaperones" accompanied me). While these interviews and factory visits were conducted primarily in Shanghai, some were conducted in factories in the industrial cities of Beijing, Chongqing, Chengdu, Dalian, Hangzhou, Luoyang, Shenzhen, Shenyang, and Hong Kong. Over the course of these interviews, I also spent time in more than 300 factories in China. The early portion of this research (1993–1998) was the basis of my book *Dragon in a Three-Piece Suit*, with the other portion coming in shorter research trips over the years since 1998. Second, in this book I also rely on official statistics to give a general picture of the economic and social trends that have defined the reform period. While there is good cause to be concerned about the veracity of official statistics, the focus here is on general trends and the magnitude of change in a given area. Official statistics are a good baseline for giving us a sense of things like how large the economy is, how much the economy has grown, per capita income, urban/rural differences, and so forth, and it is for these types of measures that I employ those data here. I also aspire to include as many specific cases as possible to illustrate the points that I am addressing throughout the book. The information in most of these cases comes from direct contact with the leadership of these organizations, though there are a few cases I use for which the information has come from secondary sources (e.g., PetroChina).

Chapter 2 lays out the logic of the pre-reform economy and the critical steps that were taken to dismantle this economy. In many ways, the reforms in China moved much more rapidly and went much deeper than the architects of the reform effort originally intended—despite the fact that China's transition to a market economy has been much more gradual than most—and it is important to begin with an understanding of exactly how the reforms unfolded in China. Command economies have a specific institutional logic, and an understanding of what has occurred in China must begin with a clear sense of the institutional structures and systems that preceded the current era of economic reform. In Chapter 2, I focus primarily on the transformation of the industrial command economy, but

I also give significant attention to the transformation of the rural farm economy. The transformation of the rural farm economy parallels the transformation of the industrial economy in crucial ways, but the experience in rural China has also diverged from the industrial economy in important ways. In Chapter 3, I look at the social institutions that define Chinese society and the ways these social institutions are changing in China today. Family, social networks, and the social systems that have organized rural and urban life will be considered in this chapter. All of these social institutions are being remade in various ways in China's new market economy, but some are proving to be more resilient under the powerful forces of change than others. I also discuss the state, the party, and markets as social institutions that are transforming the political, economic, and social worlds that Chinese citizens face.

Chapter 4 presents an analysis of China's emergence as a global economy, with an examination of global business institutions, foreign investment, and the current state of economic development in China. From foreign investment to the Internet, business relations within newly emerging markets are having a dramatic impact on the structure of Chinese society. Business institutions and relations are critical to economic development and the transformation of Chinese society, as these forces are ushering China into the global economy. Technology transfer, foreign capital, and access to international markets are all important parts of this equation. But of equal or perhaps greater importance is the extent to which Chinese managers and entrepreneurs learn about the practices of capitalism and markets through the relationships they develop in China's emerging markets. Capitalism is a socially embedded system—just as the command economy was—and understanding the operation of a market economy requires a process of learning and observation. Thus, international business relations and newly emerging markets are having dramatic consequences for the type of economy that is emerging in China. But these relations are also shaped by the new institutions that are being set in place by the state, and the emergence of Western-style legal institutions in China constitutes a fundamental shift from the structure of the command economy. I end the chapter with a discussion of China's emerging multinational corporations and the emergence of China's capital markets.

Chapter 5 engages a set of issues that has attracted a great deal of attention with respect to international relations with China: pollution, energy usage, and China's emergence as a force in the area of renewable energy. As for the issue of pollution, China clearly has serious problems in this realm. However, as with everything we are discussing here, the story is considerably more nuanced than is often reported in the popular media. There are three major issues here. First, as I try to do throughout this book, it is important to lay out the empirical reality of this situation in a systematic way. There are major problems with pollution in China, but it is actually not out of step with rapidly industrializing nations at similar stages of development (including the United States). Second, as is discussed in Chapter 2, China is extremely decentralized and there are pockets of the country that are doing horribly on this front and there are pocket doing very well. Third, China is actually fairly innovative in pushing out use of renewable energy technologies at the micro-level (especially in solar). A lot of these problems are tied up with China's voracious needs in energy usage. While we might criticize China for its rapid growth, we need to also note that this rapid growth has allowed China to lift as many people out of poverty as it has. Finally, many of the issues discussed in this and previous chapters converge in the case of China's stellar performance in the building of a renewable energy industry. This is not just an issue of innovation (indeed, most of the technological advancements come from the United States); it is an issue of state-led investment and strategizing about how to build new industries. Renewable energy is a perfect example of how and why China is surging ahead of the United States in key economic realms.

In Chapter 6, I discuss the ways in which all of these economic changes are transforming the lives of individuals in China. Stratification systems have changed in dramatic and fundamental ways in the era of economic reforms. This chapter looks at several of the critical factors that influence class, wealth, and poverty in the new economic system. Education, private enterprise, party membership, gender, inter-city migration, and the urban–rural divide all have implications for the changing life chances for individuals within China's new economy, and I discuss each in this chapter.

In Chapter 7, I examine the rule of law and the prospects for democratic institutions in China. The rule of law is a critical part of the emergence of a modern rational economy and society in China. However, the extent to which a rule-of-law society has been gradually under construction in China has not been widely understood. This chapter examines that process. In order to focus the analysis, I concentrate on the implications the rule of law has had for workers in China's economy. The reality is that although it is a part of a gradual process of reform, a rule-of-law society is emerging in China, and it has radical consequences for the rights of workers and citizens throughout the country. With respect to democratic institutions, there is a certain teleological view of the future of democracy in transforming communist societies such as China's. The view here is not only that democracy is an inevitable outcome of progress, but that democracy must emerge if China is to be truly welcomed into the international community of nations. However, democracy is not an inevitable outcome. Indeed, many scholars, pundits, and popular writers believe China will remain a one-party authoritarian system. Nevertheless, a form of democracy will emerge in China, but for reasons that are not well understood by Western politicians and pundits. While demands for democratic reform have come from both outside and within China, and while it is important to understand the role these demands have played, the structural transformation of China's political institutions has taken place on a much deeper level, set in motion by the architects of the economic reform. Yet, this is not a simple process, an inevitable outcome of the individual freedom that seems to come with a neoliberal economy. Rather, a very specific set of institutional changes set this process in motion at the beginning of the economic reforms. If we are to understand the prospects for democracy in China, we must understand the nature and causes of these institutional shifts.

I conclude the book with Chapter 8's discussion of China's place in the global economy. As this massive nation lumbers toward the position of being one of the largest and most powerful economies in the world, it is absolutely essential that we understand the process of economic, political, and social reform there. But it is also crucial that we understand its place within the global economic and political systems. While I discuss these issues in general terms, the primary substantive focus of the chapter is a political analysis of human rights, the implications of China's entry into the World Trade Organization (WTO), and other social issues such as the impact of China's development on the environment. With respect to human rights, this chapter continues this discussion with an exploration of the actual progress that has occurred in the realm of human rights in China, as well as a discussion of the trade-offs between communism and capitalism in the realm of human rights. On the one hand, China has made significant progress in the realm of human rights. As laws such as the Prison Law of 1994 and the National Compensation Law of 1995 transform social relations and spaces that marked the greatest abuses in human rights, a great deal of progress has been made in this area. On the other hand, the government seems determined to continue to take a hard line on such popular activities as membership in the Falun Gong movement. However, lest we think that the government's seemingly divergent approaches to these issues are simply authoritarian caprice, there are fundamental issues underneath the surface here, and they are shaped by the larger issues of the economic reforms. As a neoliberal ideology has spread across the globe and come to be associated with freedom and equality in markets, so too have we seen a convergence between the concepts of individual civil liberties and human rights. Individual civil liberties are certainly important aspects of human rights, and they happen to fit very well with the neoliberal idea of markets that is sweeping across the globe. However, there are tradeoffs here as well, and some people— including many Chinese citizens—see these trade-offs as complications to the issue of human rights that Western nations like the United States tend to ignore. Access to health care, guaranteed jobs and wages—all part of the old system of China's command economy—are also believed by some to be part of the larger bundle of rights that fall under the rubric of human rights. This final chapter will explore some of these trade-offs and how they are emerging in the era of economic reform. As scores of workers are laid off from old state-owned factories with no guaranteed alternatives for employment, and as migrant workers (the so-called floating population) have no guarantee for education for their children, the trade-offs of the market economy become increasingly clear, and they are trade-offs that are experienced disproportionately, if not exclusively, by the poor. These trade-offs are important, because they lay bare the challenges and contradictions that circumscribe the transition to a market economy. Indeed, it is in this context that the government's crackdown on the Falun Gong movement must be understood: this movement, which has the largest organizational membership in China (larger, even, than the Communist Party)—a fact that surely strikes fear into the hearts of party leaders—is filled with constituents who are being left behind by the economic reforms. And when the movement leaders staged a sit-in in April 1999 in Tiananmen Square, this was, in part, a political statement about the nature and direction of the reforms. The state perceived this movement, then, as representing a direct threat; the ensuing crackdown was, in this context, as predictable as it was atrocious. A careful analysis of human rights abuses in China needs to carefully analyze the trade-offs among stability, economic growth, and a rapid push toward democratization; it also must engage the question of how institutional change and democratization most effectively evolve. In addition to the general discussion of human rights and the rule of law in China, I will also address the specific issues of sovereignty with regard to the issues of Tibet and Taiwan.

With respect to China's entry into the WTO, when we stack up all of the evidence surrounding the political deals that have shaped this crucial issue of globalization, it is increasingly clear that this was not primarily a battle over human rights abuses in China. Rather, it was a battle between two geopolitical powerhouses; it was a battle over China's ascendancy as a world economic power and the desire on the part of the United States to restrict and contain what now seems like an inevitable process. Despite the rhetoric over concerns about extending economic relations with an authoritarian government, the United States has had economic relations with far too many authoritarian governments to make this claim credible. Further, if this were really the reason behind blocking China's entry into the WTO, US support of Taiwan during these years should have been suspect too, as Taiwan was run by an authoritarian government until 1996. The late North Carolina senator Jesse Helms, who for many years was a leader of the anti-China relations camp, likely cared much more about the impact on tobacco and textiles, two of the sectors that would be hit hardest with China's entry into the WTO—also, not coincidentally, two of the primary sectors fueling North Carolina's economy. Within China, agendas and behind-the scenes strategizing were also in play: Zhu Rongji's play for China's entry into the WTO was, at its very core, about a political battle between hard-liners who still believe in an ideological communism and reformers who have used China's continued integration into the world economic system as a means to defeat the hard-liners. The reformers rightly believe that the best strategy for long-run radical reform in China is to gradually and continually integrate China into the international community. As the norms that are widely associated with business practices and economic transactions of the international community—transparency of economic practices, the rule of law, respect for individual civil liberties—become the norms by which China must operate, the changes within China will continue to be dramatic and deep.

As China grows in stature and power, it has also begun to play a major role in global geopolitical tensions around issues like international human rights and the environment. The quest for resources has led China into the Sudan, where the catastrophic bloodshed in Darfur has led to calls from various activist groups and individuals for China to use its influence to help stop the carnage. But the need for oil is a crucial element in China's economic development, and China's position in this crisis has certainly been influenced by that need. Add to this that the firm in question, PetroChina, is now one of the largest corporations in the world, worth, for a brief period, more than $1 trillion, and we have a complex intermingling of national interests, growing economic power, multilateral institutions (with resolutions by the Security Council in the mix), and human rights. These issues of energy consumption are not unrelated to environmental concerns, either. Currently, China is the largest consumer of coal in the world, and the sulfur dioxide produced by coal combustion as well as the carbon dioxide produced by the process will certainly contribute to environmental problems that extend far beyond China's borders.

China's role as a global economic superpower is intensified by its increasingly central role in geopolitical discussions in issues ranging from human rights to the environment. As that role continues to expand and grow, the intermingling of politics, economics, and social issues will continue to be a central part of that story.

2

SETTING THE STAGE: A PRIMER TO THE STUDY OF CHINA'S ECONOMIC REFORMS

The first time I visited Mao's mausoleum in the spring of 1995, I was surprised to realize that this icon of Communist ideology had quietly become kitsch. The mausoleum sits in the middle of Tiananmen Square. In the time of the dynastic emperors, you could stand in the middle of the Forbidden City, looking South, and have a clear vision through all of the great gates of the City and straight across the Square to the "Front Gate" on the opposite side of Tiananmen Square and down Qianmen Road. Today, the building that is Mao's resting place sits right in the middle of that view. The story is that this building was placed there in order to remind the world that this society no longer belongs to the emperors but instead belongs to Mao and his legacy. The process of entering the mausoleum projects the tone of reverence that one might expect for the resting place of the "Great Helmsman." Long before the opening hour, the line to enter the mausoleum winds back and forth, with hundreds of tourists— mostly Chinese people—waiting to pay their respects. As you near the viewing hall, people remove their hats, become very quiet, and look expectantly toward the door; once in the viewing hall, people file past the embalmed body in the glass case with a mixture of reverence and awe. The scene is somewhat dreamlike. As you file out the backdoor of the mausoleum, the scene transforms from dreamlike to surreal. As soon as you exit this memorial to communist ideology, you are immediately assailed by entrepreneurs selling the kitschiest Mao memorabilia imaginable; you move from the somber mood of respect and reverence for the leader of China's Communist Revolution to trying to decide which Mao cigarette lighter you should buy. Small-scale entrepreneurs place Mao-adorned playing cards in front of you, saying in broken English, "How much? How much? Very cheap, very cheap."

As jarring as the scene was in 1995, it is actually reflective of key aspects of the economic reforms in that period of time. At that time, China was in the middle of dismantling the command economy that had been established under Mao's leadership. As part of that transition, in the 1980s, the government allowed for the emergence of small-scale entrepreneurs so that displaced workers would have some avenues for economic viability in the face of closing options in the state sector. But the fostering of entrepreneurship in the 1980s and early 1990s involved a delicate push and pull, with the government allowing the private sector to grow without allowing it to grow too rapidly or become too powerful of an independent force. In this context, one can see why the state would want to allow (or even quietly promote) the practice of small-scale entrepreneurs cozying up to the back door of Mao's mausoleum to sell images of the old icon: much better to have them hawking cigarette lighters with images of Mao on the front that hum "The East is Red" when lighting up than being rogue entrepreneurs. It was around this time that you also began to see taxi drivers hanging little plastic portraits of Mao from their mirrors—some of them surely purchased from the entrepreneurs selling his image outside the mausoleum. Suddenly it seemed like kitschy representations of Mao were everywhere, and they often seemed to be tied to small-scale entrepreneurs or operators.

A decade later and two thousand miles across the country, I was struck by the further transformation of Mao's image. Across the street from Lijiang's Office of Cultural Exchange stands a 50-foot tall Mao statue. (Lijiang is a small town in Southwest China's Yunan Province at the foot of the Tibetan plateau.) It is one of the classic Mao statues that were built during the Communist era, an image of Mao standing erect, right hand raised, proclaiming the founding of a new nation, the People's Republic of China. The image is familiar to all Chinese and to anyone who has followed Chinese history over the last fifty years—the statue can be found in many cities and the actual scene it represents can be found in virtually any documentary that depicts the history of the PRC. I had seen this statue before on a trip to Lijiang in the summer of 2000 and found it interesting if only because the architects of this particular scene had gone to the trouble of constructing a backdrop for the statue that looks like the stage at the mouth of the Forbidden City, overlooking Tiananmen Square, where Mao stood in that famous pose on that victorious date of October 1, 1949.

When I passed by the statue on a trip to Lijiang in 2007, I couldn't help but notice that you hardly detect Mao at all anymore; his presence here is the backdrop for a different scene. The scene was overwhelmed by the presence of a balloon arch advertising the launch of the Geely Auto Company's new line of cars. Underneath the arch sat five new models, all just off the assembly line of Geely's main plant in Zhejiang Province. As I chatted with the on-site Geely representative, he was very quick to point out that Geely is a Chinese-only brand. "We are not a joint venture," he proclaimed proudly. "We are a Chinese company, and our cars are at international standards." Behind the line of cars, there was another layer, a different kind of advertisement, a sign that was not a part of the Geely expo, but had been placed in this public space recently, presumably by the

Figure 2.1 Geely Auto Expo under Mao Statue, Lijiang, Yunan, 2006.

Photo by: Tim Barner.

Lijiang City government. This sign was an advertisement of the recently passed Public Safety Law; the billboard contained the entire text of the law, and it was meant to make available to and educate the population on the concepts and rights associated with this new law. To the right of this informational legal billboard were several cartoonish billboards depicting different aspects of the legal and moral aspects of responsible driving. Finally, if you studied the scene long enough, you were forced to return to Mao, whose outstretched hand, ironically, appeared to be blessing the entire scene—a scene filled with capitalist production and new laws.

Economic change, new policies and laws, and the image of Mao's founding of Communist China all wrapped into one scene; the layers and implications were fascinating then, and these conflicting images can be found in China every day. In this chapter, I examine the thirty-year gradual transition from planned to market economy. To illuminate these processes of reform in China, throughout this text, we will need to focus on three levels of analysis—macro, organizational, and individual. By macro, I mean issues like national such as the "economic opening up" [*jingji kaifang*] (e.g., the Coastal Development Strategy), national laws (e.g., the Joint Venture Law [1979], the Labor Law [1994], and the Company Law [1994]) and national level policy decision around issues like decentralization and taxation. By organizational, I mean the firm- or factory-level changes that are redefining work-unit life in China. And by individual, I mean changes that affect people at the individual level, like labor markets, labor mobility, labor force changes, and changing life chances for mobility within the economy.

The New Society under Mao[1]

When the Communists proclaimed the founding of a "new China" on October 1, 1949, Mao Zedong and his fledgling government set in motion the creation of a new society. The emergence of communism under Mao fundamentally altered the social, political, and economic structure of Chinese life. While the chapters that follow are primarily about the ways in which Deng Xiaoping's economic reforms transformed life in Communist China, it is useful to contrast those changes against a backdrop of the social, political, and economic order that preceded them. In this chapter, I will give a brief outline of the structure of society under Mao and then an outline of the changes that were set in motion by Deng. While the short descriptions here will not do these topics justice, it is important to give a basic outline of this background. The basic theoretical points that guide the discussion of this chapter can be stated simply: (1) under Mao, the Communists set in place a system that intimately wove together political ideology, economic production, and social control; (2) the task for Deng was to unravel this interdependent system; and (3) Deng's government undertook this task in a gradual fashion, experimenting widely with many policies that would gradually rationalize and cede governmental control over the economy and society.

When the Communists took power, they were largely a rural movement. The control of the cities was the crucial next step in taking control of the country. The strategy of the party, at this point, became the mobilization of the population through mass campaigns in which communist ideology would be spread, and people energized by the ideology and commitment to the party would emerge as urban cadres. In 1950, in a campaign called the Resist America and Aid Korea Campaign, the party ordered searches of all alleged spies—all foreigners—and investigated all public associations that were in any way connected with foreigners; many individual Chinese were also investigated for contact with foreigners. The party also moved against foreign businesses, freezing all assets in December 1950. Workers were encouraged to rise up against their exploitative employers. Companies were charged back taxes for all the business they had been doing in China up until the Communist Revolution. In no uncertain terms, foreigners were forced out of China.

The government followed this movement with a second mass campaign in 1951 directed at domestic "counterrevolutionaries." The targets of this mass campaign were officially the individuals who had served under or supported the Nationalist Party, but the target, more generally, was anyone who was suspected of not supporting the party. A large number of public executions took place: in Guangdong Province alone, 28,332 people were executed in 1951. Many of these were staged as public executions. An important development of this campaign was the setting up of neighborhood associations and committees to monitor members of society. Along with the work unit, these associations became one of the most important structures of social control in Communist China. The "Three-Anti" and "Five-Anti" campaigns followed in 1951 and 1952, respectively. The first of these was directed at three sets of vices, which were associated with three groups: corruption, waste, and obstructionist bureaucracy, directed at Chinese Communist Party (CCP) officials, the wider spectrum of bureaucratic officials, and managers of factories. Ironically, though directed at corruption among officials and business leaders, this movement was also used to gain greater control over labor: government took over all labor unions and made them a part of the party infrastructure. The second campaign was designed to ferret out and vanquish the bourgeoisie in China (similar to, and contemporaneous with, the campaign against capitalists and landlords in the countryside). The targets were those Chinese businessmen who represented the capitalist class. In addition to being arrested and forced to confess to crimes against the party, capitalists were also encouraged to denounce each other.

These campaigns not only asserted the Communist control over the people ideologically, but it also allowed the Communists to step in and take control of industrial organizations, ending the independent modes of operation and production in the Chinese economy. While these campaigns set the stage for a terror-driven ideological control, there was also an infrastructure for individual-level social control. The institutions for this individual-level social control were also integrally linked to the economy. In the urban industrial economy, these were the work unit and the neighborhood association system; in the rural economy, these were the collectives and communes. Thus, as they were creating a new order of discipline in society, the Communists were also extending their reign over the economy. The new government adopted a number of measures that would allow them to control production in both agricultural and industrial arenas. The system adopted was modeled after the Soviet Union, which was based on a combination of state-controlled industrial production and sequence of five-year plans; this type of state control was credited with the Su's emergence as a world class power in the 1930s. There was close collaboration between the Soviet Union and China during this period, as Soviet technical advisers came to China to help with factory building, industrial planning, electric power, the railway system, and urban architecture.

The country was organized into a tightly nested hierarchy in which party planning was carried out through a central government (in Beijing), twenty-two provinces, five autonomous regions, and three municipalities.[2] Under these were some 2,200 county governments, which supervised about 1 million towns, villages, and other administrative units. In rural areas, in 1952 and 1953, the government put households together into groups of thirty to fifty households, and land and labor were pooled together into cooperative units. Originally, peasants held a private component in which they were allowed to keep private plots for their own use—to raise crops for their own consumption or to be sold. Balances after government quotas were met were divided based upon how much each family contributed originally. Thus, this was not a fully socialist system as richer peasants, who had contributed more land, did better in the end. Figure 2.2 shows the relationships among levels of government in this administrative system. One scholar has described this system in the following way: "This administrative structure forms the hierarchy in which national resources and incentives [were] allocated from the central command to the various levels of local governments."[3]

Different levels of government had direct control over factories—or "work units"—in this system. The ministry of a given sector had direct control and supervisory power over factories, as did provincial, municipal, and township levels of government. In general, the industrial work units at the upper levels of the administrative structure were large-scale, heavy industry, "state-owned" organizations of the industrial planned economy. "State ownership" is a bit of a misnomer here, as it has often directed scholars to focus on state property rights versus collective or private ownership. However, as one scholar has described this system,

> In terms of the definition of property rights ... there is no fundamental distinction between state and collective enterprises.... The most important way in which government ownership rights in state and collective sectors do differ is in the extent to which they are regulated by higher levels of government.... What varies in this hierarchy is not the nature of government property rights but the composition and scale of industry and the degree to which government rights are attenuated by central regulations.
>
> (Walder 1995a, 271–273)

Within this administrative system of the planned economy, resources flow up to the higher levels of government and are then redistributed based on need. However, work units had variable access to resources in the command economy: the higher a work unit was positioned in this "nested hierarchy," the greater the access to resources it had (Walder 1992a; Bian 1994a). Work units and cooperatives within this system were much more than units of production in the planned economy, however; they were also the sites of social welfare distribution and political and social control.

The first five-year plan seemed to pay off, as industrial production rose dramatically. Nevertheless, there were still significant problems with the economy that emerged in the 1950s. For example, by eliminating the private sector, the government had gained control over the economy, yet it had eliminated market competition. In establishing production quotas, the central government placed local officials (as opposed to business owners) in charge of production. These local officials were often ignorant of economic planning and were more concerned with meeting targets than they were with running efficient factories. This pressure to meet targets often led to false reporting. As well, the elimination of markets and the bureaucratic control of distribution channels often led to hoarding, bottle-necks, and, ultimately, shortages of production goods. The government job assignment system meant that factories could not control how large their workforces should be; factories simply had to accept the number of employees that were assigned by the government to the work unit. On top of this, the connection between the work-unit system and social welfare meant that work units were often burdened with large costs to support the livelihood of their employees.[4]

Mao's response to these problems, along with political challenges he was facing in the spring of 1956, was to "deepen" the revolution.[5] In 1957–1958, Mao launched a disastrous movement called the Great Leap Forward. In rural areas, cooperatives were converted into people's communes such that, by the end of 1958, 740,000 cooperatives had been merged into 26,000 communes. These communes comprised 120 million rural households—99 percent of the rural population. One of the central problems in the rural economy was that grain was not being produced at a high enough rate. Grain was a necessary part of industrial growth, because it was the primary product China could export to the Soviet Union. As a result, in 1957, the CCP began organizing people into huge workforces for irrigation, construction projects, and the like. Mao also tailored his ideas about harnessing the peasantry for a truly communist revolution driven by the Chinese peasantry to the industrial economy, inducing the population in 1958 to create over one million backyard steel furnaces. These policies

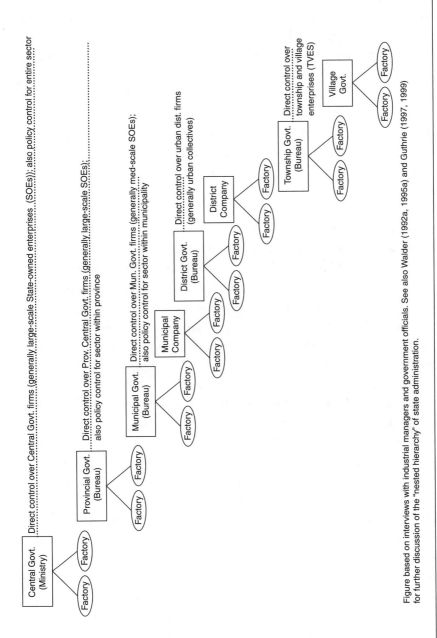

Figure 2.2 Nested Hierarchy of State Administration in China.

Figure based on interviews with industrial managers and government officials. See also Walder (1992a, 1995a) and Guthrie (1997, 1999) for further discussion of the "nested hierarchy" of state administration.

Central Govt. (Ministry) — Direct control over Central Govt. firms (generally large-scale State-owned enterprises (SOEs)); also policy control for entire sector

Factory, Factory

Provincial Govt. (Bureau) — Direct control over Prov. Central Govt. firms (generally large-scale SOEs); also policy control for sector within province

Factory, Factory

Municipal Govt. (Bureau) — Direct control over Mun. Govt. firms (generally med-scale SOEs); also policy control for sector within municipality

Municipal Company

Factory, Factory, Factory

District Govt. (Bureau) — Direct control over urban dist. firms (generally urban collectives)

District Company

Factory, Factory, Factory

Township Govt. (Bureau) — Direct control over township and village enterprises (TVES)

Factory, Factory

Village Govt.

Factory, Factory

proved disastrous, as they led to a famine from 1959 to 1962 in which an estimated 20 million Chinese citizens died of starvation.

Following some of the devastating effects of these economic policies, Mao lost political power in significant ways. Deng Xiaoping and Liu Xiaoqi were gaining political credibility, and they were increasingly critical of Mao and his policies. But Mao was still the charismatic leader of China. He was the leader of a movement that, in retrospect, is appropriately referred to as the "cult of Mao." He was seen as the leader who gave self-reliance and self-respect back to the Chinese. Despite his failed economic policies, he was still the leader of the revolution. And he was the most powerful man in China in terms of his ability to mobilize political power.

The Chaos of the Cultural Revolution

The mid-1960s saw the emergence of a group of intellectuals who were critical not just of Mao's policies but also of his isolation from the public. A well-respected Ming historian named Wu Han began to write extensively about Mao's poor judgment and policies. In September 1965, Mao attempted to begin a movement to criticize the "reactionary bourgeois ideology," but found little success because much of the state media were controlled by his political opponents. He left Beijing in November and disappeared from public view; it was later learned that he had gone to Shanghai, where he assembled a group of hard-line communist intellectuals to help him bring socialist order back to the country.

Mao called for an attack on the four "old" elements of Chinese society— customs, habits, culture, and thinking—but the Red Guards directed this movement at the local levels. As a result, the movement spun completely out of control. Eventually, everyone in power was in danger of being labeled a capitalist roader, a counterrevolutionary, and an enemy of the party. This led to clashes between the Red Guard radicals and the People's Liberation Army. By September 1967, all leaders, including those in the radical wing of the party, agreed that the chaos was threatening to tear the country apart. They began denouncing "ultra-left tendencies." It was not until the summer of 1968 that something resembling order was restored. A retrenchment movement followed, in which hundreds of thousands of Red Guard radicals were "sent down" to the countryside for "reeducation." Many of these youths spent a decade of their lives working in hard agricultural labor in the countryside. They were only able to return to their homes after Mao died in 1976.

Mao's death brought an end to the Cultural Revolution. But the chaos of the years since 1957 (when the Great Leap Forward began) had crippled the country economically. Under the terror that swept the country during the Cultural Revolution, a generation of students had lost the opportunity for high school and college education, as they were sent down to the countryside for ideological reeducation; industrial production declined precipitously during this era; and the country had become dramatically isolated from the rest of the world. For a brief time, it appeared that little would change in the wake of Mao's death, as Hua Guofeng, a conservative leader who sought to follow Mao's economic and social policies, emerged as Mao's successor. On October 6, 1976, the now infamous "Gang of Four"—Jiang Qing, Wang Hongwen, Yao Wenyuan, and Zhang Chunqiao, the radical leaders of the Cultural Revolution—were arrested on Hua Guofeng's orders. They were blamed for the excesses of the Cultural Revolution, even defying, it was alleged, the warnings of Mao himself. On October 7, Hua Guofeng was named to succeed Mao as chairman of the Central Committee of the CCP and chairman of the Military Affairs Commission. And in November, Hua formally laid the first foundation stone for Chairman Mao's mausoleum, which would be erected in the center of Tiananmen Square.

Deng Xiaoping sought refuge in Canton, where he was protected by a powerful military leader, Xu Shiyou, who despised Hua Guofeng, associating him with the Gang of Four. In 1977, Xu began pressuring the party to rehabilitate Deng, and in July of that year, Deng was reappointed to his position of vice premier. While Hua continued to champion the reforms of central planning and a more cautious version of the notions that Mao had articulated in pushing the Great Leap Forward, Deng had a different economic orientation. A pragmatist, Deng believed that economic reform was necessary and developed his political power through advocating reform. He saw central planning in industry and collectivization in agriculture as inflexible and unable to deal with the economic problems China was facing. Although the debacles of the Great Leap Forward and the Cultural Revolution were now past, several social problems now stood in their wakes. For one thing, there were the urban residents who had just returned from a decade in the countryside, with no guaranteed place in the planned economy and no plan for how the current system would absorb them. They were part of a new trend that saw unemployment rising to new highs within the system.[6] And by 1978, a ten-year economic plan—fashioned in 1976 to get the nation back on track after the Cultural Revolution—was already falling far below projected goals. In response to these challenges, in the late 1970s, Deng Xiaoping was positioning himself to lead China in a radically different direction economically and would introduce a set of controlled modifications into the structure of the socialist system. Deng advocated the implementation of a modernization plan that would incorporate foreign investment and technology and abandon state controls.

The Quiet Revolution: The Era of Economic Reform in China

When Deng Xiaoping unveiled his vision of economic reform to the Third Plenum of the Eleventh Central Committee of the Chinese Community Party in December 1978, the Chinese economy was faltering.[7] Reeling from a decade of stagnation during the Cultural Revolution and already appearing to fall short of the projections set forth in the ten-year plan of 1976, it would take much more than a new plan and the Soviet-style economic vision of Deng's political rival, Hua Guofeng. At the time, Deng's plan was to lead the country down a road of gradual and incremental economic reform, leaving the state apparatus intact while slowly unleashing market forces.

Since that time, the most common image is of an unbending authoritarian regime that has engineered a remarkable period of rapid economic growth but has seen little real substantive change politically. There is often a sense that China remains an entrenched and decaying authoritarian government run by corrupt party officials (extreme accounts depict it as an economy on the verge of collapse). However, this vision simply does not square with reality on a number of levels. While it is true that China remains an authoritarian one-party system, it is also the most successful case of economic reform of any communist-planned economy of the twentieth century. Today, as the second-largest economy in the world, it is fast emerging as one of the world's most dynamic market economies. Understanding how this change has come about requires an examination of five broad changes that have come together to shape China's transition to capitalism: (1) the *gradual* receding of the state from control over the economy, a process that brought about a shift in economic control without privatization; (2) *decentralization* of economic decisions and practices by turning control over to the provinces, municipalities and townships; (3) the steady growth of *foreign investment*; (4) the growth of a *private economy* from below; and (5) the gradual emergence of a *rational–legal system* to support these economic changes. During the 1980s and 1990s, economists and institutional advisors from the West advocated the rapid transition to market institutions as the necessary medicine for transforming communist societies. Scholars argued that private property provides the institutional foundation of a market economy, and, therefore, communist societies making the transition to a market economy must privatize industry and other public goods. The radical members of this school argued that rapid privatization—the so-called shock therapy or big bang approach to economic reforms—was the only way to avoid costly abuses in these transitional systems.[8] The Chinese path has been very different from the shock therapy approach. While countries such as Russia have followed Western advice—constructing market institutions at a rapid pace, immediately removing the state from control over the economy, and rapidly privatizing property—China has taken its time in implementing institutional change. The state has gradually receded from control over the economy, taking the time to experiment with new institutions and to implement them slowly and incrementally within the context of existing institutional arrangements.

The success of gradual reform in China can be attributed to two factors. First, as Barry Naughton has argued, through gradual reform, the government retained its role as a stabilizing force in the midst of the turbulence that inevitably accompanies the transition from plan to market. Institutions such as the "dual-track" system kept large state-owned enterprises partially on the plan and, at the same time, gave them incentives to generate extra income through selling what they could produce above the plan in China's nascent markets. Over time, as market economic practice became more successful, the plan part of an enterprise's portfolio was reduced and the market part grew. Enterprises were thus given the stability of a continued but gradually diminishing planned economy system and the time to learn the practices of setting prices, competing for contracts, and producing efficiently (Naughton 1995; see also Rawski 1994, 1995, 1999). Second, the government has gradually pushed ownership-like control down the government administrative hierarchy to the localities. As a result, the central government was able to give economic control over to local administrators without privatization. But with economic control came accountability, and local administrators became very invested in the successful economic reform of the villages, townships, and municipalities under their jurisdictions. In a sense, as Andrew Walder has argued, pushing economic responsibilities onto local administrators created an incentive structure much like those experienced by managers of large industrial firms.[9]

Even as reform in China has proceeded at a gradual pace, the cumulative changes over three decades of economic reform have been nothing short of radical. These economic reforms have proceeded on four levels. First, the transformation of China's economy begins with institutional changes set in motion at the highest levels of government; second, they have been followed by firm-level institutions that reflect the rational–legal system emerging at the state level; third, these firm-level changes have been supported by a budding legal system that provides workers institutional support for grievance proceedings, a dynamic that is heavily influenced by relationships with foreign investors; and fourth, labor relations have been shaped by the emergence of new labor markets in China, which allow workers the freedom and mobility to find new employment when necessary. The result of these changes has been the emergence of a rational–legal regime of labor, where the economy increasingly rests upon an infrastructure of rational law, and workers hold the right to invoke these laws in the legal system when necessary.

The process began with a gradual introduction of economic autonomy to enterprise managers and local officials in industrial areas and decollectivization in the countryside. As of the early 1980s, individuals increasingly had the freedom to pursue their fortunes in the newly emerging markets of the Chinese economy, and many individuals chose to do so. Enterprise autonomy for managers and officials meant that the party and industrial bureaus were no longer leaning over the shoulders of economic actors in the industrial economy. Thus, the gradual reforms hit squarely at the heart of the central institutions around which Communist China was organized. Once Deng wrested power from the conservative factions of the party, to unleash the broader forces and trends articulated above, his specific challenges included:

- transforming incentives in the agricultural economy;
- forcing the central government to give local bureaucrats some measure of economic control over the localities they govern;
- creating a system that kept in place the planned economy while at the same time giving autonomy over to the local enterprises;
- beginning a process that would address the economic burden that the social security system posed for Chinese enterprises;
- facilitating the development of a private economy;
- attracting foreign direct investment.

Several of these goals began to emerge explicitly onto the agenda at the Third Plenum of the Eleventh Central Committee of the Chinese Communist Party in December 1978. For example, on December 15, the party announced that it would establish full diplomatic relations with the United States on January 1, 1979. During this time, the party also laid the groundwork for the passage (in 1979) of the Law of the PRC on Chinese–Foreign Equity Joint Ventures, which would allow foreign firms to enter the Chinese economy for the first time since the founding of the PRC. It would also signal a reversal of Mao's "revolutionary" governance structure with the passage (again in 1979) of the Resolution of the Standing Committee of the National People's Congress Authorizing Provinces, Autonomous Regions, and Municipalities Directly under the central government to Change Revolutionary Committees to People's Governments.

Following his political breakthrough in 1978, Deng symbolically signaled these changes with a crucial visit to the United States in January 1979. During this trip, Deng officially normalized relations with the United States, which in turn officially ended formal U.S. diplomatic relations with Taiwan and explicitly conceded China's position on the "one-China" policy.[10] Many nations in the international community would follow by normalizing relations with China.[11] During that trip, Deng also visited Atlanta, Houston, and Seattle to see the facilities of the first two companies with which agreements would be signed—Coca-Cola and Boeing.

Developing an Independent Mindset in the Rural Economy

Initially, Deng's reform agenda aimed to loosen the central government's control over the economy, stimulating economic growth, controlling unemployment and inflation, and improving the Chinese citizens' living standards. It was not clear, in these early years of reform, that Deng had in mind the creation of a market economy; instead, he seemed to have in mind a one-step-at-a-time approach to creating a more robust economy in China. It was under these auspices that Deng became famous for the notion of "groping for stones to cross the river [*moshitou guohe*]." In other words, "We don't know yet how we are crossing this river, but we will get there one step at a time."

One thing that was clear, even in the early years of the economic reforms, was that, if the central government was going to successfully break down the planned economy and allow the economy to be kick-started by the gradual emergence of markets, it would need to develop an economy of (semi-) independent market actors. One of the early keys to developing such an economy was to gradually allow individuals to harness individual-level incentives to participate in the market economy. With the breakup of the commune system and the establishment of the Household Responsibility System in the early 1980s, peasants in rural areas were allowed to lease land and produce agricultural goods on a household basis as if they were running a household business. They still had to deliver a minimum quota of grain to the government—usually to the collective from which the land was leased—but beyond that amount, they were free to sell the surplus in emerging rural markets. Rural markets were thus opened to a large portion of the Chinese populace (about 80 percent of the population at that time), the first step toward establishing a grass-roots movement to a market economy. The "dual track" nature of this arrangement would also become a model for enterprise reform in the industrial economy.

This system had three immediate positive consequences. First, it allowed an infusion of cash to flow into individual households, which were still, by world standards, extremely poor. Annual per-capita net income in rural areas of China in 1978 was 133.6 yuan (about $16.25), or about $70 in total annual household income. Individuals were still reliant on the state for the provision of goods and services, so a low per-capita income overstated the poverty (because individuals had access to nonwage bene-fits), but the economy at this point was still extremely poor. As local governments began to withdraw the social support that was the hallmark of the "iron rice bowl," individuals would need new sources of income to cover those costs. The Household Responsibility System provided those sources of income. Second, although there were concerns that rural production of grain would suffer as a result of this semi-privatization effort, the system actually stimulated grain output significantly: from 1978 to 1984, grain production grew by over 100 million tons, from 305 to 407 million tons.[12] Third, by creating incentives for individuals to produce and then creating the autonomy for them to do so, Deng Xiaoping created a large constituency that supported the economic reforms from its early stages.

Local Governmental Autonomy

One of the interesting differences between China's planned economy and that of the Soviet Union was that China's was much more decentralized. This fact has played a crucial role in the success of China's economic reforms, as a number of scholars have argued.[13] Nevertheless, despite the relative decentralization in China, giving autonomy over to localities was still a key factor that guided the economic reforms forward. Economic decentralization ushered in two forces that have been key to the economic reforms: (1) local officials, who were much closer to the economic strengths, opportunities, and necessities of their localities, would be given the autonomy to pursue various development strategies, and (2) this measure would introduce a level of competition among local officials vying for different economic opportunities. Deng Xiaoping clearly recognized the importance of these potential forces by passing the elaborately titled Resolution of the Standing Committee of the National People's Congress Authorizing the People's Congresses of Guangdong and Fujian Provinces and Their Standing Committees to Formulate Separate Economic Regulations for Their Respective Special Economic Zones.[14] This resolution, one of the early resolutions passed in the era of Deng's economic reforms, clearly recognized the importance of political decentralization in the reform project. National development has proceeded along these lines throughout the era of the economic reforms. Individual provinces and municipalities have had the autonomy to make economic decisions and innovations in developmental strategies to gain advantages over neighboring regions and provinces. It is also the case that individual regions, provinces, and municipalities were given the power to create small-scale special economic zones for the localities within their jurisdictions.

New Autonomy and Incentives for Factory Managers

While creating a fledgling market economy mindset among the peasantry and local officials was a crucial first step in the gradual creation of a market economy, tackling the industrial economy was an equally important, though exceptionally more complex, next step. Even before the Third Plenum, Sichuan Province had begun experimenting with giving autonomy to factory managers, a fact that would position Zhao Ziyang to emerge as one of Deng's early partners in the reform agenda. The basic strategy here was to turn autonomy over to economic organizations. There were a number of specific institutional reforms that pushed the development of enterprise reform in China forward. I will discuss a few of these reforms as examples here.

The Dual-Track System

One of the early enterprise reforms institutionalized by the Chinese government was the dual-track system, characterized by the coexistence of two coordination mechanisms (plan and market) within the state sector.[15] This economic policy maintained the elements of the planned economy while attempting, at the same time, to give state-owned organizations incentives to develop market-oriented strategies that would work above and beyond the plan. Continuing to govern each sector in the economy allowed the government to continue using direct controls over finance and investment and provided a degree of stability during the transition process. However, instituting the dual-track system also allowed the existence of a two-tiered pricing system for goods and allowed the state firms to sell the goods above plan quotas and keep extra profits. This two-tiered system greatly stimulated the incentives of the enterprises, as anything that firms produced above the plan could be sold within China's newly emerging markets at a market price. The system also provided valuable flexibility by allowing the state firms to transact and cooperate with non-state and foreign sectors. Economic growth was thus concentrated in the market "track," and, over time, the "plan" became proportionately less and less important in the transition process.

Allowing new firms into the marketplace was crucial, and reformers could not have anticipated how rapidly the non-state sector would grow. But even more important, they had little sense of the profound political and economic impacts the growth of this sector—combined with enterprise autonomy—would bring about.[16] As the market replaced the plan, the state fiscal system eroded, putting further pressure on reformers to experiment with new paths toward marketization; the pressure of the market and the fiscal crisis pushed bureaucrats to seek ways to help firms become more productive. Thus, the economy "gradually grew out of the plan" as the plan itself and the state sector became less important parts of the economy. Some of this may have been unintentional: as Barry Naughton (1995) describes it, China's reform effort is characterized by an interaction between early governmental policies and the "unforeseen consequences of economic change." While economic reformers adopted early strategies to make the initial move away from a purely command economy, it was only in the later stages of the reform period that the goal of a market-based system emerged. In other words, early policy decisions began the process of reform, but soon the consequences of this early reform effort caused the system to unravel, pushing the reforms far beyond leaders' original intentions. However, the gradual nature of this process allowed the state sector to remain, at least in the early years, the anchor of the economy that it had been in the pre-reform era, creating some degree of stability throughout the process.

Property Rights

In the realm of enterprise autonomy, it is also useful to examine the institutional transformation of property rights in China. On one end of the spectrum, the view of property rights in market transitions has been unequivocal: the rapid privatization of property is necessary in the successful transition to a market economy. This view is partly ideological, but it is also grounded in theory and experience. For decades, the planned economies of the Soviet Union and China were rife with the inefficiencies that accompany state ownership. State-owned factories operated on the principles of a redistributive system, whereby revenues were turned over to the government and input costs were drawn from state coffers and "redistributed" to the factories owned by the state. This system of "soft budget constraints," in which factories could draw endlessly from state coffers regardless of revenues, led to problems of rent seeking, a lack of connection between input and output costs, and the absence of pressure within factories to operate efficiently. Thus, the privatization of property, which places fiscal responsibilities squarely within the firm, came to be viewed by many

Western economists as a necessary step in reforming the inefficiencies of the planned system.

The Chinese experience belies this view. As China has marched through two decades of double-digit economic growth, the rapid and complete privatization of property has not been part of this story. Property rights have played a complex role in reform-era China, in fact. In an insightful essay on this topic, Andrew Walder and Jean Oi begin by rejecting the notion that property can be adequately understood in the crude categories of private or state owned. Drawing on earlier work in this area (especially Demsetz 1967; Furubotn and Pejovich 1974), Oi and Walder (1999) argue that property should be conceived of as a "bundle of rights," where questions of managerial control, the ability to extract revenue, and the ability to transfer ownership must all be addressed in a full understanding of this institution. The view of property rights as dependent upon shifting politics and relations has a long history in legal scholarship (Singer 1982, 1988), dating perhaps as far back as Hohfeld's (1913) re-conceptualization of rights nearly a century ago. Unfortunately, however, the field of economics has, until only recently, been blind to a more nuanced view of institutions such as property rights. The central point here is that while many firms in China are still officially state owned, individual parameters within these bundles of rights have been reformed to various degrees, so firms are often free to act independent of state control, despite the fact that they are still officially state owned. This perspective helps us resolve the puzzle of how it is that China has successfully reformed its planned economy—though this process is far from complete—without relying on the mandate of rapid privatization: the state has gradually allowed for the reform of some parts of these bundles of rights, while leaving others intact. To systematize this analysis, Oi and Walder (1999) also outline five ideal types of ownership arrangements that exist along a continuum, with state-owned enterprises occupying one end of this spectrum and fully private enterprises occupying the other. Between these ends of the continuum, we find firms that have incorporated innovative reforms including management incentive contracts, government–management partnerships, and leased public assets.

Local Governments as Industrial Firms

The central government kept control over policy making and shifted economic decision-making down to local governments and to the management of the enterprises. One key effect of this policy is that it allowed local officials to aggressively pursue development strategies for the firms under their jurisdictions. The earliest sector of the Chinese economy to surge in growth and output in China's reform era was that of the township and village enterprises (TVEs). Indeed, the rapid growth of China's economy in the 1980s was largely due to the exceptional growth rates of the rural industrial economy, where the vast majority of TVEs are. As the primary segment contributing to China's high economic growth in the 1980s, the TVE sector expanded to 24,529 in 1993, almost fifteen times its size in 1978. By 1998, however, the number had dropped to 20,039 due to the informal privatization processes led by the local governments in the 1990s.[17] These organizations were essentially state owned. Though not controlled by the national or provincial governments, they were still controlled by the state, as township and village governments owned the property. Local governments were the residual claimants, and they controlled managerial decisions and the rights of transferring assets. However, after the economic reforms began, TVEs faced few of the institutional and organizational legacies of the planned economy that larger state-owned organizations controlled by higher levels of government faced.[18]

As the economic reforms progressed, managerial and ownership control were quickly decentralized to give local officials direct control over the firms under their jurisdictions. This strategy was partly borne out of necessity: as the central government sought to gradually dismantle the redistributive economy, firms in the rural economy were the first to be cut off from funds from state coffers. However, local officials were also given free reign to generate income as they could. Thus, local officials were given incentives to behave like managers and run their TVEs like local industrial firms (Walder 1995e). From this frame of reference, TVEs rapidly came to resemble business organizations in crucial ways, yet the property rights still resided in the hands of the local state. As a result, decentralization has greatly stimulated the rural industrialization driven by the development of TVEs. These sectors have been pushed to respond more to the market forces and less to the governmental plan. With harder budgets, the non-state sectors (which also include the private and foreign sectors) have become the most competitive firms and today contribute to over 70 percent of China's gross domestic product.

Organizational Structure: Dismantling the Old and Creating the New

Chinese industrial firms have been transformed in dramatic ways over the course of China's economic reforms. Perhaps the most important change set in place over the course of the economic reforms in China came when the state handed economic decision making over to industrial managers (Naughton 1995; Guthrie 1999). While some of the organizational changes occurring in industrial firms are in direct response to the hundreds of new directives and economic laws being promulgated by the state, many of the changes occurring in Chinese industrial firms come from decisions made by autonomous managers who are transforming their firms by force of creativity, will, and, in some cases, pure desperation. In the uncertain environment of China's newly emerging markets, managers have been impelled to innovate, create, strategize, and improvise their way through the economic reforms. For many of these managers, they learned the ways of markets, competition, and economic survival through experimenting with and implementing the new organizational strategies and structures their firms were adopting in this period.

Innovative managers within the organizations carried out these firm-level changes as organizational strategies. The transformation of Chinese industrial firms is just as much a reflection of managerial decision making, then, as it is some abstract notion of organizational strategies, because it is largely the general managers (along with the local bureaucrats in some administrative jurisdictions) who are running the show in China today. These firm-level changes are very much about innovation, experimentation, and finding creative solutions to organizational problems; they are thus driven by entrepreneurial decisions of the general managers who run these firms. The first dramatic change that aggressive managers are implementing in their organizations is a clearing of the decks. Wiping out the old system has been an important step in aggressive enterprise reform in China, but it has not been an easy one. Inasmuch as industrial enterprises under the command economy served as the nation's social security system, dismantling this system of extensive benefit packages amounted to nothing less than a fundamental transformation of the labor relationship and the meaning of work in China. Although these changes are often not commonly acknowledged as such, they comprise a dramatic shift that is occurring in Chinese firms, leading to newly emerging organizational structures and forms. Since the late 1980s, we have witnessed the emergence of bureaucratic structures that look strikingly like the type of organizational structures we find in Western economies. The construction of these new "intra-organizational" structures in Chinese firms over the last decade has required innovation, experimentation, and imagination from industrial managers.

Today, the evidence of these new institutions and structures abound in the Chinese economy, yet industrial managers have embraced these changes at varying rates. Three key factors have driven this transformation forward. First, the background of the general managers has a significant impact on the extent to which they are actively reshaping the organizations they are running. Firms that are run by managers with backgrounds in business and economics are more likely to adopt the economic structures that are associated with the economic reforms. General managers with backgrounds in business and economics are also more prone to act in an entrepreneurial fashion with respect to organizational restructuring than their counterparts with training in other areas or no formal training at all. Second, the social world and the economic models present in that social world play a significant role in the aggressive adoption of new organizational forms in China. Firms that have joint ventures with foreign companies are significantly more likely to adopt the economic structures associated with the reforms. Third, the institutional structure in which a firm is embedded also plays a significant role in the adoption of new organizational structures and forms. Firms that are positioned under the jurisdiction of municipal companies tend to be aggressive adopters of the new organizational forms.[19]

The Company Law: Adopting New Corporate Forms

A second area of aggressive development can be seen as general managers lead their firms to take advantage of the institutional opportunities created by the state. As the state inundates society and the market with a horde of new laws and institutional rules, the really interesting question becomes which of these institutional changes have meaning for society. Which of these institutional reforms managers have adopted and which they have ignored is a key question in the reform era. In the end, the institutional reforms that really have meaning for the economic reforms are those that are aggressively adopted by actors in the economy. And it is often entrepreneurial managers taking advantage of—or, in some cases, avoiding—the institutional changes that breathe life into these reforms.

A fascinating case in point is that of the Chinese Company Law. Adopted by the National People's Congress on December 29, 1993, the Company Law provides the first legal basis in the history of the PRC for private, collective, and state enterprises to exist as autonomous legal entities. It is an institutional change that continues the process of separating—both legally and operationally—enterprises from the state redistributive system of the former command economy. Yet, while the law now exists in China, there is still considerable variation as to whether or not organizations have chosen to incorporate this change into their daily operations. Managers must actively choose to transform their firms into companies if they want to take advantage of the Company Law—they must apply to the Economic Commission to take on company status—and aggressive managers have seen this as an opportunity to become part of the "modern enterprise system." They must act as entrepreneurs with respect to this new institution, applying for this change in status, figuring out what it means for their organization, and adopting the changes that come with this economic transformation. As one general manager described this process,

> In 1986, business in our factory really started picking up. Before [that] we were a planned economy. But after the economic opening, our factory was one of the earliest to integrate a market economic approach. That year was actually the year that our profits really started picking up. Then last year we applied to have our factory changed from an enterprise to a company. So now we are under the Company Law, and our scope of business is much wider. It's really a much better situation for us in terms of development now.
>
> (Personal interview)

What types of managers and firms are transforming their organizations in this way? First, managers whose organizations are embedded in formal relationships with foreign companies are more likely to adopt the Company Law. Firms that are engaged in relationships with—and therefore under the influence of—foreign partners are more likely to pursue economic strategies that the state has defined as a "modern enterprise system." A general manager's decision to adopt the Company Law is not significantly related to the profit margins of the firm or the firm's overall organizational health—other variables that would presumably be proxies for economic success; in other words, this change itself has little to do with past economic success. I think the stronger interpretation of the joint-venture effect is that a foreign partner provides a Chinese firm with detailed examples of how foreign firms operate. The "modern enterprise system" is, in many ways, a rhetorical stand-in for Western-style management practices. Managers who are exposed to the concept of the "modern enterprise system" through contact with foreign companies and through setting up a joint-venture company are more likely to see the institutional advantages (real or perceived) of broadening the organization's scope of operation and becoming an independent legal entity. Entrepreneurial managers pursue this change as a way of helping to shepherd their firms into the modern economy.

Second, Chinese organizations that are at the highest level of the government administrative hierarchy are more likely than those under more local governmental offices to adopt the Company Law. Central- and provincial-level government offices, with jurisdiction over many enterprises, do not have the administrative resources to monitor and offer administrative advice or help to the firms in the large organizational fields under their jurisdictions (Guthrie 1997, 1998a, 1999). As a result, firms under these levels of government experience a greater sense of being set adrift in the economic transition. They are thus encouraged—or they feel the impetus—to pursue economic strategies on their own. Adopting the Company Law and thereby broadening the scope of action in China's growing markets is one such strategy that firms, especially those under bureaus, are taking. Firms under the jurisdiction of district companies, on the other hand, are much more closely monitored by their government organizations (relative to those under bureaus), and these firms are offered a significant amount of administrative help and attention in the economic reform. The result is that when the opportunity to apply to become a company and adopt the Company Law arose, managers under high-level governmental offices had the autonomy (and the impetus) to move their firms toward adopting this institutional change.

Price Setting: Flexibility and Competition in the Market

A crucial issue in the transition from a command to a market economy pertains to the setting of prices. Under the command economy, all price setting in large industrial organizations was controlled by the state.

Reforming price-setting practices would prove to be a central issue of the economic transition. Price reform has followed the course of gradual reform that is indicative of China's reform process, laden with politics, experimentation, and piecemeal implementation. Government control of pricing began to change officially with general reforms in 1979 and then, more specifically, with the October 1984 Reform Declaration. Implementing a market pricing system may not have been a central part of the financial rationalizing system that was being promoted by Zhao Ziyang, but it was an important issue that was on the table for many years of the reform and often advocated by Zhao himself. The "price reformers" certainly saw the issue as crucial to the success of the reforms, and even if the "enterprise reformers" were antagonistic to the idea, the liberalization of prices was an issue that was central to the debates that raged between these two reform-minded groups. But if the debates over price control and liberalization were central to the reforms, progress on the issue was slow. By the end of 1984, factor prices were still unreformed, and product prices had still not yet been realigned.[20] Managers, for their part, have responded to the price reforms in China in a variety of ways—some have simply remained passive, following the market but pursuing few strategies in the negotiating that can often allow prices to shift in a market, while others have viewed price reform as an opportunity to aggressively negotiate with customers in the market (Guthrie 1999, Chapter 5).

Transforming the Social Security System: Ending the Institution of Lifetime Employment

Command economies were typically known for having small variation in wages while offering a range of living benefits that were tied to the workplace. In the pre-reform era, China sat on the extreme end of this spectrum, because wage differentials were extremely narrow, and virtually all social security was tied to the work unit. Further, in China, lifetime employment was the very essence of the labor relationship that existed between enterprises and workers.[21] Workers entered their work unit, and, from that moment on, the work unit was the social system that dispensed their salary, housing, medical insurance, and any other benefits the unit might offer. In different periods, especially in the late 1970s, a small fraction of the population was classified as "waiting for employment," but for the most part, the state still fulfilled its promise of finding employment for everyone. This relationship would extend through the worker's retirement. This system was colloquially referred to as the "iron rice bowl."

Although by 1980, state sector jobs had become more competitive than ever before (only 37 percent of workers were assigned jobs in state-owned enterprises), still 80 percent of workers were assigned jobs in either state enterprises or collectively owned enterprises in that year (Walder 1986a, 57, 68–74). Once jobs were assigned, the job assignment was for life, except in rare cases of disciplinary firing and even rarer cases of layoffs (which were often followed by reassignment to another enterprise). This is not to say that workers never changed jobs or resigned from a given enterprise, but once workers were assigned to a work unit, except in unusual circumstances, they had the option of staying at that organization for life. With tightening fiscal constraints in the reform era, the heavy burdens of social security coupled with lifetime employment have crippled enterprises, and redefining the social security commitments of enterprises has become a central issue for the industrial reformers. Even in the reform era, it is not uncommon to walk into a factory, department store, or bank and see far more employees than are necessary to accomplish the tasks of that workplace. Why? The reason is that, under the planned economy, workers are simply assigned to work within various work units, and these units are responsible for supplying social security benefits. In the reform era, these work units have been reluctant to simply fire workers or cut pensions for retired workers as a way to cut costs. As one manager explained,

> Many of these employees have been working for this factory for twenty or more years; they have spent most of their lives working for this factory, but they just haven't reached retirement age yet. To suddenly cut these people off would be cruel. Suddenly they would have no retirement security; that would be very unfair to them . . . It's no way to treat people who have been working for you for so long.
>
> (Personal interview)

Another manager assessed the challenges that are associated with this mindset:

> The biggest problem that our state-owned enterprises have is the retired workers. We are taking care of so many people in comparison

to other private companies. We can't compete with them in terms of development. They take all of their profits and put them back into the company; we have to use all of our profits to take care of workers who are no longer working here. And many of these retired people are now working at other companies, but they still come here every month to get their pay.

(Personal interview)

Nevertheless, many broad institutional changes have emerged to redefine the labor relationship, including the new pension system (which does not really function to cover the costs of retired workers), labor contracts, the Labor Law (PRC 1994), and the existence of Labor Arbitration Commissions, which give workers some recourse against the factories where they are employed (these issues will be dealt with in Chapter 6). The emergence of labor contracts in China marks an important turning point for the socialist system created under Mao, as it marks the effective end of lifetime employment in China. This fact relieves work units of a large future burden of lifetime commitment to the workers they employ while, at the same time, breaking the commitment of the iron rice bowl for individuals.

Developing a Private Economy

While many scholars have argued that privatization is a necessary step in the transition from plan to market, the case of China belies this claim in important ways. However, an important distinction is necessary here: despite the fact that China did not move quickly along the road of privatizing state-owned enterprises, the government did allow a private economy to emerge, and this private economy has played an important role in the reform era. As Barry Naughton (1995) has pointed out, the private economy in China played an important role in teaching the state sector how to compete. State-owned factories were not privatized, but they were subjected to market competition from below by the emerging private sector.

It is important to note here that the private sector in China actually consists of three components. First, there are the small-scale entrepreneurs of the household economy (the "household enterprises"), which occupy a legal category that demands that they do not grow beyond seven employees. These small-scale organizations were very important in the early years of the economic reforms, as they provided opportunities for the large numbers of individuals who were "waiting for employment," including those who had returned home to urban areas after being "sent down" to the country-side during the Cultural Revolution. Some scholars have also suggested that this sector of the population provided a much-needed outlet for inno-vation and political resistance in the early years of the reforms (Gold 1989a, 1989b, 1990, 1991; Wank 1999). Second, the private enterprises have also played a crucial role in the development of the private economy in China. Private enterprises are different from household enterprises because they are allowed to grow beyond seven employees. It is this group of enterprises that has grown to challenge the state sector across a number of sectors in the economy. Like their smaller-scale counterparts in the household economy, this sector of the economy has also been an important force in social change. Some scholars have argued, for example, that this sector played a crucial role in the evolution of the Tiananmen Movement of 1989, as they had the resources to help the students organize in signifi-cant ways (Guthrie 1995; Perry and Wasserstrom 1992). A third sector of the private economy has to do with the publicly listed companies on China's stock exchanges in Shanghai and Shenzhen. These companies are becoming "privatized" in some ways; as some 30 percent of shares enter the free-floating market, however, the ownership and control of these compa-nies still largely rests in state hands, as it is typical for a firm listed on either of China's stock exchanges for the government to maintain control over 40–50 percent of the stock issued by the company.

Enticing Foreign Investment

By the early 1990s, it was still premature for China to claim that its economic system was an established market economy, but it had already made impor-tant strides away from the planned economic system. The long-term debate on whether China should focus on a plan-track policy or a market-driven policy between "hard-liners" (e.g., Li Peng) and "pragmatists" (e.g., Hu Yaobang and Zhao Ziyang) among Chinese leadership ended in the spring of 1992, when Deng Xiaoping took his "southern tour" to Shenzhen and officially declared the Chinese economic system as a market economy with socialist characteristics. One of the most important forces that pushed toward the building and maturation of market institutions came from the influence of foreign capital, driven by the opening-up policy in late 1979.

The establishment of Special Economic Zones in the 1980s in coastal areas greatly contributed to the inflow of foreign capital into China. China has taken a more aggressive view toward FDI than most other developing countries in recent years. The magnitude of foreign investment in China is greater, and it is also the case that foreign-invested firms in China play a very significant role in the growth of exports. The level of foreign investment in China is significantly greater than that of Japan in comparable development eras.[22] China's foreign investment regime is also far more liberal than that of South Korea. At the same time, the state-led project of building a rational–legal system is helping the Chinese market system to get on track with the international community, deal better with its foreign partners, and introduce advanced technology (Guthrie 1999).[23]

It is still too soon to give a definite picture of, or evaluate, how open China's markets are today, but it is very clear that China's market for goods has developed significantly, driven by the export-oriented development strategy and the rise of consumption within China. Clearly, labor markets have developed in significant ways, which has resulted mainly from the restructuring of the state sector, the booming of the non-state sectors, and state-led law building. The openness of China's economy is also evidenced by its liberal legal provisions facilitating exports based on processing or assembly activity. In addition, over the last two decades, China has become one of the major trading nations of the world. Despite claims that markets in China have been closed to foreign producers, for the first decade of the reforms, China ran a trade deficit with the world, which meant that more goods were being sold in China than the country was able to sell to the rest of the world. However, today China does enjoy a trade surplus with respect to the United States. The ratio of U.S. imports from China relative to U.S. exports is somewhere around 3.5 to 1. Nevertheless, the main point here is that even at their early stages of development, domestic equities markets in China are significantly more open than those in Japan, South Korea, and Taiwan at comparable stages.

Beyond the openness of the export economy, which has been a crucial factor in attracting foreign capital, the Chinese economy has also attracted investors of another type—those interested in capturing the internal market in China. The lure of the billion-person marketplace has been a key factor in attracting the likes of Coca-Cola, DuPont, General Motors, Kodak, Motorola, and many other blue-chip foreign firms that have been positioning themselves for years to capture the internal marketplace in China. These investors have also played an important role in China's economic reforms, because they have something to offer in return for access to China's internal markets: technology transfer is a central point of negotiation in the joint venture and licensing agreements they negotiate.

Taxation

Another significant change that has played a fundamental rule in the emergence of China's market economy lies in the area of taxation. One of the features that defined the redistributive economy was the fact that administrative offices collected the revenues and were therefore in a position to extract excess revenues from the factories under their jurisdictions; they would then redistribute these resources as they saw fit. In China today, however, this is largely a thing of the past. Three key changes have transformed this system. First, the extraction of revenues has been standardized in the taxation system (i.e., governing organizations are no longer permitted to simply extract all "excess" revenues), a change that officially came about with the Second Phase Profits Changed to Taxes Reform of 1985.[24] Second, today taxation is basically standardized—with value-added tax (17 percent of turnover) and income tax (33 percent of net income) as basic standards for firms and individuals. Third, most firms pay their taxes directly into the Government Tax Bureau, which has one bureau office for each district and each municipality, instead of to their governing organization.[25] Tax breaks and subsidized loan repayment make the concept of standardized taxation less meaningful, and it is often the case that implementing these internal policies is a problem (i.e., they exist on paper but not in practice). There are still ways for governing organizations to extract revenues from firms, such as negotiations over profits and "management" fees. But the main point here is that taxes are now being paid to a central office—rather than the administrative organization extracting revenues. Without the convenience of revenue extraction across a wide base of firms, the ability of governing organizations to skim or extract excess amounts of revenue is significantly reduced.

Constructing a Rational–legal System

Under Deng Xiaoping, Zhao Ziyang brought about radical change in China by pushing the country toward constitutionality and the emergence of the rule of law to create "rational" economic processes in China. This project would be carried on by Zhu Rongji after Zhao was ousted in 1989. These changes, which were set forth ideologically as a package of reforms that were necessary for economic development, fundamentally altered the role of politics and the role of the party in Chinese society. The early years of reform not only gave a great deal of autonomy to enterprise managers and small-scale entrepreneurs but also emphasized the legal reforms that would undergird this process of change. However, creating a body of civil and economic law, such as the Labor Law (1994), the Company Law (1994), and the National Compensation Law (1995), upon which the transforming economy would be based, meant that the party elites themselves would be held to the standards of these legal changes. Thus, in a number of ways, the rationalization of the economy led to a decline in the party's ability to rule over the working population.

In recent years, the next step in this process has come from global integration and the adoption of the norms of the international community. By championing global integration and the rule of law, Zhu Rongji also brought about broader political and social change in China, just as Zhao Ziyang did in the first decade of economic reform in China. Zhu's strategy has been to ignore questions of political reform and concentrate instead on the need for China to adopt economic and legal systems and norms that will allow the country to integrate smoothly with the rest of the global economy. From rhetoric on "linking up with the international community" (a very popular phrase among Chinese managers today) to laws such as the Patent Law (2000) and institutions such as the State Intellectual Property Office and the Chinese International Economic Trade and Arbitration Commission, this phase of reform has been oriented toward creating the standards of the international investment community. Thus, Zhu's objective was to intensify all of the reforms that have been discussed above, but at the same time to begin to hold these changes up to the standards of the global economy.

After two decades of transition, the architects of the reforms have set in place about 400 new national laws, administrative laws, 10,000 local regulations, and over 30,000 administrative procedures; compare this to the decade of the Cultural Revolution (1966–1976) when the government passed nine new laws. These legal changes and many more regulations, along with experiments with new economic institutions, have driven forward the process of reform. A number of laws and policies in the 1980s laid the groundwork for a new set of policies that would redefine labor relations in fundamental ways. Take, for example, the policies that set in motion the emergence of labor contracts in China, which were officially introduced in 1986. The labor contract was further institutionalized by the Enterprise Law (PRC 1988, Chapter 3, article 31), which codifies workers' rights for fair treatment and the right of due process in the event of unfair treatment. There are economic incentives behind the embracing of labor contracts by Chinese firms (the most important being the end of lifetime employment), but this institution, nevertheless, places the rationalization of the labor relationship, a guarantee of due process in the event of unfair treatment, and, ultimately, workers' rights at the center of the labor relationship. Other policies and laws also push this process forward (Guthrie 1998a). For example, the Labor Law (1994), Prison Reform Law (1994), and National Compensation Law (1995) are all examples of laws tied to labor that place the protection of individual civil liberties front and center. And the Company Law (1994), which has its roots in American and German corporate law, places much more emphasis on employee welfare than does the American version, to be sure. These laws and many others provide the legal infrastructure that allows workers to file grievances against managers, and individual citizens to file for compensation for past wrongs committed by the government. Laws such as these are a crucial part of the changes occurring in the conception of individual rights in China.

The obvious and most common response to these changes might be that they are symbolic rather than substantive in nature, that a changing legal and policy framework has little meaning when an authoritarian government still sits at the helm, but the scholarship that has looked extensively at the impact of these legal changes largely belies this view. For example, the rationalization of labor relations in the workplace is directly tied to institutional changes, such as the Labor Law, and other legal institutions that emphasize the individual civil liberties of workers (Guthrie 1999). Workers and managers take these new institutions seriously, and they have had a dramatic impact on the structure of authority relations and the conception of rights within the workplace. Research has also shown that legal and policy changes that place an emphasis on individual civil liberties matter in significant ways in other arenas as well. The most systematic and exhaustive study of the prison system to date shows that changes in the treatment of prisoners have indeed emerged in the wake of the Prison Reform Law (Seymour and Anderson 1998). And, although no scholarship has been done on the National Compensation Law, it is noteworthy that under this law, 97,569 suits were filed against the government in 1999, including such recent high-profile cases as a suit against the government for its hand in producing cigarettes and a suit against the government for the deaths in the Tiananmen Square massacre. These rational–legal institutions guarantee that, for the first time in the history of the PRC, individuals can now receive their day in court, and it is under this system that lawsuits against the government specifically have risen over 12,000 percent since the beginning of the economic reforms.[26]

The Labor Law (PRC 1994) and the Labor Arbitration Commission (of which there are branches in every urban district) work hand-in-hand in guaranteeing workers their individual rights as laborers. Chapter 10 of the Labor Law, entitled "Labor Disputes," is specifically devoted to articulating due process, which laborers are legally guaranteed should a dispute arise in the workplace. The law explains in an explicit fashion the rights of the worker to take disputes to outside arbitration (the district's Labor Arbitration Commission, or LAC) should the resolution in the workplace be unsatisfactory to the worker. Further, many state-owned enterprises have placed all of their workers on fixed-term labor contracts, which significantly rationalize the labor relationship beyond the personalized labor relations of the past. This bundle of changes has fundamentally altered the nature of the labor relationship and the mechanisms through which authority can be challenged (both within and outside the factory). For more than a decade now, it has been possible for workers to file grievances against superiors and have their grievances heard at the LACs, and, in 1999, out of 120,191 labor disputes that were settled by arbitration or mediation, 63,030 (52 percent) were decided wholly in favor of the workers filing the suits. These are official statistics, and we should be skeptical of their veracity. However, even if the magnitude is off, these numbers illuminate an important trend toward legal activity regarding workers' rights.

Many of these changes in labor practices were not originally adopted with workers' rights in mind, but the unintended consequence of these changes has been the construction of a regime of labor relations that emphasizes the rights of workers. For instance, extending upon the example of labor contracts, which were being experimented with as early as 1983, these were originally intended as a form of economic protection for ailing enterprises, allowing enterprises a formal way of ending lifetime employment. However, as the terms of employment were codified in these contracts, workers began using them as a vehicle for filing grievances when contractual agreements were not honored. With the emergence of the LACs in the late 1980s and the further codification of these institutions in the Labor Law of 1994, the changes that were afoot became formalized in a set of institutions that ultimately benefited workers in the realm of rights. In a similar way, workers' representative committees began as an institution formed in the state's interest, but once in place became an institution that workers claimed as their own. These institutions, which many managers I have spoken with refer to as "our own little democracy," were adopted early in the reforms as a compromise, a way of heading off the growing agitation for the creation of independent labor unions. These committees do not have the same power or status as independent labor unions in the West, but workers have nonetheless made them their own, and they are much more significant in factories today than they were originally intended to be.

Setting the Stage for Entry into the Global Economy: Capital Markets and SASAC

In the 1990s, the focus was on building the institutions that would continue to push along the reforms of the state sector while, at the same time, attracting foreign capital through capital markets (Guthrie *et al.* 2007; Guthrie and Wang 2007). Accordingly, coinciding with the legislative changes of the 1990s was the founding of the Shanghai and Shenzhen Stock Exchanges. The first of these, the Shanghai Exchange, opened for business on December 19, 1990, with the Shenzhen Exchange opening shortly thereafter. By the end of 2004, the number of domestically listed companies in China had risen to 1,371 with a total market capitalization of 525.6 billion U.S. dollars (SSEa 2005; SSEb 2005; Hertz 1998; Gao 2002). Following the gradualist model, the Chinese government's construction of the institutions that govern public ownership has been spread across the period. After a series of regulations such as "the Opinions on Standardizing the Joint Stock Limited Companies" and "the Provisional Regulations on the Administration of Issuing and Trading of Stocks," the Securities Law of the People's Republic of China (PRC 1999) was adopted in 1998 at the Ninth National People's Congress and took effect in July of 1999, thus institutionalizing the legal basis for the standardized operation of listed companies. The Company Law (PRC 1993) laid the foundation for this standardization. The law itself contains twelve chapters, covering a range of issues from stock issuance and stock transactions to the rules governing ownership and shareholding of publicly listed companies. Finally, in 2001, the central government passed The Tentative Measures for Decreasing State Shareholding (PRC 2001). Yet, as China has been systematically constructing the institutions of a publicly traded economy, even in the area of public ownership of listed companies, we must acknowledge the complexities of enterprise–state relations in the Chinese model, as the government's receding from control over publicly-listed state enterprises has, like every other institutional change in the Chinese economic reforms, been a gradual process. The companies listed on China's domestic stock exchanges are becoming "privatized" in some ways. A typical ownership transformation for a state-owned enterprise would allow the state to retain between 30 and 40 percent of the company's shares; between 30 and 40 percent of the shares are designated for institutional shares; the remaining 30 percent of shares are designated for public consumption as free floating shares.

Another critical institution in China's next phase of development has been the emergence of the State-Owned Assets Supervision and Administration Commission (SASAC), a state asset management organization that has offices at the Central and all provincial-level jurisdictions. This organization owns controlling stakes in the vast majority of China's blue-chip companies. As with virtually all cases of institution building in reform-era China, the emergence of SASAC has been a gradual and experimental process, dating back to the first decade of the economic reforms. In 1988 the State Council established a national state-owned assets authority—the State-owned Assets Management Bureau [*guoyou zichan guanli ju*] to coordinate the management of all state-owned assets in the People's Republic of China. The State-owned Assets Bureau will exercise its power under the guidance of Ministry of Finance. Over the course of the 1990s, many reforms that would target state-owned enterprises (SOEs), would increasingly involve the group of organizations that would eventually become SASAC. These reforms included: the principle of state-owned asset management was "unified guidance, decentralized

management" [*tongyi lingdao, fenji guanli*]; "national unity, classified monitoring, and autonomous operation" [*guojia tongyi suoyou, zhengfu fenji
lueguan, yinye zizhu jingying*]: unified ownership by the state; separate
supervision by local governments; independent management by the enterprises themselves. During this period, the central government emphasized
the notion of listing large SOEs on the stock markets, including domestic
and overseas stock market, while small enterprises were encouraged to
become private. In 1998, Zhu Rongji merged the State-owned Asset
Management Bureau System into the Finance Ministry System. Then, in
1999, the State Council passed key decisions that emphasized the strategic
restructuring of the state sector. Between 1999–2003, in order to manage
better state-owned assets, the State Council gradually announced several
documents to set up a specific department to supervise and administrate
the state-owned assets and some relevant documents to further emphasis
on the responsibilities of this department. As a result of the 16th CPC
National Congress Government Reform Plan [*jichang gaige fangze*]
the State-Owned Assets Supervision and Administration Commission
(SASAC) was formally established (after more than a decade of gradual
development). The supervision scope of SASAC is the assets controlled
under central state-owned enterprises. Assets owned by local state-owned
enterprises are managed by local SASACs, which were set up and governed
by provincial- and municipal-level governments. Thus, the system of separately owned, separately supervised was set up among central SASAC and
local SASAC. Today, SASAC is the most powerful state organization
managing across industries in China.

Conclusions: Gradual Reform and China's Quiet Revolution

Much like the advocates of rapid economic reform, those demanding
immediate political and social reform often take for granted the learning
that must take place in the face of new institutions. The assumption most
often seems to be that, given certain institutional arrangements individuals
will naturally know how to carry out the practices of capitalism. Yet, these
assumptions reflect a neoclassical view of human nature in which rational
humankind will thrive in its "natural" environment—free markets.
Completely absent from this view are the roles of history, culture, and
preexisting institutions, and it is a vision that is far too simplistic to
comprehend the challenge of making rational economic and legal systems

work in the absence of stable institutions and a history to which they can be tied. The transition from a command economy to a market economy can be a wrenching experience not only at the institutional level but also at the level of individual practice. Individuals must learn the rules of the market, and new institutions must be set in place long enough to gain stability and legitimacy; these are processes that occur slowly and over time. The government's methodical experimentation with different institutional forms and the party's gradual receding from control over the economy has brought about a "quiet revolution" in the Chinese economy. Yet this is a slow and gradual process and must be placed in the context of China's recent institutional history: when there is no immediate history of a rational–legal economic system, it is impossible to create it in one dramatic moment of institutional change. Thus, the architects of China's transition to capitalism have had success in reforming the economy. They have recognized that the transition to a radically different type of economic system must occur gradually, allowing for the maximum possible institutional stability as economic actors slowly learn the rules of capitalism. Capitalism has arrived in China, and it has done so under the guise of gradual institutional reform under the Communist mantle.

It is not by coincidence that the Geely representatives in Lijiang set their expo up under the symbolic blessing of Mao Zedong—the Chinese government is great at using symbols and hidden messages. And, to be sure, the notion of Mao blessing emerging domestic multinationals is an important one and one that, once again, illuminates the Chinese government's savvy use of gradual economic change with classic symbols of the past. For one thing, the Chinese government is no longer ambivalent about embracing the capitalist class. While Jiang Zemin's decision to admit "capitalists" into the CCP in 2001 raised opposition from the conservative wing of the party at the time, that debate is long past. The private sector has come to be viewed as a critical constituency that the CCP leadership must actively court. Second, with China well on its way to achieving the status of global economic superpower, the story is no longer about a successful export-led economy and the gradual emergence of a grassroots private sector. China's power in the global economy today is about companies like Geely, PetroChina, Hier, Lenovo, CNOOC and many more—companies that are ready to compete on the global stage and they do so with the full blessing and backing of the CCP and its leadership.

As a final note, thinking back to the CCP's use of Mao's image to legitimize the gradually emerging capitalist modes of production and livelihood, this has certainly been a strategy of the party. However, there is also something deeper going on, which has to do with gradual political reform. It is widely acknowledged that the economic reforms in China have led to economic growth that has been nothing short of astonishing, but the world is much more skeptical about political reform. China's government has been viewed widely as a group of authoritarian economic elites clinging desperately to power as they buy the population off with steady economic growth. This view, however, is incorrect. China's economic *and* political reform has been gradual, and the lack of a sudden break from the past has led many observers to believe that there is not a commitment to real political change. For the last fifteen years, the Chinese leaders have been quietly pushing forward institutional change. Through the passage of hundreds of new national laws and thousands of local laws, the institutionalization of democratic elections at the village level, the gradual emergence of a nonprofit sector, and many other institutional changes that are gradually sweeping across the nation, Chinese society is being transformed.

While China's political leaders do not openly advertise these changes—it has proven to be politically imprudent to do so in the past—a distancing of the party from its past is clearly in the making. And these political changes are also reflected in the further diminishing of Mao's image—and not only in the kitschified and overshadowed scenes of the Tiananmen Square mausoleum and the Lijang statue. Perhaps the most extreme version of this diminishing came in the fall of 2006, when Shanghai high schools began teaching from a new standard textbook that was curiously silent on Mao and his Communist movement. With little fanfare or press, the central government quietly wrote Mao (and Communist history) out of the history books. The ideologically driven version of communism, which dominated China from 1949 until the economic reforms began in 1979, and Mao himself receive little attention in the textbook. Topics such as technology, economics, and the New York Stock Exchange and figures such as J.P. Morgan and Bill Gates are given significantly more attention and space than Mao, his revolution, and Marxist ideology. While China watchers like Joseph Khan of the *New York Times* have wondered about Mao's sudden diminishing status, this particular change is but one of a long line of gradual changes that are quietly redefining China's political system.

It is unlikely that China will ever openly reconsider Mao's legacy in the fashion that the Soviet Union disavowed Stalin's legacy under the leadership of Khrushchev. For thirty-two years of economic reform, the Chinese model has been to gradually adopt new systems, laws and policies without ever openly overturning the past. In many cases, they have actively employed the images of the past to act as symbolic handmaidens of the new policies. And with his seemingly authoritarian stances on a number of issues, many have worried that President Hu Jintao would leave his once-liberal image behind, showing instead his true colors as the leader of "China's new authoritarianism." But, as we will discuss in Chapter 7, under President Hu we have seen a fundamental transformation of private property rights and the right to form independent unions, two issues which have been central to criticism of China's political reform process. As reform-minded elites emphasized the need for a rational system for economic development, they were also altering the politics of the party system. And, in the end, President Hu, with his quiet authoritarianism, had the political will to close the history books on the Maoist era.

3

CHANGING SOCIAL INSTITUTIONS

When I was doing my doctoral research in China in the early 1990s, like most graduate students, I did not have much money.[1] Overall, China was still much cheaper than the United States, but Shanghai was fairly pricey, so the organization that sponsored my research, the Shanghai Academy of Social Sciences, helped me find a job teaching English to supplement my income. In the class I taught, I had one student, a middle-aged man named Mr. Zhang, who was extremely friendly and asked me often if he could take me out for an evening. It felt odd to me to accept the invitation, because the student had made clear that he wanted to treat me to a night out, and average people in China in the early 1990s had even less money than I did, but eventually I accepted. The evening began with dinner in a private room of an expensive Shanghai restaurant, where we were joined by another individual the student introduced to me as a friend of his, Mr. Li. When the bill came, I offered to pay, but Mr. Zhang insisted on treating. He leaned in close at one point and said cryptically, "Maybe you can help me in another way sometime." A few days later, I received a call from Mr. Li, the "friend" who had accompanied us at dinner. He said that he was interested in practicing his English and that Zhang had told him I would be willing to help him. I was a little confused, as I did not recall making such agreement, but, remembering Zhang's comment about helping him in "another way," I decided to meet with Li and help him with his English. As the discussion unfolded over three or four meetings, I gradually came to understand that our transaction (me teaching Li

63

English for free) was part of an extended series of social obligations and debts. In short, Zhang had treated me to an expensive dinner in order to manufacture some level of obligation with me, so that I could then be called upon to give Li English lessons. Li, it turned out, was the doctor of Zhang's ailing mother. And while Li did not have enough money to afford English lessons from a foreign teacher, he did control a very valuable asset—the allocation of beds in his overcrowded hospital. Zhang's mother was often sick enough that she required hospital care, and Zhang spent a lot of time worrying about whether she would receive the proper treatment when she was hospitalized. I came to understand that, in essence, my free English lessons to Li were helping to manufacture the debt that would ensure a hospital bed and quality hospital care for Zhang's mother. By the time I understood the web of social relationships and obligations I was entangled in, I was fascinated at the extended plans that lay behind what I initially thought was a simple invitation to dinner. It left me wondering about the rules of the gift economy in China. It also left me wondering what would happen to the gift economy as the economic reforms progressed.

This system of exchange—the gift economy—is a social system that is not uncommon in nonmarket economies, and it has played an extremely important role in Chinese society. It is but one of several key systems around which Chinese society was organized when the economic reforms began, one of the consequences of the institutional structure of Chinese society. Social scientific definitions of the word institution generally settle on three characteristics: institutions are organizations, structures, or systems that (1) involve two or more people; (2) involve rules—either formal or informal—that govern behavior; and (3) are stable over time.[2] If we are to understand the ways in which society is transforming as China becomes more integrated into the global economy, we must begin with an examination of the crucial social institutions that governed this society on the eve of the economic reforms. One scholar, Anthony Oberschall, made this point lucidly in an academic symposium on China's transition from plan to market, succinctly laying out the key institutions he observed when living in China in the early 1980s:

> [In the early 1980s] there were three institutions at the core of Chinese society: the family, the work unit in the city and the collective farm in rural China, and the communist party-state. Each

Chinese citizen belonged to a family, and every family had been a permanent member of a work unit (*danwei*) or a collective farm. The party-state, accountable only to itself, penetrated and controlled every work unit and collective farm, and thus also every family and every individual. Chinese social organization was rigid and hierarchic. Work units were isolated from each other—even physically bounded by brick walls—with solidarity, loyalty, and collective identity encapsulating members against outsiders.

(1996, 1028)

This set of institutional arrangements helped to create a type of dependence—a reliance by individuals on the party-state system—that Andrew Walder (1986a) has called "principled particularism," meaning that individuals were forced to develop personal relationships that would mitigate their reliance on the organizations and institutions that governed their lives. Individuals were engulfed by the institutions that governed their lives in Communist China, as there was very little private space that was not shaped by these institutions in one way or another. As Oberschall put it, it was a "world of total institutions."[3] In this chapter, I introduce some of the key institutions that govern life in China and discuss the ways in which they have changed as economic reforms have unfolded. I will look at the party-state, systems of allocation (such as work units), and the family. I will also introduce some of the consequences of these institutional arrangements, such as corruption and the gift economy. All of these are social institutions that are important in Chinese life, and all have undergone dramatic changes in the era of economic reform.

The Family as a Social Institution

For more than 2,000 years, the family has been the central organizing unit of Chinese society and one of the most important social institutions organizing individuals' lives. Yet the twentieth century has witnessed dramatic changes in the structure of the Chinese family. There were two major points of rupture at which the family was dramatically transformed, the first being the transition to the Communist system after 1949, and the second being the changes that occurred in the era of economic reform. The traditional structure and values of the Chinese family were significantly weakened during the Communist Revolution and the early years of the

Communist regime and were further weakened in the era of economic reform. Today, some elements of traditional China have survived and have been interwoven with the new structures and values of the reform era; however, the family as a social institution in China has undergone dramatic changes in the last half century.

Family Structure Before 1949

Throughout the imperial period and before the fall of the Qing Dynasty in 1911, the values of the Chinese family were stipulated by Confucian teachings. In very basic terms, Confucian thought can be characterized as a secular moral philosophy with a strong emphasis on social responsibility. Though often thought of as a religion, Confucianism is not built upon notions of heaven and hell, or sin and redemption, but, rather, on a simple sense of doing that which is ethical and right in the world (such as trustworthiness, propriety, altruism, filial piety, and having a sense of shame). Confucius was suspicious of law, believing that laws were for restraining and that a just moral society should emanate from individuals who acted morally and ethically within their family settings. Thus, he believed that morality stood in the realm of family, and family rules governed the lives of individuals (Mote 1989).

With the goal of building a peaceful and harmonious moral world, Confucius saw a family-centered system as the pillar of Chinese society, where an individual's primary duty was to the family, and then to the community or society, and finally to the state. These links among individuals and their families, and eventually the state, were realized through five fundamental relationships among individuals: (1) affection (*qin*) between parents (primarily fathers) and children (primarily sons); the rules regulating these relationships centered on the concepts of filial piety and respect for elders; (2) righteousness (*yi*) between ruler and subject (the notion of righteousness between ruler and subject parallels the relationships between fathers and sons, and the rules regulating it include loyalty and respect for the authority); (3) distinction (*bie*) between men (husbands) and women (wives), a rule that stipulates women's compliance to men; (4) the pecking order (*xu*) between old and young siblings; and (5) sincerity (*xin*) between friends. These basic concepts encapsulated social relationships within the Chinese family for more than 2,000 years.

The family in the pre-Communist era was a patriarchal institution in which fathers ruled with complete authority. When the state intervened in the realm of the family, fathers were heavily favored. For example, within the family structure, fathers committing a given crime against their sons were punished far more lightly than sons who committed the same crime against their fathers. The same was true of husbands harming their wives. Extended families became the social fabric of a society in which the state was significantly removed from the lives of individuals. Functioning as a social security system of sorts, several generations often lived under one roof, creating a self-sufficient institution that provided mutual support among family members, including the care of children and the elderly. A certain amount of wealth would be pooled in the form of lineage land, the income from which would pay for the upkeep of ancestral temples and graveyards, and for teachers who served as instructors of lineage schools.

Arranged marriage was common, with matchmakers arranging marriages for the benefit of both families. Marriages between children of powerful lineages were carefully negotiated by the parents, and great care was taken to preserve lineages and bring together powerful clans. Marriage transfers in traditional China usually consisted of direct and indirect dowries—the groom's family made a contribution, which was returned with the bride as part of the dowry. Bride prices varied across classes, and marriage transfers were often built upon social prestige. While elites used dowries to maintain their wealth and enhance their status, poor families often "sold" their daughters to finance their sons' marriages. Elites in the imperial period organized their extended families around immense patriarchal power, smothering the younger generation's pursuit of individual freedom. During the Imperial Period, the state was conspicuously absent within the Chinese family before the building of the modern Chinese state in 1911. However, following the Nationalist Revolution, the established relationships and family structures prescribed by Confucian thought were disrupted by the rising militarization of Chinese society with the warlord period (1912–1927), the period of Nationalist Party control (1927–1949), and the occupation of China by the Japanese Army (1937–1945), each of which established their own social controls. Despite more intervention by state power into Chinese families during this time period, the state still largely relied on family-run social control much more than state-based social control. As an "official" (*guan*) space with limited social control, the state was still removed from the "private" (*si*) realm of individuals and families, and also the "public" (*gong*) field where the clan systems prevailed.

The Post-1949 Family

Following the Communist Revolution, the Chinese family underwent considerable changes. The revolution and the mass movements under Mao Zedong's regime set out to break up traditional familial bonds and establish an ideologically based egalitarian social order. Confucian ideals were recast as the "Four Olds" (*sijiu*)—old ideas, old habits, old customs, and old culture—and were attacked, destroyed, and replaced by communist ideology. During this period, the Communist state began to encroach upon all aspects of individuals' lives to a much greater extent than ever before.[4] In the Maoist era, the targets were ancestor worship and lineage organization, which changed the extended family on cultural and religious levels. Individuals and their families were subjugated to the greater goal of running a communist country. Collectivization and the elimination of private property destroyed many of the economic motivations that had shaped family loyalties for millennia. In urban areas, both men and women were organized by the work-unit systems that provided them with social welfare (income, housing, medical care, and the like) and also facilitated the Chinese Communist Party's centralized political control over individuals. In rural China, communes were set up and rural families were organized around collectives that functioned as the basic units of agricultural production until the late 1970s. Thus, the state destroyed the power and authority of patriarchs and the material basis for the clan-based system.

These institutions and organizational practices continued to break down family bonds throughout the Communist period. The fates of individuals and their families were tightly tied to the state through party membership and party loyalty. This was most dramatically demonstrated during the Cultural Revolution (1966–1976), when Chinese families were broken apart and family members were encouraged to favor state ideology over the shared family values inherited from Confucian ideals. The Red Guards, supported by Mao during the early period of the Cultural Revolution, were encouraged to challenge the older generation and their traditional authority. Many people had to separate themselves from "class enemies" within their families in order to show their loyalty to the party. After Mao betrayed his revolutionary followers and sent them to the countryside for "reeducation," many families fell farther apart, as family members spent years away from each other.[5]

Beyond tightening the ties between the individuals and the party-state, the Communist state eliminated many family rituals and ceremonies, as well as the traditional social order that arose out of them. The most striking characteristic of the family in Communist China was that women—at least in theory—were elevated to a position equal to men. Women were assigned to work in the urban work-unit system or the rural collectives. The Marriage Law of 1950 outlawed many practices targeting women: arranged marriages, concubinage, dowries, and child betrothals. Article 2 of the Marriage Law stipulates, for example, that a marriage must be "based on the free choice of partners ... and on equality between man and woman...." Article 3 declares, "Marriage upon arbitrary decision by any third party ... shall be prohibited." And Articles 9 and 13 entitle women to the same status within their families as men, stipulating, "Husband and wife shall have equal status in the family," and, "The property acquired by the husband and the wife during the period in which they are under the contract of marriage shall be in their joint possession ..." Women were granted the right to file for divorce. Marriage transfers still existed, but they became less predictable. Marriage was commonly delayed until somewhat later in life, with the encouragement of the law. In addition, lavish dowries and wedding feasts were stigmatized as feudal extravagance in both urban and rural areas under Mao's rule. The land reform changed the ability of rural elites to transfer land as part of a dowry. Even though second-generation families in the Mao era began to revert to some of the old traditions surrounding marriage, most of the rituals and ceremonies fell out of practice in Communist China.

Since the late 1970s, the economic reforms have brought about another revolutionary change to the Chinese family, with the party's control being gradually withdrawn from the lives of individuals. In urban China, most people have continued to receive housing and health care from their work units, but younger generations depend less on the state redistributive system, as increasing numbers find work in the private and foreign sectors. Economic liberalization, the resulting economic boom—especially in the coastal areas—and changes in the restrictions against migration have led rural men and women to migrate into cities (see Figure 3.1) to seek employment often far away from their homes. Young women form a big part of the labor force that is steadily migrating to urban and coastal areas—a fact that has fundamental consequences for the structure of the

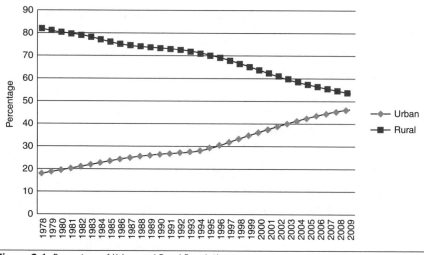

Figure 3.1 Percentage of Urban and Rural Population.

Source: National Statistical Bureau of China (2010, 95).

Chinese family in rural areas. The liberalization of state policies in the reform era has also led to the reemergence of many traditional practices that were eliminated by the Communist regime. Wedding ceremonies and dowry practices, for example, have returned in rural regions as a way of reinforcing social status for new elites of the reform era. Marriages and deaths are marked by important rituals that foreground the centrality of family lineage, especially in rural China.

State Control over the Family and Population

Despite the reduction of the state's direct control over family life during the reform era, state control over population growth has nevertheless continued to play a significant part in shaping the Chinese family and economy.[6] Since 1949, the Chinese population has more than doubled, from 565 million in 1953 to nearly 1.3 billion at the 2000 Census. The country has undergone five stages of population growth during this period. The first baby boom in China occurred between 1949 and 1957, when the birth rates were fairly high (32–38 per thousand). During this time period, death rates were remarkably reduced due to a more egalitarian distribution of food and universal (albeit rudimentary) medical care. Consequently, natural growth rates were high (16–25 percent). The first real push for population control began in 1953, with the passage of laws legalizing abortion. Following that, a series of propaganda campaigns—such as the formation of birth control study groups in 1954—made it very clear that the state would control all aspects of individuals' lives, including their family plans. In 1956, the government actively pushed for limitations on childbirth but to little real effect. Overall, this period saw the creation of a new environment for Chinese family planning.

The period 1958–1961 witnessed high death rates caused by the catastrophic policies of the Great Leap Forward, along with decreasing birth rates and natural growth rates.[7] But as normal conditions were restored, the death rate fell to 10 per thousand in 1962 from 25.6 per thousand in 1960, and the post-crisis birthrate and natural growth rates were very high, causing the period to be known as the second baby boom. The birth rate in 1963 was 43.3 per thousand, and it remained high until 1970. The natural growth rate remained at about 25–33 per thousand. The Chinese government attempted a new family planning program in 1964, but it was disrupted by the Cultural Revolution, which began in 1966.

It was not until the 1970s that real attention was paid to the problems of population growth. The *wan xi shao* ("late" marriage, "long" birth intervals, and "fewer" children) campaign was enforced and led to rapid reductions in the birth rate (down to 18 per thousand during this period) and natural growth rate (down to 12 per thousand). Following this campaign, the fertility rate declined from 4.2 in 1974 to 3.2 in 1976 to 2.2 in 1980. The solution to the population problem, known as China's one-child policy, was launched by the government in the early 1980s. In 1982, a national census advised by the United Nations counted the Chinese population at over 1 billion; but even earlier than this, officials had a sense of the magnitude of the problem, which was that China's population would soon be too large for the country to feed itself. In September 1980, Hua Guofeng announced this policy, and austere measures were subsequently enforced. Over the next two years, in addition to a propaganda campaign, the State Planning Commission oversaw compulsory intrauterine device insertion and, in some cases, compulsory sterilization of 16.4 million women, as well as sterilization of 4 million men. In addition, the Chinese government created various disincentives through the work-unit system to enforce the one-child policy in urban areas, particularly in the 1980s. The couples that violated the one-child policy were subject to high taxes, loss of jobs, decrease in wages, loss of benefits from the work units, and loss of bonuses for the entire work group, in some cases. In rural areas, the household incentive system was set up to offer a premium on family-based labor for those families who would comply with this policy.

While China's one-child policy has decreased the population growth rates and arguably contributed to China's rapid economic growth in the past thirty years, it has remained a subject of considerable controversy both in academia and in the population policy field. There is little doubt that the enforcement of the one-child policy in the reform era has brought about crucial social changes in family structure, as well as a series of social problems. Family size has decreased, and an entire generation of "only children" is expected to support a disproportionately old and retired population in the near future. With the gradual withdrawal of state support for the elderly, their care has grown to depend more on the family system, thereby exacerbating this demographic problem. Among the social implications is also a generation of "only children," who have been nurtured by their parents and four grandparents, leading to a phenomenon that some authors have referred to as the "little emperor syndrome."[8] Some demographers note that China also faces the prospect of an insufficient labor force in the decades to come.

The most serious and often noted social problem linked to the one-child policy is female infanticide and abandonment of female children. Historically and culturally, sons in Chinese families are responsible for taking care of the elderly, along with carrying the family name and inheriting the family property. As a result, male offspring are preferred in Chinese families, especially in rural areas, and female offspring suffer accordingly. For a time in the 1980s and early 1990s, female infanticide became relatively common—it has been estimated that 200,000 female babies have been killed each year since the 1980s. (For obvious reasons, there are no official statistics on this topic, but this number has certainly gone down dramatically in the last decade.) Abandonment of female children is also common, though no estimates on the numbers are available. Many of the girls' births go unregistered, causing them to lose access to many legal benefits, including educational opportunities and other forms of social welfare. In addition, the use of advanced technologies such as ultrasound has increased the numbers for female infanticide, thus leaving China with a significant gender gap. Official statistics placed the sex ratio at birth (male/female) in China at 116.86 in the 2000 Census, a figure

Table 3.1 Demographic Changes in China

	1978	1989	1997	2001	2005	2009
Family						
Total number of households	206,410,000	270,780,000	328,900,000	353,300,000	395,590,000	401,520,000[1]
Average household size, urban areas	NA	3.55	3.19	3.1	2.96	2.89
Average household size, rural areas	NA	4.86	4.35	4.15	4.08	3.98
Marriages and Divorces						
Registered number of marriages	5,978,000	9,372,000	9,141,000	8,050,000	8,231,000	12,124,000
Number of divorces	285,000	753,000	1,198,000	1,250,000	1,785,000	2,468,000
Housing						
Per capita living space, urban areas (sq. ft.)	72.11	145.31	191.6	269	280.94	NA
Per capita living space, rural areas (sq. ft.)	87.11	185.14	242.19	300.32	319.69	361.67

Sources: National Statistical Bureau of China (2006, 915 1978–2005 data; 2010, 10, 101, 2009 data)[1]
[1]Source: http://www.stats.gov.cn/was40/gjtjj_en_detail.jsp?searchword=census&channelid=9528&record=5 2010 data.

Table 3.2 Basic Statistics on National Population Census

	1953	1964	1982	1990	2000	2010*
Total Population	594,350,000	694,580,000	1,008,180,000	1,133,680,000	1,265,830,000	1,339,724,852
Male	307,990,000	356,520,000	519,440,000	584,950,000	653,550,000	NA
Female	286,360,000	338,060,000	488,740,000	548,730,000	612,280,000	NA
Sex Ratio	107.56	105.46	106.3	106.6	106.74	106.74
Average Family Size	4.33	4.43	4.41	3.96	3.44	3.10
Population by Age Group (%)						
0–14	36.28	40.69	33.59	27.69	22.89	16.6
15–64	59.31	55.75	61.5	66.74	70.15	74.53
65 and Over	4.41	3.56	4.91	5.57	6.96	8.87
Nationality Population						
Han Nationality	547,280,000	654,560,000	940,880,000	1,042,480,000	1,159,400,000	NA
Percentage to Total Population	93.94	94.24	93.32	91.96	91.59	91.51
Minority Nationalities	35,320,000	40,020,000	67,300,000	91,200,000	106,430,000	NA
Percentage to Total Population	6.06	5.76	6.68	8.04	8.41	8.49
Population by Residence						
Urban Population	77,260,000	127,100,000	210,820,000	299,710,000	458,440,000	665,570,000
Rural Population	505,340,000	567,480,000	797,360,000	833,970,000	807,390,000	675,150,000

Source: National Statistical Bureau of China (2010, 98),

*Source: *Press Release on Major Figures of the 2010 National Population Census*, Year 2010, population percentage of age group 15–64 for year 2010 was calculated by subtracting percentage of 0–14 and 65 and over from total population percentage. http://www.stats.gov.cn/english/newsand-comingevents/t20110428_402722237.htm, accessed June 19, 2011.

outrageously high compared to the natural ratio of lower than 105.[9] This is up from 108.5 in 1982, 110.9 in 1987, and 111.3 in 1990.[10]

Entering into the new century, the Chinese government has not yet officially relaxed its one-child policy, but in 2002, the Population and Family Planning Law was passed to rationalize the state's control over family planning. According to the law, equal importance is attached to measures providing contraception services and promoting the one-child policy, beyond simply ensuring the control of the country's population. Those who have an extra child, according to the law, must pay for the extra burden they impose on society because they will use more public resources.

The State and State Allocation Systems

The state is a crucial institution in Chinese society. In a state-dominated society such as China, on the eve of the economic reforms, the state is forever present, setting the rules by which individuals live and finding more subtle ways to control behavior and command loyalty. From the fall of the Qing Dynasty through the building of the People's Republic of China following the Communist Revolution, the role of the state in Chinese society has changed in critical ways over the course of three periods: (1) in the pre-Communist era, the state was an instrument of symbolic and cultural power, with some limited elements of social control, but it was far removed from the private realm of individuals and families; (2) in the Communist era, the state steadily penetrated down to the level of the individual; and (3) in the period of economic reform, the state's control over society has been steadily receding.

The Imperial Period

Before the establishment of Mao's Communist regime, the imperial government ruled largely through a cultural power and family-centered social system that Confucian thought prescribed. After the fall of the Qing Dynasty, more direct systems of coercion were imposed upon the Chinese. For instance, in rural China, gentry began to use access to government offices to build up networks of power, becoming "buffers" between the modern Chinese state and individual families in rural society (Fei 1946). Despite more intervention by the state into the life of the Chinese family during this period, the state still relied primarily on family-run social control. The *baojia* system was the key link between the state and family in late imperial China. Stemming from the Qing judicial system and strengthened by the Nationalist Party's rule, the *baojia* system was a locally autonomous institution that made the rural elite responsible for enforcing public order and collecting taxes for the state. Ten families (households) formed a *bao*, and ten *bao* formed a *jia*, which contained 100 hundred families. The heads of each *baojia* were responsible for social control within their *baojia*. Based on the family as the primary unit, the *baojia* system placed "the collective responsibilities for the proper and law-abiding conduct of all its members" (Yang 1959, 103).

The Communist Era: The Party and the Political System

Originally established in 1921, the Chinese Communist Party (CCP) is China's only ruling party, holding exclusive political and institutional power over the country. From 1949 until very recently—the mid-1990s—the party and the state overlapped in almost every aspect of governance, as the party exercised firm control over state bodies through interlocking organizations. In practice, all decisions of central government units had to be approved by the party, which meant that de facto political power rested in the hands of the party. All top positions are held by Communist Party members, further bolstering the party's power. In addition, Communist Party branches exist within all central and local government organizations. In the pre-reform era, these branches were the actual decision makers. In the early years of the economic reforms, they removed themselves from direct decision-making, but they still kept a watchful eye over the decisions of virtually every governmental office. Today, the role of Communist Party offices is receding further and further from direct control over the governmental offices they used to run; however, all key officers of government organizations are Communist Party members. And, although recently the residents in more and more villages have begun to elect non-party members as chairs of the Village Automatic Administration Committees, all of the leadership positions from the township governments on up are still occupied by party members.[11]

Within the CCP, the Political Bureau and its Standing Committee are the real centers of political power of the People's Republic of China (PRC). Although the Politburo Standing Committee (PSC) has existed since the beginning of the PRC, the actual power wielded by the PSC has varied over time. During the Cultural Revolution, the PSC was essentially

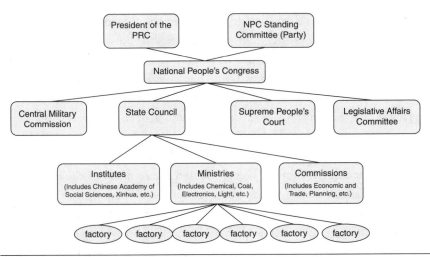

Figure 3.2 Structure of the PRC Government.

powerless, while real power was exercised by the Revolutionary Committees set up by Mao Zedong. Deng Xiaoping revived the PSC's political power after he took over and built the second generation of CCP leadership. Recently, the former president of China, Jiang Zemin, stepped down from this powerful committee to make way for a fourth generation of leadership led by Hu Jintao. Currently the PSC, elected by the CCP's Central Committee at the 2002 Sixteenth Party Congress, is composed of nine members: Hu Jintao, Huang Ju, Jia Qinglin, Li Changchun, Luo Gan, Wen Jiabao, Wu Bangguo, Wu Guanzheng, and Zeng Qinghong.[12] Among them, Hu Jintao is president of the People's Republic of China, general secretary of the Communist Party of China, and Chairman of the Central Military Commission, as of 2004; Wen Jiabao is premier of the State Council of the PRC; and Wu Bangguo is Chairman of the Standing Committee of the National People's Congress. Although Hu Jintao has begun to institute certain changes within the CCP, Jiang's influence may continue, given that six out of the nine new members of the PSC—Huang Ju, Jia Qinglin, Li Changchun, Wu Bangguo, Wu Guanzheng, and Zeng Qinghong—are Jiang protégés.

The Reform Era: From Revolutionary Party to Governing Party

In the past thirty years, there have been two major transitions within China's political institutions, both of which demonstrate the CCP's attempt to maintain its political legitimacy in the reform era through self-transformation. One is the changing relationship between the party and the government. Though he did not publicly express an intent to make radical changes within China's political system at the beginning of the economic reforms, Deng did move to rationalize the government by replacing Mao's dictum of "politics in command" (*zhengzhi weigang*) with "economics in command" (*jingji weigang*), essentially reversing Mao's creation of a "revolutionary government" in 1957. To ensure the success of the economic reform agenda, Deng effected the removal of the party from the daily management of the state system and economic enterprises (*dangzheng fenkai* and *dangqi fenkai*). Although the party remains the ultimate institutional authority and there are still conservative voices within the CCP leadership, reforms within China's political system have achieved critical changes.

The encouragement of grassroots democracy (discussed in greater detail in Chapter 7) is among the important reforms influencing China's political institutions today. Faced with serious local corruption in the late 1980s, the CCP realized it was losing legitimacy in rural areas. As a result, a law on village committee organization, stipulating that directors, deputy directors, and members of village committees would be chosen by direct democratic elections, was introduced in 1987 on a trial basis. In 1989, a similar law, defining neighborhood committees in cities as autonomous organizations, took effect. Since then, village leadership has changed five times through direct elections in most provinces, autonomous regions, and municipalities across China,[13] and urban community leaders have been directly elected in twenty Chinese cities. Apart from the heads of autonomous organizations, deputies to the People's Congresses at county and township levels are also chosen through direct elections, in accordance with the election laws for local organizations. The deputies at county and township levels, who serve for five years and three years, respectively, number about three million nationwide. According to the Ministry of Civil Affairs of China, to date, more than 700 million Chinese have been involved in voting for their community leaders and deputies to the People's Congress at county and township levels though direct elections.

The National People's Congress (NPC), China's legislature, has moved far from the "hand-raising machine" or "rubber-stamp" institutions that have historically operated in Leninist political systems. By turning party decrees into state laws, Leninist legislatures functioned to provide the party with "a veneer of legal–democratic legitimacy" (Tanner 1999, 100). Although China's NPC today is far from a liberalized legislature with genuine accountability, and it is still subject to the party's manipulation and intervention, the NPC's lawmaking and policy influence has been greatly transformed in the past two decades. Tanner (1999) cites a number of new phenomena revealed by NPC voting data that show the increasing institutional capacity and influence of the NPC. First of all, it is now rare for proposed laws to pass unanimously, as before. Second, it is no longer the case that all laws pass. In addition, large dissenting-vote totals are becoming relatively common. As Murray Tanner notes, of the full NPC's twenty-three known votes on personnel appointment and other motions in the 1990s, six of them received dissenting vote totals of over one-fifth. The political power and leadership position of the NPC over the State Council only appeared on paper before, but today the State Council has had little choice but to make changes in its legislative drafts in order to get approval by the NPC deputies and leadership.

In 2001, the CCP made another notable stride in the form of the "three representatives" theory proposed by Jiang Zemin—the former president and general secretary of the CCP. By permitting private entrepreneurs to be recruited into the party, the CCP announced that it not only represents the traditionally represented group of workers and peasants but also the interests of capitalists ("advanced social productive forces") and intellectuals ("advanced cultural forces"). Over 100,000 private entrepreneurs reportedly applied to join the party in the weeks immediately after Jiang's announcement (Dickson 2003). At the Sixteenth Party Congress in 2002, this theory was enshrined in the CCP's constitution. The moment indicated a remarkable change in CCP ideology, even if it seemed out of date with China's rapid change. Yet, this recognition also took the CCP one step further away from the revolutionary party it claimed to be. The CCP and its new generation of leadership can hardly claim them to represent a "revolutionary" party after thirty years of economic reforms and social change occurring in China.

The Communist State and the Work Unit System[14]

The Chinese state under Mao was often referred to as a totalitarian regime under which society was atomized to a large extent and the social ties between individuals and families were destroyed.[15] Political pressure from the state down to the individual, secret police surveillance, and the intensive mass campaigns (discussed in Chapter 2) initiated by Mao were the main tools by which the totalitarian regime functioned. While the party-state itself is a large-scale institution that has shaped life in Communist China, it is impossible to fully understand the role of the communist state without understanding the fundamental institutions around which communist societies are organized.

In the Chinese setting, the work unit was the key institution of state allocation that organized Chinese urban society for over thirty years of Communist Party rule. In the pre-reform era, the work-unit system of China functioned as a unit of economic production, social welfare, and political control. Economically, when the Communists came to power, one of the first things they did was eliminate private ownership of economic organizations and establish different levels of state-owned industries in urban areas. The work-unit system was developed to bring together a centrally planned economy with the redistribution of social welfare benefits. It was through their work units that urban citizens could obtain housing, medical care, and job opportunities. Moreover, the system allowed the party-state to directly monitor and supervise individuals within the work unit. Work units established security surveillance and secret dossiers (*danan*) on individuals, thus playing an important role in maintaining political stability in Communist China. Martin Whyte and William Parish's classic book on the subject, *Urban Life in Contemporary China*, describes the ways in which work units and neighborhood committees shaped life in China from 1949 to the early 1980s. Through work units and neighborhood committees, Chinese Communist bureaucracy permeated urban society, leaving few barriers between the individual and the state. The Communist state had managed to largely eliminate urban poverty by restricting migration into the cities, maximizing urban employment, and maintaining a relatively egalitarian distribution system and a high degree of economic security. The system led to high stability in jobs and residence, involvement and familiarity with neighbors and coworkers, minimal differentiation of consumption patterns and lifestyles, and high female work participation. But it was also a system of intense monitoring and social control by the party-state. As Whyte and Parish put it, "Chinese urban residents [were] victims rather than masters of their own fate" (1984, 295).

Another classic book on this topic, Andrew Walder's *Communist Neo-Traditionalism: Work and Authority in Chinese Industry*, provides insightful analysis into the ways in which work units established the economic, political, and personal dependence of workers on their work units and their leaders, a set of relationships that formed the basis of authority relations and political stability. The creation of patron–client relations between managers and workers became the primary way that state power was exercised in Communist China. Walder (1995b, 1995c, 1995e) has further explored the institutional mechanisms that served to maintain order within this system, including organized dependence (the dependence of subordinates on their superiors for the satisfaction of needs and career opportunities), monitoring capacity (the capacity of superiors to obtain information about the activities of subordinates), and sanctioning capacity (the ability to reward or punish the political behavior of subordinates). These relationships were central to the ways in which the Communist state institutionalized control over society, maintaining stability of state power even during the chaos of the Cultural Revolution.

The Receding Role of the State in the Reform Era

It is the breakdown of these institutional bases of power that have led to the decline of the Communist state's power in the reform era. Deng's reform program, initiated in 1978, made economic development a priority for modernizing China and aimed to build a market economy while leaving the party-state intact. Despite the focus on economic reform, the fact that the political, economic, and social systems were intertwined in the past meant that reforming the economy would lead to fundamental political and social changes as well. As I discussed in the previous chapter, as of the early 1980s, individuals, collectives, and local areas were empowered to make their own economic decisions. And with the reemergence of the private sector, individuals increasingly had the freedom to pursue their fortunes in the newly emerging markets of the Chinese economy. Through these two critical changes, the party-state removed itself as the key economic decision maker, and, with the emergence of the private sector, it broke the dependence of individuals on the state because it no longer held monopoly control over livelihoods. The party and government offices no longer stand over the shoulders of economic actors in the industrial economy. State officials still hold—and can use—their power to trade official favors for other benefits (e.g., housing) and pursue personal profits, but they have lost most of their control over the distribution of goods. In today's markets, individuals can access nearly all necessities in their everyday lives. Thus, the relations of authority based on the patron–client ties in the workplace have broken down, and the organizational dependency of individuals on their work units and superiors has been largely eliminated.

In rural areas, decollectivization in the late 1970s transferred production decisions from the commune to the family. The establishment of the "household responsibility system" afterward provided peasants with more economic resources, opportunities, and choices than could be obtained through the party in the pre-reform era. The collective industrial sector emerged especially in towns and villages in the 1980s, offering peasants new job opportunities in the emerging rural industrial sector. Once peasants began to farm land rented from the state on a household basis, establish their household enterprises, and make their own economic decisions, the bases of Communist power and the grassroots mobility of the Communist Party in rural areas greatly eroded. These declining institutional mechanisms, which once organized Communist urban and rural worlds in China, have triggered a "quiet revolution from within" (Walder 1995b, 1995c, 1995e) in China's reform era.

Unintended Social Consequences

The declining role of the state in economic activities in the reform era has had unintended consequences, confronting the party-state with a series of challenges from within and outside the political system. Official corruption is among the most serious crises with which the Chinese government has had to deal. Corruption comes in two primary forms—economic and noneconomic (Lu 2000). Within each of these two categories are three additional subtypes of corruption—graft (bribery), rent seeking (resource extraction), and prebendalism (perquisites and benefits connected to a public office). China was rated one of the most corrupt countries in the world by Transparency International in the 1990s. Though recently China has been removed from this blacklist, the CCP in the reform continues to struggle with corruption (in fact, today, China is not far off from other countries including India, Mexico, Brazil, and is far better than a number of other emerging markets, like Russia).[16] The massive scale of official corruption in the late 1980s was one of the catalysts of the 1989 Tiananmen student movement, and many commentators explain the initiation of village-level elections as a response to the widespread corruption among local officials in rural areas. In the past decade, the CCP has initiated a number of political campaigns to curb official corruption, and today the central government seems more determined than ever to eliminate the problem. However, among the challenges China faces in dealing with official corruption is the very nature of its political system. The CCP still holds enormous and exclusive political power in China, which provides many opportunities for officials to abuse their power and trade favors for profitable deals. There is strong evidence that China is well on the way to rationalizing its rule by law, but during the long-term transition toward that goal, there has been much room for abuse of the emergent system.

Xiaobo Lu's (2000) work in this area provides an insightful explanation of why a revolutionary party like the CCP has trouble institutionalizing a modern bureaucracy that should bring about impersonal, rational offices and functions. Lu argues that corruption among Communist cadres is not a phenomenon of the post-Mao reform period, nor is it caused by purely economic incentives in the emerging marketplace. Rather, it is the result of a long process of what he calls "organizational involution," which began as the Communist party-state embarked on the path of Maoist "continuous revolution." Lu argues that there is a fundamental contradiction inherent in the routinization of revolutionary movements. After a revolutionary party comes to power through a wave of change, and political offices are occupied by the same revolutionary personalities who brought about the change, these individuals are often more committed to the revolutionary goals and the process of change that brought them to power than they are with maintaining a strict organizational structure. Eventually, the prescribed organizational norms become unglued from the value system of the party members who brought about change in the first place. These members continue to act through personalistic, informal modes, and organizational deviance becomes inevitable.

In the CCP's case, after the Anti-Rightist Campaign of 1957, when many of the party's policies of the early years were questioned, Mao adopted an aggressive policy of revolutionary reform as a way of furthering his Communist legacy. This period made it impossible for revolutionary goals to be routinized in organizational norms and practices. The

1966–1976 Cultural Revolution that followed nearly eliminated China's bureaucratic system and made it very difficult to develop institutionalized routines. The CCP gradually lost its ability to sustain officialdom with either the Leninist-cadre or Weberian bureaucratic modes of integration. Instead, the party unintentionally created a neotraditional ethos, mode of operation, and set of authority relations among its cadres that have fostered official corruption. Apart from the internal crisis, the CCP has had to deal with challenges from the societal level, even under so-called totalitarian controls. In order to institutionalize political control, the CCP established the dual institutional structure of the state–society relationship in the Communist era: strong organizational control over the society by the state (Whyte and Parish 1984), and the organizational dependency of the individuals on socialist economic institutions (Walder 1986a). By monopolizing the resources for organizing private interests, the Communist state effectively denied the legitimacy of any organized interests outside its control. However, according to Zhou (1993a), such an institutional structure of state socialism actually facilitates collective action based on "unorganized interests" and systematically transforms individual behavior into "collective action." The structure of the system reduces barriers to collective action by producing "large numbers" of individuals at structurally similar positions vis-à-vis the state and with similar sets of experiences and interests.

Zhou's theory explains the puzzle of why, without any independent organization, large-scale social movements have repeatedly erupted in Chinese society during the period of Communist Party rule. On a number of occasions, massive numbers of individuals were able to spontaneously converge to express their common interests despite the tight control exercised by the Communist state. For example, when Mao encouraged the intellectuals to speak out on the ideologies and policies of the CCP in the spring of 1957, the immediate groundswell of discontent was largely unanticipated by the CCP. Mao put an immediate stop to this "collective action" by labeling intellectuals as rightists and sending many of them to the countryside for "reeducation." Seemingly spontaneous moments of collective action also seemed to occur during the Cultural Revolution; upon the death of Zhou Enlai in 1976; during the Democracy Wall movement in 1978–1979; and during the reform era, when a million students occupied Tiananmen Square for six weeks in 1989 in pursuit of political freedom. In all of these cases, individuals in structurally similar positions vis-à-vis the state came together with common interests and common grievances to rebel against the party-state system.

Social Networks (Guanxi) and the Gift Economy

It is nearly impossible to travel to China and avoid being confronted by the view (if not the reality) that *guanxi* is a central part of social life in China. There are two distinct concepts, both of which are important for discussing the role of *guanxi* in Chinese society. The first is that of social relations, or *guanxi* itself. This concept is often used to denote some type of friendship, kinship, or other type of social tie—as in, "I have a [good] relationship with him" [*wo gen ta you guanxi*]. A second concept, which is sometimes used interchangeably with *guanxi* but is more accurately referred to as *guanxi xue* (literally, "the study of *guanxi*"), is the gift economy. The gift economy is a concept that implies the use of social relations to "manufacture obligation and indebtedness" in order to accomplish some set of future tasks (Yang 1994, 6). The Chinese can hardly claim to have the only society where social networks (*guanxi*) or a gift economy (*guanxi xue*) play important roles in social life, but China scholars have, in general, not questioned the centrality of *guanxi* in Chinese society, culture, and everyday life. There are two major theoretical orientations toward understanding *guanxi* in Chinese society. One is the cultural perspective, which views *guanxi* and *guanxi xue* as products of deep-seated aspects of Chinese culture; the second is an institutional perspective, which maintains that *guanxi* and *guanxi xue* arise from specific types of institutional relationships and constraints.[17] Recent debate around these two approaches is based upon disagreement over the extent to which *guanxi* is something unique to China and Chinese culture or whether it is an outgrowth of the institutional arrangements that are common to command economies.

The cultural orientation is based on the concept of *guanxi* as a distinctly Chinese phenomenon, inextricably linked to Chinese culture and social structure (e.g., Yang 1994). The scholars adhering to this approach trace *guanxi* to its enduring significance in traditional Chinese philosophy, in particular its stress on the centrality of social interaction in the formation of the individual's identity. Among the Confucian-based discourse that placed social relationships at its center, Liang Shuming's relations-based (*guanxi benwei*) perspective (King 1985) and Fei Xiaotong's model of "different mode of association" (*chaxu geju*) (Fei 1992) are often cited to demonstrate the centrality of *guanxi* as a cultural element of being "Chinese" regardless of time or place. According to this view, Chinese culture creates a deep psychological tendency for individuals to actively cultivate and manipulate social relations for instrumental ends. In the context of China's economic reforms, the cultural approach stresses the increasing roles of *guanxi* and social networking in doing business and attributes the practices of *guanxi xue* in contemporary China to the cultural characteristics of Chinese society. The scholars holding this view contend that *guanxi* and *guanxi xue* will not decline over the course of China's economic transition, since they are something fundamentally Chinese, or alternately, that *guanxi* practice may decline in some social domains, but it may find new areas in which to flourish, such as business transactions, and may display new social forms and expressions (Yang 2002).

The institutional orientation considers *guanxi* to be a general phenomenon less related to Chineseness and more a response to specific institutional and historical conditions that happen to exist in China. It is the institutional structure of Chinese society at certain time periods that facilitates or encourages the reliance on networks to accomplish tasks in Chinese society. *Guanxi* practice is thus no different from the gift economy in other societies that are at similar or analogous stages of development. Particularly during the Communist era, a shortage economy combined with a weak legal infrastructure facilitated the reliance on networking and trust as fundamental parts of transactions in Communist China. Andrew Walder's (1986a) institutional analysis of the work-unit system, as discussed above, illuminates the use of *guanxi* in the form of patron-client relations as a response to a situation in which powerful officials controlled access to scarce necessities and job opportunities during the Communist era. It follows logically that as the institutions of these developing economies and societies change, so too should the reliance on social networks. Thus, from the institutional perspective, *guanxi* is an institutionally defined system—a system that depends on the institutional structure of society rather than on culture—that is changing alongside the institutional changes of the reform era (Guthrie 1998b, 2002a). In general, culture offers important perspectives in understanding the ways in which *guanxi* and *guanxi* practice function in Chinese society, and it would be inaccurate to claim that *guanxi* does not matter in China. However, the empirical reality of the industrial and commercial economies in China today suggests that practices and perceptions of *guanxi* are changing in important ways in the urban industrial economy, and these changes suggest a trend that does not fully fit with theories that emphasize the cultural importance of *guanxi* in Chinese society or that see an increasing role of *guanxi* and *guanxi* practice throughout China in the economic transition.

Guanxi *and* Guanxi *Practice in the Urban Industrial Economy*

In the urban industrial economy, there is a growing emphasis on the distinction between social relationships (*guanxi*) and the use of these social relationships in the gift economy (*guanxi* practice), and managers in the industrial and commercial economies are increasingly likely to distance themselves from the institution of *guanxi* practice in the economic transition. While managers often view social connections as important in business transactions, they view the importance of *guanxi* in market relationships as secondary to the market imperatives of price and quality. Increasingly today, managers will often say things like, "*Guanxi* only helps if you are competitive" (Guthrie 1999). In addition, managers do not view the use of personal connections in China as being any different from the ways in which business is conducted in economies throughout the world.

Currently, the Chinese government is engaged in the project of constructing a rational–legal system that will govern the decisions and practices of economic actors. This is especially true for large-scale organizations that are more closely monitored by the state administrative offices than are individuals or small-scale entrepreneurs. Through the construction of this rational-legal system, the state pushes actors—especially large-scale industrial firms—to approach economic activities in ways that are sanctioned by the rational–legal system. In addition, as the government continues to place economic responsibilities directly on the shoulders of firms, organizations are forced to consider many factors that make economic sense, many of which often lie in conflict with the use of social connections. Once again, the argument here is not that *guanxi* and *guanxi xue* are insignificant in Chinese society. Clearly these practices are important in many aspects of Chinese society. However, whether they are important for "all types of commercial transactions" and whether their importance has "increased at an accelerated rate" (Yang 1994, 167, 147) in the economic transition are empirical questions. To a large extent, the empirical data indicate that the "art" of *guanxi* (i.e., *guanxi* practice) may in fact occupy a diminishing role in China's urban industrial and commercial economies as the economic transition progresses.

In China today, powerful economic actors often pay increasing attention to the laws, rules, and regulations that are part of the emerging rational–legal system. Many managers of large industrial organizations increasingly view *guanxi* practice as unnecessary and dangerous in light of new regulations and prohibitions against such approaches to official procedures. Understanding how the system of *guanxi* interacts with the rational–legal system at the state level and formal rational bureaucratic structures that are emerging at the firm level is important for understanding how this system is changing in the reform era, and it is important for understanding the reforms more generally. Changes surrounding *guanxi* in the reform era vary with a firm's position in the state administrative hierarchy (Guthrie 1998b, 1999, 2002a). The higher a firm is in China's administrative hierarchy, the less likely the general or vice general manager of the firm is to view *guanxi* practice—that is, using connections to get things done—as important in the economic transition. Conversely, the lower a firm is in the administrative hierarchy, the more likely the firm's general manager is to view *guanxi* practice as important to success in the economic transition. Attitudes toward *guanxi* practice also vary with a number of organizational factors, ranging from the background of the firm's general manager to whether or not the organization has a joint venture with a foreign company.

Of the two types of *guanxi* that shape action in China today (i.e., *guanxi* and *guanxi* practice), *guanxi* practice lies in conflict with the rational–legal system emerging at the state level (i.e., formal laws, policies, and rational procedures), while *guanxi*, more broadly conceived, is often viewed as a necessary part of the market reforms and business transactions in a market economy. The importance of this distinction is increasing in the urban industrial economy for two reasons. First, large industrial organizations are monitored by the state much more closely than individual actors in the economy are. Given that the official discourse surrounding *guanxi* practice is negative, it is not surprising that large-scale industrial organizations are more careful about the extent to which they engage in this institution. In addition to the fact that markets are becoming increasingly competitive, the very existence of markets changes the meaning and significance of *guanxi* in China's transitional economy. In China today, emerging markets and the transition from a command to a market economy allow actors the freedom to make economic choices in an open market. If one element of *guanxi* practice for industrial managers under the command economy was the necessity of gaining access to distribution channels (input and output) that were controlled by state officials under that system, in China's transitional economy, officials have no such control over the distribution of resources and products. In the economic reforms, in many sectors, an open market increasingly controls the flow of goods. This change has profound implications for the transition away from a focus on *guanxi* practice to a more general focus on *guanxi* as business relationships. Industrial managers no longer need to curry favor with state officials to overcome bottlenecks or gain access to resources, and, as a result, they do not view *guanxi* practice as an important part of decision-making in China's industrial economy.

Guanxi *Practice and Hiring Decisions*

While managers often express views that imply a declining significance of *guanxi* practice in China's economic transition, we are still faced with the problem of rhetoric versus empirical reality in the analysis of qualitative evidence. Are these managers simply presenting normative statements— or an official party line—on the way the economic transactions in China should be, irrespective of how things really are, or do their words reflect the empirical reality of changes that are actually occurring in China's transforming economy? Evidence that might help adjudicate between these two possibilities would be whether these managers, despite their views of *guanxi* practice, still use connections to accomplish specific tasks in the transition economy. If managers espouse views that the significance of *guanxi* practice is declining while still using *guanxi* to accomplish specific tasks, we should approach their views skeptically; if, on the other hand, managers who present a picture of the declining significance of *guanxi* do not use *guanxi* in accomplishing specific tasks, this fact would lend credence to the picture these managers paint.

One specific task or practice that has been analyzed in depth with respect to *guanxi* practice is the use of connections in hiring decisions. While industrial managers in China often acknowledge that connections figure into hiring decisions to some extent, many managers describe a scenario that fits with the declining-significance-of-*guanxi*-practice theory (Guthrie 2002a). The positions taken by these managers square with those presented on the more general issue of *guanxi* practice presented above: in

China's economic transition, some organizations have constructed formal rational bureaucracies that transform organizational practices in fundamental ways; other organizations are responding more directly to market constraints, hiring individuals who are most qualified for the job, irrespective of social connections. Both types of transformations suggest the declining significance of *guanxi* practice.

Conclusions

In this chapter, I have given a brief introduction to some of the key institutions around which Chinese society is organized. The family, the party-state, and the work-unit system are all important institutions in the structure of life under communism. However, key changes in each of these institutions have brought about fundamental changes in the lives of individuals. The economic reforms have transformed the family and its relationship to the state. Following the Communist takeover in 1949, the state methodically broke down the boundaries that had isolated families from state control in the Imperial period. Breaking up clans and extended families, and placing individual families in state-controlled organizations such as neighborhood associations in urban areas and collectives (and later communes) in rural areas, institutionalized an unprecedented level of control over Chinese families. With the economic reforms, decollectivization, and the receding of the party-state from organizations like neighborhood associations, the party-state's control over family life has steadily diminished—it is no longer the force of ideological or social control that it was prior to the era of economic reform. However, state control over the family in the current era has taken a different form of control. Beginning with the austere measures of the one-child policy, the state's control over families took the form of official policy. Austere measures of forced sterilization and the threat of job loss have been replaced by more subtle policies, such as tax penalties, but the state control over family size remains a key issue in China today.

The economic reforms have also transformed the party-state itself. Official reforms, such as removing the party from economic control over organizations, creating democratic elections in villages, reforming the National People's Congress, and allowing private entrepreneurs into the party ranks, have all gradually transformed the party from within. Most important, perhaps, has been the transformation of the party-state's ability to control individuals by breaking its monopoly over the allocation of social services. As the party-state receded from direct control over the economic decisions of enterprise managers, it became less and less of an ideological force at the organizational level. And with the concurrent emergence of a private economy and the opening of labor markets, individuals no longer solely rely on the party-state for the allocation of jobs and social welfare benefits.

There have been many consequences of the changes in the institutions that govern Communist society in China. In this chapter, I have named only a few. Corruption has been one immediate consequence of the party-state's receding from direct social control. Removing itself from direct control over local officials left open new opportunities for local officials to behave unchecked. New laws have been set in place to deal with these issues, but establishing control over the situation has been gradual, just as the economic reforms have been. Social networks and the gift economy have changed as well. Where the gift economy constituted one of the basic ways in which individuals dealt with the shortage economy, the reforms have opened up new channels for economic exchange for people living in China today. People no longer need to curry favor with officials or other individuals in their lives who control resource allocation.

4

CHINA IN THE GLOBAL ECONOMY

In the first half of 2011, I took two trips to Shenzhen, both at the invitation of the leadership of powerful global companies that are significant players in the region—one a foreign company that is increasingly centralizing its operations in the region; the other a Chinese company that has grown up there and is increasingly looking outward. The first trip was to visit the primary operations of Colgate-Palmolive's toothpaste and toothbrush production facility. Toothpaste production is a funny business; for someone who is not familiar with the intricacies of the production process (like me, prior to this trip), it might seem somewhat mundane as a business. It does not, at first glance, have the complexity of automobiles or high tech businesses; it does not seem to hold the scientific "importance" of pharmaceuticals. But, as it turns out, importance of this industry cannot be overstated, as everyone needs these products and they actually track very closely with health and hygiene, which, in turn, track closely with education, and several other socio-economic indicators. And the production process within a toothpaste plant is actually incredibly complex and fascinating to see in action. The complexity and efficiency of CP's fully automated plant is truly amazing, and this is the company's première production facility in the world. The majority of CP's production for the world comes from China, but the company is also very much focused on China's internal market. The decision to link the company's future so closely to China—both in terms of production and in terms of growth—is indicative of the multilayered advantages China has as a destination for foreign companies: China has become the company's factory for the world, but dominating China's internal market is also crucial to the company's future.

Later that spring, I visited the headquarters of China's largest private company, Huawei (which is also the 397th largest company in the world and the second-largest telecommunications infrastructure company behind Ericsson). In today's economy—in the world of smart phones, tablet computers, wireless connectivity, and cybersecurity—this company has garnered a significant amount of attention as of late; it has begun to flex its muscles and the rest of the world's telecommunications companies are feeling the impact of its growth; and it one of only a handful of private companies that are on the Global 500 list. On a personal level, this trip was different from most of my China company visits: During the visit, I fell down some stairs and broke my shoulder while touring Huawei's headquarters, and I spent the next six days having my shoulder reconstructed in a nearby Shenzhen hospital. Throughout the experience, I was fortunate to be under the watchful eye of senior Huawei executives, engaging in conversations about the strategy and structure of the company, as they sat bedside working to ensure that I received the best treatment available. It was an odd way to learn about one of China's most powerful global companies. But it was also a time that allowed me to look deeply inside this enigmatic global powerhouse. This company is deeply misunderstood in the United States, a fact that has led the U.S. government to step in twice to stop deals that would have major positive financial implications for the U.S. economy. And Huawei is just one of many powerhouses in China's economy that has emerged to play a powerful role in the global economy. Understanding how these corporations have come to play the roles they have in China—and how China has transformed from an isolated nation on the verge of bankruptcy in 1978 into the second largest economy in the world with many powerful multinationals—is the purpose of this chapter.

China began with an export-led growth strategy but also oversaw the growth of an entrepreneurial collective and private sector from below; the transformation of the state sector from above; the attraction of foreign capital and the transfer of technology and the learning of management practices from their new foreign partners. It has been a complex process with many moving parts. However, while counterparts in Russia and Eastern Europe followed simplistic prescriptions about rapid privatization and the selling off of assets to foreign investors, China carefully balanced all of these moving parts to build a powerful and complex economy. In this chapter, I examine how it has come to be that China's transition to a market economy has produced remarkable growth rates and fundamental changes in the organization of economic action. Though lacking the basic institutional shifts that have defined many transforming socialist economies around the world, China's gradualist reforms have nevertheless been radical and deep. In order to understand the process of economic transformation in China, it is necessary to examine a few key areas of development. This list is by no means exhaustive, but it does comprise some of the key areas in which economic development has transformed China in fundamental ways. I look first at China's engagement in global markets. Second, I examine the varieties and types of organizations that have been successful in transforming themselves in China's market economy. Third, I look at the forces of change that have contributed to this success.

The basic thesis of this chapter is that economic development in China has been shaped by three key factors. First, the central government has driven reforms forward through several key policies that have allowed China to engage fully in the global economy. These policies of engagement have had both external and internal orientations. In terms of China's external focus, the most important policy has been the export-oriented coastal development strategy, which has played a key role in helping China to emerge as the second-largest trading economy in the world in 2010 (behind the United States), with total trade of $2.97 trillion ("total trade" is a sum of imports and exports). In terms of internal focus, the government has adopted a surprisingly open stance vis-à-vis foreign direct investment (FDI), liberalizing internal markets to a degree greater than is commonly understood and certainly to a greater extent than in India and Japan, for example, at similar stages of development. The reasons for aggressively attracting FDI range from capturing advanced technology through technology transfer agreements and studying management practices from advanced market economies to attracting foreign capital. Second, the government decentralized decision making in significant ways. This point cannot be overemphasized: the decentralization of economic decision-making is one of the key factors that has pushed China's reform effort forward. This economic decentralization had several key effects, including giving incentives for local development to local officials and creating competition among localities. Third, while the government has reformed industrial organizations without privatization, it has, at the same time, allowed a private economy to emerge from below. This is an important distinction: in the sector controlled by the Chinese state, state-owned enterprises (SOEs) (*guoying qiye* or *guoyou qiye*), urban collectives (*jiti qiye*), and township and village enterprises (TVEs) (*xiangzhen qiye*) remained state owned throughout much of the reform era (though collectives and TVEs have increasingly been sold off or bought out by local entrepreneurs and employees in the last decade). Though the incentives for such enterprises shifted downward and were placed in the hands of local officials, they remained state property in the early years of the reform. They have been transformed through a process of reform *without* rapid privatization; something many observers of transforming planned economies argued was not possible. However, the government did allow a private sector to emerge, and these private sector firms became an important factor in the creation of competition for state-owned firms and in the creation of new markets.

The Early Years of Reform and the Coastal Development Strategy: Creating an Export Economy

A fundamental part of the economic reforms has been the move to recast China as being part of the global economy. At the same time that it was embarking on the domestic reforms that transformed the economy in the 1980s and 1990s, China was opening itself to the global economy. This transformation included:

- the construction of new institutions, both nationally and internationally;
- the development of new industrial strategies;
- the creation of special economic zones (e.g., Pudong, Shenzhen, Zhongguancun), which allowed firms (domestic and foreign) to take advantage of specific tax incentives and other types of policy goals in targeting specific kinds of investment in China;
- the adoption of trade and aggressive export strategies;
- the adoption of development strategies that were regionally specific within China.

The 1979 Joint Venture Law was the first in a series of regulations allowing the flow of foreign capital into China. In 1980, China enforced its opening-up policies in a small part of the coastal region where four special economic zones (SEZs) in Fujian Province (Xiamen) and Guangdong Province (Shantou, Shenzhen, and Zhuhai) were established. After witnessing the rapid growth of these SEZs, in the mid-1980s, Zhao Ziyang implemented a coastal development strategy to accelerate the flow of FDI and expand foreign trade to a wider region, including eastern and southern provinces in coastal areas.[1]

Zhao Ziyang had good revolutionary credentials. Born in 1919 to a land-owning family, Zhao joined the Communist Youth League as a schoolboy in 1932. At the age of nineteen, he entered the Chinese Communist Party (CCP) and served the Communists in a military capacity through the revolution. After the revolution, Zhao was transferred to Guangdong Province, where he steadily rose in power. In 1975, he was transferred to Sichuan and proved to be a strong, reform-minded voice in the party. Then, in 1978, when Deng Xiaoping began consolidating his own position of power by surrounding himself with reform-minded politicians, Zhao was among the first to whom Deng turned. By the early 1980s, it was clearly perceived that Zhao would play a major role in the economic reforms on a national level and that he could potentially be the successor to Deng. In December of 1987, Zhao was elected secretary general of the CCP. Economic policies have always intertwined with political power in Communist China, and the situation for Zhao was no different. He was best known for the rationalization of enterprises and price reform, but he also championed and implemented the critical policy known as coastal development strategy.

As with all economic strategies in Communist China, it is important to view the coastal development strategy in a political light. One of the primary reasons this strategy was launched was to give Zhao more power in defining the direction of China's reform and thus shift the balance of power away from the more conservative voices in the party. Conservatives were pushing for a slowing down of economic reforms. Zhao's main challenger here was the conservative Li Peng, and Zhao urgently needed new initiatives to prove that he was a worthy successor to Deng Xiaoping. In addition, money was needed in the reform process for Zhao to solidify his power base, and he also needed support from local officials as well as the intellectual community in China. The coastal development strategy would allow him to achieve all of these ends.

The goal was to allow coastal regions greater autonomy in the area of export trade. These regions included Beijing, Fujian, Guangdong, Guangxi, Hainan, Hebei, Jiangsu, Liaoning, Shandong, Shanghai, Tianjin, and Zhejiang. There was precedent for this development strategy in the region, as Japan, South Korea, and Taiwan had prospered through an export-oriented development strategy. The strategy provided an enticing solution to two of China's major problems: employment of the surplus labor from the rural areas and improvement in industrial competitiveness; it would also provide much-needed income for industrial enterprises. However, implementing the strategy meant further decentralization of China. The decentralization of development that China had adopted was not only tied to a lack of political control at the center (which led to corruption in the provinces) but also a lack of economic control over prices, raw materials, and the like. Trade decentralization contributed to inflation, which was already moving in a startling direction as a result of the price reform initiative of 1988.[2]

Nevertheless, by this time, China was deeply enmeshed in this process; for reasons of employment, growth in gross domestic product (GDP), and cash for foreign technology, even the conservative reformers could not hold back foreign trade for long. As a result, behind Zhao's leadership, China launched the coastal development strategy in early 1988. Since that time, China's exports have soared. By 2009, $1.2 trillion worth of goods a year were being pumped into the global economy. This is compared to imports of about $1 trillion, creating a trade imbalance with the rest of the world of about $200 billion. As Table 4.1 shows, China's export economy grew at an average annual rate of nearly 27 percent over the period 1978–2009. The import of goods grew at a rate of nearly 26 percent over the same period. These goods have overwhelmingly been in the category of manufactured goods, as opposed to those classified as "primary" goods (agricultural products and raw materials).[3] Figure 4.1 shows graphically the rapid rise in imports and exports but also how sensitive China is to the health of the global economy—the sharp decline in 2008 is clearly a result of the global recession.

The coastal development strategy has transformed China's economy in dramatic ways. It has transformed what was an isolated country thirty years ago into the primary producer of goods across a number of different sectors. It has brought a huge infusion of cash into the economy. And it has led the way in an open-door policy that has had fundamental consequences for other aspects of internal growth across a number of sectors in the economy. Despite claims that markets in China are closed to foreign producers—an allegation that is often raised in the face of the growing trade deficit with the United States and the rest of the world—it is important to think through the complexities of this claim. First, the magnitude of foreign investment in China dwarfs that of Japan in comparable development periods. In the early stages of reform, China's foreign investment regime was far more liberal than that of Japan or South Korea (Lardy 1994). Second, as U.S. trade with China has grown, its trade with other East Asian economies has shrunk. This is not surprising, given that countries such as South Korea and Taiwan have moved production units to China to take advantage of cheaper labor there.[4] Under these circumstances, exports from China grow; however, this commodity-chain cooperation amounts to a reorganization of export flows across the region rather than a simple net growth of exports from China. In other words, in order to really think accurately about the trade imbalance with China, we need to also account for the fact that as production in Taiwan has declined, many of the Taiwanese businesses have moved their factories over the China's eastern seaboard.

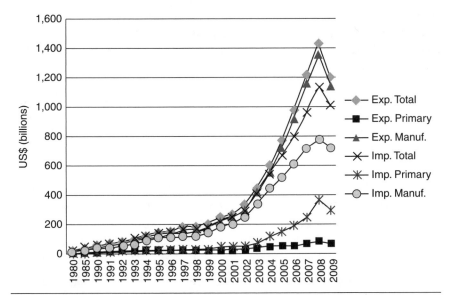

Figure 4.1 Imports and Exports by Category, Primary and Manufactured Goods (US$, billions).

Source: National Statistical Bureau of China (2010, 231, 232).

Table 4.1 Total Trade, 2009 (U.S.$, billions)

	Total Imports and Exports	Total Exports	Total Imports	Balance
1978	20.64	9.75	10.89	-1.14
1980	38.14	18.12	20.02	-1.9
1985	69.6	27.35	42.25	-14.9
1989*	111.68	52.54	59.14	-6.6
1990	115.44	62.09	53.35	8.74
1991	135.7	71.91	63.79	8.12
1992	165.53	84.94	80.59	4.35
1993	195.7	91.74	103.96	-12.22
1994	236.62	121.01	115.61	5.4
1995	280.86	148.78	132.08	16.7
1996	289.88	151.05	138.83	12.22
1997	325.16	182.79	142.37	40.42
1998	323.95	183.71	140.24	43.47
1999	360.63	194.93	165.7	29.23
2000	474.29	249.2	225.09	24.11
2001	509.65	266.1	243.55	22.55
2002	620.77	325.6	295.17	30.43
2003	850.99	438.23	412.76	25.47
2004	1,154.55	593.32	561.23	32.09
2005	1,421.91	761.95	659.95	102
2006	1,760.4	968.94	791.46	177.48
2007	2,173.73	1,217.78	955.95	261.83
2008	2,563.26	1,430.69	1,132.56	298.13
2009	2,207.54	1,201.61	1,005.92	195.69

Source: National Statistical Bureau of China (2010, 230), *National Statistical Bureau of China (2006, 734).

Third, of the top forty exporters from China, ten are U.S. companies.[5] Multinational corporations such as Dell, Motorola, and Walmart benefit tremendously from producing in China and exporting to the rest of the world—benefits that include healthy profits, which boost stock prices and, thus, market capitalization. These exports, however, count on China's side of the export ledger, because the goods are produced in China. The shift from gross national product (GNP) to gross domestic product (GDP) in 1991 had critical implications for this accounting.[6] By GNP accounting anything made by a U.S. corporation *anywhere* figures into the U.S. side of the trade balance; by GDP accounting, anything produced outside the United States does not. Thus, although Walmart is one of the largest importers to the United States from China, those imports count as Chinese exports in the balance of trade. Fourth, these trade imbalance figures do not account for recent changes in the flow of information around the globe. As reporter James Flanagan has noted,

> [In the garments industry] patterns and instructions are sent over the Internet to factories in China, where the garments are made. They are then shipped back through the ports of Los Angeles and Long Beach and on to stores. Although the patterns that go out over the Internet don't count as "exports," the garments that come back in through the ports count as "imports." . . . The pattern is the same in toys. Jordan Kort's Northridge-based What Kids Want Inc. designs toys under license from Walt Disney Co. and the Nickelodeon division of Viacom Inc. Princess dolls and other toys are manufactured in China, but the lion's share of the proceeds from making and selling the toys go to Kort's firm, the retailers and Disney and Viacom. Indeed economists estimate that the Chinese manufacturers earn only 20 percent of the value of the goods they make for export.[7]

The bottom line is that, while the trade deficit is clearly a problem for many U.S. policy makers, it is a complicated development that encapsulates many more commodity–chain relationships than the statistic itself reveals.

Enterprise Reforms and the Rule of Law

Over the course of the reforms, the central government has transformed its role as the country's economic decision maker into one of macroeconomic policy maker, passing a battery of key laws and regulations that changed the practices of organizations. For example, in 1979 the Chinese government passed the Joint Venture Law, allowing foreign firms to enter the Chinese economy for the first time since 1949. Decollectivization policies in rural areas and the creation of the categories of household business and private enterprise stimulated the emergence of the private enterprises. The entry of these startup firms quickly gave rise to increasing market pressure on the state sector. In 1986, the State Council passed regulations that changed the nature of employment relationships, essentially marking a formal end to the institution of lifetime employment.[8] Also in 1986, the Chinese government passed the Enterprise Bankruptcy Law, which for the first time established that insolvent enterprises may apply for bankruptcy. Two years later, with the passage of the Enterprise Law, the state not only underscored the government's policies toward hardening budget constraints for SOEs but also stipulated the government's policies and legal guarantee for protecting the non-state sector, through regulations such as the Rules of Foreign Invested Enterprises and the Provisional Regulations of Private Enterprises.[9]

In 1992, coinciding with Deng's "southern tour," the State Council further specified that enterprises were entitled to up to fourteen rights: decision making in production and operation, price setting for products and labor, selling of products, material purchasing, import and export, investment decision-making, disposition of retained bonuses, disposition of property, decision-making on joint operation or mergers, labor employment, personnel management, distribution of wages and bonuses, internal structuring, and refusing apportioning. Since then, SOEs have been expected to operate independently in the market according to law and be responsible for their own profits and losses. Two years later, the Company Law was passed. As mentioned earlier, this law governed the process of converting enterprises into shareholding companies and stipulated that companies funded by investing bodies of different ownerships were all equal under the law. More important, the Company Law encouraged enterprises to build new corporate structures and standardize organizational bodies (mainly with regard to shareholder meetings, corporate boards, and managers) in order to further block political interventions in the decision making process. By the mid-1990s, the government would formally define its role in the economy as "creat[ing] the conditions for all sectors of the economy to participate in the market competition on an equal basis, and guarantee enterprises from all sectors to be treated indiscriminately."[10]

Coinciding with these legislative changes was the founding of the Shanghai and Shenzhen Stock Exchanges in the early 1990s. Since 1993, the number of listed companies rose from 10 to 1,718 with a total market capitalization of U.S.$3.7 trillion. Following the gradualist model, the Chinese government's construction of the institutions that govern public

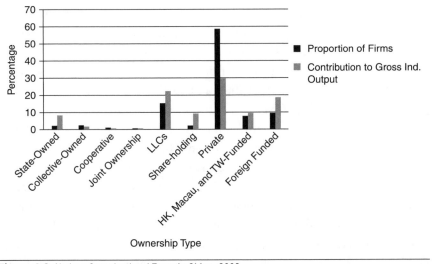

Figure 4.2 Various Organizational Types in China, 2009.

Source: National Statistical Bureau of China (2010, 507).

ownership has been spread across the period of economic reform. After a series of regulations, such as the Opinions on Standardizing the Joint Stock Limited Companies and the Provisional Regulations on the Administration of Issuing and Trading of Stocks, the Securities Law was passed in 1998, forming legal guaranty for the standardized operation of the listed companies. Yet, even in the area of public ownership of listed companies, we must acknowledge the complexities of enterprise–state relations in the Chinese model, as the government's receding from control over publicly listed state enterprises has, like every other institutional change in the Chinese economic reforms, been a gradual process. A typical ownership transformation for a state-owned enterprise would allow the state to retain between 40 and 50 percent of the company's shares; between 20 and 30 percent of the shares are designated for institutional shares; the remaining 30 percent are designated for public consumption (Guthrie *et al.* 2007).

Since 1979, the non-state sectors have also been increasingly entitled to the legal acknowledgment and protection from the capricious whims of the state. In 1997, at the Fifteenth National Congress, the government issued the significant formal statement that "the non-state sector is an important component part of this country's socialist market economy," and the statement was incorporated into the Constitution in 1999. At this point, the status of the non-state sector—especially the private sector—in China's economic system was officially legitimated. In 2004, the government further amended its constitution to protect private property rights for the first time since the People's Republic of China (PRC) was founded in 1949; under Hu Jintao, the National People's Congress further bolstered property rights in 2007. Over the course of China's market transition, the law-building process of the central government, especially since the 1990s, has gradually rationalized the institutions that govern autonomous business practice in China. These changes have brought about the rapid growth of the non-state sectors and intensified the transformation of the state sector in the reform era. They have also codified the autonomy of organizations operating as businesses in China. As a result, all types of China's business organizations have been more or less driven toward independent market behavior with diminishing reliance on the government system.

Fiscal Reforms, Decentralization, and the Rise of Local States

While it is certainly true that the state has gradually withdrawn from economic management and control of enterprises in the reform era, it is premature to conclude that the Chinese state has become insignificant in its relationships with business organizations. In particular, it is important to note that local governments have risen to play important roles in the development of local enterprises and the economic development of their regions more generally (Huang 1995a; Walder 1995e; Lee 1991), though this has occurred at varying rates depending on a given locality's relationship to the central government (Li 1997). Since the beginning of the reform era, policies of *economic decentralization* have transferred most economic decision-making power from the central government to localities by a series of tax and fiscal reforms. In 1980, the fiscal reforms started with the implementation of a fiscal responsibility system, under which the central government and provincial-level governments signed revenue-sharing contracts. According to this contract, taxes collected by local governments were to be divided into two parts: (1) central fixed revenues, which were to be remitted to the central government and (2) local revenues, which the central and local governments were to share in terms of various standards across regions. This revenue-sharing system provided local governments both strong incentives and institutional means to increase their revenue base by allowing them to retain more when they collected more revenues and guaranteeing the rights of localities to income from their assets. The direct outcome of these reforms was an explosion of local revenues in the 1980s, which lasted until 1994, when the central state was forced to enforce new fiscal reforms (Wang 1995; Wong 1997; Wong *et al.* 1995). In addition, economic decentralization policies have involved local governments in a number of responsibilities for carrying out national social policies and a variety of economic activities. For instance, the governments at the city level are responsible for 100 percent of expenditures for social security, unemployment insurance, and social welfare, and the governments at the county and township levels account for 70 percent of education expenditures and 55–60 percent of health expenditures.[11]

The increasing responsibilities in the reform era have made local governments actively involved in economic activities and business affairs in the localities. Lower levels of local governments have played significant roles in the development of TVEs, which became the most dynamic sector in China's transitional economy in the 1980s and early 1990s. By the early 1990s, the TVEs were contributing between 40 and 50 percent of tax revenues for local governments. As noted above, local governments, in many cases, actually came to behave like "industrial firms" themselves during the rural industrialization process, engineering the development of collective enterprises and forming the corporate structures to govern them. In many ways, decentralization has been the "secret sauce" of China's successful transition from plan to market: although China did not privatize property, the transference of property rights to local states created intense competition among local states, which drove local governments toward aggressive development agendas, higher levels of efficiencies, new models of innovation.

The fiscal reforms of 1994 put more duties on the localities and requested the lower levels of local governments to be responsible for expenses and social welfare. At the same time, the early 1990s liberalization policy of foreign investment and foreign trade increased local government responsibility for managing the foreign sector in localities. These conditions created both fiscal pressure and incentives for local states to be more involved in the local–global business activities for capital accumulation. Aside from directly dealing with foreign capital, local governments were given the authority to relax the rules governing foreign exchange balances, power and water fees, land prices for factory buildings, restrictions on hiring nonlocal workers, and other policies related to foreign investors.

Local governments often interpret the central government's policies flexibly and have frequently implemented them strategically for their own good.[12] As a result, foreign investors have begun to realize that "favorable investment policies issued by Beijing" are not nearly as advantageous as the "special deals" that can be crafted with local officials. Rather than dealing with the central government, foreign investors often prefer to build up long-term alliances with local officials for more stable and favorable investment conditions and cheaper local resources. In addition to directly developing enterprises for more revenues and dealing with the foreign investors for more capital, local governments have formed various relationships with local business organizations, including those in non-state sectors. The result of these macro-level policies is that the state has established the conditions under which a variety of organizational types, including those that are still state owned, have the latitude to behave like business organizations in China today.

Decentralization does have its dark side, however. The best work on this front comes from Victor Shih (2008), who examines the structure of China's political system and the ways in which factional politics have shaped the current system in fundamental ways. The conflict here begins with the tension between fiscal decentralization and central control, with the generalists advocating the former and the technocratic elite advocating the latter. Decentralization has allowed for flexibility in the implementation of policy and local initiative and local competition among provinces and local-level officials; it has allowed for market-like incentive structures despite the continuation of state ownership. However, local officials want to maximize investment in their localities and they rely on their political ties within the generalist faction to do so. They see local investment as the key source of growth and have little incentive to adhere to borrowing limits, a problem that could ultimately lead to hyperinflation. On the other hand, the technocrats, the faction led by Zhu Rongji in the 1990s, have consistently pushed for greater central control, and have thus constrained inflation. These factions coexist, because, while the technocratic elite have greater control over central resources and institutions, the generalists have a broader base and ultimate control over the vast majority of the party infrastructure. With the ebb and flow of the economy, different economic conditions determine which factions hold the upper hand in monetary policy at a given point in time. This tension of who is in control at any given point in time opens the door for much uncertainty as well as opportunities for corruption.

The Development of Market-Oriented Organizations in China

We turn now to the internal focus of economic development in China. One of the key goals of China's economic reforms since 1979 has been to transform the relationships between enterprises and the state. Under the planned economy, almost all of China's enterprises were state owned and state run (here again, state-run enterprises include collectives and TVEs). Enterprises varied in terms of the level of government under which they resided (from central to local) and in terms of the resources they were able to extract from the government, but there was no question that the state was the residual claimant, exercised managerial control, and controlled the transfer of assets. There was a small number of collective enterprises, but their managerial system was not essentially different from that of state-owned enterprises. These organizations—state-owned and collectively owned enterprises alike—served not only as production units of the governmental system but also as redistribution units for the goods of social welfare. Enterprises before economic reform were essentially inseparable from the government and highly dependent on it.

As discussed briefly in Chapter 2, Deng's reforms transformed enterprises in two significant ways: (1) relieving them of the responsibility for social benefits and (2) turning economic autonomy over to both economic organizations and the managers who ran them. In the 1980s, the decentralization of economic responsibilities for TVEs and the local officials who governed them transformed the responsibilities and rights of both governments and the enterprises they governed. In similar ways, the "dual track" policy rebuilt the incentive structures of the SOEs and the responsibilities and rights of both the government and enterprises, though, as discussed earlier, this process occurred in a much more gradual fashion.

Thus, these enterprises obtained, in many cases, enough financial control and freedom from the burden of social welfare costs to transform their practices in the market economy. In addition, as the party and the administrative arm of the government—the administrative bureaus—receded from direct control over enterprise behavior, managers throughout the

Chinese economy have become the key decision makers of TVEs and SOEs, along with their counterparts in the private and foreign-funded economy.

It is far too simplistic, then, to think of business organizations as only covering the private enterprises in the economy; this sector, while important, constitutes only one of the organizational types that are behaving like business organizations in China today.[13] SOEs, TVEs, private enterprises, and foreign-funded enterprises are all part of the group of Chinese organizations that have, to varying degrees, become oriented toward the market in China. In this section, I focus on the institutional changes that have shaped business organizations in China today, specifically looking at (1) the evolution of government–enterprise relationships, (2) the impact of foreign direct investment (FDI), (3) the transformation of social relationships in China's market economy, and (4) the emergence of business associations. Through each of these areas of change, I address the question of the forces that have transformed Chinese economic organizations.

By classical definitions of markets and firms, only private enterprises and some foreign-funded enterprises in China would fall under the category of business organizations. However, strict classifications of business organization do not capture the variety of organizations that behave like capitalist firms in China. An analysis of economic development in China must focus on what it means to operate like a capitalist firm rather than on official categories or types. The evolution of the study of property rights is illustrative here: Where classical studies of property rights defined the institutional arrangements into basic categories (private, public, or state owned), more recent work in this area has focused on the specific practices that define property rights as a "bundle" of rights, including (1) the right to residual income flows, (2) the right of managerial control, and (3) the right to transfer assets (Demsetz 1967; Furubotn and Pejovich 1974; Oi and Walder 1999). The property rights issue is especially important in this case, because many firms in China have long operated like private firms while still retaining a state-owned status (Walder 1995e; Oi and Walder 1999). In China, beyond private and foreign-funded enterprises, SOEs and TVEs have also evolved to behave like market firms in various ways. As of 2004, China had 25,339 state-owned and state-holding enterprises, occupying 2 percent of total enterprises; these organizations contributed 15 percent of the output value to the total gross industrial output of the country. The 141,772 collectively owned enterprises (11.1 percent of the total) contributed just over 8 percent of the output value to the total gross industrial output; 102,392 limited liability corporations (8.1 percent) contributed 28.4 percent to the total output; 902,647 private enterprises (71.1 percent) contributed nearly 32 percent to the total output; 17,427 shareholding corporations (1.4 percent) contributed 14.9 percent to the total output; 54,910 firms funded by Hong Kong and Taiwan money (4 percent) occupied 11 percent of the total output; and 51,255 firms funded by foreign sources (3.7 percent) contributed 19.2 percent to the gross industrial output.[14]

TVEs and SOEs as Market Firms

In Chapter 2, I introduced the concept of local governments and the TVEs they preside over as behaving like industrial firms. SOEs were slower to see true reform than their counterparts in the rural industrial economy. In the early stages of the economic reforms, the "dual track" policy provided a degree of stability for the early enterprise transitions when the state sector was still evidently dominant in China's economic system. According to this policy, SOEs were allowed to sell the goods above the "plan" quotas and keep extra profits, a system that significantly shifted the incentive structures for these organizations. Thus, even in the early period of the economic reforms, when SOEs still largely operated under the rubric of the planned economy, managers were given incentives to direct their enterprises to behave like business organizations in the emerging market economy.

In 1992, the Chinese government made clear its market-driven reform direction and shifted its policy making toward creating the rules, laws and institutions that govern a market economy, and from this point forward, the dual track system was phased out. Since then, substantial restructuring of state-owned industry has been central to the reform agenda. By the mid-1990s, SOEs were increasingly being pushed to restructure their operations in fundamental ways, causing them to be treated—and to increasingly behave—like business organizations in practice if not in legal form. Firms were placed on independent budgetary systems, many were cut off completely from the redistributive funds of central government coffers, and many were given full latitude to make decisions over how they would govern themselves in China's emerging markets. Laws like the

Enterprise Bankruptcy Law (1986), the Enterprise Law (1988), the Company Law (1994), and the Labor Law (1995) established a framework for these changes. But the key point here is that although the transition away from the planned economy was a gradual process, managers in many of China's SOEs were increasingly being handed the key responsibilities that fit with the management of business organizations: although they did not possess the right to transfer assets, they increasingly had the rights to residual income flows and the power and responsibility of managerial control.[15]

In addition to the declining scale of the SOEs, their contributions to China's GDP and total industrial output have also significantly decreased. In 1978, the SOEs generated about 80 percent of China's GDP, while in 2004, the contribution of the SOEs dropped down to 15 percent and the collective, private, and joint-venture sectors generated over 70 percent. In 1978, the state sectors contributed over 75 percent of China's industrial output and collective sectors accounted for about 22 percent (Naughton 1995). In 1995, the state sectors' portion in industrial output had declined to 35 percent, while collective sectors contributed over 36 percent of industrial output values and private sector and other non-state sectors produced the rest (*Statistical Yearbook of China* 1996). By 2004, the shares of gross industrial output being produced by the private firms, combined with foreign funded enterprises, rose to 52 percent, while the share of the SOEs was only 18 percent and the share of collective sectors was down to 10 percent (*Statistical Yearbook of China* 2006). It is very clear that through the reform era, the non-state firms have been growing at a strikingly faster rate than the state sector. However, even today, SOEs still remain a massive force in China's economy. They provide basic employment and social welfare for the majority of urban workers and the bulk of fiscal revenues for most levels of government. They still control more than half of China's industrial assets and dominate vital industries such as financial services, power, telecommunications, steel, and petrochemicals, among others. China cannot fully accomplish its market reforms without successfully restructuring and further reforming the state sector. It is also worth noting that state-owned firms officially only account for 2 percent of firms. It is also important to note that this is a conservative estimate of the state-owned firm category, as many of the firms in the "private" or "limited liability" or "shareholding" categories could just as easily be thought of as state-owned (many publicly trading shareholding corporations, which are officially categorized as shareholding corporations, are firms in which the state controls up to 70 percent of the shares). Finally, it is worth noting the strong contribution to industrial output by the relatively small proportion of firms funded by Hong Kong and Taiwanese money.

Private and Foreign-Funded Enterprises

In the era of economic reform, however, the entry and success of large numbers of collectives, private firms, joint ventures, and foreign firms have significantly driven China's market reforms and sharply overshadowed the status and roles of SOEs in the industrial sector and the national economy. The organizations that populate these categories of economic organization are the closest to the classic definitions of market firms. Private firms, for their part, are fairly clear cut: they are organized around relationships between principals (owners) and agents (managers and workers), and they are basically oriented toward the pursuit of profits in exchange for the production of goods and the provision of services. There are a couple of key distinctions among types of organizations within this sector—namely, that between household businesses and private enterprises: household businesses employ a maximum of seven employees, while private enterprises employ eight or more workers. In addition, private enterprises are subject to the Enterprise Law (or the Company Law, depending on whether the organization has made this transition), while household businesses are not. It is worth emphasizing again here that while the Chinese government has allowed private firms to emerge, this process is different from the process of privatization. SOEs, urban collectives, and TVEs have remained largely in state hands, but a private economy has also emerged to coexist with the state economy. This private (and foreign-funded) economy has competed with—and built markets in conjunction with—the state sector.

Foreign-funded organizations are a little more complicated than private organizations. In general, these organizations come in two primary forms. First, wholly owned foreign enterprises (WOFEs) are private organizations that are funded by a foreign parent or benefactor. However, these organizations are different from private business organizations in that they are largely extensions of the parent organizations that formed them. Thus, while these organizations may appear to be the most similar to private organizations in the Chinese economy in terms of property rights, they are most often closely tied subsidiary organizations. Further, especially for larger organizations in this category, their operation in the economy depends in part on their relationships with other organizations and with the local or national government (depending on their scale and scope). The second form that appears within this category is the joint-venture firm. Joint ventures are usually fully independent entities from the parent organizations that have contributed resources to their formation. However, these parent organizations may control their business decisions to varying degrees. In some cases, joint ventures operate as fully independent entities, exercising managerial control and control over residual income. In other cases, parent companies from both the foreign and Chinese partner sides can occupy significant managerial control over these entities.

In the 1990s, private and foreign-funded firms replaced TVEs as the most dynamic sectors of the economy. With respect to foreign-funded firms especially, these organizations have seen the highest levels of labor productivity, ratio of output to assets, and ratio of profits to cost (see Figure 4.3 and Table 4.2) (Guthrie 2005). In contrast with the decline of the SOEs, the non-state sectors have become the most dramatic driving forces of China's market-led reforms, the most competitive firms, and the most important force in supporting the high-speed growth of the national economy in the past thirty years.[16]

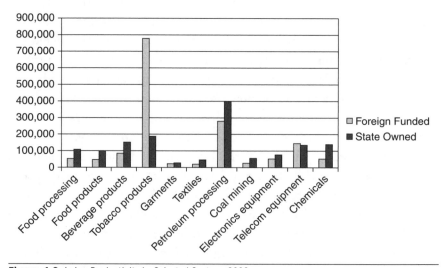

Figure 4.3 Labor Productivity by Selected Sectors, 2003.

Source: National Statistical Bureau of China (2004, 533, 543).

Table 4.2 Comparison of State-Owned and Foreign-Funded Firms

	Foreign–Funded			SOEs w/ no foreign funds		
	2001	2003	2009	2001	2003	2009
Ratio of Assets to Output (%)	9.83	11.46	13.08	8.17	10.09	11.29
Ratio of Profits to Cost (%)	5.85	6.83	7.25	5.75	7.25	6.73
Labor Production (Yuan/ Person-Year)	75,913	92,158	NA	54,772	87,095	NA
Number of Times of Turnover of Working Capital	1.89	2.20	2.18	1.36	1.69	2.05

Sources: National Statistical Bureau of China (2002, 446, 456; 2004, 553, 543; 2010, 522–523, 542–543).

FDI, Global Business, and Organizational Change

Since the early 1990s, China has become a major recipient of foreign direct investment (FDI), which occupies the major part of total foreign capital (including foreign loans, FDI, and other investments) that China has received. Beginning in 1991, the amount of FDI in China rose precipitously. In 1993, China received more FDI than any other country and, since then, has been the second largest recipient in the world, behind only the United States (see Figure 4.4). By 1999, FDI in JVs and WFOEs exceeded 250 billion U.S. dollars (Lardy 2002). In 2002, China's total inflow of FDI reached near half a trillion U.S. dollars, making it the world's largest recipient of FDI. According to Nicholas Lardy (1996), four factors contribute to such dramatic increases of FDI that China attracted in the early 1990s: (1) the increasing magnitude of aggregate FDI flowing to developing countries in the 1990s; (2) China's political stability in the post-Tiananmen Square era, combined with the explosive growth of domestic economy, rebuilt the confidence of foreign firms and investors; (3) after one decade of economic liberalization, and the practice of the coastal developmental strategies, China's foreign investment regime had been systematically liberalized, and more sectors had been opened to foreign investors;

and (4) it is widely believed that Chinese firms disguised their money as "foreign investment" to take advantage of the special policies only provided to those enterprises that attracted foreign investment. (This final point likely accounts for the high rates of FDI flowing in from Hong Kong.)

With the country's rapid economic growth in GDP and its explosive growth in foreign trade, China's business organizations have experienced dramatic changes. The nation's economic architects aspired to force rational economic actions and organizational structures onto the development agenda of business organizations through initiating several waves of enterprise reforms at different time periods. From Zhao Ziyang in the 1980s to Zhu Rongji in the 1990s, Chinese leaders have clearly focused on the creation of rational accountability and the embracing of international standards. The enterprise reforms in the current era have concentrated on building a "modern enterprise system" and forcing enterprises to restructure their accounting practices so that they comply with international models and standards.

Both the government and the enterprises recognized the need for foreign capital, advanced management experience, and technology. The

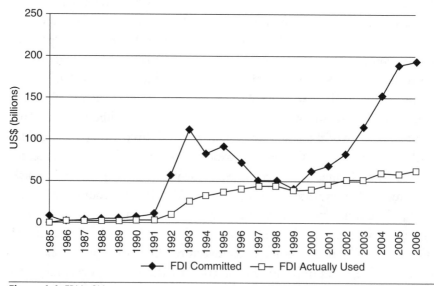

Figure 4.4 FDI in China.

Source: National Statistical Bureau of China (2010, 250).

Table 4.3 Utilization of Foreign Capital (U.S.$, billions)

Total Amount of Foreign Capital to be Utilized through Signed Agreements and Contracts

	Total		Foreign Loans		Direct Foreign Investments		Other Foreign Investments Value
	Number of Projects	Value	Number of Projects	Value	Number of Projects	Value	
1979–1984	3,841	28.13	117	16.978	3724	9.75	1.398
1985	3,145	10.27	72	3.53	3,073	6.33	0.40
1986	1,551	12.23	53	8.41	1,498	3.33	0.50
1987	2,289	12.14	56	7.82	2,233	3.71	0.61
1988	6,063	16.00	118	9.81	5,945	5.30	0.89
1989	5,909	11.48	130	5.19	5,779	5.60	0.69
1990	7,371	12.09	98	5.10	7,273	6.60	0.39
1991	13,086	19.58	108	7.16	12,978	11.98	0.45
1992	48,858	69.44	94	10.70	48,764	58.12	0.61
1993	83,595	123.27	158	11.31	83,437	111.44	0.53
1994	47,646	93.76	97	10.67	47,549	82.68	0.41
1995	37,184	103.21	173	11.29	37,011	91.28	0.64
1996	24,673	81.61	117	7.96	24,556	73.28	0.37
1997	21,138	61.06	137	5.87	21,001	51.00	4.18
1998	19,850	63.20	51	8.39	19,799	52.10	2.71
1999	17,022	52.01	104	8.36	16,918	41.22	2.43
2000	22,347	71.13			22,347	62.38	8.75
2001	26,140	71.98			26,140	69.20	2.78

(Continued overleaf)

Table 4.3 Continued

Total Amount of Foreign Capital to be Utilized through Signed Agreements and Contracts

	Total		Foreign Loans		Direct Foreign Investments		Other Foreign
	Number of Projects	Value	Number of Projects	Value	Number of Projects	Value	Investments Value
2002	34,171	84.75			34,171	82.77	1.98
2003	41,081	116.90			41,081	115.07	1.83
2004	43,664	156.59			43,664	153.48	3.11
2005	44,001	192.59			44,001	189.07	3.53
2006	41,473	198.22			41,473	193.73	4.49
2007	37,871				37,871		
2008	27,514				27,514		
2009	23,435				23,435		
1979–2009	684,918	1,661.62	1683	138.54	683,235	1,479.4	43.68
Total Amount of Foreign Capital Actually Used							
1979–1984		18.19		13.04		4.10	1.04
1985		4.76		2.51		1.96	0.30
1986		7.63		5.01		2.24	0.37
1987		8.45		5.81		2.31	0.33
1988		10.23		6.49		3.19	0.55
1989		10.06		6.29		3.39	0.38
1990		10.29		6.53		3.49	0.27
1991		11.55		6.89		4.37	0.30

Year			
1992	19.20	7.91	11.01	0.28
1993	38.96	11.19	27.52	0.26
1994	43.21	9.27	33.77	0.18
1995	48.13	10.33	37.52	0.29
1996	54.81	12.67	41.73	0.41
1997	64.41	12.02	45.26	7.13
1998	58.56	11.00	45.46	2.09
1999	52.66	10.21	40.32	2.13
2000	59.36	10.00	40.72	8.64
2001	49.67		46.88	2.79
2002	55.01		52.74	2.27
2003	56.14		53.51	2.64
2004	64.07		60.63	3.44
2005	63.81		60.33	3.48
2006	67.08		63.02	4.06
2007	78.34		74.77	3.57
2008	95.25		92.40	2.86
2009	91.80		90.03	1.77
1979–2009	1141.62	147.16	942.65	51.82

Source: National Statistical Bureau of China (2010, 250).

desire to attract foreign investment and technology has led to institutional accommodations that support rational–legal accountability and the rule of law within the firm. Coupled with the reformers' intentions, the inflow of foreign capital and global corporations into China exerted significant pressure on the evolution of Chinese business organizations to adapt to the rules of the global market. These influences from foreign investors and global corporations are evident not only in the nation's macroeconomic policies but also in organizational changes that can be observed at the firm level. Western investors—many of whom are more interested in long-term investments to capture market share than they are in cheap labor—generally seek Chinese partners that are predictable, stable, and knowledgeable about Western-style business practices and negotiations.[17] This pressure from international organizations and Western investors has accelerated the rationalization of China's economic system not only at the state level but also within firms.

The Emergence of Capital Markets, Homegrown Multinationals, and the Rise of SASAC

China was never going to be on the path to becoming a dominant economic power in the world based on the size of its labor pool alone. It was always necessary that China make the transition from an economy built around supplying labor to the world's largest corporations, to one built around the development of great corporations of its own. Fortunately for China, and challenging for the rest of the world's corporations, China's domestic corporations have arrived. Two of China's corporations have cracked the Global top ten in terms of revenues (Sinopec and CNPC at 5 and 6, respectively), but the tremors are being felt more widely than this statistic indicates. Companies around the world would readily admit to the competitive pressure they feel from Chinese companies: Lenovo's purchase of IBM's Thinkpad division; Haier's bid to buy Maytag; CNOOC's bid to take over Unocal; Huawei's tense competition with Cisco and, more recently, its proposed alliance with Sprint and bid to take over 3Leaf; the international public listing of PetroChina, ICBC, China Unicom, China Mobile, Aluminum Corp. of China, among others. China's arrival at this position has been the next step in the process of developing a first-rate economy. In some cases, the state's role in supporting the gradual growth of companies like PetroChina, ICBC, and China Unicom has been a central feature of these companies' emergence. In others, the process of securing technology transfer through joint venture agreements or the growing power of private companies in the cases of Lenovo and Huawei, has allowed China to develop an indigenous high-tech sector that is growing in influence around the world.

However, this system does not work without the growth of two more institutional systems that have been crucial to China's growing economic power. The first is a central feature of all of mature capitalist economies—capital markets. China's domestic stock exchanges in Shanghai and Shenzhen were founded in 1990 and 1991 respectively. China's nascent stock market has since grown tremendously, and by the end of 2009 the number of domestically listed companies in China had risen to 1,718 with a total market capitalization of 3.8 trillion U.S. dollars. As one of the key market mechanisms, China's stock market was introduced in order to restructure SOEs through corporatization and simultaneously to attract private and foreign capitals to finance the SOEs in transition. Thus, building a stock market was not out of step with the broader logic of China's gradual reform. Following the gradualist model, the Chinese government's construction of the institutions that govern public owner-ship has been spread across the period. First, the Company Law [1994, 2006] pushed enterprises to standardize governance structures by codi-fying the process of converting SOEs into corporations and of limiting political intervention. During the period of the 1990s, the legal basis for the standardized operation of listed companies in the stock market was gradually developed, and a series of regulations and laws such as "the Opinions on Standardizing the Joint Stock Limited Companies," "the Provisional Regulations on the Administration of Issuing and Trading of Stocks," and the Securities Law of the People's Republic of China were instituted. In 2001, the central government passed The Tentative Measures for Decreasing State Shareholding; then in 2006, amended versions of the Company Law and the Securities Law came forward to deepen these reforms.

As China has been systematically constructing the institutions of a publicly traded economy, it has been widely reported that the government has significantly decreased its stake in the state-owned firms that have been listed on the Shanghai and Shenzhen Stock Exchanges, and these companies are becoming "privatized" in some ways. Woo (1999), for example, saw the Fifteenth Congress of the Chinese Communist Party (CCP) in September of 1997 as a watershed moment, as the state passed key resolutions to accelerate privatization of the state sector. And as scholars have watched this process unfold over the decade following the Fifteenth Congress, many have come to the conclusion that the state has indeed proceeded in the process of privatizing the state sector, particularly those firms listed in the domestic and international stock exchanges. As Beamish and Delios describe the trend: "Along with ... growth in the number of listed companies has come a change in ownership, in which formerly state-owned companies have had their shares transferred into the hands of private interests ..." (2005, 310)

This view, however, lacks a nuanced understanding of the complexities of enterprise-state relations, as the government's receding from control over publicly listed companies has, like every other institutional change in China's economic reform, been a *gradual* process. In this study we argue that because the state maintains a controlling interest in these publicly traded firms in variety of ways, state-ownership of publicly traded firms has declined only by degrees. First, over the course of the Initial Public Offering (IPO) process, the state office overseeing a large group company [*jituan gongsi*] usually has a heavy hand in deciding which part of the group will be spun off for the IPO. Most often the strongest performing factory or group of factories goes public. The state maintains the basic state–firm relationship with the remaining part of the group company—it remains on as the advisory administrative office, playing a significant role in the strategic decisions the firm or group makes as well as maintaining a hand as the partial residual claimant on firm profits (Guthrie *et al.* 2007). In some cases in which firms are not part of a group, the entire factory may go public. However, IPO processes more often involve a spin-off situation. In the initial stages of the IPO, the state administrative office and the group company will maintain control over between 20 and 60 percent of the shares, though in the early years of the stock exchanges these numbers were closer to 70 percent. The remainder of the shares is divided between various types of institutional and free-floating shares. A typical ownership transformation for a state-owned enterprise would allow the state to retain between 40 and 50 percent of the company's shares; between 20 and 30 percent of the shares are designated for institutional shares; the remaining 30 percent of shares are designated for public consumption as free-floating

Table 4.4 Evolution of China's Domestic Stock Markets

	Market Capitalization (US$, billion)	Total No. of Firms	No. of Firms, Shanghai	No. of Firms, Shenzhen	No. of Firms, A Shares Only	No. of Firms, A&H Shares	No. of Firms, A&B Shares	No. of Firms, B Shares Only
1990	–	10	8	2	10	–	–	–
1991	–	14	8	6	14	–	–	–
1992	–	53	29	24	35	–	18	–
1993	–	183	106	77	140	3	34	6
1994	–	291	171	120	227	6	54	4
1995	47.65*	323	188	135	242	11	58	12
1996	–	530	293	237	431	14	69	16
1997	–	745	383	362	627	17	76	25
1998	–	851	438	413	727	18	80	26
1999	363.45*	949	484	465	822	19	82	26
2000	660.30*	1,088	572	516	955	19	86	28
2001	597.56*	1,160	646	514	1,025	23	88	24
2002	526.29*	1,224	715	509	1,085	28	87	24
2003	656.23	1,287	780	507	1,146	30	87	24
2004	572.74	1,377	837	540	1,236	31	86	24
2005	501.24	1,381	834	547	1,240	32	86	23
2006	1,381.82	1,434	842	592	1,287	38	86	23
2007	5,056.28	1,550	860	690	1,389	52	86	23
2008	1,875.83	1,625	864	761	1,459	57	85	23
2009	3,770.31	1,718	870	848	1,549	61	85	22

Source: National Statistical Bureau of China (2010, 742, 743, 744)

Calculated at 6.47 Yuan /USD

www.xe.com 6/23/2011

*Source: National Statistical Bureau of China (2006, 789, 790).

shares (Guthrie *et al.*, 2007). More importantly, the above-mentioned popular view that former SOEs have had their shares "privatized" neglects the roles that the newly built state-owned asset management companies (SOAMCs) in the mid-1990s have played in masking continued state ownership over publicly-listed firms. Over the course of the last 20 years, there has been a rapid proliferation of SOAMCs that act like investment companies or "funds." Some of these are effective and think like capitalist shareholders; others are nothing more than a mask for classic state ownership.

By far the most important of these organizations is the State-Owned Assets Supervision and Administration Commission (SASAC), a central government agency that now owns a controlling stake in 151 of the largest, most powerful Chinese corporations. When SASAC was founded in 2001 (which was the end of a long gradual process of governmental reorganization that dated back to 1988), it was initially set to manage about 6.9 trillion *yuan* in assets (about $866 billion); with several high-profile initial public offerings (IPOs) on the books—including PetroChina's recent IPO, which gave it (briefly) a market capitalization of over $1 trillion, the value of SASAC's assets is likely to be over several trillion dollars. The emergence of SASAC has been a crucial step in China's gradualist model of economic reform process, yet surprisingly little has been written about this key institution. This institution is, without question, the most powerful asset management institution shaping China's economy. SASAC emerged for two reasons. First, SASAC was set with the difficult task of creating profitable entities out of China's still-lagging largest SOEs. Even beyond the scope of SASAC, however, as Chinese firms sought to become more international (e.g., attracting the interest of institutional investors from abroad), they began to experience pressure from abroad to clean up the soft budget ties that ran throughout the state sector. The first movement in this area related to banks: The large banks could not be taken seriously as international financial institutions with the number of bad loans they had on their books. Through the SOAMCs these banks set up new institutions—which were owned by the banks—that were, in theory, separate places to deposit the loans but in reality still subsidiary to the same organization. As governmental agencies sought to list the firms under their jurisdictions on the stock exchanges around the world (including, but not limited to, the Shanghai and Shenzhen exchanges), institutional investors from abroad often raised the question of to what extent these firms were still owned by the state. With the premium placed on privatization as the "correct" institutional arrangement to produce efficiency and profitability, many institutional investors from abroad pressed the issue of whether the state owners had adequately divested themselves from ownership and control over state-owned organizations. The state's approach to this issue was to form SASAC and move the ownership accounts of these organizations over to the Central and local SASACs. The catch was that, unbeknownst to many investors, the same state agencies that previously owned the SOEs also owned SASAC. In this sense, the divestment of its ownership stake in publicly traded SOEs was part of an accounting move by the government agencies to make these firms more attractive for institutional investors from abroad.

While this account might be taken as a cynical view of the state's effort to maintain property rights and governance over the firms under their jurisdictions, there is a second force at work. The logic of what the Chinese government has done with the transfer of ownership to SASAC is not out of step with the broader logic of gradual reform. Gradual reform is fundamentally about experimenting with new institutional forms that allow for stability and connection with past institutional forms while at the same time encouraging new management models. SASAC can be seen in this light, though it may simply be too early to see the positive effects on firm performance. Under the logic of gradual reform, asset management companies are organizations that may be an interim model of corporate ownership and governance—it is likely the case that these organizations will act more and more independently from the state agencies to which they report and, eventually, act fully independent of their influence. These state organizations devoted to the performance of the firms under their jurisdictions helped buffer transforming SOEs from the shock of the market reforms, stabilizing the firms under their control and offering administrative resources and advice where needed. The real question for SASAC is not whether it is still ultimately owned by the state, but, rather, whether it manages and governs firms differently from the government agencies that were formerly the direct owners. The interesting reality here is that that SASAC companies actually perform more like private firms than their classic state-owned counterparts (Guthrie *et al.* 2009; Wang *et al.*, 2012). Further, SASAC serves the important function of working as an agent of the state to think about cross industry strategizing. As the largest shareholder in many of China's blue-chip firms, SASAC serves as the intermediary between the pressures of international capital markets (where many of these firms are listed) and the strategic goals of the Chinese state.

The Macro-Level Impact of Multinational Corporations

Attracting foreign investment has been a basic part of China's economic development in the reform era. On March 25, 1997, in the City of Shanghai, the automotive giant General Motors (GM) announced a joint venture with the Shanghai Automotive Industrial Corporation (SAIC).[18] For China, the positive aspects of this deal were many: GM agreed to commit a large amount of capital, even compared to other large-scale joint-venture deals;[19] it brought technology to China in a highly competitive industry; and it brought international cachet and branding from the largest automotive company in the world (at the time). For GM the potential upside was significant as well: the ability to gain access to the world's fastest-growing automobile market would position the company well for the future. Yet, despite these many advantages for both sides of the partnership, both sides also take on significant risk. The risk for GM was largely economic: given that many of the joint ventures involving multinationals in China have reported losses for the entire time they have been in operation in China, it is unlikely that GM would see a return on its investment anytime soon. This was an investment for the future, and the future is always somewhat unpredictable in developing countries like China. The risk for China is, in some ways, more fundamental: when the State Council endorses a deal of this size, it is giving up some amount of control over the development of the sector in which the venture is occurring. In other words, investments such as these pierce the veil of the authoritarian government's sovereign control over the nation and the economy. Presidents and chief executive officers of multinational firms investing large sums of money in China expect to be heard. In Beijing, the mayor has established an advisory council, made up of presidents and chief executive officers of companies with significant stakes in China, so that these high-powered individuals can have an official forum through which to express their views.[20] Sometimes, company executives are afforded even higher access to air their concerns. For example, following an incident that involved theft of intellectual property, DuPont used what bargaining power it had to pressure government officials to set forth policies that would safeguard against the recurrence of a similar incident in subsequent investments. In 1994, on the brink of embarking on another joint venture in China, DuPont's chairman Edgar Woolard met with Chinese president Jiang Zemin to discuss formal policies that would protect foreign investors. It is unlikely that Woolard was able to elicit any guarantees from Jiang or that this meeting was a direct precursor to the law protecting intellectual property, which was promulgated in 1995 (the law had been in the works for a long time prior to the meeting). Yet, as China needs foreign investment to develop, such high-stakes negotiations require the Chinese government to create an environment in which these investors feel that their assets are somewhat protected. This requires giving up sovereign control over industries and sectors of the economy.

There are a number of ways that negotiations over foreign-invested joint venture agreements have an impact on Chinese state sovereignty. For example, if companies specify arbitration clauses in their joint-venture contracts, the Chinese government no longer has jurisdiction over disputes that may arise in these deals. Beginning in 1979, for the first time since the founding of the PRC, foreign parties have input on decisions that affect Chinese internal affairs. Enforcement still lies in the hands of Chinese authorities. But for a country that only a few years ago operated fully on the institution of administrative fiat, turning over decision-making power to a third party is somewhat problematic. In other words, negotiations with foreign parties require the Chinese government to give up some power and control over Chinese society. The extent to which the Chinese government is forced to give up sovereignty varies with the value of the joint venture investment: when the Chinese government is facing a large multinational company that seeks to invest a significant amount of capital and technology, both of which China desperately needs, it must give up control over the venture to a significant extent. And if that company uses arbitration clauses in its joint venture contracts, as most large multinationals operating in China do, the government gives away control of the economic venture in question to a still greater extent.[21]

Foreign investment has played an important role in China's reform effort since it reopened its doors to foreign investment in 1979. From Deng's visit to the United States in 1979 to the Law on Chinese-Foreign

Equity Joint Ventures—one of the first laws passed to usher in the economic transition—the attraction of foreign capital and technology has played a central role in the economic changes occurring in China. Table 4.3 puts the General Motors venture into perspective: despite the size of the venture, this sum of money, while significant, is only one part of an investment trend that has been occurring for the last three decades in China. This venture is only the most recent in a long line of investments that have placed the Chinese government in a partnership with Western multinationals. It remains to be seen whether deals such as these constitute fundamental encroachments on state sovereignty in the realm of foreign investment, but this challenge to the state is only the most recent in a long line of sectoral transformations that have occurred throughout the economy over the last twenty years.

Changes in Productivity at the Firm Level

In the 1980s and early 1990s, many prominent economists advising nations in the construction of markets assumed that institutional change was a relatively simple process. The institutions of capitalism and democracy reflected the natural state of rational economic actors, and if we could just get the institutions right, individuals in these societies would know what to do. Further, the inefficiencies of state planning and the shackles of an authoritarian government ran counter to this natural state, and there was no way to configure the institutions of planned economic systems to work with the instincts of human nature. Accordingly, during the period of China's transition to a market economy, economists and institutional advisors from the West have advocated the rapid transition to market institutions as the necessary medicine for transforming communist societies. Many scholars have argued that private property provides the institutional foundation of a market economy, and, therefore, communist societies making the transition to a market economy must privatize industry and other public goods. Further, the radical members of this school have argued that rapid privatization—the so-called shock therapy or big bang approach to economic reforms—is the only way to avoid costly abuses in these transitory systems. According to scholars in this camp, the institutional goals of these transitions are clear, and the architects of these transitions should not waste any time in pushing their economies toward these goals (Kornai 1980, 1990; Sachs 1992, 1995a, 1995b; Sachs and Woo 1994a, 1994b, 1997).

Much like the advocates of rapid political reform, those demanding immediate economic reform often take for granted the learning that must take place in the face of new institutions. The assumption among rapid-reform advocates is that, given certain institutional arrangements, individuals will naturally know how to carry out the practices of democracy and capitalism. Yet these assumptions reflect a neoclassical view of human nature in which rational man will thrive in his natural environment—free markets and a democratic system. Completely absent from this view are the roles of history, culture, and preexisting institutions, and it is a vision that is far too simplistic to comprehend the challenge of making markets and democracy work in the absence of stable institutions and a history to which they can be tied. The transition from a system of a planned economy and authoritarian rule to one of free markets and democracy can be a wrenching experience, not only at the institutional level but also at the level of individual practice. Individuals must learn the rules of the market, and new institutions must be set in place long enough to gain stability and legitimacy. These are processes that occur slowly and over a long period of time.

Two sectors of the Chinese economy have outperformed others over the course of the reforms: in the 1980s, it was the township and village enterprises (TVEs) in the rural industrial economy; in recent years, it has been those firms that have been shaped by foreign direct investment (FDI). The first fact corresponds to the changes that have reshaped state–firm relations in the reform era. Even though the command economy is virtually nonexistent today, where a firm was positioned in the industrial hierarchy of the former command economy has had profound consequences for how it experiences economic reforms. The central issue here is the level of attention firms receive in terms of monitoring and support from the state administrative offices to which they report. The second case of elevated productivity corresponds to the impact that relations with foreign firms have on Chinese corporations. Many scholarly and popular accounts have focused on either the exploitative role of foreign firms in the Chinese economy or on the importance of technology transfer in the economy. Here, however, I examine the ways in which a particular group of foreign multinationals is playing a critical role in the transformation of organizational practice in China.

The market economy is not simply a natural state that will magically emerge in the face of private property or "shock therapy." Rather, successful navigation of an emerging market economy is a learned set of practices and behaviors, and actors in transforming economies must be exposed to the models of economic action and the guidance from different organizational actors in the marketplace to institutionalize the successful models of the new economic system. Managers of Chinese corporations learn the rules of the market from the organizations that provide the best lessons for the successful transition to a market economy. As Chinese firms deal with the uncertainties of China's emerging marketplaces, they are influenced by the organizations—whether local state offices or foreign multinationals— from which they learn the successful practices of a market economy. Transfers of knowledge occur in three ways in the development of market economic practices in China's transforming economy. First, they sometimes come from above: local state offices offer guidance to the firms under their jurisdictions, helping them implement the new management practices that are necessary for survival in China's transforming markets. Second, heightened expectations and standards come from close relationships with powerful foreign investors. Chinese managers want desperately to land the lucrative joint-venture deals that will bring access to technology and investment resources, and when they are in a position to compete for those resources, they raise their level of production accordingly. The attention to productivity, quality, and "efficient" management all become signals in the marketplace that these organizations know the meaning of doing business in China's emerging market economy; they know what it means to "link up" with the international world. These kinds of relationships with foreign investors stand in contrast to those in which foreign investors are simply seeking cheap labor. Third, close collaboration with foreign multinationals through the negotiation of joint venture deals and sitting on joint boards of directors with their foreign partners are also important mechanisms through which transfers of knowledge flow. Interlocking directorates become a conduit through which senior management of a Chinese company has constant access to the input and advice of a successful multinational partner in its own sector. Various combinations of these transfers of knowledge can be observed in the cases described below.

Three Case Studies of Chinese Industrial Firms

In the following section, I present three examples of Chinese firms that illuminate different aspects of China's evolution as a global economic power. In the first example, we consider one of the more famous cases of the transformation of a large SOE in the oil and gas industry. This case allows us to trace the evolution of a large, inefficient state-run SOE as it transforms itself into a more efficient organization that is built, at least in part, around capitalist values, as part of the organization eventually becomes a listed entity on the NYSE. This case is important not only as an example of the transition from SOE to global publicly traded multinational but also because it highlights the importance of alliances with global corporations like Goldman Sachs, McKinsey, PricewaterhouseCoopers, among others. The second example focuses in on a company that relied heavily on a multinational alliance that gave it key technological and managerial advantages in the marketplace. In the third example, we consider a case in which successful transformation has come from the bottom up, with little guidance from the state. In this case, the company grew organically from small-scale converted collective to multinational.

The Chinese National Petroleum Corporation and the Formation of PetroChina

In 2001, China launched its first international IPO, a listing on the NYSE that was backed by Goldman Sachs. Today PetroChina is, by some accountings, one of the most efficient oil companies in the world. This statement is a little complicated because the numbers look very different if PetroChina is regarded as part of its parent organization as opposed to independently (PetroChina is very efficient; its parent, CNPC, is not). Nevertheless, the evolution of PetroChina is a case that gives us a window onto the evolution of China's massive SOEs.

In 1988 the Chinese government disbanded its Ministry of Petroleum Industry and formed three state owned companies to oversee and modernize its petroleum-related activities. The China Offshore Oil Corporation (CNOOC) was formed to handle offshore production, the China Petrochemical Group (Sinopec) focused on refining and petrochemical production, and the China National Petroleum Corporation (CNPC) took over all onshore exploration and production of oil and gas. The reforms leading to the abolition of the Ministry of Petroleum Industry represented one of the first major steps the Chinese government took towards reform of heavy industries. Up until that point, most economic reform efforts were primarily focused on agricultural, light manufacturing and commercial industries. The government had been more conservative with companies engaged in the manufacture of steel, machines, trucks and other heavy industrial goods because of their importance to the economy as a whole. During the 1980s, heavy industries were the largest employers and providers of social services to urban residents. They were also the primary source of revenue at many different levels of the government.

While the government made some incremental reforms in the energy industry by shifting production from government ministries to state-owned enterprises, the large number of people that were dependent upon these companies for their livelihoods made the perceived consequences of any potential errors very serious. As a result, the newly formed state-owned enterprises continued operating as if they were still parts of the Ministry of Petroleum Industry because the government was willing to overlook the systematic failure of such companies to turn a profit due to overstaffing and low productivity (Wu 2002). When CNPC was formed as a state-owned enterprise it inherited responsibility for nearly all aspects of its employees' lives. This imposed both operational and financial burdens, as the lack of market mechanisms made it necessary for CNPC to establish and operate its own social services such as hospitals, schools, court systems, and police departments. In fact, many of the oil fields the company operated were effectively self-contained cities presided over by its general manager, with around 500,000 employees working in social services positions unrelated to oil exploration or production. The *danwei* system made it all but impossible to fire workers, and CNPC's payroll had ballooned to 1.54 million employees and 400,000 retirees by the early 1990s. Additionally, workers had ample opportunities to take advantage of the system. For example, Smyth *et al.* (2001) found that at Fushun CNPC, employees could apply for *li gang* status ("leaving their post") when they reach age 45 for women or age 50 for men, and over 7,500 employees had secured such status in 1999. These workers continued to receive 80 percent of their salaries as well as all social benefits given to normal employees. The system is even more generous at some subsidiaries such as the CNPC's Fushun Catalytic Plant, where *li gang* workers also receive private medical and property insurance. Programs of this nature exacerbated the burden of providing social services to the point that nearly all of the revenues from the company's oil businesses were used to provide social services.

This led to dramatic problems in productivity. To put the productivity in perspective: When a CNPC delegation visiting international oil companies found that the Norwegian state-owned oil company Statoil employed 80,000 people and produced 130 million tons of oil annually. CNPC had comparable annual production of 140 million tons, but at the time it employed around 1.4 million workers (Rowe 2006; Dyck and Huang 2006). While not all of these workers were directly involved in oil exploration or production activities, CNPC was still employing over 11 times as many people to produce a comparable amount of oil. Some of the difference in staffing between the two companies can be explained by the fact that it was Statoil's standard practice to outsource any aspects of it business not directly related to oil exploration or production. CNPC on the other hand used in-house divisions to provide all of its construction services, well logging, drilling, and engineering services. Such a large and varied organization was made even more difficult to manage profitably because the company's legal structure afforded senior executives relatively little influence over their regional counterparts. While CNPC and its subsidiaries were technically operating as one company, in reality the level of integration between the various entities was very low.

The first step the government took was to remove the artificial functional segments that had been created when the production of oil was overseen by government ministries. This was seen as a crucial step towards achieving the government's twin goals for the reorganization: first, to separate the industry oversight and business management functions, and second, to better position CNPC and Sinopec Group as efficient, competitive companies (Wu 2002). To establish new market segments, the government organized a series of asset transfers between CNPC and Sinopec Group that significantly increased vertical integration at both companies. However, the management at the newly restructured CNPC realized that to become an efficient and competitive organization after operating for so many years as a government ministry would require a radical transformation. While CNPC had been established in 1988 to improve the competitveness of China's oil and gas industries, in the ten years leading up to the 1998 reforms the company had been unable to make a break with its past as a government ministry. Though no longer formally part of the government, it had continued to face many of the same problems and inefficiencies the Ministry of Petroleum Industry had encountered before it was disbanded.

As government financial support continued to decline throughout the mid-1990s, it became increasingly clear to many at CNPC that unless they acted quickly the firm could be facing some very serious problems. Executives realized it was no longer feasible to rely on the government for financing, and the company began searching for new sources of capital. In 1997, the company's president Zhou Yongkang formed a ten-person team headed up by Gong Huazhang that was tasked solely with raising enough new capital for the company to continue its development. The team's analysis quickly revealed that, as an intact company, CNPC would almost certainly be unable to raise sufficient capital for three key reasons: first, the company's outdated management practices, social burden, low efficiency effectively disqualified it from holding an international equity offering; second, because of its vast size it was also highly unlikely that it could raise enough through an offering on the still-immature domestic market, and third, very few banks were willing to lend any significant amount to CNPC because of its high debt–equity ratio and its projected capital shortfalls (Smyth *et al.* 2002).

CNPC first began exploring the idea of creating an international oil company within the model of the Chinese oil and gas industry when its senior management established the Enterprise Reform Office in 1992. The management team knew that it was in need of a serious restructuring to eliminate the multiple legal entities and levels of management, refocus the company on its core businesses, expose the company to external pressures to drive reform, and to increase the efficiency with which the company used its resources. Shortly after a state government reform proposal was drafted in 1995, China International Capital Corporation and Goldman Sachs Asia approached CNPC with a proposal to provide advice regarding the restructuring and potential IPO. (CICC is a joint venture between four companies including the Construction Bank of China and Morgan Stanley.)

Shortly thereafter the Enterprise Reform Office made a formal proposal to CNPC's president that the company should split itself into three sectors then hold an IPO for the oil and gas division. In 1997 the proposed changes were approved by Zhou Yongkang, the president of CNPC, and CICC, and subsequently brought before the State Council for approval. The government voiced strong support for the deal and encouraged CNPC as well as other large SOEs to enter the international capital markets.

Coinciding with the government's broader reforms in the oil and gas industry, the Ninth People's Congress named Zhou Yongkang the Minister of National Land and Resources. His successor at CNPC, Ma Fucai, continued to push the restructuring plans forward, eventually creating the Public Listing Preparation Team, led by Jiang Jiemin, in February of 1999. The Public Listing Preparation Team identified four steps for the company's restructuring: first, CNPC's social functions would be returned to government; second, the CNPC's non-core services would be consolidated into a company still owned by CNPC; third, transfer all the core oil and gas operations to a new subsidiary (PetroChina); and fourth, to publicly list PetroChina in the United States, Europe, and Hong Kong.

Returning Social Functions to Government

The first step of this plan presented several potential pitfalls. Because the company was relying on many different local governments to take over its social services, CNPC needed to negotiate the transfer terms with each government individually. This was often difficult because the governments wanted assurances that taking over CNPC's social functions would not increase their financial burdens, especially because the elimination of the multi-level legal entity system would shift a significant portion of the tax revenue from CNPC away from local governments to the central government.

Non-Core Services

To maximize efficiency at PetroChina, it was decided that the non-core services operated by CNPC would not be publicly listed, but would instead remain a part of the parent company. To determine which of its businesses would be considered parts of non-core services CNPC's senior management identified three different categories of non-core businesses. The management team classified all of the businesses as companies focused on oil engineering/technical/production services and property management, companies only engaged in oil engineering/technical/production services, or companies involved only in property management and logistics.

Core Services PetroChina

To establish PetroChina as a separate entity, all non-core social services as well as five chemical production facilities remained part of CNPC, all core oil and gas exploration and production businesses were transferred to the newly formed company. CNPC believed it was important that PetroChina have a complete value chain, and in late 1999, the company took over RMB 144.4 billion of CNPC's debt and 480,000 employees, as well as thirteen oil and gas exploration and production businesses, two research institutions, production sharing contracts, one pipeline company, fifteen petrochemical and refinery businesses, and twenty-one marketing companies.

The PetroChina IPO

After CNPC received approval of its plans from the State Council in 1999, it initially planned to take PetroChina public that same year. However, several unexpected challenges caused the company to delay the IPO until April 2000. One of these problems was that the low price of oil, coupled with lack of knowledge and interest in Chinese SOEs on the part of international capital markets and investors, meant that demand for the newly listed shares would be uncertain. To boost demand, CNPC sought out substantial investments from companies it believed would be strategically beneficial. The most notable of these investments was the purchase of 10 percent of the available shares by BP (Wu 2002). After making these changes, CNPC went ahead with the IPO on April 6, 2000 and raised U.S. $2.456 billion after listing H-shares in Hong Kong and ADSs in Europe and the United States. While shifting ownership of its controversial projects in Sudan enabled the IPO to go forward, PetroChina has faced continued criticisms by groups that claim transferring ownership back to the parent company does not excuse PetroChina's activities in Sudan. The campaign led by these groups was successful in pressuring several large investors such as state pension funds and the Harvard endowment fund to divest themselves of PetroChina shares.

Much of the opposition to PetroChina's IPO stemmed from the fact that 86 percent of the company is owned, and controlled, by a Chinese national SOE (PetroChina 2007). Many potential investors and analysts raised concerns about the company's ability to act in the best interests of its public shareholders in the event that the CCP's interests diverged from those of CNPC or PetroChina. A separate but related issue concerned many potential business partners as well. The widespread opposition to the IPO by labor unions and NGOs raised the possibility that doing business with PetroChina might lead to labor problems or a customer backlash. Such problems actually materialized for BP Amoco and Talisman of Canada, as both found themselves the targets of divestment and boycott movements aimed at pressuring the companies into ending their business dealings with PetroChina (Hiebert and Saywell 2000). Despite the challenges the government's involvement posed to PetroChina's IPO, the company's overall relationship with the government has been very beneficial.

PetroChina's initial public offering was backed by Goldman Sachs, UBS, and CICC. It was also coached along by McKinsey, Pricewaterhouse Coopers, and a number of foreign law firms. The cynical view of this team of firms was that they simply brought the legitimacy that top investment banks, consulting and accounting firms could bring to a project like this and that legitimacy would be necessary for the IPO roadshow that PetroChina would embark upon. However, the reality is that the Chinese learned much more from the firms they engaged in restructuring PetroChina, as they studied the officials governing the firm worked to create the incentive systems that would make the company more efficient. As Dyck and Huang (2004, p. 4) point out, "In the roadshow, aside from questions about future strategy, the reform that garnered the most attention was the innovative compensation scheme that offered strong incentives for managers to focus on stock performance and, it was hoped, provided a mechanism to refocus management from volume-based to profit-based goals." And the structure of these incentives was specific and closely tied to cost reduction, attainment of profit targets, and return on capital. All employees from department general managers and above would be compensated through a combination of stock options, performance bonus, and salary. The approach was nothing short of revolutionary in the Chinese context: it fundamentally altered the approach to the link between performance and compensation that was heretofore accepted practice in the PRC.

The use of stock options as an incentive for senior executives and high-level skilled employees in Chinese SOEs has not been without controversy inside China. And it is still a system under development. Some reports have indicated that the Ministry of Finance was only appointing senior executives who understood that they would never exercise their options; at the very least, it was taboo to discuss the issue or publicly acknowledge that options were being exercised (Wen and Ming 2009). New official policies followed in 2006—a regulation released by SASAC called the Measures for State-Owned Overseas Listed Companies—which stated that options should not exceed 10 percent of a state-owned corporation's capital base; the regulation also instituted a two-year wait for exercising options. (It is worth noting here that, while such restrictions may seem overly-controlling to U.S. observers, the recent crisis of capitalism in the United States and, in particular, the pondering of run-away executive compensation, raises the question of whether the Chinese approach is a more balanced way to handle incentive-based pay.)

There is still risk. While PetroChina has thus far benefited from working closely with the central government, both the rapid cooling of China's economy and the company's relatively spotty environmental/safety record have increased the risk of the central government intervening or regulating the market in a disruptive manner. The declining economy has brought to the surface what some investors believe is a conflict of interest between PetroChina and its state owned parent company. These investors believe that the large number of assets transferred between CNPC and PetroChina at bargain prices indicate that CNPC sees PetroChina not necessarily as an independently operating investment asset, but instead as a back door to global capital markets. The IPO was initially met with high profile resistance in the market, as powerful institutional investors such as TIAA-CREF and CalPERS vowed to steer clear of the stock based on human rights, environmental, and transparency concerns. Besides risks associated with the possibility of direct government intervention in PetroChina's operations, the company is also significantly vulnerable to the consequences of the CCP's macroeconomic policies. For example, throughout much of 2007 the central government kept retail prices for domestic gasoline and diesel in line with their targeted levels. As a result of these policies, PetroChina was forced to sell its refined products for as much as 2,000 RMB/ton less than the prices quoted in the Singaporean market. However, some institutional investors saw an opportunity: as a holder of nearly ten percent of the available shares, Berkshire Hathaway is now one of the company's key principals. Its holdings are dwarfed by CNPC's stake—about 40 percent of available shares—but both investors are principals with significant resources tied up in PetroChina. CNPC has a specific set of economic goals for PetroChina that fit with the developmental goals of the Chinese government and likely diverge somewhat from the economic models typical for a principal like Berkshire Hathaway. However, while Berkshire Hathaway almost certainly has very different ideas about development, profitability, and performance from CNPC, it is also certainly the case that, with a significant stake in PetroChina, Warren Buffett exerts some level of influence over the firm's decisions about the implementation of efficient business practices.

Motorola and the Hangzhou Telecommunications Factory

In 1988, Motorola set up one of the first large-scale Wholly Owned Foreign Enterprises (WOFEs) in China, Tianjin Motorola. Set in Tianjin's special economic zone, this venture would become one of the early models for companies testing the waters of entry into China's markets in the early stages of the economic reforms. In the early stages, WOFEs were a way of protecting intellectual property. In joint venture negotiations, one of the key factors of the negotiation in asset or technologically intensive industries is the transfer of technology. For companies that were concerned with the protection of the proprietary technology in the joint venture entity, it was often a significant challenge to safeguard intellectual property at levels that were common in home countries. In one famous example, when DuPont opened an agricultural chemicals plant in Shanghai, local entrepreneurs infiltrated the company, copied one of DuPont's herbicidal formulas, and brazenly started a rival company to produce it. Despite the passage of the Patent Law of the PRC in 1985, DuPont found that Chinese courts would not protect the intellectual property rights of its products.[22] To avoid such situations, some multinationals set up WOFEs, which can easily protect proprietary technology, and then establish licensing agreements with Chinese factories that produce prepackaged technology. With these arrangements, Chinese factories do the assembly and production, but they do not have access to the technology from start to finish. While the advantage of these arrangements lies in the protection of the technology, there is a disadvantage: if the multinational corporation wants access to internal Chinese markets (as opposed to just production for export), the export ratio is also part of the joint-venture negotiation. Firms that do joint-venture deals generally receive better export ratios (i.e., they are able to sell a greater percentage of their product to internal markets) than those that simply engage in licensing agreements.

Though licensing agreements do not demand the same level of commitment as joint-venture relationships—they are "cooperative" agreements rather than joint ventures (*hezuo xiangmu* as opposed to *hezi qiye*)—they do require a commitment over time. The distinction here is between contractual production agreements that are between a Chinese and a foreign firm that are commitments over time and those contractually bound ventures in which a completely separate legal entity (a joint-venture firm) is established as part of the deal.[23] Thus, on the spectrum of the intensity of the relationship between a Chinese firm and a foreign partner, joint-venture agreements are the most intensive and usually require long-term commitments (most deals are for twenty years); they include the joint establishment of a new entity, which almost always has board members from both contributing organizations, and they usually involve some form of technology transfer. The next-closest arrangement is the cooperative licensing agreements, which are commitments over time but do not include the establishment of a new organization or the transfer of technology. Beyond licensing agreements, farther down the spectrum of Chinese-foreign relations are other types of contractual relations between foreign and Chinese firms that are not commitments over time. For example, the piece-rate production agreements that prevail in the garment and shoe industries tend to be per project and are renegotiated and shopped on a competitive production market in each round of production. Thus, the commitment of a company such as Liz Claiborne or the Gap to an individual factory is marginal, as they are always shopping for cheaper production prices. This is fundamentally different from a licensing agreement or a joint venture, as these commitments are long-term agreements.

When Motorola set up its WOFE in 1988, it needed a well-placed partner with which to sign a licensing agreement. Motorola worked with a number of factories, but the one it worked with most closely was the Hangzhou Telecommunications Factory. In terms of this firm's position in the administrative hierarchy of the former command economy, as the name suggests, this organization sat directly under the Telecommunications Bureau of Hangzhou Municipality. The organization was a sprawling factory complex, a classic "little society" socialist work unit facility under that system—a campus containing all of the necessities of life for the individuals who were employed by this organization in the old system. There are many large-scale factories such as this one throughout China, and many of them are among the group of organizations that are struggling to find the road to efficient production in the era of economic reforms.

The Hangzhou Telecommunications Factory, however, is much different. Walking through the grounds of this factory in the mid-1990s, it was amazing to see just how far down the road of market reform this firm was. Banners and signs hung across the main thoroughfare running through the complex advertising the firm's identity as part of the "modern enterprise system," a catchall phrase indicating an organization's alignment with the institutional changes of the reform era. Similar banners exhorted workers to familiarize themselves with the Labor Law, which had been passed in 1994 and pushed workers and management alike into a new era of intra-firm labor relations. Impressive new buildings stood side by side with old buildings constructed during the pre-reform era, giving a sense of newness built on top of the old. At each appointed stop within the factory, managers would greet visitors (in my case, an academic researcher) with a friendly seriousness, giving a sense that, while they were very happy—even proud—to open the doors of their well-run facility, time was money, and there were many things yet to be done in the day. When the tour finally reached the center of the factory, I was ushered into a new building and allowed to slowly browse the assembly-line production going on within. Moving at a rapid clip down the line was their prized product— the Motorola cell phones that were, at that time in the mid- and late 1990s, becoming ubiquitous symbols of status and style throughout China. Workers were undistracted by our presence, moving quickly and efficiently as they assembled, tested, and packaged the phones for the outside world.

This factory benefited tremendously from its relationship with Motorola in a number of ways. First, the revenues generated from the production of the cellular phones licensed from the Motorola Corporation made this old state-owned factory wealthy in comparison to other large-scale SOEs in China. As distribution grew and Motorola handsets spread throughout China, as the central node of production for these handsets the Hangzhou Telecommunications Factory gained significantly from the infusion of the cash that came in from these products. The added income, while important, was secondary to the ways the factory changed as a result of its relationship with Motorola. The critical ways the factory changed had to do with a transformation of management practices and the level of standards to which management and workers aspired. Managers spoke openly of their relationship with the Motorola Corporation and how much they had learned about "international business" through that relationship. They spoke of Motorola's role in helping the factory "link up with the international [business] community." At this point, that learning was primarily through advice given and standards set by the Motorola Corporation and, more directly, Tianjin Motorola. Also important, to be sure, was the fact that Motorola had set up an in-house training system, dubbed Motorola University China. Established in 1988, MU-China was established to train senior and middle management from Motorola's suppliers and business partners (Borton 2002). Thus, through active engagement in the education of managers of firms within its supply chain—the Hangzhou Telecommunications Factory among them—Motorola was teaching the principles, practices, and standards of participation in the emerging market economy.

In the mid-1990s, the limited nature of that relationship began to change. After several years of watching Motorola enjoy solid returns for its handset production in China, the Chinese government began to pressure the corporation to expand its relations with its primary partner in China. As mentioned above, the WOFE-licensing agreement configuration allows the foreign corporation to protect intellectual property. However, for exactly this reason, the Chinese corporation is often written out of one of the things it covets most in the Chinese-foreign joint-venture relationship— technology transfer. In the mid-1990s, the government began pressuring Motorola to set up a joint-venture relationship with the Hangzhou Telecommunications Factory. In return for the schedule of technology transfer that would be incorporated into the agreement, Motorola would receive greater access to internal markets and, more important, the corporation would continue to receive "favorable" treatment from the government in matters of approvals and the like. As one highly placed Motorola employee put it to me,

> We really didn't have much choice in the matter. We have been doing well over here for a while, and now the government wants us to share the wealth a little. Ideally, we would keep things the way they are, but, at this point, it's clear that that's really not an option. But we will get better market access through it. And Hangzhou has been a good partner for us. So it should be fine.

> (Personal interview)

In 1996, the two companies established the Hangzhou Eastern Telecommunications Company, or Eastcom. When I visited the Hangzhou factory in 1995, this deal was already well under way. As such, the top-level managers with whom I spoke had already benefited from extensive experiences of sitting on a joint board with Motorola management and going through the details of negotiating a complex joint-venture deal, not to mention the years of joint work in the production of Motorola handsets through the previous licensing agreement. In many ways, the managers of the Hangzhou Telecommunications Factory had learned the ins and outs of market-driven production from Motorola. The factory had finally been "married off"—a term state officials often used to describe the Chinese-foreign equity joint-venture deal. The joint board and the close contact with their foreign partners facilitated the flow of knowledge between foreign and Chinese management.

Then in November of 1996, EastCom went public on the Shanghai Exchange. It was in this period that broader changes were also occurring in the governance structure of this industry as well. Signaling the move from "bureaucratic" to "economic" governance, the Posts and Telecommunication Industrial Bureau [*youdian gongye ju*], which was directly under the Ministry of Posts and Telecommunications, changed its name to the Potevio Corporation—same organization, though now possessing a different mission. As of 1998, 63 percent of EastCom was owned directly by the Zhejiang Eastern Telecommunications Group through "state shares" [*guojia gu*]. In 2001, the Zhejiang Eastern Telecommunications Group Company changed its name to become the Putian Eastcom Group; more important than simply a change in name, however, is the change in status from group company to institutional investor—it was at this point officially an SOAMC. Now, by 2003, while it appeared on paper that the state has officially fully divested itself from any interest in EastCom as all of the "state shares" had been sold, a closer look reveals a shift in accounting. Because the transformation of ZETGC into Putian Eastcom Group allowed the organization to take on the function of institutional investment, the government essentially took its 63 percent interest of state shares, transferred 52 percent of those shares to the category of "state institutional shares" (*guojia farengu*) and sold off 11 percent of those shares. However, of that 11 percent, 6 percent went to the Zhuhai Eastcom Investment Company, which is almost completely

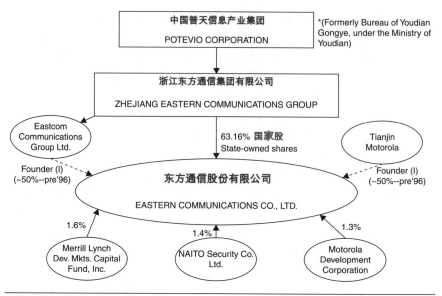

Figure 4.5 EastCom Ownership, 1998.

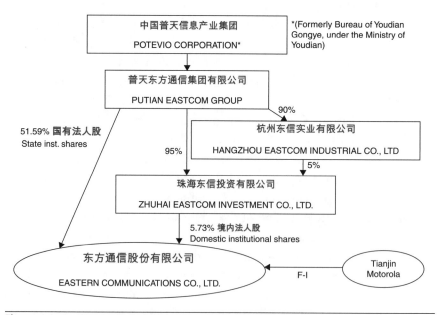

Figure 4.6 EastCom Ownership, 2003.

owned by the Putian Eastcom Group. Thus, while it looks like the state has almost completely divested itself of its controlling interest in EastCom, a deeper analysis of the organizational transformations show this not the be the case.

Over the course of the last two decades, the Hangzhou Telecommunications Factory has been an organization that has transformed significantly. Its relationship with Motorola has been a significant part of that transformation as has the public listing of EastCom. In this case, we see the flow of technology that has benefitted so many Chinese companies over the years. Joint-venture agreements almost always resulted in the transfer of technology and the Chinese government often requires these transfers as quid pro quo for access to the internal market. We also see the flow of management practices between Motorola and the Hangzhou Telecommunications Factory. Chinese companies have studied and learned from their foreign partners, and this has afforded them great advantages in the marketplace. We also see the ways in which the state has maintained ownership and control, even through a public offering of stock.

Emerging Power From the Private Sector: Geely

In this final case, we look at a company that emerges from the private sector, without the advantages of state resources that come with state ownership and without the advantages that come through alliances with powerful multinationals. In this case, we see the gradual transformation of a small startup enterprise and the steady industrial upgrading that has given this company a decent status in an extremely complex and competitive industry. Geely has not yet achieved the international status or success of Haier or Huawei, but it has moved through the process of industrial upgrading in an impressive fashion nonetheless. Most recently, Geely shocked the world in 2010 with its purchase of Volvo from Ford Motor Corporation.

Geely Automobile Holdings Limited (Geely) is the premier privately owned entrant in the Chinese sedan market. It was formed in 2003 after Guorun Holdings Ltd. became Zhejiang Geely Holding Group Ltd. and restructured by establishing joint venture companies with its factories in Ningbo and Shanghai. The newly formed company is headquartered in the Hangzhou Hi-Tech Industry Development Zone with 9,498 employees worldwide. Geely further consolidated its operations related to the automotive industry by establishing a parts subsidiary in Taizhou. The consolidation process continued in May 2004 as another round of acquisitions brought all of Geely's automobile assets under one roof.[24] Today, Geely is one of the most prominent Chinese automobile brands, and is often identified as one of the "young tigers," a group of car companies known for their lofty ambitions and unconventional practices. The young tigers' aggressive plans to sell their vehicles in the West have garnered significant media attention, both in trade publications and in the mainstream news. The widespread coverage of their successes in the developing world has forced the established players in the automotive industry to see Geely, and the other young tigers, as viable competitors. The appearances made by Chinese automakers at several recent international auto shows signaled not just their strength as competitors, but the changing nature of the automotive industry as well; Geely's recent purchase of Volvo makes the point and the more emphatically. Geely's rise against all conventional wisdom is proof of the dynamic shifts in the way the automotive industry considers specialization, outsourcing, product architecture, globalization, and the flow of technical information. It is also proof of the dynamic growth process in China's emerging private sector.

Li Shufu, the founder of the Geely brand, continues to play an active role in the company, serving as chairman and executive director responsible for overall strategic planning and corporate policy. Geely Automobile Holdings Ltd. is listed on the Hong Kong stock exchange with market capitalization of $672 million and $8.5 million in revenues for the first half of 2007. Mr. Li, however, remains the principal shareholder through his investment company, Proper Glory Holding Inc.[25] Through investment holding companies Geely owns interests in higher education, real estate, hotels, tourism, securities, and most recently, VoIP technology. The evolution of Geely Automobile Holdings Ltd.'s parent company from its inception up until its entry into the automobile market can be conveniently divided into three periods. First, Mr. Li's founding of the company and initial entry into refrigeration component manufacturing. During the second phase, Geely left the decorating materials industry to enter the motorcycle market. The third period saw Geely focus on the diversification of its assets and investments, as well as develop an interest in the auto industry.

Refrigeration

Mr. Li recognized that the economic reforms of the 1980s would lead to significant increases in demand for consumer products, especially white goods. In 1986, with this in mind, he went into business manufacturing refrigerator-evaporator components in Taizhou city, Zhejiang Province. Mr. Li grew up as a peasant and had no experience in the refrigeration industry, so Geely was forced to rely on outside technology. The firm found success in the expanding economy and quickly achieved nationwide sales and distribution. However, Mr. Li's newfound prosperity was cut short by the 1989 military crackdown in Tiananmen Square. In the state of flux immediately following the incident, the permanence of economic reform came into question. Mr. Li felt running an entrepreneurial organization without any state ties during such a time of uncertainty would be foolhardy, and citing his lack of a manufacturing license, he turned over his refrigeration business and his entrepreneurial income to the local government.

Decorating Materials

Later that same year, Geely entered the building materials industry. The production of advanced decorating materials continued as the company's main focus until April 1994, when Mr. Li decided to enter the rapidly expanding motorcycle industry. The company maintained its involvement in the building materials business today through its subsidiary Zhejiang Geely Decorating Materials Company, Ltd.

Motorcycles

Geely manufactured its first scooter two months later, and went on to sell 60,000 and 200,000 scooters in 1995 and 1996 respectively. The company changed its name to the Geely Group Co., LTD in May 1996 and became the primary manufacturer and exporter of motorcycles in China. During 1996, the company began to explore the possibility of entering the automotive industry. The next year, Geely began developing its first car, and after a very short development period, launched the first Geely Car on August 8, 1998 in Linhai City, Zhejiang Province.

Cars

Geely entered the Chinese domestic automotive industry using an unconventional strategy considering its position as an inexperienced company without its own technology or capital. The majority of the Chinese automotive industry is comprised of FDI-backed JVs and SOEs backed by government subsidies that rely on direct technology transfer from partnerships with major international automotive companies. Product development contracts with Fiat and Daewoo, and an offering on the Hong Kong stock exchange, provided alternative sources of technology and capital for Geely. Focusing on developing its own intellectual property as an independent company has created four significant advantages for Geely, namely lower technological development costs, smaller manufacturing facilities costs, more flexibility in creating localized products, and greater focus on organizational improvement (Lee 2003; Jin 2006).

The low cost of Chinese labor extends to development engineers, making the domestic development of technology much more cost effective than importing existing technology from joint ventures or other sources. Chinese engineers are more inclined than their foreign counterparts to use domestic equipment and materials, a distinction that leads to further cost advantages for companies like Geely that focus on developing their own intellectual property. Overall, Geely benefits from freedom to determine its own product development strategy not shared by its competitors that have JV partners. This freedom to determine its own production strategy extends to the construction of manufacturing facilities more suited to Chinese production. JV companies, on the other hand, are often forced to use technology developed by their partners for use in other markets. These production technologies are often designed to lower labor costs through automation, but the low cost of Chinese labor usually negates the benefits such manufacturing techniques might have. Geely employees build its cars by hand while the GM JVs nearby use robots, but price of each unit is roughly enough to pay the salaries of a few hundred of Geely's laborers.

Because they import preexisting models from abroad, companies with JV partners often spend most of their engineering resources retooling existing designs to meet the needs of local markets. Over the long run, this puts Geely and other companies with experience developing their own models at a significant advantage because they are better able to use their understanding of the local markets. Additionally, long-term success in the Chinese automotive industry depends on a firm's ability to create value through new offerings and product upgrades, areas in which Geely and other independent companies are far more capable. The final benefit of developing technology independently comes from the opportunities for organizational improvement the product development process provides. The process of overcoming obstacles to independent technological development generally enhances organizational efficiency and the ability to find innovative solutions to operational, technological, and organizational problems in the future.

Along the way, Geely developed several important advantages in the manufacturing process to expand its margins and compete in both the foreign and domestic markets at the same time. The first step to improve the manufacturing process was to develop relationships with diverse suppliers, especially those with foreign JV technology, both through partnerships and through mergers and acquisitions. In partnership with the JV suppliers, Geely was able to both improve the quality of its cars and perform reverse engineering analyses to learn more about the technology. In other cases, Geely took over factories or production facilities that produced parts for JVs, and then used the technology in its own components production. By creating a standardized and effective method for dealing with suppliers, Geely minimized the risk of supply chain problems. It was able to entertain bids from more suppliers, and used careful management of the purchasing process to quickly realize a cost advantage. Geely also expanded into auto parts production to facilitate vertical integration, thereby raising efficiency and keeping the value-added chain within the firm. The development of its engine product line clearly exemplifies Geely's strategies for vertical integration and supplier relationships. In the early stages of its business, Geely sourced its engines from Toyota because its experience in the motorcycle industry had not developed the technology necessary to produce its own drive trains. At the same time, Geely began an effort to internalize its engine procurement by reverse engineering the Toyota model. Beginning with the in house production of low-tech components, Geely began the vertical integration of the Toyota engine and eventually produced 30 percent of the components used in the drive trains it sourced from Toyota. After changing the design to both comply with intellectual property regulations and orient the engine to the Chinese market (where performance over 110 km/h is irrelevant), Geely began producing the MR4970Q model engine at one third the price it had been paying to use Toyota's engines. This process of reverse engineering took place in tandem with a focus on developing beneficial relationships with its suppliers.

China's accession to the World Trade Organization (WTO) has generated a host of opportunities and benefits for Geely and the Chinese automotive industry in general. Geely was able to significantly expand its export business because, as a condition for accession to the WTO, China was forced to eliminate regulations posing challenges for international business. China's membership in the WTO has allowed Geely significant access to the markets of the developing world, greatly expanding the company's ability to export its vehicles as well as access to more efficient international suppliers (Lee 2003; Luo 2005). Geely has suffered abroad due to the lack of strong brand recognition outside greater China and some developing nations. During the early stages of its export initiative, Geely made critical errors that had their root in the company's misunderstanding of the Western market. Geely failed to organize an effective international distribution network for its cars, and during the product launch phase discovered that its car did not not only meet consumer expectations in the developed world, but also was too small for generally taller Europeans. Additionally, the number of defects per car has been rising in China as automakers cut costs to stay competitive in the price war.

In March of 2010, Zhejiang Geely Holding Co. (the parent company of Geely) paid $1.8BN for a Volvo. The deal would have many of the elements that have been central to economic development in China over the course of the last three decades. As one analyst surmised the situation, this move will be yet another example of the balancing act between the incorporation of foreign capital, brand-power, management knowhow and the opportunities that lie in China's domestic market:

> Volvo will keep its own management team, board of directors and headquarters in Gothenburg, Sweden. That would indicate that Volvo will keep its Swedish heritage and cachet. European and American Volvo loyalists will still be buying cars engineered in Gothenburg and built in Europe . . . What that would mean, however, is that Geely is buying Volvo and lingering on with the same money-losing structure. That's where China comes in. The Chinese luxury market is booming and still has room for some other players to come in and build a brand. Geely will assemble Volvo cars in China using cheaper manufacturing, Hall says. The brand is upscale and Geely ownership might even be seen as preferable by Chinese consumers.

So the company can grow sales and get fatter margins in China. That makes the business case work better than it ever did either under Ford or as an independent carmaker. After so many failed auto deals, this one has the makings of a success. Of course, it means Geely can't manhandle Volvo. They need to rely on Ford and the Swedes for technology that will make the Chinese cars real Volvos. In short, they should manage it as a separate subsidiary the way Volkswagen Group runs Audi AG. Give it autonomy and let the tiger run. Volvo is a niche brand and will never be a cash cow. But it certainly could work if Geely gives it some independence.

(FN: "Geely buys Volvo: Believe it or Not, It Could Work," David Welch, *Bloomberg Businessweek*, March 29, 2010)

The Geely case presents us with an example of an organization that has grown up from more humble origins than the previous two cases. Where PetroChina had its origins as a powerful (if inefficient) state-owned organization at the highest levels of the state administrative hierarchy and EastCom benefited from a favored relationship with a provincial government and a powerful foreign partner, Geely had no such benefits. It began as a private company and gradually worked its way through technological and industrial upgrading to eventually enter the international market through the acquisition of a major international brand.

The Underpinnings of Success

The Chinese government's gradual and methodical experimentation with different institutional forms and the party's gradual receding from control over the economy and political processes has brought about a quiet revolution in the Chinese economy. Recognizing that the transition to a radically different type of economy must occur gradually, the state has allowed for maximum institutional stability as economic actors slowly learn the rules of the emerging market economy. And, to the frustration of many institutional advisors from the West, China has undergone the most successful transformation of any economy making the transition from a planned to market system. While the government has achieved this end by gradually introducing new laws and institutional reforms that have guided the reforms forward, of equal importance to the success of this model is the fact that capitalism is a learned set of practices, where economic actors shape themselves after the available models in the marketplace. In other words, policies of gradual reform have been important, because they have maintained stability in the face of radical institutional change, and they have allowed economic actors to learn the rules of the game gradually, rather than assuming that they know the rules intuitively.

Many state-led development strategies have pushed the process of economic reform in China forward. The government has been behind the construction of more than 700 new federal laws and regulations that govern the economy and society and over two thousand new local laws and regulations (Pei 1994, 1998). It has done this through a process of gradually introducing changes into the economy, experimenting with their implementation through on-the-ground practice, implementing them on a larger scale, and, finally, institutionalizing them in formal declarations through laws and regulations. It has gradually allowed for the emergence of a private economy, slowly moved enterprises off of the dual track system, and gradually rationalized production processes and labor relations within firms (Naughton 1995; Guthrie 1999). While these forces of change have been important in the evolution of the Chinese economy, both types of institutional change—the state-level policies and regulations and the growth of a private economy—do little to explain the ways that firms will actually respond to institutional change or increased competition in markets.

Some firms in the Chinese economy had important advantages. First, some benefited from the changing distribution of responsibilities within the industrial hierarchy of the former command economy, because, at certain levels of the hierarchy, state firms were given the autonomy to take advantage of new opportunities in the urban industrial economy. Second, alliances with foreign firms played a critical role here as well. These two issues will be discussed in greater detail below. The focus of this discussion will be on the ways that relationships within the economy give rise to a transfer of knowledge, helping to guide Chinese firms through the turbulent waters of the transition to a market economy.

The Importance of State Structure

If we return for a moment to Figure 2.1 (in Chapter 2), we find a key factor that defines state- firm relations in reform-era China. A number of scholars have identified the importance of the industrial hierarchy of the former command economy as one of the key legacies shaping China's path through the economic reforms (Bian 1994a; Guthrie 1997, 1998a, 1999; Oi 1989, 1992, 1995; Rawski 1994; Walder 1989a, 1989b, 1992a, 1992b, 1994a, 1994b, 1995a). One of the key features of the economic reforms that would emerge from the vision of gradual reform was that the bureaucratic sector slowly pushed economic responsibilities down the hierarchy of the former command economy, placing economic responsibilities on the shoulders of local officials and individual managers. As economic responsibilities were shifted onto the shoulders of enterprise managers and the local offices who governed them, local-level economic actors were to be responsible for the industrial upgrading and strategizing of the firms they governed. Those administrative offices that had the fewest factories to govern were also the most subject to tightening fiscal constraints (in large part because of their distance from the central government). The combination of tightening fiscal constraints and the close monitoring and attention these lower-level governmental offices could give to the few factories under their jurisdictions allowed these factories to receive the most hands-on attention and guidance through the turbulent waters of the economic reforms. Oi (1989, 1995) and Walder (1995a) have argued that it is the combination of closer monitoring and tighter fiscal constraints in rural areas that led to the higher levels of productivity among the TVE sector, which was, in many ways, the most dynamic part of the Chinese economy in the 1980s.

Close monitoring by local officials meant a level of security and continuity, even as budget constraints were being hardened and the competitive pressures of China's emerging markets were proceeding apace. Walder argues that, as economic burdens are shifted down to local areas, local governments have increasingly acted like local firms. The fact that they were overseeing only a few firms under their jurisdiction gave them the advantage of being able to pay close attention to how firms were strategically making their way through the turbulent markets of China's transforming industrial economy. In stark contrast to the arguments about the impossibility of a gradual transition (Kornai 1990), it was the local officials—the former agents of the planned economy—who were actually the teachers (or perhaps collaborators is a better word) of the market economy to the local managers under their jurisdiction. In other words, a firm's position in the industrial hierarchy of the former command economy matters tremendously to the ways that the reform process transpired.

Even though we have not seen equal rates of growth in productivity in the urban industrial economy, there is, nevertheless, evidence of similar patterns of state-firm relations. Namely, firms under the jurisdiction of municipal bureaus were much more likely to be losing money and to adopt "lifeboat" strategies of economic reform (such as renting out factory space to the highest bidder) than their counterparts under lower-tier urban government offices. The primary issue here was the extent to which firms were able to gain stability from the close monitoring by officials from a local administrative office. With hundreds of firms under their jurisdiction, bureau officials had little ability to soften the shock of hardening fiscal constraints; however, with only a few firms to watch over, officials from municipal and district company offices were able to provide stability, guidance, and leadership for the firms under their jurisdiction, encouraging them, for example, to focus on upgrading machinery or pooling resources with other firms to avoid shortfalls.

The success of the Township and Village Enterprises in the 1980s and early 1990s could be traced to this dynamic of the benefits of close monitoring from the government. The central point that comes across in that case is that where a firm was positioned in the industrial hierarchy of the former command economy had dramatic consequences for the guidance and collaboration it received in learning the rules of the market economy. Although local offices had little to offer firms under their jurisdiction in the way of fiscal bailouts, those with few firms to govern could deliver to their firms another asset—careful guidance through the turbulence of China's emerging markets. This view directly contradicts economists who predicted that state officials would always act in corrupt ways without the incentives provided by rapid privatization (Kornai 1980). In the Chinese case, local officials became collaborators in firms' gradual adaptation to the rules of the market. Following the logic of the above arguments, we might expect that firms under lower-level government offices would have higher levels of productivity.

The Impact of Foreign Influence

A second key feature driving the learning of successful practices in the market economy among transforming organizations in China was the entry of foreign capital into the Chinese economy. With the passage of the Chinese-Equity Foreign Joint Venture Law in 1979 and Deng

Xiaoping's symbolic trip to the United States (discussed in Chapter 2), foreign corporations were granted entry into the Chinese marketplace, and the foreign capital that flowed into the Chinese economy from this point on grew steadily over the course of the economic reforms. From 1997 to 2001, the average annual commitment was on the order of $64 billion, and by 2001, the amount of foreign capital committed to economic projects in China would total over $70 billion annually.

There has been some debate over the impetus behind the dramatic investment in China. On the one hand, Yasheng Huang (2003) has recently argued that FDI has been attracted to China because of a distorted institutional environment: artificial suppression of the private sector in order to protect the state sector has created the opportunity for extraordinary growth in the FDI sector. Others (e.g., Fu 2000) have argued that the state has purposefully set in place the institutions to attract FDI, because of the variety of positive externalities that come along with it: both the government and the enterprises recognized the need for foreign capital, advanced management experience, and technology. In either case, the impact on Chinese business organizations has been significant. While much of the focus on the firm-level impact of foreign investment has been on the issue of technology transfer and the opening of new markets (e.g., Zhu *et al.* 1995; Shi 1998; Fruin and Prime 1999), one of the critical aspects of FDI has to do with the transfer of knowledge in the learning of new economic practices. Much the way certain organizations in the industrial hierarchy of the command economy benefited from different levels of monitoring and support throughout the process of gradual reform, those with direct contact with foreign firms have learned the practices of a market economy as well. It is not simply the opening of markets or the transfer of technology that allows Chinese firms to transform into capitalist entities; of equal importance are the new management practices that Chinese organizations observe in the marketplace, and one of the critical places they learn these practices is through contact with foreign companies (Santoro 1999; Guthrie 1999, 2002b, 2002c). The general impact of contact with foreign investment can be observed in the differing levels of productivity between firms that receive foreign capital or some form of foreign involvement and those that do not. Table 4.2 shows that, according to a number of different economic indicators, Chinese firms that have some kind of funding coming from foreign sources do significantly better on a number of different economic indicators. These firms have better ratios of output to assets, profits to cost, and they are nearly 40 percent more productive than firms with no foreign funding.[26]

Not surprisingly, there is variation across regions of China with respect to this effect, and it may be useful to think about whether the effect of foreign investment is tied to specific regions or sectors of the economy.[27] While there are a few interesting anomalies in the relationship between foreign involvement and productivity, such as in tobacco, where foreign-invested firms do worse than their non-invested counterparts, the relationship generally holds: across a number of economic sectors of the economy, firms that have direct contact with foreign corporations fare significantly better across several key economic indicators. However, we should be careful not to view outliers such as the tobacco industry as simply anomalies in this relationship: indeed, in China today, tobacco is the only industry that, by Chinese law, does not allow a majority stake of foreign ownership in joint-venture firms. Thus, it may be the case that foreign majority ownership is an important factor in the productivity of firms that have foreign involvement. Yet, suggestive as the results are, from this industry-level data it is difficult to interpret the meaning of such a series of relationships.

One obvious argument behind the higher labor productivity among foreign-invested firms is that foreign corporations arrive on China's shores seeking cheap labor, thus inducing firms they have contact with to raise production while driving down labor costs (hence producing higher levels of labor productivity, by these calculations). However, while this view is likely correct for certain sectors of the economy—such as garments, where piece-rate, project-by-project contractual relations prevail—the figures in Table 4.2 also include firms that have joint-venture relationships, which pay significantly higher wages than their peers who have no such relationships (Guthrie 1999). While these figures give us a sense of the sectors of the economy that fare better or worse in terms of productivity, they are aggregate-level data. Aggregate-level data, whether at the sector or regional levels, give us little sense of the changes that are actually taking place at the organizational level. What changes actually occur at the firm level? In what ways does foreign investment matter for these changes? Beyond the type of monitoring activity that occurs through government–state relations, what are the transfers of knowledge that occur between Chinese firms and their foreign partners?

I have argued elsewhere that relationships with foreign investors result in significantly different practices in the ways that their Chinese partners define labor relations and economic practices within their organizations. We might extend this analysis beyond a strict focus on organizational practice to an analysis of how practice translates into productivity. The argument here is that Chinese firms learn from their foreign partners through institutionalized relationships like joint boards of directors, joint decision-making processes, and through the process of negotiating a joint venture deal, as is illustrated in the case of the Hangzhou Telecommunications Factory and its relationship with Motorola. They learn what capitalist firms from advanced market economies look like in terms of internal structures, systems, and norms, and they often implement these changes as a way of attracting further investment from the foreign community.

Conclusions

The Chinese government has driven the reform process forward in three ways. First, through gradual reforms, the state has created an institutional environment that has integrated China into the global market, both externally and internally. Externally, the development of an export-led economy—especially in the early years of the reforms through the coastal development strategy—allowed China to emerge as an economic juggernaut, becoming one of the largest suppliers of manufactured goods in the world. Internally, the government opened its markets enough to attract massive amounts of foreign capital. Foreign capital has been important for economic development in China in a variety of ways. Beyond supplying capital and, in many cases, the transfer of important technologies, there is a learning process that has occurred in the transfer of management knowledge across organizations. Aggregate data shows that across a variety of sectors and regions of the Chinese economy, those firms that have benefited from foreign direct investment are significantly more productive than their counterparts that have received no such investments. While one might assume that some of these gains in productivity surely come either from a selection effect or from pressure to squeeze labor for greater production at lower costs, these two scenarios are only part of the story of gains in productivity. Also important are the ways that firms learn to survive and thrive in the market today. Beyond the labor squeeze, it is clear from organizational-level data that, when productivity is measured as output-per-unit labor, firms that have greater exposure to the export market (a proxy for piece-rate contract relations) have significantly lower levels of productivity.[28] Foreign investment helps guide firms through the process of economic development and the learning of the dynamics of a market economy.

Second, decentralization has been a crucial factor in the government's management of the transition to a market economy. In the 1980s, we saw the strength of this method in the rural economy through the thriving TVE sector. But even in the urban industrial economy, we also see the advantages of local government offices taking direct control over the firms they are governing. Following the logic of the previous arguments, local offices have greater administrative resources to help guide the firms under their jurisdiction through the reforms. However, administrative status— that is, the level of government—actually does matter, and perhaps in crucial ways. For example, as described above, the basic levels of Chinese government are the central, provincial, municipal, township, and village governments. Within urban areas, there are also local district governments, but these are ultimately under the primary category of the municipal government. While municipal and district companies in the urban industrial economy have similar monitoring capacities—both having jurisdiction over only a few firms per office—municipal companies ultimately report to the municipal rather than the district government. This difference gives these offices greater administrative clout in their areas, compared to district companies of the same size. Position in the state hierarchy— particularly in a way that allows Chinese firms to receive significant attention from the government offices that oversee them—is a critical factor in the success of firms in the economic reforms.

Third, while the government did not undertake a process of full-scale privatization of the state-owned economy, it did allow a private economy to emerge. This growing private economy has played an important role in the creation of a competitive marketplace in which the state sector must now compete. The balance of these strategic approaches has allowed China to emerge as the economic juggernaut that it has.

5

POLLUTION, ENERGY CONSUMPTION, AND RENEWABLE ENERGY

Spend a hot summer day in Beijing, Shanghai, Wuhan, or any of China's sprawling urban metropolises, and you can easily sense how serious China's pollution issues are. And the well-known urban centers are not even where the pollution is the worst; there are parts of rural China where industry is concentrated and regulation is lower that are exceptionally polluted. In Shanghai, in the late-1990s, if you ever took a stroll in the northern part of Shanghai and walked along the Suzhou Creek, the fetid smell of pollutants was overwhelming. This should not be a surprise to anyone, as China has received much scrutiny on this issue over the last decade. For example, the *New York Times* is just one of many periodicals that regularly report on the environmental degradation occurring in China, noting recently that the country's "pollution problem has shattered all precedents. Environmental degradation is now so severe, with such stark domestic and international repercussions, that pollution poses not only a major long-term burden on the Chinese public but also an acute political challenge to the ruling Communist Party. And it is not clear that China can rein in its own economic juggernaut."[1] Or, more recently: "China, the world's most prodigious emitter of greenhouse gas, continues to suffer the downsides of unbridled economic growth despite a raft of new environmental initiatives . . . Other newly released figures show . . . an epidemic of pollution in waterways."[2] Similar articles have appeared in nearly every major periodical. China scholars have taken on the issue as well. Probably the most prominent among them is Elizabeth Economy of the Council of

Foreign Relations, who has built her reputation on lambasting China for its environmental record (Economy 2007, 2004).

In this chapter, I have two objectives. The first is to lay out the empirical reality of China's environmental problems. There are of course major problems with environmental degradation in China, but China has also taken major steps forward in certain areas, and it is important to recognize the problems as well as the areas of improvement. The second is to introduce the reader to some of the aggressive moves China has made in the area of environmental reform in the last five years. Criticism of China's environmental record often strikes me as lacking nuance on a couple of different levels. First, as we have discussed in previous chapters (Chapters 2 and 4), China is an extremely decentralized country—indeed, the logic of the economic reforms have depended on this decentralization. One of the consequences of that decentralization is that there is tremendous variation, and this variation extends to environmental performance; places such as Linfen, Yangquan, Datong or Zhanglidong are among the most polluted places you will find on earth; and places like the Suzhou industrial park have some of the highest environmental standards for industrial parks in the world. Second, China's problems in this area are inextricably tied to rapid economic development and industrialization. While the country has done a remarkable job of lifting people out of poverty over the last thirty years, pollution and environmental degradation have been one of the costs to this process. The country does not completely ignore issues of pollution and environmental degradation as is often portrayed in popular accounts, but controls are definitely lagging behind the speed and magnitude of development and change. The question for China will be whether it will be able to construct a regulatory framework before too much damage is done. There are bright spots, however: on the positive side, China is doing better than is often acknowledged on diversification of energy usage. The fact that China has a unified energy policy actually gives it some advantage in this area. It is widely acknowledged, for example, that China has surged ahead of most of the world in the area of renewable energy, and understanding how and why this development has occurred provides a fuller picture in the area of environmental reform. It also links nicely to the issues of industrial and economic development raised in the previous chapter.

It makes little sense to talk about pollution without talking about energy usage as it relates to economic growth. Accordingly, this chapter will unfold in the following manner. First, I will present the basic context of energy usage in China. I will then follow that with a discussion on the basic empirical situation of pollution. Finally, I will discuss the ways in which China is surging ahead in the building of a renewable energy sector.

Energy Consumption

To accurately assess energy consumption in China, it is first important to have a basic understanding of the key players in the field. Figures 5.1 and 5.2 depict the percentage of global energy consumption of the top economies in the world from 1990 to 2010. A quick glance distinguishes China and the United States as the world's two leading energy consumers. In 2010, China alone was responsible for more than 20 percent of the world's energy consumption, which totaled 2.4 billion tons of oil equivalent. That same year, the United States consumed 2.3 billion tons of oil equivalent, accounting for 19 percent of global consumption. In 1990, just a decade into China's economic reforms, the United States and Russia led the world in energy consumption, with the United States consuming nearly a quarter of all the energy consumed and Russia consuming just over 10 percent. By 2000, China had surpassed Russia as the second-largest consumer in the

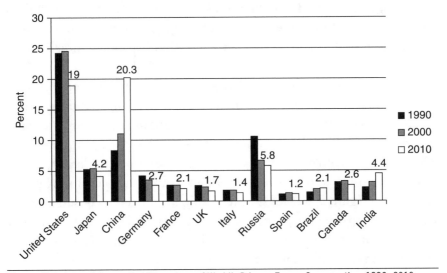

Figure 5.1 Largest Economies' Percentage of World's Primary Energy Consumption, 1990–2010.

Source: *BP Statistical Review of World Energy* (2011) http://www.bp.com/statisticalreview

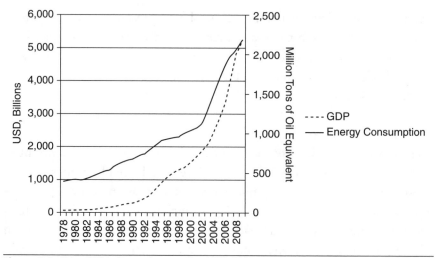

Figure 5.2 China GDP to Energy Consumption 1978–2009.

Source: National Statistical Bureau of China (2010, 38), *BP Statistical Review of World Energy, 2011* http://www.
bp.com/statisticalreview

world, and today it has surpassed the United States as the leading energy
consumer. Industry has been and continues to be the country's largest
source of energy consumption in China. In 2008, industry consumed more
than 2 billion tons of coal equivalent. Household consumption, a distant
second, accounted for 318 million tons of coal equivalent. Not only does
industry represent the largest portion of energy consumption in China, it
also accounts for the largest growth in energy use, expanding from 1 billion
to 2 billion tons of coal equivalent from 2000 to 2010.

China's energy demand has increased alongside its economic development. Figures 5.3 and 5.4 show the energy demand and GDP of China
and the United States, respectively. An important trend to note is the close
connection of the GDP in China compared with energy consumption.
Although China has now surpassed the United States as the largest energy
consumer in the world, it is also important to take into account the population size. Figure 5.4 sheds a different light on energy consumption in
China by comparing the per capita energy consumption of the two largest
economies in the world. China's per capita consumption rate is less than a
quarter of that in the United States.

Historically, China has depended greatly on coal to support their energy
consumption. The country leads the world in the production and

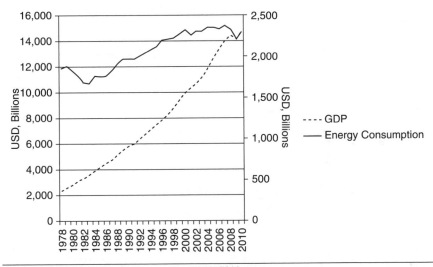

Figure 5.3 US GDP to Energy Consumption 1978–2010.

Source: GDP from Bureau of Economic Analysis, Accessed 7/12/2011 http://www.bea.gov/national/index.htm#gdp, BP *Statistical Review of World Energy, 2011.* http://www.bp.com/statisticalreview

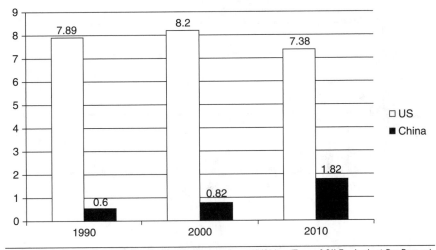

Figure 5.4 Energy Consumption Per Capita Comparison US/China (Tons of Oil Equivalent Per Person).

Source: BP *Statistical Review of World Energy* (2011) *http://www.bp.com/statisticalreview,* World Bank *Indicators* http://data.worldbank.org/indicator/SP.POP.TOTL

consumption of coal, and houses the world's third largest coal reserves (Energy Information Administration 2010). China accounts for nearly half of the world's coal power consumption, seconded by the United States, consuming 14.8 percent. China currently supplies a very large portion of its

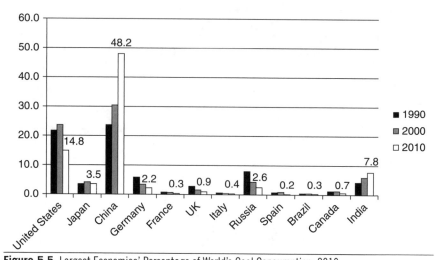

Figure 5.5 Largest Economies' Percentage of World's Coal Consumption, 2010.

Source: *BP Statistical Review of World Energy* (2011) http://www.bp.com/statisticalreview

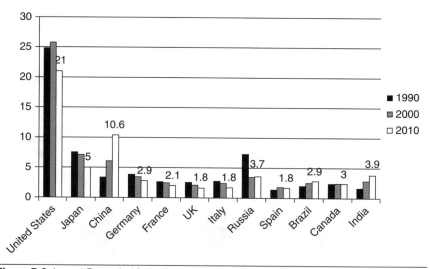

Figure 5.6 Largest Economies' Percentage of World's Oil Consumption, 2010.

Source: BP *Statistical Review of World Energy* (2011) http://www.bp.com/statisticalreview

energy through coal power. Though China has made considerable efforts on diversifying its energy consumption, the country has continued to increase its coal consumption. From 1978 to 2010, China increased its reliance on coal from 70.3 percent to 77.3 percent. In the last few years, China has increased its oil consumption. In 2010, China accounted for just over 10 percent of the world's total oil consumption, with just over 9 billion barrels of oil. This is still less half the amount of the United States, which consumed over 19 billion barrels of oil, making up 21 percent of the world's total oil consumption.

So where does all this consumption leave us? On the one hand, it has been the engine behind China's rapid economic development and growth. On the other hand, it has led to the environmental degradation that is so widely scrutinized. We turn now for a brief look at the levels of pollution in a couple of key areas.

Air Pollution

Air pollution is a terrible problem in China today. A couple of years ago, on a trip to China, my traveling companion came down with a serious respiratory infection that could only be traced to the poor air quality in the major urban centers we were visiting. Unfortunately, the experience is not uncommon in China today. According to the *New York Times*, "Only 1 percent of the country's 560 million city dwellers breathe air considered safe by the European Union." In 2007, a World Health Organization study estimated that air pollution in China kills over 600,000 Chinese citizens each year.[3]

So how bad is air pollution in China? First of all, air pollution in China has been linked to widespread health problems. It is increasingly common to see deaths due to pollution-caused diseases in China. In 2003, premature deaths related to air pollution cost the country 157.3 billion yuan (World Bank and SEPA 2007). However, to give an accurate assessment of the air quality in China, it is useful to take a step back and look briefly into the major air pollutants in China and some of the ways they are affecting the country. China's system for rating air quality establishes pollution levels for five prominent air pollutants (SO_2, NO_2, PM_{10}, CO_2, and O_3) on an air pollution index (API) and correlates that index number to a grade level for the air quality. For example, in Beijing, The API ranges from 0–500, relative to the concentration of a specific pollution. The air quality grading then assigns a grade of 1–5 (1 being excellent and 5 being heavily polluted) to the air quality based on the API (Andrews 2009).

In beginning the discussion of air pollution it is probably best to first address the most widely discussed pollutant, CO_2. China's insatiable thirst for energy to supply its fast-growing economy has had tremendous consequences on the country's air quality, as CO_2 emissions in China have risen almost hand in hand with the country's GDP (Figure 5.1). Not surprisingly, China recently replaced the United States as the world's leading greenhouse gas (GHG) emitter (though on a per capita basis, the United States is still far ahead of China) (Zissis 2008). In 2010, China emitted 8.3 billion tons of carbon dioxide, accounting for more than a quarter of world's total CO_2 emissions (BP 2011).

Nitrogen Oxides

Nitrogen oxides contribute to the presence of both ozone and PM 2.5. They are known to cause bronchitis and asthma (WHO 2008). NO_X in the atmosphere is both natural and anthropogenic in origin. Anthropogenically, it is mostly formed when generating heat through biomass or coal combustion, though research has also shown a correlation between the increasing number of automobiles and the emission levels of NO_2 in China (Zhang *et al.* 2007). In 2008, China emitted 20 million tons of NO_X, 45 percent of which were from the coal power industry, making the country the leading emitter of NO_X in the world (*China Daily* 2011). 2003 data showed that China accounted for 8 percent of total global NO_X emissions (Zhao *et al.* 2006). In addition, NO_X is a precursor to the formation of surface level ozone (O_3), which is one of the major contributing factors of smog and causes an array of respiratory problems (WHO 2008). Increase levels of surface ozone could also be linked to reduced crop yields (Aunan *et al.* 2000).

Carbon Monoxide

Carbon Monoxide is an odorless gas that mainly comes from mobile energy combustion. CO causes damage to the body by depriving the body of its needed oxygen (EPA 2010). In the 1990s, CO emissions increased yearly by roughly 3 percent. CO is a very large contributor to ozone in China, accounting for 54 percent of ozone production. Data from 2003 showed that China accounted for 10 percent of total man-made emissions of CO in the world (Zhao *et al.* 2006).

Sulfur Dioxide

The most common source of Sulfur Dioxide (SO_2) is the combustion of fossil fuels, seconded by industrial facilities (EPA 2010). SO_2 causes inflammation in the respiratory system and an increased production of mucus.

This can irritate asthma and bronchitis, and increase the occurrence of respiratory infections. Environmentally, SO_2 is a major contributor to acid rain (WHO 2008). China's extensive SO_2 emissions are not a recent phenomenon, as China has been the leading SO_2 emitter in Asia since the 1970s. The SO_2 emissions in China have been closely tied to the energy industry. The high levels of SO_2 have caused the country to experience an increased frequency of acid rain. Nearly one third of the country experiences acid rain and the pH level of rain has fallen below 5.6, the natural pH for rain, for 40 percent of the country (Fang *et al.* 2008). Annual SO_2 emissions in China increased from 22.5 million tons in 2004 to 25.9 million tons in 2006. SO_2 levels began to drop in 2007 and have continued to decline. There were emissions of 22.1 million tons of SO_2 in 2009. The majority of SO_2 emissions are from industrial sources. Of the total 22.1 million tons of SO_2 emitted in 2009, 18.66 million tons, or 84 percent, came from industrial sources (including energy production), the remaining 3.48 million tons of emissions came from domestic sources. 2003 data show that China accounted for around 30 percent of total world SO_2 emissions (Zhao *et al.* 2006). China has recognized the environmental and health problems that SO_2 has caused and has made a considerable effort to curb SO_2 emissions. SO_2 levels have dropped considerably in Chinese cities. Many cities in China now have SO_2 levels below WHO recommendations (World Bank 2007). Both the tenth and eleventh five-year plans had goals to reduce SO_2 emissions. The sulfur dioxide goal of the eleventh five-year plan was to reduce emissions by 10 percent. From 2005–2009, China saw a 13.14 percent reduction in SO_2 emissions (*China Daily* 2011).

Particulate Matter
PM 10 and PM 2.5 refer to particle pollution in the air that is smaller than 10 micrometers and 2.5 micrometers respectively. Particles this small can easily bypass the nose and throat and enter the lungs, potentially causing serious health repercussions. The smaller size of PM 2.5 allows it to penetrate further into the respiratory system, making it the more harmful of the two pollutants. Particulate matter is more detrimental to health than any other form of air pollution. Exposure to PM causes respiratory disease and lung cancer. Data from the EU has shown that life expectancy is noticeably lower in areas with higher levels of PM pollution (WHO 2008). The WHO air quality guidelines, released in 2005, suggest that human

exposure levels of PM 10 remain below a mean of 20 micrograms per cubic meter per annually (WHO 2005). Particulate matter represents a serious problem in China. Levels of particulate matter in the air in China are dangerously high. However, it should not be overlooked that the country is making efforts to get levels of PM under control. From 2000 to 2008, China was able to reduce the levels of particulate matter from 85 to 66 micrograms per cubic meter.

Sources of Pollution

There is no doubt that pollution is a major problem in China today. In 2008, China's State Environmental Protection Agency announced that it would systematically collect data on the sources of China's pollution problems. In recent years, the government has given more attention to this topic than in years past. And there is great variation across China in how the issue is being handled. However, there are basic empirical questions that still must be answered, the most important among them being: what are the true sources of China's pollution problems?

Energy and Industry

Energy production and industry are the largest contributors to air pollution in China. China's energy needs are continually increasing. Total energy consumption in China nearly tripled in three decades, reaching over 2.9 billion tons of standard coal equivalent in 2008. China is the largest consumer of energy in the world, accounting for 20.3 percent of the world's total energy consumption, followed by the United States, which accounts for 19 percent of the world's total energy consumption (BP 2011). China's thirst for energy is largely satisfied by coal power. It produces and consumes more coal than anywhere in the world. The 3.5 billion short tons of coal that were consumed in China in 2009 made up 46 percent of the world's total coal consumption. That same year, coal power accounted for 77.3 percent of China's total energy consumption. Coal power is the largest contributor to air pollution in China. A large majority of energy in China is consumed by industry. The increase in energy consumption from industry shot up with the booming economy of the past few decades. In 2007, industry accounted for 75 percent of total energy consumption. Iron and steel, chemical, and cement and mineral production accounted for more than 50 percent of total industry energy demands. Due to China's heavy reliance on coal, the energy demand from industry made up 73 percent of total carbon dioxide emissions from energy related sources (Oshita and Price 2010).

Automobiles

China's economic growth has brought millions of people out of poverty in the past few decades. Accompanying an increase of the population's expendable income has been an increase in car sales. The number of personal vehicles has grown exponentially in the past few decades, increasing from roughly 100,000 in 1990 to around 25 million in 2007. However, even with the dramatic increase in automobile ownership, the number of cars in China barely makes a dent on the amount of cars in the world, with an estimated 1.5 percent of the total number of cars in the world. This is hardly comparable to the 230 million automobiles in the United States (Gallagher 2010, p. 15). Though the number of vehicles in China is much smaller than that in the United States, the prominent fear is that the number of automobiles will continue to grow, causing increased stress on the environment. The number of motor vehicles in Beijing alone more than tripled from 1995 to 2005, accounting for 46 and 35 percent of total emissions of volatile organic compounds (VOCs) and nitrogen oxides (NO_x) in the city, respectively (Feng *et al.* 2008). Vehicular emissions of these pollutants, two components of surface level ozone, contribute to 45.9 percent of surface level ozone in Beijing (Liu 2008).

In 2009, China produced 13.79 million motor vehicles, making it the largest automobile producer in the world. In an attempt to control the increase in automobile production and ownership in the country, China has been proactive on developing cleaner technology and establishing higher standards for automobile emissions. The country has established strict fuel economy standards and a testing system to determine if cars meet the standards before the manufacturer can begin production. In 2007, China denied construction of 444 models from 44 different car makers because they did not fully meet the fuel efficiency standards. The 2008 fuel economy limits for automobiles under 1,667 pounds were 42.9 and 40.3 mpg for manual transmissions and automatic transmissions (SUVs included), respectively (Cao *et al.* 2010).

Chinese leaders understand that increasing the fuel economy of automobiles is not a complete solution to the problem of GHG emissions from cars. In order to further address the situation, the country has also implemented non-technology-based regulations, including taxes to promote the purchase of smaller vehicles, and policies to improve public transportation. For example, in September of 2008, China increased the percentage of excise tax on passenger vehicles according to engine size. To purchase a vehicle containing an engine with a volume 4 liters or more, consumers must pay a 40 percent excise tax on the price of the vehicle. Also, a regulation on public transportation is in the works that will hold city governments accountable for developing a framework to support public transportation. Such frameworks will require that local city governments allocate funding to establish public transportation systems.

Water Pollution

In early 2010, the Chinese government put forward the results of its most detailed survey ever on the issue of water pollution, acknowledging that "water pollution in 2007 was more than twice as severe as was shown in official figures that had long omitted agricultural waste" as a source of water pollution.[4] The issues of food/agriculture and water are among the most significant health and development issues China is facing today. Many of China's lakes and rivers are at hazardous pollution levels and no longer support fish or wildlife. Of the major rivers in China 16.4 percent do not meet the lowest standard of water quality (Blanchard 2011). In 2006, the World Bank reported that nearly one-third of the water in all of the monitored sections of China's river systems fell into the category of very restricted functionality and only 28 percent was potable (World Bank 2006). In 2009, none of the lakes in China met Grade I standards for water quality, only 3.9 percent of lakes met Grade II standards and 34.6 percent of lakes in China did not meet Grade V standards (RSE 2009 [2010]).

There are three main sources of water pollution in China: industry, municipalities, and agriculture. The discharge of wastewater in China has increased from 48.2 billion tons in 2004 to 58.9 billion tons in 2009. The majority of wastewater is from the municipal areas. China has been active on pursuing solutions for these areas of pollution. Two of the major pollutants clogging the waterways are chemical oxygen demand (COD) and ammonium nitrogen. In 2009, 12.8 million tons of COD and 1.2 million tons of ammonia nitrogen were discharged into the waterways. These levels are down from the 2006 levels of 14.3 million tons and 1.4 million tons, respectively (RSE 2009). A serious problem in China that pertains to water pollution is the emergence of algae blooms in lakes around the country. In 2008, 75 percent of the lakes in China were eutrophic. Eutrophication occurs when water sources have excessive amounts of nutrients, particularly phosphorus, causing low oxygen levels, bacterial growth, and algae blooms; it is most often associated with pollution from agricultural runoff. Pesticides, fertilizers, and domestic animal wastes drain into waterways from over-saturated agricultural fields, thus causing excessive amounts of nitrogen and phosphorus in waterways. In an effort to increase the efficiency of fertilizer use, the country has been promoting technology that will help establish standards for the amount of fertilizer needed and used for different types of soil. If successfully implemented, it will increase soil efficiency by 5 percent. The over-fertilization of agriculture not only causes pollution but also causes detrimental effects on the soil. Chinese chemical fertilizer has an efficiency rate of only 15–30 percent. The excessive fertilizer not only negatively affects climate change, but also causes the soil to harden, reducing the ability of the land to survive natural disasters that often accompany climate change. Encouraging the habit of over-fertilizing crops are the perverse incentives that emerge from subsidies to the fertilizer industry.

Water scarcity is also a serious issue, especially in Northern China. The world average per capita water availability is 8,513 m³/year. In Northern

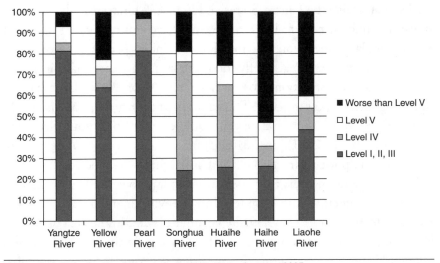

Figure 5.7 Water Quality of China's Seven Major Water Systems, 2007.

Source: *The China Environment Yearbook*, Vol. 4, p. 339. (Level I = Suitable for nature reserves; Level II = Drinking quality w/o treatment; Level III = Drinking quality w/ treatment; Level IV = Agricultural and landscaping only; Level V = Toxic).

China, the average water availability is 725m^3. As urban populations increase, China will have to pay more attention to its water resources and establish new methods of reusing, conserving, and cleaning available water. The majority of water used in China is to supply agricultural needs. In 2005, agricultural, industrial, and residential use of water accounted for 63.3 percent, 22.8 percent and 12.5 percent of total water use in China, respectively (World Bank 2006).

What's Being Done: Energy Diversification and Investment in Renewable Energy

Though the majority of the country's energy, about 77 percent, comes from coal, China has not overlooked the importance of energy diversification. Initial areas of diversification begin with natural gas and nuclear power. Though China has been increasing its consumption of natural gas, the country still consumes very little in comparison to the United States and Russia. In 2010 China's natural gas use only represented 3.4 percent, as compared to 21.7 and 13 percent for the United States and Russia, respectively. China accounted for 98 million tons of the 2.9 billion tons consumed worldwide, whereas the United States and Russia used 621 and 372.7 tons, respectively. In the last two decades, China has begun investing in nuclear power, though its total output is still relatively small compared to nuclear giants like the United States and France. China currently has plans for twenty nuclear power plants in the works, accounting for almost half of all nuclear plants under construction globally. China's plans for these nuclear power plants were stopped briefly following the 2011 earthquake in Japan, but continued construction shortly thereafter. As of 2011, China had 13 operating nuclear power plants. The addition of twenty more plants should increase their capacity from 2 percent to 5 percent of their total electricity generation (Biello 2011). In 2010, China accounted for 2.7 percent of global nuclear power, a fraction of the United States' 30.7 percent.

The real game in energy diversification today, however, lies in the area of renewable energy. And despite China's environmental woes, over the last decade, the country has actually become a leader in the area of renewable energy. It is interesting to note that during the time that China has taken a leadership position in this industry, the United States has fallen dramatically behind. In wind-generated energy, from 2005, China doubled its capacity each year, becoming the world's leader in this renewable in

2009.[5] In solar power, Germany is the world's leader, with the United States running second, and China third, though China has increased its capacity in solar heating dramatically in recent years. In hydroelectricity, China is the world's leader by a long shot. (It is an interesting irony that China has received a tremendous amount of criticism for its development of hydroelectric power because of populations that were displaced due to the building of the Three Gorges Dam.) As the well-known "green" venture capitalist John Doerr of Kleiner Perkins described the situation, "China's growth in renewables is astounding. The results of their policies are really staggering. My conclusion is that we are barely in the race today. My conclusion is that China is winning."[6]

Since 1978, China has more than doubled the proportion of energy that comes from renewable energy sources, including nuclear. Hydroelectric, nuclear, and wind power make up 7.8 percent of total energy production in China. In 2009 China became the world leader in clean energy investment, with investments totaling at $34.6 billion. China has shown a continuation of this trend with a five-year growth of investment rate of 148 percent in clean energy. Clean energy produced 52.5 GW of electricity, accounting for 4 percent of the total power capacity. China has set a high goal to have 15 percent of its energy production coming from renewable by the year 2020 (Gallagher 2010, 20). In 2010 China's share of the total world consumption of hydroelectricity was 21 percent, making it the largest consumer of hydroelectricity in the world. China nearly tripled its consumption of hydroelectric power, from 50.3 to 163.1 million tons of coal equivalent, in ten years from 2000 to 2010. China has also greatly increased its solar energy capacity. In 1996, the solar capacity of China was 76.6 MW. In 2010, the country reached a capacity of 2,516 MW (BP 2011).

China's clean energy investments in 2009 totaled $34.6 billion, nearly double the $18.6 billion of clean energy investments in the United States (Pew 2010). The country is a world leader in the area of hydroelectricity, as projects like the Three Gorges Dam have greatly increased the country's hydroelectricity capacity. The country currently holds the leading position in hydroelectricity consumption with 21 percent of the world's total. China is followed by Brazil, which accounts for 11.6 percent of the world's total. The United States trails far behind China with only 2.5 percent of world hydroelectricity consumption. China's focus on wind power has expanded exponentially in the last decade, putting China at the lead position in global wind power investment. From 2000 to 2010, China increased wind energy production from 352 to 44,781 MW, making up 22.4 percent of the world's production. This race to the top passed Germany and the United States, both major players in wind energy with 20.2 and 13.7 percent of the global market, respectively. China's solar capacity has been increasing steadily for the last decade. Though China has yet to reach the level of the solar energy production in Germany or the United States, the country has been incredibly effective in installing solar heating systems. In 2009, solar heating systems accounted for 58.9 percent of global market. That same year, China installed 80.5 percent of all new solar heating systems worldwide. Germany is currently the world leader in photovoltaic power, accounting for over 40 percent of global production. China currently makes up 2.2 percent of production in the important area of photovoltaic panels.

While Doerr's view that the United States is "barely in the race today" may be a little extreme, at least according to the data presented here, it is true that China has been effective in attracting key players in the renewable energy sector to build production facilities there. For example, in early 2011, Evergreen Solar announced that it would be shutting down its plant in Devens, Massachusetts and moving operations to Wuhan, China. Many

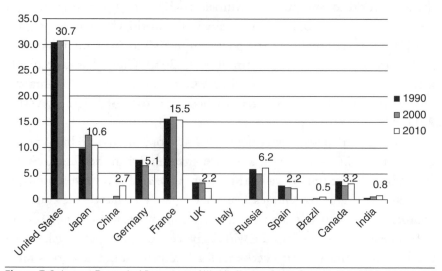

Figure 5.8 Largest Economies' Percentage of World's Nuclear Power Consumption, 2010.

Source: *BP Statistical Review of World Energy* (2011) http://www.bp.com/statisticalreview.

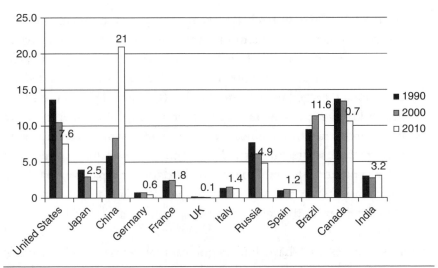

Figure 5.9 Largest Economies' Percentage of World's Hydroelectricity Consumption, 2010.

Source: *BP Statistical Review of World Energy* (2011) http://www.bp.com/statisticalreview.

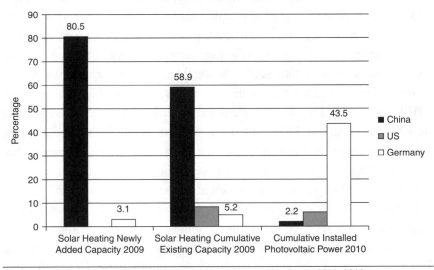

Figure 5.10 Percentage of Global Solar Heating and Photovoltaic Power, 2009, 2010.

Source: *Solar Heat Worldwide*, Weiss and Mauthner (2011), *BP Statistical Review of World Energy* (2011) http://www.bp.com/statisticalreview.

critics viewed this as a case of China stealing U.S. jobs through subsidies and lower wages; however, the harsh realities of operating in the renewable energy sector are a little more complex than this. As Evergreen Solar CEO Michael El-Hillow described the situation,

[In the US] There were challenges from the start. Lehman Brothers was our banker and had almost a third of our outstanding shares as part of a financing transaction. That disappeared in Lehman's bankruptcy and cost us about $300 million. Then we went to the federal government to get help from the TARP funds, but they said no because we weren't a financial institution . . . In December 2008 we were approached by a Chinese company, Jiawei, which was impressed with our wafer technology. The Chinese government agreed to support a loan that would cover two-thirds of our expansion in China. The subsidies we received from the government here covered less than 5 percent of the cost of our U.S. plant.[7]

Other companies that have built significant presences in photovoltaic production, such as DuPont (through subsidiary DuPont Apollo in Shenzhen, China), for similar reasons.[8]

Renewables and energy diversification have helped, but regulation has also been a necessary part of the equation. In the early 2000s, a surge in economic activity and an intensified push toward a market economy sparked energy consumption, resulting in a 3.8 percent average rise in energy intensity from 2002–2005. Since then, the country has worked to increase energy efficiency through a variety of methods (Oshita and Price 2010). With the adoption of Renewable Energy Law of the People's Republic of China in 2005, and the two most recent five-year plans, the country has attempted to step up its attention to pollution and renewable energy investment. The eleventh five-year plan (2006–2010) established ambitious goals for China's environmental agenda, including a 20 percent reduction in energy intensity and a 10 percent reduction in emissions of major pollutants (Fan 2006). Though some of the goals of the eleventh five-year plan were not met, such initiatives directly contributed to saving 250 million tons of coal equivalent in energy and reducing CO_2 emissions by 605.2 million tons (Ohshita and Price 2010). The twelfth five-year plan (2011–2015) continues high expectations on reductions and efficiency. With an expected GDP growth rate of 7 percent, China plans to cut further carbon dioxide emissions by 17 percent, reduce energy intensity by 16 percent, and increase production of non-fossil fuel energy sources by 11.4 percent (Deng 2011). In addition, one of the most prominent measures used to reduce energy has been the Top-1,000 Enterprises

Energy Efficiency Program, in which the top-1,000 enterprises in China have worked with funding opportunities and financial incentive from the government to reduce their energy dependence. The top 1,000 enterprises constitute a large portion of the energy use in China. Successful implementation of the program had possible reductions of 10–25 percent of the eleventh five-year plan goal of reducing energy intensity by 20 percent (Price *et al.* 2010).

A common criticism of the laws and regulations that the Chinese government has put into place is the practice of enforcement. The government has often been accused of lacking resources for and not placing enough emphasis on proper enforcement of environmental laws and regulations (Gallagher 2010). As a measure to address these problems, the government has formed a partnership with the United States Environmental Protection Agency and Vermont Law School to train Chinese judges in the enforcement of environmental law. The project will develop a curriculum that will help educate judges on environmental laws and principles to better address environmental protection issues. It will also help businesses that are already following environmental codes by reducing the competitive benefit for businesses that are not complying with environmental laws. With the help of academics, NGOs, and the media, China has seen a surge in the establishment of environmental courts (Cramer 2011).

Conclusions

There is no denying that China's rapid economic development has created serious problems in terms of pollution and environmental degradation. Economic development has lifted hundreds of millions of people out of poverty, but it has also come at great cost to the air, water, and land. However, as with many of the arguments presented in this book, it is important that we take an empirically driven and balanced approach to what is actually occurring in China. Just as the country has moved efficiently and effectively in building infrastructure, it has also shown that it can move effectively addressing issues of pollution and the environment. Of particular interest is how aggressively the country has been moving in the area of renewable energy in the last half-decade.

A little perspective with respect to China's environmental woes is important on two levels. First, the balance between economic development and bringing people out of poverty on the one hand and environmental stewardship on the other is a difficult one. China has moved about 800 million people out of poverty in the last 30 years, and perhaps even as many as 1 billion depending on whose statistics you trust (under World Bank standards, abject poverty is considered to be $1.25 per person per day). It has been a truly remarkable shift in global resources to the impoverished of a nation that was on the verge of bankruptcy just three decades ago. And one can understand the government's prioritization of rapid economic development and moving people out of poverty over the environment, at least in the short run. Second, although we readily lambaste China for its pollution of the air, land, and water, global comparisons tell an interesting story here. For example, the United States is still one of the most heavily polluting nations in the world in a couple of key categories. And it was not so long ago (within the last half century) that residents of Pittsburgh, Pennsylvania, could barely see through the smog that was generated by the city's steel industry or that the Cuyahoga River in Ohio caught fire outside Cleveland because it was so toxic with waste.[9] The United States acted with outrage over those occurrences and environmental protections have been taken more seriously since then. Similarly, despite its problems with environmental degradation, there are pockets of China that have actually taken stewardship of the environment seriously.

Most interesting, however, is the country's aggressive movement in the area of renewable energy. In a few short years, China has become a global leader in renewable energy. If you add together solar, hydro, and wind production and consumption, China is the world's leader in renewables. Hydroelectricity is the main contributor here; and this itself is a double-edged sword, as the country has come under much scrutiny for the Three Gorges Dam Project. China still lags far behind in solar energy, however, several key producers of solar energy (in particular photovoltaic panels), including major players like DuPont, have recently moved operations to China; China's own domestic powerhouses, like Yingli Solar are also significantly influencing China's surge in this area. The government's aggressive courting of this industry with guaranteed loans and guaranteed procurement prices should make clear how serious China is about development of the renewable energy sector.

6

CHANGING LIFE CHANCES

One hot day in June 1995, I was conducting an interview at a factory in the Caohejing district of Shanghai, a thriving economic area in the southern part of the city, mostly populated with small, dynamic factories that report to the economic bureaus of the Caohejing district government. As I sat with the general manager of this factory, he spoke at length about how committed he was to living like the workers of his factory. He pointed out repeatedly that his salary was "exactly the same" as that of the line workers in his factory. "I am just like them," he said, "I make the same amount of money as they do. That is what it means to be a socialist factory . . . We believe in equality." As the interview was drawing to a close, I began to think about my long ride back to the city center on my one-speed bicycle. It was a hot day, and I was dreading it. I mentioned something about this to my host, who then suggested eagerly that I leave my bike at the factory and let him drive me back to the city center, as he had business there anyway. As he suggested this course of action, he pointed across the parking lot to his company car, a large, expensive-looking Mercedes.

I declined the offer. But as I rode back to my dorm room, I thought about the encounter. What do the economic reforms actually mean for individuals working in China's transforming economy? If we measure socioeconomic status by income, as is common in many studies, we may mistakenly think that this general manager does indeed live like the workers in his factory, as he claims. But if we think about access to nonwage benefits, like an apartment or a company car (a Mercedes, no less), the situation might look much different. And how are these factors changing in the era of economic reforms? Who is getting access to more, and who is getting access to less? Who is gaining wealth, and who is falling behind? Further, the interaction described above occurred at an early phase of the economic reforms; inequality has risen rapidly since then. How has this rapidly rising inequality changed society? This chapter will address these questions through an exploration of the changing stratification order of Chinese society in the era of economic reform.

Two Families, Two Radically Different Tales[1]

To bring these questions into graphic relief, let us consider the lives of two individuals in Chinese society on the eve of the economic reforms (originally reported on by Dexter Roberts in 1999). When China's economic reforms began, Fengtong Liu, a welder from Beijing, and Frank Liu, a university student in Shanghai, were in similar situations economically and socially. By the standards of living in China in 1979, they were both positioned to live comfortable—though by no means luxurious—lives. Fengtong had just landed a job at a large, state-owned coal factory, known as the Beijing Number 3 Coal Plant, where he would meet his future wife, a fellow employee. In the China that these young men came of age in, landing a job such as this placed Fengtong at the top of the socioeconomic heap. With employment at a large, state-owned enterprise came social status; extensive benefits packages, including housing, paid vacations, child care, and early schooling; meal subsidies; and, above all, stability. Wages were not high, but they were not high anywhere in China, and employment came with a lifetime guarantee, so a job in a high-status "work unit" such as this meant long-term security.

At about the time that Fengtong Liu began working at Beijing Number 3, Frank Liu was beginning his studies in management administration at the Shanghai Engineering Technological University. When he finished his education, he would have a degree of higher education, while his compatriot in Beijing had only a high school diploma; but in pre-economic reform China, this would mean little in terms of potential for income and social status. Indeed, if anything, in the wake of the Cultural Revolution (1966–1976), when many from the intellectual class—including Frank Liu's parents—were punished as "bourgeois capitalists," a welder's social position and future might have seemed more secure than that of an "intellectual." According to the rules of Communist China, the likely outcome, it seemed at the time, was that Frank and Fengtong would live very similar lives in terms of wealth, material comfort, opportunity, and social status.

The economic reforms would, however, change everything. As the reforms explored in the previous chapters unfolded in the 1980s, the situations of these individuals would shift dramatically. In 1998, after nineteen years of service at Beijing Number 3, Fengtong Liu would lose his job, and his wife Jie would be placed on a waiting list for the same fate. Their secure futures crumbled like the walls of the now run-down, state-owned factory to which they had given their adult lives. That factory was simply one of the casualties of China's transition from command to market economy: deeply embedded in the inefficient ways of the Soviet-style command economy, this factory, like thousands of other factories in China, would find itself unable to survive in China's emerging market economy. Today, Fengtong works as a dance instructor, making about 90 dollars a month—half of his pay at Beijing Number 3—with no benefits and no job security. He and his family live in a 600-square-foot apartment on the grounds of Beijing Number 3. Today, the dreams of Fengtong and Jie are unassuming: to make ends meet long enough so that their daughter, Wei, can be provided with a solid education and have a secure future—something the couple once took for granted.

Frank Liu's life trajectory proved to be very different. When the economic reforms began, Frank was completing his education, after which he began teaching; he continued to do so for six years. With a degree in management administration, Frank was equipped with the skills and knowledge that would give him an advantage in China's new market economy. Market economies reward skills and knowledge differently from command economies, and Frank Liu's education positioned him well to reap the benefits of China's changing economic landscape. In 1990, after six years of teaching, Frank found a job in a government organization that manages the development of one of Shanghai's many "free trade zones." This organization is now a semiautonomous "company," and Frank is a vice president, managing the district's development—which means he spends a lot of time working with foreign investors, including such multinationals as Dell, Hewlett-Packard, and Intel. His wife, Lily, who has a degree in engineering from a university in Shanghai, works for Intel. Their son attends an exclusive private school, and they just recently purchased a 1,260-square-foot, three bedroom high-rise apartment with all the amenities you would expect to find in an apartment of an upper-middle-class family in the United States. While they began the economic reforms in relatively similar situations, Fengtong and Frank have fared very differently in the economic reforms, and the differences in their experiences bring to light many of the economic and social changes I have been exploring throughout the pages of this book. First, there is the fundamental restructuring of China's economy—the transition from a command economy to a market economic system. Under the command economy, employment in a large, state-owned factory was a high-status position in Chinese society, in part because of the excellent benefits employees of these units received, but also because these work units were so closely protected by the government. These large factories were the back-bone of China's command economy, and they were heavily subsidized by the government; there was never a question of profits, losses, or covering costs. In the era of economic reform, this system has been completely transformed. Now these organizations operate under the constraints of China's newly emerging markets and, in many cases, with no subsidies from the state at all. Many of these factories are struggling to survive, ending the once sacred social contract of lifetime employment and laying off longtime employees such as Fengtong Liu. The restructuring of the command economy in China has been nothing less than a complete transformation of the economics of production and the rules by which production units survive, prosper, and die in China's industrial economy. At the same time, as changes sweep across industrial markets, new markets are opening up. For example, the development of the computer industry throughout China—a sector that Frank and Lily Liu have both capitalized on—is creating new opportunities for individuals who are equipped to ride this wave.

A second shift illuminated by the lives of Frank and Fengtong Liu relates to the impact that foreign capital and globalization are having across China. China's economy is transforming in significant ways, and it is not only because the government has consciously worked to dismantle the command economy and allow markets to emerge. The entry of foreign capital into Chinese markets has also had important consequences for the kind of economy that is emerging in China. As discussed in earlier chapters, foreign multinationals bring with them technology, capital, and, above all, ways of doing business that are shaped by the market economies from whence they came. Chinese citizens who are positioned to be a part of this process have immediate access to higher salaries, benefits, travel, status, and, most of all, on-the-ground experience in the practices of a market economy. That Frank Liu spends much of his time dealing with and courting foreign capital has important implications for his social and economic position in China. Everyone in China is struggling to master the ways of survival in the unfamiliar—and often harsh—realities of the market, and Frank is learning his strategies from executives at Dell, Intel, and Hewlett-Packard. That Frank and his wife Lily have adopted English names and shift easily between Mandarin and English is indicative of their ability to deal in the new global economy.

Third, Fengtong and Frank's stories illuminate fundamental changes in the mechanisms of social stratification, the factors that shape the life chances and outcomes of individuals in China. In the China that Fengtong and Frank grew up in, class credentials were extremely important— intellectuals and capitalists were always at some degree of risk for political persecution. There was little difference in wages across the industrial sector, but stratification did occur—primarily through the benefits a given factory was able to secure for its employees. In this system, factories like Beijing Number 3 were the wealthiest and most powerful organizations in the country, and employees reaped the benefits of working for these high-status organizations. In the China of today, political credentials and class position are of little help in competing in the markets of the transforming economy. Knowledge, educational credentials, language skills, and, above all, the ability to adapt to the new rules of the market are rewarded in the form of high wages and open doors to the wealth of opportunities that exist for the few in the new global economy.

Finally, it is important to note that as different as the stories of Fengtong and Frank are, they do not even represent extremes in the spectrum of possible outcomes for citizens of China. Indeed, the comparison of these two individuals and their families is interesting precisely because their social and economic positions were so similar at the beginning of the reforms. But there are also the millions of indigent farmers in the country-side and nouveau riche of the economic reforms—those who drive luxury cars and have become millionaires virtually over night. There is the so-called floating population—the migrant workers, who are the castoffs of the industrial economy—a population of people estimated at about 100 million. There are more people in this impoverished position in China than there are people in Germany, France, or all of Northern Europe. There are the government bureaucrats, many of whom are struggling to adapt to the rules and necessities of China's emerging market economy and many of whom are making out quite comfortably. In order to understand how China's reforms have shaped the lives of these different groups of Chinese citizens, we must understand how China's transition to a market economy has unfolded.

Education

Before 1949, the overwhelming majority of the Chinese population was illiterate. In the decades since, the country has made great strides in providing a basic education for a substantial portion of the population, as the substantial gain in literacy of the great masses of its population shows (see Figure 6.1). Shortly after the founding of the PRC, a national system of education was built, and the policy of universal primary education was one of the main agendas of the national education system at that time. In

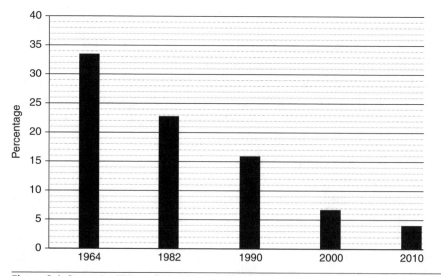

Figure 6.1 Decreasing Illiterate Rates of the Total Population in China, 1964–2010.

Source: National Statistical Bureau of China (2010, 98). 2010 Illiteracy Rate from *Press Release on Major Figures of the 2010 National Population Census* http://www.stats.gov.cn/english/newsandcomingevents/t20110428_402722237.htm.

1955, the state attempted to facilitate literacy by standardizing language (*putong hua*) and creating a common set of simplified Chinese characters.

In 1957, the national education policies took aim at developing professional education institutes, based on the Soviet model, in order to facilitate research in, and the development of, technical areas that would help build the economy. However, the commitment to technical and scientific development was short-lived. The 1957 Hundred Flowers Reform initiated by Mao led to an outpouring of criticism from intellectuals, which gave rise to a deep suspicion of the intellectuals and a radical shift in Mao's education policies. Following that, the goals of education were driven toward political and ideological ends. Mao initiated large-scale social movements and mass campaigns, including the Cultural Revolution, and mobilized the active participation of the masses. Political education would become the primary content in those movements, and Mao's *Little Red Book* became the most important textbook. During the Cultural Revolution, an entire generation of college students—Mao's "Red Guard"—was sent down to the countryside for "reeducation" with manual labor. Few from this generation of students would find the opportunity to recapture what was lost in educational opportunities during that period. As Figure 6.2

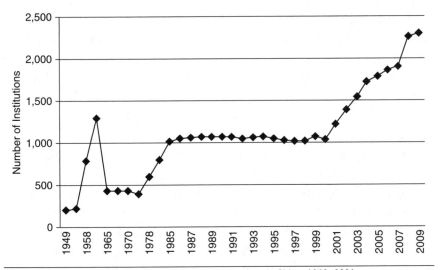

Figure 6.2 Number of Regular Higher Education Institutions in China, 1949–2001.

Source: 1949–1983 data from Tsang, M., (2000); 1985–2009 data from National Statistical Bureau of China (2010, 755).

shows, where institutions of higher education expanded rapidly in the years following the founding of the PRC, most of these institutions were shut down in the years following the Great Leap Forward (1958–1960) and during the Cultural Revolution (1966–1976).

The education policies of the 1960s and 1970s were reversed in the late 1970s with the launch of economic reforms. While the average amount spent on education amounted to only 6.5 percent of government expenditures in the years 1950–1978, that figure rose to an average of 11 percent of total government expenditures in the years 1979–1992 (Tsang 1996). The status of intellectuals and professionals has been upgraded in accordance with their better living and working conditions, and they have been able to play more and more important roles in the transformation of China in the reform era. The national examination for merit-based university entry resumed in 1978, and the lower levels of education systems were also reoriented toward improving educational quality. Political ideology is still part of the curriculum at all levels of education and one of the mandatory subjects in the college entrance examination, but it is an area of learning that carries less and less weight today. The emphasis of education today is placed on "expertise" (*zhuan*), in line with the goals of economic development and the building of a market-oriented economy.

Since 1985, the Chinese government has enforced a nine-year compulsory education policy and expanded the scale of the education system to provide full access to children from various backgrounds. On the other hand, the Chinese government supports a highly stratified education system to prepare people for diversity of vocational tasks that will best serve the goals of economic development (Tsang 2000). Various secondary technical and skilled workers schools have been established to satisfy the increasing demand for technical and skilled personnel in this period of rapid economic growth. One of the key policies in this area sought to merge small-scale universities into more effective, larger universities; it was a policy that led to a slight decline in the number of higher-education institutions from 1988 to 1998. In 1995, Jiang Zemin proposed that the current development strategy "must focus on science, technology, and education." Since then, the education reforms have concentrated on the development of one hundred key universities in key disciplines. Then, in May 1998, after more than a decade of discussion on the topic, a formal reorganization of the higher education system was set in motion. The first change was that ten universities were named as "international-level universities," and the central government would concentrate its resources on the development of these universities. The remaining twenty-six universities under the central government would be gradually turned over to provincial and municipal governments. Within this first-tier group, in addition to the usual funds that the institutions under the central government would receive, the top four universities would receive extra funds to help them develop as international-level universities.[2] Under this reform, universities were free to raise funds on their own, develop relations with foreign universities, and generally develop the programs that would make them competitive with top-tier research universities around the world. Table 6.1 and Figures 6.3 and 6.4 show the growth and changes in this sector since 1980. Since that time, the number of university students in China has increased by almost 200 percent; the number of faculty in universities has increased by almost 75 percent; the number receiving postgraduate education has grown by about 1,600 percent; the number of students studying abroad has increased by more than 1,000 percent; and the number of study-abroad students who have returned to China has increased by more than 4,500 percent.

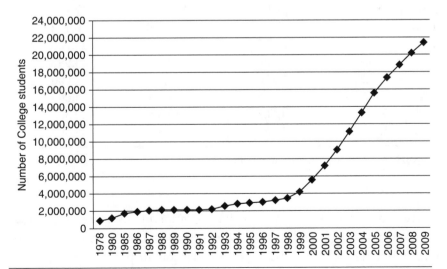

Figure 6.3 Undergraduate Enrollments of Regular Higher Education Institutions in China by Period.

Source: National Statistical Bureau of China (2010, 756).

Table 6.1 Vital Statistics on Higher Education in China

	No. of University Graduates per 10,000 Pop	No. of Faculty (Higher Ed.) per 10,000 Pop.	No. of Students Studying Abroad	No. of Students Returning from Abroad
1980	14.7	24.7	2,124	162
1985	31.6	34.4	4,888	1,424
1986	39.3	37.2	4,676	1,388
1987	53.2	38.5	4,703	1,605
1988	55.3	39.3	3,786	3,000
1989	57.6	39.7	3,329	1,753
1990	61.4	39.5	2,950	1,593
1991	61.4	39.1	2,900	2,069
1992	60.4	38.8	6,540	3,611
1993	57.1	38.8	10,742	5,128
1994	63.7	39.6	19,071	4,230
1995	80.5	40.1	20,381	5,750
1996	83.9	40.3	20,905	6,570
1997	82.9	40.5	22,410	7,130
1998	83.0	40.7	17,622	7,379
1999	84.8	42.6	23,749	7,748
2000	95.0	46.3	38,989	9,121
2001	103.6	53.2	83,973	12,243
2002	133.7	61.8	125,179	17,945
2003	187.7	72.5	117,307	20,152
2004	239.1	85.8	114,682	24,726
2005	306.8	96.6	118,515	34,987
2006	377.5	107.6	134,000	42,000
2007	447.8	116.8	144,000	44,000
2008	511.9	123.7	179,800	69,300
2009	531.1	129.5	229,300	108,300

Source: National Statistical Bureau of China (2010, 755, 757).

These changes created a sector that is autonomous from the central government in ways fundamentally different from the situation of the pre-reform era. Thus, the 1990s education reforms in the higher-education institutions have substantially brought about massive expansion of college and postgraduate opportunities, as Figures 6.3 and 6.4 show.

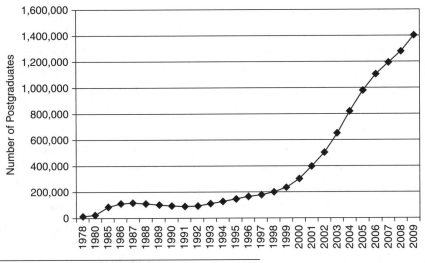

Figure 6.4 Numbers of Postgraduates in China, 1978–2009.

Source: National Statistical Bureau of China (2010, 757).

Despite these successful achievements in education in the reform era, the Chinese government today is still faced with significant challenges in creating more educational opportunities for its citizens. As of 2009, less than 4 percent of the population hold a college degree; 38 percent receive only primary schooling, and half of the population finish the nine years of education; 8 percent of the population have not received any schooling at all. In addition, it is widely noted that the nine-year schooling requirement is difficult to meet in the impoverished countryside. About 10 percent of the children in the poor hinterlands—mostly girls—cannot even attend the primary schools.

Gender

The Communist Revolution and the decades following changed the roles of women in the Chinese society in unprecedented ways. Women have entered into agrarian and industrial production and into the professional spheres, and the changes have created a relatively high rate of female employment. Women accounted for 8 percent of the total workforce in 1949; this rose to 31 percent in 1978 and reached 46 percent in 1995.[3] Female access to education and income significantly improved as well: the post-1978 economic reforms have greatly shifted gender inequalities by bringing about opportunities to women and men and slowing down the state-driven socialist movement aiming to eliminate the gender inequalities.

The research on gender inequality in the reform era has led to inconsistent conclusions about the direction of change, though all scholarship is clear about the gender inequality that exists in reform-era China. Beyond the widely acknowledged female infanticide driven by the one-child policy (discussed in Chapter 3), some scholars observe the labor-market discrimination against female workers in hiring and layoffs, job placement, and wages, and the worsening working conditions for female workers in southern China (Honig and Hershatter 1988; Lee 1995; Liu *et al.* 2000). Others find that the declining gender gap in household income contributions—driven by the off-farm employment opportunities—has improved the status of rural women in the reform era (e.g., Entwisle *et al.* 1995; Matthews and Nee 2000). Findings by Yanjie Bian and colleagues (2000) indicate that in urban China, the gender gap in earnings and other work status has remained stable from the 1950s to the 1990s. Despite the indeterminacy of these findings, there are some clear tendencies of the changing gender inequalities that help us understand the changing status of men and women in the reform era. First, in recent decades, with the increase in educational opportunities for the Chinese population as a whole, the influence of gender on educational achievement has gradually decreased. Table 6.2 shows that the percentages of female students in the total student population, and in each type of educational institution (including regular

Table 6.2 Changing Percentages of Female Students in Chinese Education Institutions, 1980–2001

% of Female Students	1980*	1985	1990	1995	2000	2001	2002
Total Students	43	43.4	44.9	46.5	47.1	47.1	47.1
Institutions of Higher Education	23.4	30	33.7	35.4	41	42	44
Specialized Secondary Schools	31.5	38.6	45.4	50.3	56.6	57.4	56
Regular Secondary Schools	39.6	40.2	41.9	44.8	46.2	46.5	46.7
Vocational Secondary Schools	32.6	41.6	45.3	48.7	47.2	47.5	47.6
Primary Schools	44.6	44.8	46.2	47.3	47.6	47.3	47.2

Source: National Statistical Bureau of China (2003, 726;* 2002, 680).

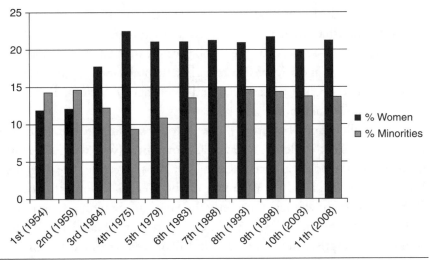

Figure 6.5 Composition of National People's Congresses, 1954–2009.

Source: National Statistical Bureau of China (2010, 883).

and specialized institutions), have all increased. Among them, the percentage of female students in specialized secondary schools and in institutions of higher education has increased the most.

The gains in access to education for women have, to some degree, reduced gender inequality, but there are still significant inequalities in the allocation of social, economic, and political resources. For example, a recent study on social stratification of contemporary China conducted by the Chinese Academy of Social Sciences shows the striking gender differences in each of these spheres. According to those findings, men account for about three-fourths of the dominant positions in the most advantageous occupational classes, including state officials (cadres) at the management level, high-level managerial positions in industrial enterprises, and private enterprise owners. At the middle level of the occupation classes—those positions occupied by professional technicians, low-and mid-level functionaries, managerial personnel, and self-employed individuals—the distribution of men and women is relatively even. However, at the upper level (higher-level professional technicians), the ratio of men to women is much higher. For those in social groups with comparatively low social economic status, the distribution of men and women is relatively even, with men holding a higher ratio among industrial workers (accounting for three-fifths). Women account for about 70 to 80 percent of urban unemployed, laid-off, and "half laid-off vagrants." In addition, women face more difficulty than men in being hired and gaining promotion in both public and private sectors. In the public sector, for instance, women are forced to retire at age 55, five years earlier than are men. In many cases women are laid off first by factories and often have to take work outside the regulated formal market.

As to the allocation of political power in today's China, gender inequalities are particularly evident. Among CCP members (who form the major social base of the political elite in China), only 14 percent of the membership is female. And only 7.5 percent of the Central Committee of the CCP is made up of women. Currently the Politburo Standing Committee (PSC)—elected by the CCP's Central Committee at the 2002 Tenth Party Congress—comprises nine members, and all of them are male. Within the current National People's Congress (NPC), about 21 percent of the representatives are female, and only 9 percent of the NPC Standing Committee is made up of women. The most influential woman in China's political hierarchy, Wu Yi, is currently one of the vice premiers of the State Council. Thus, at all levels of the political system, from the highest echelon of government down to that of the townships and villages, women, in general, experience low participation. The policy of early retirement in the government and public sectors also greatly decreases the opportunities for women to get promoted or hold the leadership positions in the political system.

In rural areas, women comprise 60–70 percent of the agricultural labor force. Many women become the heads of their household when their husbands migrate to the cities for work. Rebecca Matthews and Victor Nee (2000) argue that such a position brings greater household decision-making power to female family members. With the development of the private sector in rural China, the opportunities for working in family business have also been opened to women, but men are currently more likely than women to run the family business. The 1995 study by Barbara Entwisle and colleagues finds that households with a large pool of female labor have no advantage in starting and running small businesses. Instead, business involvement depends on the male labor pool—especially the presence of older men.

More traditionally female industries—such as those of textile, shoe, and garment making—have opened up a number of opportunities for off-farm employment for women from the rural areas. With the sizable export economy and the resulting creation of more off-farm employment opportunities for women, especially in the coastal areas, female workers' contributions to household income have significantly increased, and the relative size of contributions to rural household income for male and female nonfarm workers has narrowed (Matthews and Nee 2000). To some degree, this fact may help enhance women's status in Chinese rural households. In addition, the significant migration from inland to coastal areas in the reform era has provided women with more autonomy than they had in previous eras. Overall, however, the situation in reform-era China is still one of significant gender inequality across a number of socioeconomic and political settings.

Rising Inequalities Across Sectors and Regions

Communist China was a hierarchically organized economy where the government redistributed resources to different levels of organizations and the individuals tied to them.[4] In theory, those resources were allocated and redistributed evenly throughout the society as a whole, such that all individuals were compensated in similar ways. In fact, however, while wages were similar across Chinese society, work organizations varied widely in the nonwage benefits they could offer employees. An enterprise's position in the hierarchy of the command economy was the strongest predictor of the benefits the firm would be able to offer its workers. Those at the upper end of the nested hierarchy—under the jurisdiction of the central, provincial, or municipal governments—were able to extract the most resources from their government offices and were thus able to offer their workers the most extensive packages of nonwage benefits (Walder 1992a). Benefits ranged from housing to localized medical clinics, meal services, kindergartens, and the availability of commuter buses and group vacations.

One of the key changes in the economic reforms sought to relieve enterprises of some of the economic burden of providing social welfare for their employees. As enterprises have looked for ways to cut costs, Chinese workers are no longer guaranteed lifetime employment, as many are placed on fixed-term labor contracts (Guthrie 1998a), and the provision of extensive nonwage benefits has also diminished significantly. Wages are now more directly connected to the performance of the firms. There have been considerable differences in the rise of wages in the reform era. In the urban industrial economy, wage distribution was fairly tight even as late as the early 1990s. However, over the course of the last decade, wages have grown at differential rates. In 1978, employees of state-owned enterprises and urban collectives had average annual incomes of 644 and 506 yuan, respectively (there is no data for foreign and joint venture factories, as they did not exist as a category in 1978). By 2009, individuals in these organizations were making 34,130 and 21,706 yuan, respectively, while individuals in the foreign sector were making just over 30,287 yuan.

Income in urban areas has risen much more rapidly than in rural areas. In rural areas, income has risen from an average household level of 133 yuan in 1978 to 5,163 yuan in 2009; during the same period, the overall average income for urban households has risen from 343 to 17,174 yuan. By official measures (i.e., according to the Chinese government), the proportion of poverty-stricken households—those households that have a net annual income of 600 yuan and below—has decreased from 87 percent in 1985 to about 4 percent in 2000. However, the rise of rural household income is strikingly small when compared to that of urban China. Rural incomes in China are about 40 percent of urban incomes, when, in most

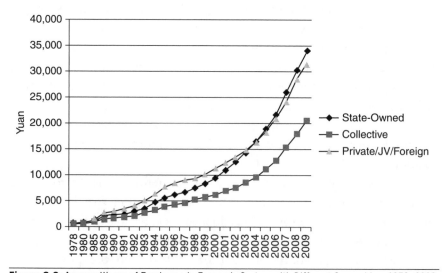

Figure 6.6 Average Wages of Employees in Economic Sectors with Different Ownerships, 1978–2009.

Source: National Statistical Bureau of China (2010, 131, 1995–2008 data; 2006, 157, 1978–1994 data).

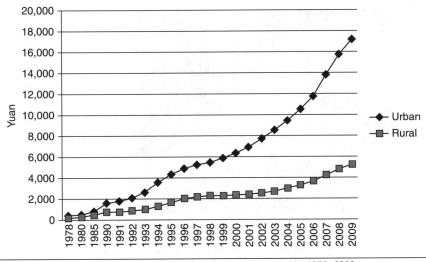

Figure 6.7 Per Capita Annual Incomes of Urban and Rural Households, 1978–2009.

Source: National Statistical Bureau of China (2010, 342).

countries, rural incomes are 60 percent or more of urban incomes in the mid-1990s (World Bank Report 1997). Further, this figure is a low poverty-line estimation. Using the international standard of one dollar per person per day would produce a higher figure, as would a poverty estimate based on calorie intake (UN in China 2005).

Regional disparities are also significant in reform-era China. In the Communist era, differences between regions were small. However, as economic reforms have concentrated development in the coast region, the uneven development between the coastal and inland areas has been extreme. Per-capita annual income in urban Shanghai in 2009 was 32,403 yuan, far ahead of other urban areas. When we compare the average annual income of eastern seaboard provinces with those of the lowest income provinces in the Western region, the differences are significant. For urban areas in 2009, the lowest per-capita annual income in the nation, that of urban Gangsu, was 12,918 yuan, less than half of the per-capita annual income of urban Shanghai. For rural areas, in 2009, the highest per-capita net income in the nation, that of rural Shanghai, was 12,483 yuan, which is more than four times the per-capita net income of rural Gansu, the lowest in the nation. In each provincial-level region, the per-capita annual income of urban areas is between two and four times that of rural areas. There were nine provincial-level regions where the per-capita annual

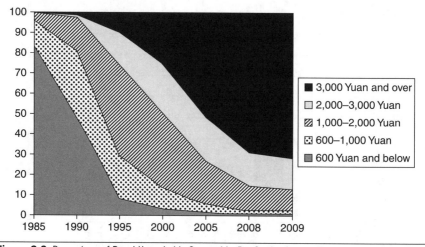

Figure 6.8 Percentage of Rural Households Grouped by Per Capita Annual Net Income, 1990–2009.

Source: National Statistical Bureau of China (2010, 363, 1990–2009 data; 2002, 343, 1985 data).

income in urban areas in 2009 was above the national average of 6,907 yuan; these include Beijing, Fujian, Guangdong, Jiangsu, Shandong, Shanghai, Tianjin, Tibet, and Zhejiang. Except for Tibet, which is located in the Western region and has received special subsidiaries from the central government, the other eight provinces are in the Eastern region. As for rural areas, there are ten provincial-level regions with per-capita annual income above the national average of 2,366.4 yuan. They are Beijing, Jiangsu, Fujian, Guangdong, Hebei, Liaoning, Shandong, Shanghai, Tianjin, and Zhejiang; all except for Hebei are, again, in the Eastern region.

Rural-to-Urban Migration

Throughout the Communist era, the household registration (*hukou*) system has been one of the mechanisms of social control employed by the Chinese state. Beyond a system of providing population statistics and identifying individual status, the *hukou* directly regulates population distribution, blocks rural-to-urban migration, and, most important, defines accessibility to state-provided benefits. In the pre-reform era, economic development strategies placed an emphasis on heavy industry and thus created significant inequality between the agricultural and industrial sectors. The work-unit system of urban industrial economy provided full employment and a range of nonwage benefits to urban residents, while the rural population was basically outside the state welfare system. To avoid the flows of individuals between industrial and agricultural sectors, as well as between rural and urban areas, the state instituted the *hukou* system as a strict measure of migration control.

Under this institution, Chinese citizens were forced to live in the place where their "household registration" was kept. Citizens were required to register in one place of regular residence. Prior to 1998, *hukou* registration was a "birth-subscribed" status inherited from a child's mother. Reforms to the policy in 1998 allowed children to inherit *hukou* status from their parents (Chan and Zhang 1999). Once assigned a residential location, individuals cannot elect to change their *hukou* registration. By 1955, all citizens of China were listed with either an urban or rural household registration. This classification was then used to determine whether or not a citizen was entitled to state-subsidized benefits and a variety of other social goods, such as public education. Holding an urban *hukou* gave a citizen access not only to the supply of food, housing, and other basic life necessities provided by the state in the pre-reform era, but also to many types of urban jobs. With proper paperwork, in some instances, individuals could legally migrate to urban areas, for example, but few people would choose to do so because it was so difficult to survive outside their *hukou* registration locations since urban job recruitment and job transfers were controlled by the government. Thus, the *hukou* system was not simply about migration control alone; it was also a fundamental part of the state monopoly over the distribution of goods and services.

In the beginning of the economic reforms, the barriers between urban and rural areas began to break down. There were at least three major reasons for this change. First, the receding state control over economic decisions led to diminishing control over social policies as well. The institutional mechanisms once maintaining the communist order in both urban (the work-unit system) and rural areas (the collective production units) declined with the withdrawal of the party-state's roles in the reform era. The *hukou* system still exists and functions in some important ways even today, but it is not the only channel through which Chinese citizens obtain their resources, goods, and services. The market economy provides more people with these resources outside their formal *hukou* location. In addition, state-subsidized welfare for urban citizens has been greatly

Table 6.3 Per Capita Annual Income of Rural versus Urban Households by Region, 2009

Eastern Provinces	Rural (yuan)	Urban (yuan)	Central Provinces	Rural (yuan)	Urban (yuan)	Western Provinces	Rural (yuan)	Urban (yuan)
Beijing	11,668.59	30,673.68	Hebei	5,149.67	15,675.75	Shanxi	4,244.10	14,983.15
Tianjin	8,687.56	23,565.67	Heilongjian	5,206.76	13,689.85	Gansu	2,980.10	12,918.04
Liaoning	5,958.00	17,757.70	Jilin	5,265.91	15,155.16	Ningxia	4,048.33	15,550.75
Shandong	6,118.77	19,336.91	Inner Mongolia	4,937.80	16,951.35	Sichuan	4,462.05	15,323.76
Jiangsu	8,003.54	22,494.94	Shaanxi	3,437.55	15,311.29	Yunnan	3,369.34	15,680.27
Shanghai	12,482.94	32,402.97	Henan	4,806.95	15,408.04	Guizhou	3,005.41	13,793.38
Zhejiang	10,007.31	27,119.30	Anhui	4,504.32	15,691.94	Qinghai	3,346.15	14,150.25
Fujian	6,680.18	21,692.35	Hubei	5,035.26	15,698.11	Xinjiang	3,883.10	13,602.18
Guangdong	6,906.93	24,116.46	Hunan	4,909.04	16,078.12	Tibet	3,531.72	14,978.95
Guangxi	3,980.44	17,032.89	Jiangxi	5,075.01	15,047.19	Chongqing	4,478.35	16,990.30
Hainan	4,744.36	14,909.28						
Averages	7,748.97	23,619.29		4,832.83	15,470.68		3,734.87	14,797.10

Source: National Statistical Bureau of China (2010, 352, 365).

reduced when compared to the pre-reform era. Second, the rapid growth of China's economy has produced increasing need for low-wage, temporary labor in developing urban areas (mainly in construction) and for more permanent labor in the export-led economy. These economic developments have become a significant driving force behind migration between rural and urban areas as well as between inland and coastal areas. Rural population began to migrate to cities for temporary jobs and money, despite the lack of state-guaranteed benefits attached to urban *hukou* status. Third, rapid growth in unemployment in rural areas since the 1980s also accounts for the increasing mobility from the countryside to towns and cities.

By 1984, the central government began to relent on the strict control over population regarding household registration, acknowledging the need for some level of rural-to-urban migration. Key changes were made by the central government to adjust its policies on migration control and household registration. In 1985, the Ministry of Public Security (MPS) published Provisional Regulations on the Management of Population Living Temporarily in the Cities. This regulation stipulated that people of 16 years of age and over who intended to stay in urban areas other than those of their *hukou* registration for more than three months could do so by applying for a temporary residence certificate. As an attempt to aid local authorities to monitor and control this temporary population, the 1985 regulation created a new category that fitted into the household registration system. One year later, it became legal to sell grain to peasants at work in the cities, and thus this temporary population was allowed to actually live in those cities on a long-term basis. Since then, almost all provincial and city governments have created their own policies for the regulation of the temporary population within their jurisdiction. In 1988, the State Council and the Ministry of Labor recommended that impoverished provinces in the hinterland export their labor to more advanced regions where there was an increasing demand for low-cost labor.

In 1989, the MPS introduced citizen identification cards in order to deal with the new population mobility; it was then mandatory for everyone over the age of sixteen to carry a citizen identification card. For peasant migrants, the citizen identification card is no longer necessary, as the "introduction letter" from the home village where the citizen's *hukou* is held now suffices (Solinger 1999b). Those who permanently change their residencies of regular *hukou* registration are now required to formally change their citizen I. D. cards (Chan and Zhang, 1999). This new system of photo identification provides the local governments with a more efficient way of regulating outsiders within their jurisdiction because the outsiders' statuses are easily identified. In 1989, the State Council permitted state enterprises to sign labor contracts directly with individual workers, as long as they report the employment to the local labor bureau and enter their individual records into the citizen identification databases.

One of the most significant products of the loosening of *hukou* regulations was the emergence of the "floating population"—those urban-dwelling and unlicensed laborers migrating from rural areas (Solinger 1999a). It is estimated that over one hundred million people constitute this floating population in today's China.[5] The existing *hukou* classification between urban and rural citizens has placed peasant migrants at the lowest level of the urban social stratification system, making them "secondary citizens" in urban areas (Solinger 1999a, 1999b). As Dorothy Solinger argues, migrant laborers are not treated like urban citizens there, despite the ability to move and work within the system. The state has allowed them the ability to move, but it does not afford them the "rights" that go along with an urban household registration in a given area. They are ineligible for welfare, medical, educational, or housing benefits to which urban residents of a given area have access. For example, migrant laborers have no access to urban housing allocations, but they are also not allowed to build or buy houses or to occupy land in urban areas; nor do they have access to government-sponsored health care or educational institutions. Since the 1990s, migrant laborers have unofficially bought land and built housing in urban areas, giving rise to growing shantytowns built by migrant laborers in urban areas. In recent years, migrants' shanty-towns have begun establishing their own schools, hospitals, and other unofficial institutions. Yet the existence of these shantytowns is precarious at best, as they can be subject to the local government's supervision and even mandatory removal.

Conclusions

A brief stroll down Nanjing East Road, one of Shanghai's posh shopping thoroughfares, gives an immediate sense of the changes that have reshaped life for Chinese citizens. Wealthy nouveau-riche couples stroll down the street, dressed in expensive suits and shopping at Shanghai's most expensive department stores, sometimes holding miniature dogs (a new accessory of the wealthy in China). Some of these people have chauffeurs waiting for them, no more than a block away, in their luxury Audis. Many of them will return to new homes in the suburbs of Shanghai, or to their large houses within gated communities, with private schools nearby. But in these same blocks, one will also run up against the reminders that capitalist economies are rife with inequality: small children from the countryside will run up, with the signs of poverty written on their faces and on their clothes, hands outstretched for any help that one can give them. They are part of the underclass of rural migrants who have made their way into China's booming metropolises to beg for a living. In some ways, the statistics reported in this chapter do not convey the true gulf in inequality that is emerging between the rich and the poor in China. However, it is important to note that China's Gini Coefficient is actually slightly lower than that of the United States, both in the low to mid 40s. (The Gini Coefficient is a scaled measure from 0–100 of the level of inequality in a country—larger numbers indicate greater inequality, smaller numbers more equality.) Thus, while China is experiencing radical inequality on some levels, it is not out of line with the level of inequality experienced in other capitalist economies (though both the United States and China are significantly more unequal than the Democratic Welfare States of Western Europe).

Life chances for individuals have changed dramatically over the course of China's economic reforms. Pre-reform Chinese society was one in which wages were very tightly controlled, and there was relatively little variation in annual incomes and little ability for mobility within the society. There were, nevertheless, certain pathways toward elite status. Party membership and government jobs created an administrative class that had significantly greater access to resources and positions of authority in the pre-reform era. In the reform era, party membership is still important, but paths to power have opened up substantially. College education has expanded significantly since 1979, and wages of college-educated individuals have risen significantly as well. And the reforms have opened a number of different pathways to middle-class status throughout the society: state bureaucrats and managers of large enterprises are still powerful in Chinese society, but so are many entrepreneurs who have made their fortunes in China's growing private economy. Individuals with the credentials that have currency in the global economy, such as college educations and English language skills, also have the ability to get ahead in today's China.

The expansion of college education and the private economy have opened up avenues for success for a larger portion of the population, but there is also growing inequality. Those in sectors that are trimming the social benefits they formerly offered people are finding themselves without health-care coverage or without the pensions that they expected would carry them into old age. Those in the countryside and, more generally, in the western provinces, have gained significantly less than those in the eastern urban centers. The loosening of migration laws has mollified these differences to some degree, as individuals from rural areas and from the west can travel to jobs in the export economy of the eastern seaboard. These individuals may do better in eastern factories or in construction jobs in urban centers like Shanghai than they do in their rural villages, but they are nevertheless the system's underclass. As China's economy makes its way on the path toward capitalism, there will be many winners and many losers within this system—but then, this is the fate of virtually all market economies around the world.

7

ECONOMIC REFORM, RULE OF LAW, AND THE PROSPECTS FOR DEMOCRACY

In the late 1980s, after nearly a decade of economic reform in China, many observers believed that political evolution would be part of an inevitable process. The liberalization of the economy had led to a new and dramatic sense of freedom in Chinese society. New laws brought a new sense of structure to social and political worlds, which only two decades before had been dominated by totalitarian caprice. Although the political elites in China maintained that they were not sure where the reforms were headed, it seemed increasingly clear what the endpoint would be. The direction of the reforms was toward a liberal economy and a democratic political system. And, although the world did not know it (though perhaps many sensed it), 1989 would be a watershed year in the transformation of political systems around the world. After a decade of economic reform in China, the country, like those in Eastern Europe, was poised for a radical transformation, one that would redress the ills that had been visited upon the population by the capricious authoritarian rule of the 1960s and 1970s.

In 1989, these visions were crushed by the images of tanks rumbling through the streets of Beijing, unleashing a destructive terror on student activists who had pushed the regime one step too far. In response to their bid to push this regime through the door of democratic reform, the Chinese government showed the students—and the world—that democratic reform was nowhere on the agenda. We were reminded with clarity that this was still an authoritarian regime and that its leaders would do as they pleased on the road to economic and political reform. As victorious images of peaceful regime changes in Eastern Europe followed in the wake of the Tiananmen Square massacre, the world was left to wonder what the fate of political reform in China would be. Those events unfolded during the first year of my life as a China scholar. As an undergraduate at the University of Chicago, I was on my way to completing my first year of intensive Chinese when the reform-minded Hu Yaobang's funeral march became the catalyst for this democracy movement. The images from CNN are still so clear in my mind from those six weeks in the Spring of 1989. When that optimistic moment suddenly transformed into images of tanks, wounded students, and blood, I felt devastated. But I was also hooked; there was so much to learn, so much to understand. Three weeks after that event, I had taken a leave of absence from Chicago and was on a plane to Taiwan to spend a year immersing myself in Chinese language and culture.

A few years later, when I was living in Shanghai in the mid-1990s conducting my doctoral dissertation research, I constantly ran up against the contradictions and tensions of a radically changing system built on the foundations of an authoritarian regime. Sometimes, it would seem that I could move about with the same freedom that I could in any democratic society. But then, when my comfort had risen to a level that would allow me to forget that I was living in an authoritarian society, a warning would come from some quarter, that I was being tracked by the Public Security Bureau. These experiences were always profoundly disturbing, as they often left me wondering who among my acquaintances was reporting on my behavior to higher authorities. Most foreign researchers have a similar sort of tale. Yet, I could not deny the fact that the China I was operating in was so much freer than the closed society foreigners had begun to enter in the late 1970s. It was a place where I was able to visit factories without a chaperoning government official, and the authorities would not restrict or limit my behavior. Still, they would watch very closely. It was a society with many new formal laws and regulations, where managers of state-owned enterprises were exhorted to take advantage of new opportunities—to "link up with the international community"—but their actions would be monitored by the watchful eye of the state.

This is the way of reform in China; a gradual measured process that begins with broad, sweeping changes from above, as the state reshapes the institutional frameworks that govern society. But these broad, sweeping changes are often vague and experimental, and they have always stopped short of a program that might threaten the one-party government. And within the context of these new institutional frameworks, the party-state itself remains conservative and seemingly averse to change. But these institutional changes have also created the space for a gradual and incremental transformation of the world from below. In our desire to see something dramatic, as we did in Eastern Europe in 1989, we have ignored the extent to which, and the ways that, political change has come about in China. In this chapter, I will examine the political changes that are occurring within the country. I will look at the process of democratic reform, in general, but I will be especially concerned with how this process is related to the economic reforms. The economic reforms are, in a very basic sense, the catalyst that set this "quiet revolution" in motion.[1] And while the state took a very strong—and brutal—position against radical political change in 1989, the transformation of Chinese politics and society has continued unabated since the economic reforms began in 1979.

While my focus throughout this chapter will be on the relationship between economic and political change in China, I will begin with a discussion of the Tiananmen movement of 1989, as any discussion of the transition to democracy in China would seem incomplete without a discussion of the Tiananmen movement and the subsequent governmental crackdown. I will follow that discussion with a more general examination of the relationship between economic and political change and will then explore other areas of institutional change, including the emergence of new legal regimes and the emergence of democratic institutions and practices at the local level and the role of political elites within these processes of change. Finally, I will discuss the emergence of a democratic society as it relates to the building of institutions that support democracy, namely, a legal infrastructure that supports the rule of law. In our rush to see transitions to democracy in this country, we often forget that democracy is a complex system that rests on many institutions that must be built and learned over time. Some of these institutions take a generation to build and even longer to settle in to the everyday practices of the society they govern.

Popular Movements for Democracy in China

China has a long history of agitation for democratic reform from below. Since the May Fourth Movement of 1919, when some 3,000 students

organized a protest in Tiananmen Square objecting to the Warlord government's acceptance of the terms of the Treaty of Versailles, public demands
for political and social reform have been an integral part of the Chinese
political process. Indeed, on the eve of the economic reforms in China,
Deng Xiaoping actually rode one such popular movement to power, the
Democracy Wall Movement of 1978–1979, until the movement turned a
critical eye on Deng himself, at which point Deng turned on the movement. As Deng was securing his position of power, the most radical participants in that movement, which included the now-famous dissident Wei
Jingsheng, were extending the protest beyond a call for economic reforms
to a criticism of China's ruling elite and the political system. While a call
for economic reform benefited Deng Xiaoping as he shored up his position
of power over Hua Guofeng, a call for democratic reform was a threat, and
the radicals of this protest were jailed.

In 1989, a protest for democratic reform followed in this tradition, but
it was a protest that substantially diverged from its predecessors. In the
spring of that year, as the world's attention turned toward Beijing, we
watched, riveted, as a million Chinese students occupied Tiananmen
Square in a struggle for democracy.[2] At first glance, this student-led movement looked simply like another movement in a long history of student-
led advocacy for democratic reform, dating back to the May Fourth
Movement. But the broad participation and sustained activism of this
movement was of a different order of magnitude from the recent movements of 1976, 1979, and 1986. More important, beyond the students
themselves, this movement engaged millions of "ordinary citizens" (Strand
1990) in ways that previous movements had not. The result was a political
movement of unprecedented proportions in the People's Republic of
China.[3]

In the aftermath of this movement, as its images spread across the
globe—images of the young dead, of bloody students being carried to
makeshift ambulances, of giant tanks rolling callously over bicycles and the
other articles left behind by the student demonstrators—the world was
left to wonder what the events of 1989 meant for China. The issues I raise
here are useful starting points for a general discussion of democratic development in the era of China's economic reforms, for several reasons. First,
an understanding of this specific social movement is critical for a discussion of the emergence of democracy in China because it was, by its very

nature—both in terms of its content and the state's ultimate response to this movement—about the road toward democratic reform. Understanding what happened in this movement brings to bear many of the issues that surround democratic reform in China's transforming economy and society. Many of these issues have been explored by prominent scholars who have studied this moment of social protest. Second, the symbols and images of this movement have become inextricably linked to the struggle for, and transition to, democracy. The images have, for many, been etched in our minds: Tiananmen Square overflowing with more than a million students, all committed to waiting there until the government heard their cries for reform; the students standing by as the "Goddess of Democracy" was installed in Tiananmen Square; the student hunger strikers, tired, ragged, and hospitalized; the People's Liberation Army marching on Tiananmen Square; and a lone student staring down a phalanx of tanks on Changan Avenue. Third, and perhaps most important for my discussion here, this movement itself is a window into the societal transformation that occurred as a result of the reforms that had taken place over the first decade of economic transition in China. A decade after Tiananmen Square, it still seemed, on the surface, that little progress had been made. The summer of 1999 saw the crackdown on the religious movement Falun Gong and the jailing of Democratic Party organizers Xu Wenli and Qin Yongmin. During that decade, China was subjected to the annual wrangling over its trade status with the United States. In many ways, this movement reveals fundamental things about the structural changes in Chinese society over the course of the 1980s and beyond.

A Timeline of the Events of the Tiananmen Movement of 1989[4]

The 1989 Tiananmen movement erupted with the death of Hu Yaobang, a former handpicked successor of Deng Xiaoping and the governmental scapegoat for the 1986–1987 democracy demonstrations. Because of Hu's political demise in 1987, many in China viewed him as a symbol of democratic reform, and his death brought about a groundswell of renewed support for reform. On April 17, two days after Hu's death, a group of students marched to the National People's Congress with a list of demands, which included restoring Hu Yaobang's reputation, guaranteeing freedom of speech, freedom of the press, and the right to peaceful demonstrations, and ending corruption among party officials. Over the next week a number

of small demonstrations occurred: one was linked to Hu's memorial ceremony on April 22; one involved a sit-in at Xinhuamen, the governmental
compound, and ended in police beating the students; and one was a gathering of some 10,000 students at Beijing University to discuss strategies.
On April 27, the movement took on a scale of a different order, as protesters
led 150,000 students through police lines to Tiananmen Square; according
to some reports, some 350,000 Beijing residents lined the streets offering
support for the students (Shen 1990). On May 4, several hundred journalists from several Beijing publications joined the students in a march to the
square, calling for freedom of the press; the occupation of Tiananmen
Square extended from this point onward. That same day, intellectuals from
several universities submitted a written manifesto in support of the movement. On May 13, some 3,000 students began a hunger strike in the
square, stating that they would fast until the government met them in
equal dialogue. Crowds swelled, and by May 17, estimates placed the
number of protesters in the square at around 1 million. The movement at
this point was not limited to students, as workers and "ordinary citizens"
were now participating in the movement in large numbers. A meeting
between Wuer Kaixi and Li Peng, which was broadcast nationally, occurred
on May 18. That same day, the independent Workers' Autonomous
Federation officially declared itself part of the movement. Li Peng declared
martial law on May 20, and on May 22, journalists and intellectuals
demonstrated in the square, calling for Li Peng's resignation. On May 26,
Zhao Ziyang was labeled an instigator of the movement and dismissed
from all of his Communist Party positions. On May 29, the students
brought "The Goddess of Democracy" statue into the square, and on
May 30 the government issued an official statement that condemned the
statue and the movement as a whole. On June 3, the government issued an
ultimatum saying that if the people did not leave the Square, they would
suffer the consequences. The government carried out a military crackdown
on the night of June 3 and in the early hours of June 4.

Institutional Change and the Decline of Party Power: Understanding the Tiananmen Movement of 1989

While the events of the Tiananmen movement are fairly straightforward,
understanding the underlying societal changes that caused this movement—or, rather, that allowed such a movement to emerge on such an

unprecedented scale—is ultimately a much more fruitful task for our understanding of the changes occurring within Chinese society. The scale and scope of this movement were intimately tied to the changes that had been occurring over the course of a decade of economic reforms in China. Andrew Walder's (1994a) essay articulating an institutional theory of regime change in transforming communist societies is relevant to the discussion here. Walder points out that while the emergence of civil societies, public spheres, economic grievances, and political instability may have contributed to movement activity in communist societies in the late 1980s, these phenomena were nothing new to these societies. And while these elements were important for the groundswell of support for movement activities in these societies, deeper changes were occurring that made these movement activities possible in the first place. As Walder puts it,

> [A] theory of political order is a necessary starting point for any theory of change. There must have been institutional mechanisms that served to maintain order in the old regime in spite of long-standing and obvious economic problems and political liabilities; and these institutions must have been eroded in ways we do not yet understand. The current emphasis upon the triumph of "society" over "the state" tends to obscure the logically prior question of how such a triumph, if it is that, could occur . . . [W]hat changed in these regimes in the last decade was not their economic difficulties, widespread cynicism, or corruption, but that the institutional mechanisms that served to promote order in the past—despite these longstanding problems—lost their capacity to do so.
>
> (1994a, 298)

Economic grievances and political struggles have played long-standing roles in communist societies, and they therefore cannot be viewed as causal agents in unprecedented movement activity or social change. The point here is that an analysis of regime change must begin with the underlying mechanisms that kept these regimes stable and, as they changed, eventually allowed for large-scale social upheavals. Walder goes on to specify the mechanisms that were crucial for maintaining order in communist societies as (1) hierarchically organized and grass-roots mobility of the Communist Party and (2) the organized dependence of individuals within social institutions—particularly workplaces. With the beginning of the economic reforms in China, both of these institutional bases of power began to erode. In the first case—the decline of party power—there are two ways this change had profound implications for the organization of Chinese society. First, the party no longer had strict control over its own agents. Party cadres operated with an autonomy that increasingly grew in scope throughout the 1980s. This was, in large part, a direct consequence of the movement away from the central planning of the command economy. As the reforms progressed, the new economic policies of the 1980s essentially mandated that local-level bureaucrats assume administrative and economic responsibilities for the firms under their jurisdictions (Walder 1995e; Guthrie 1997, 1999). As administrative and economic responsibilities were pushed down in the hierarchy of the former command economy, local-level bureaucrats exercised more and more power in the struggle to control resources and survive in the markets of China's transforming economy. In many cases, local-level bureaucrats abused this new autonomy, leading to the corruption that was one of the central problems in what has been called the crisis of succession (Calhoun 1995); this corruption was a central complaint of the student leaders in 1989. Thus, the institutional changes of the reform economy led to the decline of central party control over its own members.

Second, and perhaps more important, the party no longer exercised grassroots control over individual citizens. In pre-reform China, the party meticulously exercised grassroots control through local party meetings, usually conducted through an individual's work unit or neighborhood association (Whyte and Parish 1984; Walder 1986a). In the reform era, this centrally mandated practice eroded quickly. Managers and administrators no longer required their workers to attend meetings for the dissemination of party ideology. This change is closely related to the institutional changes of the economic transition described above: as economic imperatives replaced strict compliance with detailed directives of the party, managers and administrators began to run their organizations less around the dissemination of party ideology and more around the ideals of performance. Dingxin Zhao (1997) makes a similar point in his study of the 1989 Chinese movement. Arguing that it is problematic to place causal primacy on China's nascent civil society, Zhao, like Walder, pushes the analysis to the underlying mechanisms that allowed a civil society to emerge in the first place: the declining control of the party on university campuses, as well as in the workplace.[5] Zhao argues that "the political control system in Chinese universities was greatly weakened between the mid- and late 1980s. This weakening had changed patterns of student interaction and the nature of the control system itself; in turn, it facilitated the rise of the 1989 [movement]" (1997, 161). Craig Calhoun (1995), a firsthand observer of the movement, notes that the university campuses themselves had become an important part of the "free space" that facilitated the students' organizational activities—a situation that was very different from the era before the economic reforms began. It was only through the institutional shifts, of which the declining power of the party-state apparatus were a part, that the use of such state-controlled spaces as "free spaces" could be possible. An emphasis on the structural decline of party control over students' lives is not to eschew the importance of student agency in this movement: central to the students' understanding of democracy was an active rejection of the Communist Party's invasion into private life, and, chafing under the lingering (though much diminished) effects of party control, the students rebelled against it.

In addition to the declining role of the party on university campuses, one of the major mechanisms weakening the sanctioning power of the party was the rise of alternative paths to status attainment, which came with an expanding economic sphere (Walder 1994a; Zhao 1997). Under the command economy, students entering the labor market were assigned jobs by their municipality's labor bureau, an administrative office of the party-state. The system was highly political, and the most prestigious jobs were jobs in the party-state bureaucracy. This included upper-level management jobs in enterprises, as virtually all organizations in the command economy were state-run and university appointments; prestigious jobs across all of these sectors were essentially political appointments. Thus, the party not only had a highly functioning monitoring system on university campuses, but the incentives against rebellion were very strong: consequences were nothing less than a blocked career path for life, regardless of a student's academic performance.

With the economic reforms came alternative paths to status attainment. The growth of private, foreign, and joint-venture economies offered students many options for employment, and the managers of these organizations cared little about a student's adherence to political norms. Of the six movement leaders jailed after the Tiananmen Square protest who were interviewed in Zhao's study, none reported difficulties in finding jobs in the aftermath. In addition, Zhao reports that many other student leaders had simply left Beijing and moved to the prosperous southern provinces to find work.[6] In another example, Shen Tong (1990, 142–145, 209), a student leader in 1989, who wrote a confessional statement for his participation in earlier political activities and fretted about the effects of his political activities on his career, openly defied the government's attempt at controlling his activity in the 1989 movement. The main point here is that with the declining monitoring capacity of the Communist Party and the erosion of the party's sanctioning power, the primary incentives against political activity were largely gone by 1989.

Thus, the causal mechanisms through which we should understand the explosion of this protest for democracy are broad-based institutional changes that came with economic transition. Turning administrative and economic responsibilities over to the individual managers and workers, a coinciding decline of grass-roots party organization and surveillance, and the rise of alternative paths to status all changed the equation of protest participation. In other words, while the content of this movement—the demand for democratic reform—is important and noteworthy, the very size, scale, and form that the movement could take on in its cry for democracy were intimately tied to economic reforms themselves. With these fundamental institutional changes came a few other ancillary changes, which were critical facets of the movement that emerged.

Alternative Forms of Organization

In a tightly run command economy such as that of pre-reform China, the party-state apparatus pervades society. As the party-state receded from economic and social control, it is in the void left by declining Communist Party power that we began to see autonomous organizations and the makings of a civil society. In other words, it was a many-year trend of declining Communist Party power that led to increasingly autonomous organizations among students and citizens alike. Since the mid-1980s a number of different informal student organizations emerged to chart the path to democratic reform. "Democracy salons," "democracy associations," and various "action committees" were proliferating on college campuses at least as early as 1986; informal "conversation associations" began emerging even earlier (Shen 1990). These informal organizations served to create an indigenous organizational structure that would allow this movement to mobilize much more rapidly and gather much greater momentum than had movements of the recent past. Beyond helping to foster a type of civil society that stood outside the party structure, these organizations prepared students for more concrete organizational activity when the movement began. And at the movement's beginning, many of the students who were involved in these informal networks and organizations stepped into leadership roles in the Beijing University Student Association, the Dialogue Delegation, the United Leadership Federation, the preparatory committees from numerous university campuses, and the student-run journalism bureau (Shen 1990; Guthrie 1995). Further, these organizational structures not only allowed the students to conduct crucial practices such as fund-raising but also allowed them to strategize and deploy symbols and signals that fostered a more widespread mobilization among the citizens of Beijing (Guthrie 1995).

The rise of private entrepreneurs and enterprises also played a crucial role as organizational forces outside the party-state apparatus. The state's decision to allow private enterprises and entrepreneurs to enter the economy in the reform era also helped foster the autonomous public sphere that was emerging in the mid-1980s. These individuals stood outside the party-state and they were prepared to support and foster movement activity when the opportunity arose. The state had no control over their resources, and there were no disincentives against this group maligning the state, as they had already rejected the mechanisms and channels through which individuals are typically rewarded by the party-state. As the movement got under way, private corporations, such as the Stone Corporation, one of the largest private enterprises in Beijing, contributed significant material resources—money and electronic equipment—that proved crucial to the widespread mobilization that occurred (Perry and Wasserstrom 1991).

Economic Change of Political Reform in China: Lessons from Tiananmen Square

What, then, does this movement tell us about the prospects for democracy in China and the extent to which these changes are connected to the economic reforms? While the majority of scholarship on this movement has focused on what it reveals about divisions within the government and the ways that the students mobilized on such a massive scale, I find the movement most revealing about the nature of the economic reforms themselves. These reforms have laid the groundwork to make political reform all but inevitable.

The Declining Role of the Party

First, as I discussed in Chapter 2, economic decision-making and autonomy in markets had to be handed over to economic actors in China's newly emerging marketplaces. This was a necessary step in the reform of the command economy: if managers of state enterprises were ultimately going to survive in markets without the insurance and expectation of state subsidies, they would have to learn to make economic decisions themselves. A corollary of this economic necessity, however, was that the party was forced to remove itself from the micro-level political control it carried out in workplaces. Managers could not be expected to take seriously the notion of economic independence from the state if party officials remained present in the workplace, looking over their shoulders at every step. The thinking in Beijing was that the party's function and capacity as the nation's political institution would remain as before—that economic reform need not lead to political reform. However, a declining role of the party in workplaces meant a declining capacity of the party for micro-level social control.

The declining role of the party as an agent of social control was also a necessary precondition for the emergence of a civil society in China. Calhoun's analysis of the emergence of civil society in China prior to 1989 makes a compelling case for the inverse relationship between civil society and state control. According to Calhoun (1995, 167),

> The 1989 protest movement was possible because students were able to deploy existing organizational networks for purposes quite contrary to official policy. They were able to do so partly because individuals and groups within the government and party encouraged them, protected them, or turned a blind eye to their activities ... These middle-level officials were central to the organization of society.

But in the years preceding this movement, the students not only benefited from the existing organizational structure of Chinese society but also created civil society through alternative forms of organization. Student leader Shen Tong's report of the movement tells of many organized groups that fostered the insurgency that occurred in 1989: there were the Beijing University Student Association, the Dialogue Delegation, the United Leadership Federation, and Preparatory Committees on numerous university campuses. Perhaps more important, there were "democracy salons," "democracy associations," and "action committees" that were emerging at least as early as 1986 (Shen 1990). The gradual recession of the party-state apparatus left an opening that allowed citizens of China to create this kind of civil order.

Emergence of a Private Economy

Second, a central component in the course of China's economic reforms was the emergence of a private economy (also discussed in Chapters 2 and 4), and with the emergence of a private economy came alternative career paths for individuals (see also Figure 7.3). People no longer had to rely solely on the state for the allocation of prestigious jobs; instead, they could look to the private sector for opportunities. This change further eroded the party's capacity for social control, as it struck at the primary mechanism through which the party exercised that control. To be sure, terror has played an important role in the party's capacity for social control in China. Indeed, every decade since the founding of the People's Republic of China has been marked by at least one campaign in which innocent individuals have been crushed by the government for showing even nominal opposition to the party-state. However, the deeper level of control within the system came not from terror but from everyday incentives that worked at the individual level. Thus, when people chose not to rebel within this system, they were choosing not to sacrifice their path or opening into the institutions of the party-state system, such as employment and lifetime security. But as the party-state's monopoly over paths to employment eroded, the government lost another critical node of micro-level social control. As individuals began making money within this new private economy, we eventually saw the emergence of what amounts to an economically secure, autonomous middle class (Goodman 1999).

The Free Flow of Information: Market Influences

The final element that was crucial in the Tiananmen movement, but is also fundamental on a more general level, is access to, and the free flow of, information. In a tightly controlled command economy such as China's before the economic reforms began, the party-state's control over the flow of information is absolutely crucial to its monopoly as a political system. However, a market economy cannot exist without the free flow of information: people not only need access to multiple sources of information to make choices and comparisons in the marketplace but also must understand that the free flow of information has become institutionalized as a feature of the social system in which this newly emerging market is embedded. But as the party-state's monopoly over information erodes and the free flow of alternative sources of information becomes institutionalized, a third crucial element of the party's program of social and political control becomes compromised as well. Over the last two decades of reform in China, there has been a dramatic proliferation of alternative sources of information. Table 7.1 shows not only the rise in access to alternative forms of information outside the party-state's control, but also in the types of information and media that are available in China today. It is striking to note that as television news programs have increased significantly in Chinese society (from 7,000 in 1985 to 675,885 in 2009), access to these programs has increased in the same dramatic fashion.

Another example of the politics surrounding the evolution of information in China has to do with the extent to which this sector has remained under tighter control than in other rapidly developing industries. This sector is monitored closely by the central government for a variety of reasons. First, it is a sector in which very significant technological transfers are occurring in joint-venture deals between foreign and Chinese firms. The Chinese government knows all too well that as big as the Chinese market for IT portends to be, it is this market that foreign investors are after. Hard-line leaders would like to limit the extent to which foreign producers, such as Motorola and Nokia, are able to control that market, and the state's plan is for Chinese companies, such as Huawei and ZTE, to eventually be able to compete with these foreign companies. Yet, the government also knows that it needs the technology that companies like Motorola and Nokia can deliver. As a result, the close monitoring of this sector has become a central part of the process of development occurring within it. And when it has become apparent that certain companies are doing too well, it has not been beyond the government to step in and level the playing field some.[7] Second, and perhaps more important, because the

Table 7.1 The Flow of Information

	1980	1985	1990	1995	1997	2001	2005	2009
No. of magazines published	2,191	4,705	5,751	7,583	7,918	8,889	9,468	9,851
No. of newspapers published	188	1,445	1,444	2,089	2,149	2,111	1,931	1,937
No. of books published	21,621	45,603	80,224	101,381	120,106	154,526	222,473	301,719
News programs (radio, hours)	NA	65,995[1]	135,550[1]	353,368	429,069	483,631	1,066,800	1,116,848
News programs (TV, hours)	NA	7,444[1]	28,593[1]	80,800	116,593	235,336	637,956	675,885
Entertainment programs (TV, hours)	NA	6,957[1]	22,096[1]	109,322	225,124	191,154	382,350	402,677
TVs per 100 households	1.1[2]	17.2	59	86	90	NA	135	136

Source: National Statistical Bureau of China (2010, 348, 843, 848)

[1] National Statistical Bureau of China (2000, 712)

[2] National Statistical Bureau of China (1989, 728, refers to 1982 data).

telecommunications industry provides an infrastructure for the spread of information, the government is clearly afraid of completely losing control over individuals' access to information. Accordingly, telecommunications is the last sector to be closed to foreign capital, as Chinese law still forbids foreign capital in this sector.[8] It is for this reason that exceedingly complicated deals have been worked out in the establishment of companies in this sector, as in the case of Sina.com.[9] In addition, telecommunications is the sector that has been the target of the most aggressive regulations and control among all industries in China (with the exception of tobacco).

There has unquestionably been a great deal of activity in the IT sector in recent years. However, before looking at the development of new information technologies, per se, let us first take into account the spread of information more generally. Table 7.2 presents some indicators of the growth in access to information in China over the last two decades. For both newspapers and magazines, the growth has been exponential over the two-decade time frame, with the number of newspapers expanding from 186 in 1978 to 1,937 in 2009 and magazines expanding from 930 to 9,851 over the same period. Television programs have seen greater than exponential growth over this period, with 38,056 programs in 1985 growing to 2,653,552 programs in 2009. While these media are not typically placed in the category of new IT, they are indicative of an important trend of growing access to information and thus relevant for any discussion about information and social change.

Table 7.3 shows the growth in IT since the economic reforms began two decades ago. Use of pagers, mobile telephones, email, and the Internet, and the development of optical and digital cable lines—all important aspects of a growing IT economy in China—have expanded dramatically in this period. The growth in pager and mobile phone use has been rapid in the last couple of decades: both of these forms of technology were basically nonexistent in China in the mid-1980s, but pager use grew to about 48 million subscribers in 2000 before tapering off to the emergence of the cell phone industry. The use of mobile telephones has undergone extreme growth since 1999, growing to approximately 116 million subscribers as of June 2001, according to Lou Qinjian, vice minister for China's information industry, and to nearly 750 million in 2009.[10] The penetration of these technologies, while dramatic, is not surprising: in developing societies around the world, as mobile technology has grown, it has been much faster

Table 7.2 Access to Media of Information in China

	Magazines	*Newspapers*	*Television*
1978	930	186	–
1980	2,191	188	–
1985	4,705	1,445	38,056
1986	5,248	1,574	–
1987	5,687	1,611	–
1988	5,865	1,537	–
1989	6,078	1,576	–
1990	5,751	1,444	91,572
1991	6,056	1,524	–
1992	6,486	1,657	–
1993	6,486	1,788	–
1994	7,011	1,953	–
1995	7,325	2,089	383,513
1996	7,583	2,163	–
1997	7,918	2,149	616,437
1998	7,999	2,053	477,893
1999	8,187	2,038	526,483
2000	8,725	2,007	1,026,214*
2001	8,889	2,111	989,173*
2002	9,029	2,137	1,072,704*
2003	0,074	2,119	1,185,507*
2004	9,490	1,922	2,117,158*
2005	9,468	1,931	2,553,861
2006	9,468	1,938	2,618,034
2007	9.468	1,938	2,553,283
2008	9,549	1,943	2,641,949
2009	9,851	1,937	2,653,552

Source: National Statistical Bureau of China (2000, 712–714, 1978–1999 data; 2005, 754, 2001–2004 Television data; 2010, 848, 2000–2009 data).

and easier to implement mobile technology as the primary form of communication than it has to lay grounded lines. Given the recent introduction of mobile phone technology into China, the growth in this area has been truly dramatic—70 percent of the more than one billion phones in China are mobile phones—and virtually all industry experts agree that

Table 7.3 Growth of Information Technology in China[1]

	Email Subscribers	Internet Subscribers	Pagers[2]	Mobile phones	Land-line phones	Optical Cable Lines	Digital Lines
1978	0	0	0	0	3,868,200	0	0
1980	0	0	0	0	4,186,400	0	0
1985	0	0	0	0	6,259,800	0	0
1986	0	0	0	0	7,059,100	0	0
1987	0	0	30,900	0	8,057,200	0	0
1988	0	0	97,200	3,200	9,417,900	2,717	0
1989	0	0	237,300	9,800	10,893,300	5,670	0
1990	0	0	437,000	18,300	12,313,300	11,453	0
1991	0	0	873,800	47,500	14,544,300	23,613	0
1992	0	0	2,220,200	176,900	18,459,600	51,352	109,300
1993	0	0	5,614,000	639,300	25,673,500	162,861	298,045
1994	2,329	0	10,330,000	1,567,800	38,018,600	330,359	518,915
1995	6,068	7,213	17,391,500	3,629,400	53,993,200	484,231	677,672
1996	10,107	35,652	23,562,000	6,852,800	70,467,500	754,143	965,263
1997	15,246	160,157	32,546,100	13,232,900	87,878,300	935,835	1,139,476
1998	20,959	676,755	39,081,600	23,862,900	107,371,500	1,351,665	1,560,201
1999	19,855	3,014,518	46,744,700	43,296,000	132,378,400	NA	NA

2000	22,500,000	NA	48,843,000	84,533,000	144,829,000	NA	NA
2001	33,700,000	NA	3,606,400	116,000,000[3]	180,358,000	NA	NA
2002	59,100,000	NA	1,872,100	206,005,000	214,222,000	NA	NA
2003	79,500,000	NA	1,057,600	269,953,000	262,747,000	NA	NA
2004	94,000,000	NA	395,000	334,824,000	311,756,000	NA	NA
2005	111,000,000	NA	97,100	393,406,000	350,445,000	NA	NA
2006	137,000,000	NA	NA	461,058,000	367,786,000	NA	NA
2007	210,000,000	NA	NA	547,306,000	365,637,000	NA	NA
2008	298,000,000	NA	NA	641,245,000	340,359,000	NA	NA
2009	384,000,000	NA	NA	747,214,000	313,732,000	NA	NA

[1]National Statistical Bureau of China (2000, 543–546, 1978–1999 data).

[2]National Statistical Bureau of China (2006, 644, 2000–2005 data). National Statistical Bureau of China (2010, 658, 2000–2009 data, except where otherwise noted).

[3]*China Daily*, June 26, 2001, 5.

the country will very soon become the largest market in the world for mobile telephones. It is also likely that the figures for mobile phones are underrepresented, as the numbers listed here are those of subscribers to official services, and the unregistered mobile phone market is huge in China. Estimates on just how big this market is do not exist, but one need only go through the process of buying a secondhand phone and setting up an unregistered account to understand just how popular this practice is.

With the relatively low level of personal computer use in China, it is somewhat surprising that there are more than 3 million registered Internet users. Yet, as with the mobile phone reports, it is also likely here that the figures on the Internet are underrepresented, as the most popular Internet web sites in China are those that do not require subscriber registration. Instead, the majority of Chinese gaining access to the Internet today do so through a pay-per-minute service provided by their phone company, in which a user can log on anonymously from any phone and access the Internet or publicly maintained email accounts on one of the main Internet portals. For example, "163," "263," and "169" all allow users to gain access to the Internet without establishing a subscriber account. Table 7.3 also shows the developmental trends of the infrastructure that supports such IT as the Internet and optical cable and digital lines; the growth has been from nothing to more than a million lines each, in just over a decade. Currently China has the highest level of Internet traffic of any country in the world, and the projections of growth in this area stand to create an even more lopsided picture: with 384 million Internet subscribers in 2009, a number of market analysis firms that specialize in digital growth and e-commerce project that China will have 840 million individuals online, more than the United States, Japan, and Europe combined.[11]

The bird's-eye view of the information presented above tells us quite a bit. First, the spread of information more generally in China has occurred in dramatic ways over the course of the economic reforms; second, IT itself is spreading in significant ways in Chinese society, and this spread includes both individual users' access as well as the hardware and infrastructure that is necessary for the further development of the industry. Taken together, this means that access to information and the high-tech vehicles that facilitate communication and the sharing of information are significant forces in Chinese society. In addition, the high-tech sectors of the economy, including telecommunications, are among the most active in terms of foreign investment. The question before us now is what, if any, implications do these changes have for Chinese society, for the capacity of the Chinese state to control its population, and for the process of democratization in China?

The Free Flow of Information: Political Influences

In any society, access to information has a significant impact on general perceptions of the social and political world. In a one-party system such as China's, where an authoritarian party-state kept strict control over the media, information did not flow freely. On the contrary: in the years before the economic reforms began, the state controlled all media, so the only information available was the information that the government wanted its citizens to know. Over the course of the 1980s, the state's grip on the media—and therefore on information—began to loosen. In the Tiananmen movement, access to information proved to be pivotal in the large-scale mobilization that occurred in the spring of 1989. The 1980s saw a dramatic rise in alternative sources of information. Access to information is important because it allows individuals to find and adjudicate among different accounts of events. More than this, however, access to alternative sources of information encourages opinions. The fact that individuals had access to accounts of the student-led democracy movement that varied from the accounts portrayed in the state media allowed citizens to decide for themselves whether they believed the students' intentions were noble and good. In this particular movement, there were two additional instances of the free flow of information that proved pivotal. First, in the 1989 movement, the state-controlled media itself was not unified on its reporting. As elite factions within the party leadership struggled over how to deal with this movement—one faction, led by reformer Zhao Ziyang, sought to use this event to accelerate the pace of reforms, while another faction, led by hardliner Li Peng, sought to use this event to roll back the pace of reforms— the media were paralyzed over which party line to follow in their reporting. The result was, for a brief moment, a state press that reported as objectively and sympathetically as possible. As Walder (1989a, 38) has noted, the media's "detailed and sympathetic reporting" on the hunger strikers "riveted the city's attention on the drama . . . building a huge groundswell of popular support." Second, and perhaps more important, there was, quite coincidentally, a large contingent of foreign media present in Beijing to cover the summit meetings with Russian premier Mikhail Gorbachev and the Asia Development Bank meetings. These members of the media played a critical role not only in broadcasting the images of the movement to the world but also in spreading information and images of the movement to people throughout China. In that sense, the presence of a global media machine played a crucial role in facilitating the flow of information about the movement, thus allowing the movement itself to spin beyond the control of party officials.

While the causal roots of this movement lay in institutional changes that had been occurring for a decade, the free flow of information was also important in the evolution. In a certain sense, though, by allowing foreign media to cover the Gorbachev summit and the Asia Development Bank meetings and by giving the population access to technology—fax machines, telephones, and so on—the Chinese government had inserted itself into a global information network, and its inability to control the flow of information had important consequences for the extent to which it could control the movement. The Chinese government had, in effect, armed its opposition with the tools of resistance, and when the movement occurred, the government could not stop the flow of information beyond its borders, a fact that had profound consequences for the scale and scope of this movement.

More recently, a number of social and political occurrences involving the Internet have illuminated the new role that this form of information technology (IT) might play in the state's ability to control information. In one incident, when China's top official from the State Administration of Foreign Exchange apparently jumped from his seventh-story window on May 12, 2000, government officials were caught completely off guard as the story was posted almost immediately on a bulletin board on the widely visited Sina.com website. According to Elisabeth Rosenthal's report in the *New York Times*, "The government was clearly not prepared to release the news today, and confusion reigned for much of the day." A similar incident occurred when the story of a Beijing University student who was murdered appeared on a Sohu.com bulletin board on May 19, 2000. In the latter incident, students from all over the country staged a "virtual" protest, forcing officials to allow them to openly mourn and memorialize the student, despite the disruptions officials feared the event would cause. In both of these cases, it was clear that the government's mentality regarding control over the flow of information was lagging significantly behind the current reality in this realm. This is a new frontier for outright resistance, and it will be interesting to see, over the coming decade, what role the Internet plays in the government's ability to control the spread of information and the organization of popular movements.

Other Elements of Institutional Change

To this point, I have described the critical elements of the economic reforms that have led to a decline in the level of political and social control that China's one-party government is capable of. To summarize these: (1) economic autonomy yielded to enterprise managers led to a necessary decline in the Communist Party's capacity as an agent of micro-level social control; (2) the emergence of a private economy allowed for alternative career paths outside the system of state allocation; and (3) the free flow of information allowed individuals to have access to images and knowledge from the world outside China's borders. These key changes have had cascading effects that have led to changes in the composition of society, all of which make the continuing evolution toward political reform inevitable at this point. However, other major institutional changes have also worked hand in hand with these economic changes, and they, too, have been a necessary part of the reform process. In the sections that follow, I will discuss these critical changes and their role in what Minxin Pei (1995) has called "creeping democratization in China."

Bureaucratizing Government Institutions

The National People's Congress (NPC) and its local branches, the People's Congresses (PCs), are China's legislative organizations. In a democratic system of checks and balances, like that found in the United States, the legislative branch operates autonomously from the executive branch, a key factor in the balance of power that defines the system. One question we might be concerned with in the gradual evolution of a democratic system in China is whether governmental organizations are operating with more autonomy than in years past. Founded in 1954, the NPC was a central institution of China's governmental system, and in the early years of the reforms, the NPC was little more than a rubber stamp for the party, much the way legislatures often behaved in Leninist political systems. Indeed, the NPC became such a pro forma institution, passing whatever legislation was brought before it by the party, that Chinese people referred to it as a "hand-raising machine" (Tanner 1999), and it seemed to operate in much the same way that it did prior to the reforms. In the 1990s, however, we saw the maturing of this institution in its capacity to operate independent of—and sometimes in opposition to—the party government. Debate has become so common in the workings of this institution that it seems, in fact, to operate in many ways like a legislature of a full-fledged democracy (O'Brien 1990; Pei 1994, 1995; Tanner 1994, 1999).

While the evolution of the NPC as a democratic institution has been gradual and incremental—as has the evolution of the Chinese economy—the changes are fundamental and real, and they amount to nothing less than the gradual transition to a democratic legislature in China. As political scientist Kevin O'Brien (1990, 11) puts it, "A changing legislature attests to a changing polity ... Altered legislative involvement in law making, supervision, representation, and regime support signals a system-wide redivision of political tasks." The first major change in the NPC relates to the liberalization of the legislature from the broader political system. This is a crucial step in the democratization of a country, because a democratic government must have independent branches that act as a system of checks and balances on the decisions of any powerful group within the government. In the case of China, this transformation is essential for the continued evolution of the political system, because the party has traditionally wielded so much power in the structure of the nation's society and that power has been completely uncontested in the past. As the economic reforms have progressed, the NPC and the local PCs have slowly moved away from blanket support of the party. At the Third Session of the Eighth NPC in March 1995, fully a third of the deputies voted against or abstained from voting during the passage of the Central Bank Law, "feeling that the law would give the State Council too much power over the Central Bank and the country's monetary policy" (Pei 1995, 72). Similar numbers refused to approve the Education Law. The NPC has also, in recent years, taken a more activist approach to legislation. NPC officials have been instrumental in passing laws that protect individuals and the lawyers that defend them. In some local areas, PC officials have helped push through environmental legislation (O'Brien 1990; Pei 1995). In the 1990s, the NPC became very much a "legislative agenda-setter" and "reform activist"

(Tanner 1999), particularly in the area of economic reforms. The more this institution acts like a legislative body—allowing debate of legislation and setting a legislative agenda that is independent of the party leadership— the further the government will evolve toward a collection of democratic institutions.

A second major change in the NPC as a democratic institution also relates to autonomy from the party government but extends beyond the realm of legislation into the realm of elections. If the litmus test of true democratic liberalization is a regime's willingness to permit multicandidate and multiparty elections among the general electorate, China is not yet there. However, the NPC has helped to push the country in the direction of fair and open elections—while at the same time asserting its independence from the party—by encouraging the election to government positions of candidates who were nominated by the local PCs rather than the candidates designated by the party. In the highest-profile cases, candidates nominated by local PCs defeated two party-nominated candidates for provincial governor (in Guizhou and Zhejiang). It has done the same by encouraging local PCs to nominate their own candidates for membership in the NPC rather than simply relying on those individuals who were handpicked by the party (Pei 1994, 1995). These changes should not be mistaken for a truly open democratic system; members of the NPC and the local PCs are very much entrenched members of the government, and this system is far from one that allows for fair and open multiparty elections. However, it is one in which the NPC is, in a variety of ways, establishing itself as a governmental body that is independent of the once-ubiquitous Communist Party, and this step is a critical one in the gradual evolution of this system.

Self-Governance and Grassroots Democratization
Beyond the transformation of the NPC, there have been other fundamental changes in the institutions of governance, especially at the village level. Outside of the urban centers in China, there has been an extreme breakdown of party-state institutions. Corruption among local officials— which has followed somewhat naturally from the lack of party control— has been rampant, and the general characterization of the Chinese countryside is one of chaos rather than reform. However, two things have occurred in the Chinese countryside to make this part of the society worthy

of special note in an analysis of social and political reform. First, full economic autonomy has been a transition that has come much more quickly in the countryside than in the urban areas. When decollectivization occurred in the early 1980s, individuals were given direct control over the means of production on their land.[12] As a result, self-governance has rapidly become a way of life for Chinese farmers, who have control over what they produce, what prices they will sell their goods for, and what they choose to do with their land—all with little or no intervention from the state. They are still, in many cases, bound to selling some portion of their agricultural goods to the government, but anything they produce beyond this amount is theirs to use as they please.[13] This notion of self-governance in economic activity—along with the collapse of the institutions of the party infrastructure—has had a large spillover effect for the operation of political institutions in rural areas as well.

Somewhat in response to (and somewhat in anticipation of) the rise in corruption that has followed the breakdown of party institutions in rural areas, in 1987 the NPC established the Organic Law of Villagers' Committees, which effectively gave adult villagers the right to vote, stand for election, and run committees of self-governance (Lawrence 1994; Li and O'Brien 1999). This was a necessary step in cauterizing the wounds left by the failing party infrastructure in rural China. Placing accountability and control in the hands of rural dwellers, it was hoped, would lead to a more transparent and stable political system. For example, Article 22 of the Law on Villagers' Committees requires that elected officials openly publish financial accounts every six months. This type of institutional change forces local officials to be accountable for the ways in which they are spending local funds. The fact that they are now elected rather than appointed means that their actions must be accountable to an electorate. In many villages across rural China, individuals are forcing elected officials to participate in open planning processes. In November 1998, after eleven years of practice and experimentation with village-level elections throughout China, the Law of Villagers' Committees was given the status of permanent law. No accurate numbers are available on how many villages have held genuinely competitive elections; however, with about 930,000 villages in China, some official estimates state that half of the country's villages have implemented elections in accordance with Chinese law (Jakobson 1998). Today, village elections occur in some 700,000 villages across China, reaching 75 percent of the nation's 1.3 billion people. Twenty-five of China's thirty-one administrative regions have promulgated local laws and regulations to facilitate implementation of the law on villagers' committees.

International institutions also play an important role in this transition. For example, the Ford Foundation provided a grant in 1993 to China's Ministry of Civil Affairs to help develop and monitor fair elections. Following the Ford grant, grants also came from the United Nations, the European Union, the Carter Center, and a number of other foundations. In 1997, the Carter Center signed an agreement to observe village election procedures; to provide assistance in gathering election data, educating voters, and training election officials; and to host Chinese officials to observe U.S. elections. After the center's completion in 1999 of a successful pilot project, the Carter Center and the Ministry of Civil Affairs signed a three-year cooperation agreement. The Carter Center also began observations of township elections—that is, elections above the village level—in conjunction with the National People's Congress in 1999. In December 2002, the center observed elections at the county level for the first time. This observation followed a Chinese delegation's visit to the United States in November 2002. The impact has been dramatic: in parts of rural China, village elections have become commonplace in the 1990s; villagers have concrete experience with the process and demands of self-governance; and the gradual movement toward democracy has led to a stable learning process and an institutionalization of the norms of a democratic society.

Compared to those in rural China, the political reforms in urban areas have been much more limited.[14] This is largely because the central institutions of social control in urban areas, the industrial work unit and the neighborhood association, have remained intact throughout the economic reforms. Yet, major changes are occurring in this sector of Chinese society as well, though they are more subtle changes in the political realm than are the fundamental political reforms occurring in rural areas. First, while the rise of self-employment, private enterprises, and other forms of employment outside the state sector have eroded the centrality of the industrial work unit in the organization of urban life in China, this institution is still one of the pillars around which urban society is organized. This fact makes the changes that are occurring within and around the industrial work unit all the more important. Within the work unit, labor relations have been formalized, as work units have adopted formal organizational rules, formal grievance-filing procedures, worker representative committees (which create a democratic process in the restructuring of the firm), and formal hiring procedures. Many state-operated enterprises—the old work units that were at the core of the social security system that was constructed under Mao—have placed all of their workers on fixed-term labor contracts, which significantly rationalize the labor relationship beyond the personalized labor relations of the past. Outside of the work unit, these internal changes are supported by new institutions, formed in the late 1980s, like Labor Arbitration Commissions. This bundle of changes, which includes fundamental changes to the nature of the labor relationship (they are now formal and rationalized through labor contracts) and the mechanisms through which authority can be challenged (grievance-filing procedures and mediation committees within the firm), teaches democracy and democratic processes from the ground up. It is now possible in China for workers to file grievances against superiors and have these grievances heard at an institution outside the workplace. In fact, as I will discuss in detail later in the chapter, the majority of such disputes settled by arbitration or mediation are won by workers. This is a truly radical change.

Second, there are also more general changes afoot within the urban population outside the work unit. In the only systematic study conducted on democratic participation in urban China, Tianjin Shi (1997) finds that urban residents are anything but removed from, or apathetic about, politics and political participation. After a decade of reform, Chinese citizens clearly recognized that they were participants in a slowly changing system, but that they were willing and active participants in such a system. Forms of political participation that can be found in urban China today, according to Shi, include participation in elections (of local PC deputies and village or work-unit leaders); boycotting unfair elections; appeals through the bureaucratic hierarchy; complaints through political organizations, trade unions, or to deputies of the PCs; and letter writing to government officials. Shi finds strong evidence for high levels of participation in all of these acts and many more. The changes that might help explain the political assertiveness that Shi finds surely include the growing middle class, which can increasingly afford to act independently of state directives and demands. As was discussed earlier, the changed career choices available to individuals in urban China make this population ever less reliant on the good will of the government for life and livelihood. But beyond these changes in material reliance on the government, after two decades of economic reform in China, there is a deepening culture of democratic participation and gradual political reform there.

Reform-Minded Elites in the Global Economy

Any discussion of economic and political transformation in China would be incomplete without a discussion of the role of political elites in this process. Indeed, this process would not have begun were it not for Deng Xiaoping's political will in steering China onto the road of economic reform. Yet, in the wake of Tiananmen, few would claim that Deng Xiaoping was a backer of political reforms. In addition to Deng, however, other critical players in the government, such as Jiang Zemin, Li Peng, Zhao Ziyang, and Zhu Rongji, as well as the elite political actors below them, have all been instrumental in the pace and direction of economic reform. The struggles among political elites always seem to circle around basic ideas about the nature and pace of economic reforms in China, with liberals ("reformers") championing radical change in the organization of the economy and conservatives ("hard-liners") attempting at every stage to hold back the process of change. Elite politics certainly matter in the course of economic reforms in China.

However, as we are particularly interested in the relationship between economic and political reform here, it is relevant to ask who among these elites has had any impact on political reform. On the surface, while party elites in the National People's Congress are pushing for gradual political reform, it seems clear that the true elites of the government are united in their resistance to political reform. Historically, when party elites have gotten too close to explicitly supporting political reform, the rest of the elite circle has closed ranks on them, immediately purging them from their positions and stripping them of any political power whatsoever. Hu Yaobang and Zhao Ziyang both suffered this fate when they became associated with the democracy demonstrations in 1986 and 1989, respectively. Yet, I would like to argue here that reading China's economic reforms as a case in which political elites are willing to induce economic change but unwilling to implement changes in political realms is a simplistic understanding of the process of political reform in China. It also dramatically oversimplifies the relationship between economic and political reform and the extent to which political elites in China are using economic reforms as a way of accomplishing political reform. There have been repeated messages from antireform elites within the party that explicit suggestions about political reform will lead to retribution from the party, and the cases of Hu Yaobang, Zhao Ziyang, and, more recently, the jailing of Democratic Party founders Qin Yongmin and Xu Wenli, have made this point clear. However, certain reform-minded elites have brought about significant political change without ever mentioning political change directly. They have accomplished this through global integration and the rationalization of the Chinese economy and society.

Deng Xiaoping and Zhao Ziyang brought about radical economic change by pushing the country toward constitutionality and the emergence of the rule of law. This process, which was marketed ideologically as a set of reforms that were necessary for economic development and change, fundamentally altered the role of politics and the role of the party in Chinese society. In regularizing the economy and the state's relation to it, the architects of China's reform set in motion changes that are forcing the emergence of a more rational political system. As Joseph Fewsmith explains it,

> The recognition, even in principle, that there were laws and principles that even the party had to obey implied the end of solipsistic knowledge as a legitimating principle. It also laid the basis for later efforts to separate the party from the government, an effort that has gone forward only with great conflict and tension precisely because the principle inherent in bureaucratic rationality conflicts with the privileged claim on truth on which the party originally based its legitimacy.
>
> (1999, 55–56)

In other words, as reform-minded elites emphasized the need for a rational economy for economic development, they were also altering the politics of the party system. The rationalization of the economy and society led to a dramatic decline in the party's power to rule as an authoritarian government.

In recent years, the next step in this process has come from global integration and the adoption of the norms of the international community.

The emphasis here is still always on economic norms of the international community, but many social and political norms also come with this project. Zhu Rongji stayed away from discussions about democratization. However, by championing global integration and the rule of law, Zhu brought about gradual political change in China, just at Zhao Ziyang did in the first decade of economic reform in China. Zhu's strategy has been to ignore questions of political reform and concentrate instead on the need for China to adopt economic and legal systems and norms that will allow the country to integrate smoothly with the rest of the international community. Yet Zhu clearly recognizes that the adoption of the norms of the international community will continue to push China down the road of general societal transformation. In other words, Zhu's objective is to deepen all of the reforms that have been discussed above, all of which have, and will continue to, reform China's political system in significant ways. This view has many skeptics among Western academics. However, it is important to note that many of the laws passed under Zhu Rongji's watch, while purportedly about global integration, had at their core an emphasis on individual civil liberties. The Chinese Company Law (1994), for example, is in many areas more aggressive on affirming workers' rights vis-à-vis the corporation than American corporate law is today. Zhu avoided marketing this aspect of the reforms, at least in part, because his political career unfolded in the shadow of Zhao Ziyang's fate. However, it is undeniable that Zhu Rongji and Jiang Zemin, who incorporated entrepreneurs into the Communist Party (discussed below), have pushed forward reforms that have had an impact on political reform in China.

With his seemingly authoritarian stances on a number of issues, many have worried that Hu Jintao would leave his once-liberal image behind, showing instead his true colors as the leader of "China's new authoritarianism." But under Hu Jintao we have seen a fundamental transformation of private property rights and the right to form independent unions, two issues which have been central to criticism of China's political reform process. And, perhaps, most profoundly, it was under Hu Jintao that the party, in the fall of 2006, literally wrote Mao out the history of the PRC: as Shanghai's high school students returned to class that fall, Mao had been reduced to little more than a brief mention. And, contrary to his predecessors of the 1990s, Hu is not afraid to talk about democratization, as he showed in his speech for the Seventeenth Party Congress in October of 2007. The main point here is that, in the post-Zhao Ziyang era, an outwardly conservative façade has allowed Zhu Rongji, Jiang Zemin, and now Hu Jintao to push forward a reformist agenda of institutional change. As each of these reform-minded elites emphasized the need for a rational system for economic development, they were also altering the politics of the party system.

Business and Cooptation

In 1988, the Chinese government began to exert control over social organizations, including various business associations, by creating an official registration system for such organizations. A newly established Social Organization Management Department within the Ministry of Civil Affairs would enforce it. One year later, the Regulations on Registration and Administration of Social Organizations were issued by the State Council, along with the Measures on Management of Foundations and the Interim Rule on Management of Foreign Chambers of Commerce. These guidelines essentially stipulate that all social organizations must be sponsored by government or party organizations, even though they all have the right to independent legal status. After a period of rapid proliferation, by the end of 1992 the number of established and registered social organizations settled at around 40,000. In 1998, two new sets of regulations were issued—the Regulations on Registration and Administration of Social Organizations, and the Interim Regulation on Registration and Management of Private Nonprofit Organizations.

The 1990s' laws on social organization aimed to incorporate governmental supervision and control while transferring the function of governmental monitoring to a separate governing body. A large body of work on China's reforms has emphasized the "corporatist" model of social organization and control or "embedded" relations between social organizations and their governing agencies.[15] And beyond the formal ties between business associations and the governing system stipulated by law, there are various informal ties between entrepreneurs' groups and the state officials that directly influence the ways such business associations are run.

It is still too early to draw conclusions about the degree of independence of entrepreneur groups and business associations that are emerging in China's reform era. The reality of China's position as a still-authoritarian regime and the Chinese Communist Party's (CCP's) status as the most powerful organization in China suggests significant limitations on the relative autonomy of these groups. However, the emergence and growth of those new social groups have brought about social and political implications that cannot be ignored in today's China. While the wealth attached to the economic elites running new business organizations has not led directly to democratic values or to pressure on the CCP for radical political reforms, these economic elites and, more broadly, the emerging "middle class" have become the most important social groups that have begun to exert pressure on China's political regime.[16] Perhaps the most critical evidence of the importance of this social group comes from the government's embracing of Jiang Zemin's "three representatives" policy, discussed in Chapter 4, which permits private entrepreneurs to be members of the CCP. Proposed by Jiang in 2001, this policy was incorporated into China's Constitution at the Sixteenth Party Congress in 2002. This policy is a direct outcome of the rapid growth of private economy in the 1990s. Thus, the cooptation model becomes clear: a major part of China's economic growth and transformation has been to bring the private economy and democratic reforms into the fold of the current one-party system. By incorporating private entrepreneurs into its political camp, China's only ruling party is now announcing that it not only continues to represent the workers and peasants but all of the people's interests, including those of the capitalists, the so-called advanced social productive forces. In doing so, the CCP has ended a half-century of exclusionary policies aimed at private entrepreneurs. While these entrepreneur groups only occupy a small part of the Chinese population, the inclusion of private entrepreneurs is a clear statement by the CCP and the Chinese government that the business groups can no longer be ignored within the political community.

The Emergence of a Rule-of-Law Society

Because of the absence of a clear, radical break with the authoritarian past, China is often portrayed as a place in which institutional change has not yet occurred in any substantive way. It is much more common to speak of corruption and the authoritarian nature of the system than about the fact that these gradual reforms have, in many ways, begun the process of constructing a rational economy.[17] Yet, despite the fact that such changes are dismissed, if not ignored, China has created the foundations for an economy based on rational–legal principles and individual civil liberties.

As the state gradually receded from direct control over enterprises, it left in place a rational economy that will eventually govern the decisions of the economic actors that survive the transition. New laws and institutions have created the basis for a new conception of labor rights that few scholars of China acknowledge, much less explore.

In the second half of this chapter, I will approach the emerging rule-of-law society in two ways. First, there is empirical reality: an analysis of economic reform in China must begin with an acknowledgment of the changes and progress that have actually occurred there. Of course, it is still the case that abuses of labor, a curtailing of individual freedoms, and many other violations of human rights occur in China. However, this is only part of the story; the other part is one in which the government has sought to create a society in which individual civil liberties and a protection of labor sit at its core. Second, there is an explanation: understanding the forces driving these changes forward must avoid the simplistic assumptions of efficiency, the invisible hand, and the progress toward modern capitalist markets and, instead, strive to isolate the institutional forces and actors that are guiding this process of change. More than a simple logic of the freedom to pursue profits, the decisions and practices of managers and entrepreneurs in China are shaped by willful political decisions by the government and the economic models to which Chinese managers and entrepreneurs are exposed. Economic pressures are important in economic decision-making, but markets are more than purely economic systems; they are also political and social settings in which actors make decisions based upon the social, normative, and political pressures they experience. As state officials and economic actors are exposed to different models of institutional structures in the global marketplace—and as they receive different kinds of pressure to adopt new models of action—they implement strategies that reflect these pressures. The forces behind the changes occurring in the Chinese economy must be analyzed through this prism. As we observe the emergence of a rational economy in China, we must begin with a social, political, and normative understanding of the origins of these models of economic behavior.

The emergence of a rule-of-law economy in China is not based upon an inevitable march toward rational economic action or the result of some inexorable drive of modernization. Instead, economic actors in China are adopting Western models of economic behavior because of normative pressure to take seriously the new laws and institutions emerging from the government; as a way of attracting foreign investment; as a result of the pressure from international organizations, such as the World Trade Organization; and as a result of the changing demographics and structure of labor markets in China. The Chinese government, for its part, is willfully creating a rule-based economy as an institutional and political project that is shaped by the desire to participate in the global economy and by the success of market systems in the West. Within this framework, modern rational capitalism is not an inevitable outcome of laissez-faire economic systems, as transition economists have argued. It is the outcome of a power struggle among nations (and among ideological camps within nations) in which capitalist nations and powerful economic actors force these models onto the economic agenda. Modern rational capitalism arrives as the result of particular social and political forces in a particular historical moment. The ideas of this economy are, in cases such as China's, exported overseas to governments and economic actors within developing nations.

One might raise the question here of why it would be that capitalist nations, and capitalists themselves, would care about exporting rational-legal capitalism to China. Indeed, there are many examples of development around the world in which Western nations and capitalists have happily undercut the institutional framework as a way of supporting despotic regimes or extracting profits through the exploitation of labor. And the Chinese government has hardly been a champion of rational law—at least in the first thirty years of the PRC. But the case of China, in this particular phase of development and in this particular moment in the global economy, brings together a different set of dynamics and a different set of principles about development and the transition from socialism to capitalism. The point here is that, while it is empirically true that Chinese firms and the labor relations within them are becoming more rationalized, this is not the inevitable outcome of a march toward modernization or the inevitable outcome of market reforms.

Rather, changing labor relations in China are the unintended consequence of a particular set of power relations that involve large-scale Western capitalists, the Chinese government, and the international agencies organizing the global economy. Because Western capitalists are intent upon conquering the Chinese market (it is simply too large and lucrative to cut off, as we have done with Cuba) and they are unwilling to wait until

China's authoritarian government collapses, pressuring the government to create a rational economy—one in which rational law and contracts are respected—is the next best thing. The Chinese government and Chinese factories, for their part, know that their own survival lies in continued economic development, which, in turn, relies heavily on the attraction of powerful investors that will bring with them new technologies. Changing labor relations and, more generally, the creation of a rational environment within the firm become important markers and signals that Chinese firms can set in place to attract powerful foreign investors and thereby secure their own future.[18] In the sections that follow, I will first lay out some of the fundamental changes occurring in the Chinese economy.

There are many other critical changes occurring, but due to space constraints, I will limit my discussion here to only a few of the critical changes that are transforming labor relations in China. Following that discussion, I will explain the reasons behind these changes.

The Transformation of Labor Relations in China's Emerging Market Economy

In December of 1999, Bao Zhenmin, a former employee of the Thomson Group Jiadi Real Estate Limited Company (TGL) in Shanghai, sued his former employer for back wages that resulted from what he alleged was an inappropriate dismissal.[19] Mr. Bao had signed labor contracts with TGL in May 1994, January 1997, and January 1998. First introduced into the Chinese economy in 1983 as part of a larger effort to rationalize labor relationships and codify worker rights in the factory, labor contracts are recognized by many workers in China today as a key mechanism for knowing what their rights are in situations such as these. Though many Western scholars of China remain skeptical that reforms such as these actually fulfill their purported purpose, the reality is that many workers like Mr. Bao know their rights and they exercise them. Initially, things did not look good for Mr. Bao in his quest to win compensation. When he applied for a hearing in front of Pudong's Labor Arbitration Commission (LAC), the LAC denied his claim. So he took the only avenue left to him—suing the company in the Pudong District People's Court (*Bao Zhenmin* v. *Thompson Group Ltd*. 12/28/1999). After an initial decision, an appeal by TGL, and a second decision by the court, Mr. Bao received a favorable judgment, one that awarded him back wages, two-months' living allowance, and economic compensation for lost wages. TGL was also required to pay the costs of the trial. Mr. Bao received his day in court, and he won.

The Rule of Law

Democracy movements should be viewed as being built on the foundation of a movement toward the rule of law in Chinese society. The last decade has seen amazing changes in this area. In the Spring of 1999, several relatives of students who were killed in Tiananmen Square in the early hours of June 4, 1989 decided to sue the government for the slaughter of their children. They invoked two relatively new laws, the Administrative Litigation Act, passed in 1990, and the National Compensation Law, passed in 1995, which effectively allows Chinese citizens to sue the government for compensation for restitution for past wrongs. Passage of this law seemed to occur as a matter of course, as the National People's Congress passed many rights-based legal institutions in the mid-1990s in China, including a Labor Law, a Prison Reform Law, and many others. Yet, while the government may not have anticipated such an employment of these laws, the event marked a dramatic step forward in the evolution toward a rational–legal system in which the government is held accountable for its actions just the same as individual citizens are. In 1989, the participants in the Tiananmen Square movement were operating completely outside the institutional system they were criticizing; they were branded "counterrevolutionaries," "hooligans," and "enemies of the state." A decade later, their relatives are employing the legal system to criticize the state for its actions.

These events are important for two reasons. First, it is important to understand the extent to which this society is indeed evolving in a dramatic fashion, despite the fact that the evolution (instead of revolution) make changes seem all too slow to come about. That individuals can now sue the government for past wrongs stands in stark contrast to the society that existed even a decade ago. Second, the creation of a predictable, rational-legal system has been a central part of the Chinese government's path toward the creation of a market economy; it has also been a necessary part of China's transition to a global market economy. A number of scholars have argued that the construction of a rational–legal system to ensure market transactions that match the standards of the international community is a necessary precondition to participation in the global economy. It is possible to have an economic system that is not based on rational–legal principles—for example, an economy could be based on social ties and particularistic relations—but this type of economy is unlikely to attract significant amounts of foreign capital, as investors from overseas will be at a disadvantage in this type of market. Yet, a market still requires enforcement mechanisms for meting out justice, and if cultural norms and social ties cannot serve this function, other institutional standards must form the basis for the governance of the market. In the mid-1990s, the National People's Congress adopted a certain urgency with respect to legal reforms, affirming that legal reform would be the backbone for a stable and regulated marketplace. As Minxin Pei (1995, 68) puts it, the rule of law is "the institutional foundation of a market economy and a constitutional government," and China is hurtling headlong toward this type of institutional system.

In the two decades since the economic reforms began, the National People's Congress has written and passed literally hundreds of new laws, resolutions, and policies that gradually move the country away from the governance of capricious leaders and toward a rational–legal system in which newly defined laws and market institutions govern society. New laws, such as the National Compensation Law and the Labor Law (1994), which rationalizes the labor relationship in significant ways, have fundamentally changed the structure of Chinese society, at least on an official level. These laws and many others have dramatically transformed the institutions and rules that define labor relations and economic transactions in China's reforming economy. With regard to the Administrative Litigation Act (1990), the case of the Tiananmen Square suit is only the highest-profile example of a trend that is actually quite common in China today: with the passage of the act came a rush of suits against the government—about 25,000 per year. Perhaps more amazing is that the courts ruled with the plaintiffs in about 28 percent of the cases (Pei 1995). Also in line with the high-profile Tiananmen case, there have been many cases in which political dissidents have filed suit against the government for violation of their constitutional rights.

We might ask, at this point, whether the creation of all these new laws and institutional frameworks is having any impact on the way Chinese society is actually governed. Indeed, it could very well be the case that while these new laws and institutions exist on paper, they have little impact

Table 7.4 Evidence of the Rule of Law in China

	No. of Lawyers	No. of First Trial Cases	Criminal	Civil	Economic	Administrative
1980	NA	763,535	197,865	565,679	NA	NA
1985	34,379	1,319,741	246,655	846,391	225,541	916
1990	90,602	2,916,774	459,656	1,851,897	591,462	13,006
1995	NA	4,545,676	495,741	2,718,533	1,275,959	52,596
1996	100,198	5,312,580	618,826	3,093,995	1,515,848	79,966
1997	98,902	5,288,379	436,894	3,277,572	1,478,822	90,557
1998	101,220	5,410,798	482,164	3,375,069	1,450,049	98,350
1999	111,433	5,692,434	540,008	3,519,244	1,529,877	97,569
2000	117,260	5,356,294	560,432	3,412,259	1,290,867	6976
2001	122,585	5,344,934	628,996	3,459,025	1,149,101	6891
2002	136,684	5,132,199	631,348	4,420,123	NA	NA
2003	142,534	5,130,760	632,605	4,410,236	NA	NA
2004	145,196	5,072,881	647,541	4,332,727	NA	NA
2005	153,846	5,161,170	684,897	4,380,095	NA	NA
2006	164,516	5,183,794	702,445	4,385,732	NA	NA
2007	142,967	5,550,062	724,112	4,724,440	NA	NA
2008	156,710	6,228,831	767,842	5,412,591	NA	NA
2009	173,327	6,688,963	768,507	5,800,144	NA	NA

Source: National Statistical Bureau of China (2010, 886, 897) unless otherwise noted, National Statistical Bureau of China (1999, 2000, 2006), No. of lawyers data 1980–2003.

in practice. Table 7.4 shows evidence of the rule of law in everyday governance in a number of different spheres. At this point, China only has one-tenth the number of lawyers that we have in the United States. However, for the number of professionals in this field to have tripled over the course of a decade suggests dramatic growth in the litigiousness of this changing society. The number of cases brought before the Chinese legal system has increased by about sevenfold over two decades of economic reform. Most remarkable is the emergence and dramatic rise of economic and administrative cases: in the pre-reform era, these two spheres were simply not subject to law in any way, yet they have emerged as central features of the Chinese legal system in the reform era.

In discussing the rule of law, it is also worth considering the transformation of the prison system in China, for this is one of the primary targets of allegations about human rights abuses. The most systematic assessment of the prison system in reform-era China is presented in James Seymour and Richard Anderson's *New Ghosts, Old Ghosts: Prisons and Labor Reform Camps in China* (1998).[20] As the common form of incarceration in China, the Chinese *laogai* (literally, "reform through labor") is a network of up to 1,250 labor reform prison camps, housing perhaps 1.5 million offenders (other estimates are much higher but do not stand on the quality of research that Seymour and Anderson's estimates do). Though prisons have existed in China for thousands of years, this specific institution has its roots in Chinese communism, as people were expected to change themselves by engaging in hard labor. Corruption and a lack of state regulation in the 1960s and 1970s made this system one of the most abusive prison systems in the world, and, as a result, it was often held up as the Chinese equivalent of the Soviet gulag. Seymour and Anderson's study sets out to examine the state of this institution in the mid-1990s, exploding myths about the institution with empirical information.

With a total prison population of about 2 million (including jail populations), the rate of incarceration is about 166 individuals per 100,000 people. Even in the mid-1990s, there were still horrific conditions in some parts of the prison system, such as in the Xinjiang system. Yet, the system is improving under the new laws and regulations that emerged in the 1990s. The rule of law is changing the situation in the Chinese *laogai* in fundamental ways. While a great deal of abuse still occurs in the *laogai*, the situation is apparently changing in response to the reforms enacted by the 1994 Prison Reform Law. Institutional change is an incremental process, and if we are going to apply political pressure for reform in China, we must also recognize progress when and where it occurs. As one former prisoner put it, "Since the prison law . . . prison conditions have improved greatly. Now the *duizhang* [wardens] no longer beat prisoners, because they also study the prison law" (Seymour and Anderson 1998, 180). Rule of law is the one true hope for human rights in China, and this study makes that point convincingly.

The rule of law, which many scholars have argued is a centerpiece of the transition to a market economy, is also the foundation of a rights-based society and the gradual transformation of an authoritarian political system. The Chinese government has institutionalized so many new laws—those that govern the economy and extend to the level of individual civil rights—that it has obviously made great progress toward the creation of a rule-of-law society. Skeptics might still argue that change has not come quickly enough, that the laws are a formal shell, more symbolic than substantive, or that the only true marker of political reform is a dismantling of the authoritarian one-party system itself. To some extent, this view is right: there have been many accounts of the ways that new laws have been ignored or openly defied in practice, and, although the rule of law is often bandied about as evidence of true change, constitutional rights can still be overthrown at the party's whim. However, deeming this fledgling system a failure also places unrealistic expectations on the process of institutional change in China—which is, necessarily, a gradual process—especially given that the country was devoid of such formal institutions when the economic reforms began. In addition to the construction of new legal institutions, it is also necessary for norms, legal cultures, and general public awareness to follow these changes. These norms and cultures are being built in China gradually and over time, and they have significant implications for the rights of the population, in general, and for workers, specifically.

Labor Relations: Labor Contracts and the End of Lifetime Employment

Under Mao, labor was organized according to authoritarian principles. Workers were subject to the caprice of organizational and party authorities, and they had little recourse against this system. To the extent that labor relations in market economies are based on "independence, contract, and universalism," labor relations in pre-reform China were based primarily on "dependence, deference, and particularism" (Walder 1986a, 10). Andrew Walder's study of factories and labor relations in pre-reform China reveals a system organized around political and social relations in the firm, and central to these relations is the notion that workers are dependent upon management and supervisors. If formal rational (or rational–legal) systems imply a structure in which the benefits and rights of the worker are defined independently of personal ties, factories in the pre-reform Chinese system were decidedly informal. The relationships among workers and supervisors were personalized, and supervisors had considerable discretion over processes in the workplace.[21] In other words, supervisors within factories made decisions about worker advantages and advancement based on personal relations and personal decisions, unrestrained by formal rules or routinized decision-making systems. This system has changed radically in the reform era. While the transformation is far from complete, the fundamental building blocks for a new set of labor relations have been set in place in China.

The transformation of labor relations in China begins with the institutions that are rationalizing these relationships. Labor contracts are the first among several important institutional changes that have transformed labor relations. In Mao's China, under the command economy, employment was guaranteed by the state.[22] Workers were assigned to work units by the Labor Bureau, and, from that point on, the work unit was responsible for dispensing income, benefits, and retirement pay for the rest of the worker's life. In different periods, especially in the late 1970s, a small fraction of the population was classified as "waiting for employment," but for the most part, the state still fulfilled its promise of finding employment for everyone.[23] Although by 1980, state-sector jobs had become more competitive than ever before (only 37 percent of workers were assigned jobs in state enterprises), still 80 percent of workers were assigned jobs in either state enterprises or collectively owned enterprises in that year (Walder 1986a, 57, 68–74). Once jobs were assigned, except in rare cases of disciplinary firing and even rarer cases of layoffs (which were often followed by reassignment to another enterprise), the job assignment was for life. This is not to say that workers never changed jobs or resigned from a given enterprise, but once workers were assigned to a work unit, except in exceptional circumstances, they had the option of staying at that organization for life.

Labor contracts began a new system in which enterprises are only responsible to workers for as long as the contract specifies. If the enterprise and individual sign a one-, three-, or five-year contract, the enterprise is only responsible for the worker for one, three, or five years and is under no obligation to renew the contract at the end of this period. At the end of a contract period, the enterprise has no obligation to continue to pay income or benefits to the worker. As one manager in the chemicals sector explained the gravity of this change,

> The labor situation has changed tremendously over the last few years
> . . . I think that probably the most significant change is that we have
> everyone on labor contracts now. Now if workers violate the terms of

their contracts, they can be fired . . . We've never had this type of labor relationship before. (Personal interview)

The labor contract was officially introduced in 1986 with Document Number 77 and Decree Number 99, both promulgated by the State Council.[24] Although these institutional arrangements officially emerged in 1986, experimentation with labor contracts dates back as early as 1983, as defined by the 1983 State Council Notice for Trial Implementation (PRC 1983). Following the 1986 documents, the legitimacy of the labor contract was further enhanced by the Enterprise Law (PRC 1988, Chapter 3, Article 31), which states, "The enterprise shall have the right to employ or dismiss its staff members and workers in accordance with the provisions of the State Council." Though such a statement does not sound radical as far as enterprise rights go in market economies, in fact, turning the rights of hiring and dismissing of workers over to the enterprise was extremely radical in the context of China's recent institutional history. Other institutional changes, such as the establishment of unemployment and social security funds, set up to protect workers in the event that their organization would let them go in the "re-optimization" movement, have also given legitimacy to the use of labor contracts.[25]

The proportion of the industrial labor force on contracts has risen steadily and significantly since 1984. In 1984, 1.8 percent of workers were on labor contracts.[26] By 1994, about 26 percent of workers were on labor contracts. By sector, the labor contract has been most readily adopted in manufacturing, where 41 percent of workers were on labor contracts in 1994.[27] What this means is that a large percentage of employees are no longer guaranteed lifetime employment by the work units at which they are employed. While I have argued elsewhere that labor contracts are adopted by managers and factories as a way of protecting themselves from the economic duress of supporting a labor force with lifetime employment—in other words, they are adopted to end lifetime employment and therefore are not in the interests of workers (Guthrie 1998a, 1999)—there are positive unintended consequences of this transformation for the rights of workers. This is a common theme that will come through in many of the transformations occurring with regard to labor in China: while a series of changes have been adopted for a variety of reasons, there are positive unintended consequences for the emergence of a rational economy, in general, and the rights of the worker, specifically. Despite the fact that factories have adopted labor contracts as a cost-cutting measure, they have rationalized the labor relationship in fundamental ways. These contracts provide workers with an institutional basis upon which employment relations are defined. They lay out the terms of the labor relationship, forcing workers and managers to acknowledge that labor relations have taken on a formal, rationalized, contractual quality. If workers want to file grievances about their treatment in the firm, they can rely on a formal document to present their case. In the past, the rules of the workplace were defined solely on the caprice of authoritarian rule; today, they are increasingly based upon previously agreed-upon terms that are depicted in a formal document.

A process of rationalization is occurring in the workplace, as well, where Chinese companies are adopting a number of the rational bureaucratic systems that are most often found in Western organizations, such as grievance filing procedures, mediation committees, and formal organizational rules and guidelines. Evidence from urban Shanghai shows that Chinese factories and companies have been experimenting with a number of formal institutions in the workplace (Guthrie 1999, 2002b). Figure 7.1 shows that more than 60 percent of workplaces in industrial Shanghai have adopted formal organizational rules, formal grievance filing procedures, and formal pay scales. More than 80 percent have institutionalized worker representative committee meetings, which many workers and managers informally refer to as "our own [factory's] democratic institutions" [*women zijide minzhu zhidu*] (personal interviews). And more than 50 percent have institutionalized formal job descriptions and mediation institutions within the firm. The emergence of some of these changes is remarkable, given that many of these formalized institutions only emerged in American firms in the 1970s (Dobbin *et al.* 1993; Sutton *et al.* 1994).

The Labor Law and Labor Arbitration

Beyond the emergence of a rationalized and formalized labor relationship within the firm, other formal institutions have emerged to create an environment outside the firm that further rationalizes the labor relationship. The Labor Law (PRC 1994) and the LACs are two governance structures that have had the largest influence on firms' institutional environments and, by extension, the internal practices firms adopt in the period of economic reform. For example, Chapter 10 of the Labor Law, titled "Labor Disputes," is specifically devoted to describing the process laborers are legally entitled to follow should a dispute arise in the workplace. The law explains in an explicit fashion the rights of the worker to take disputes to outside arbitration (the district's LAC) should she be unsatisfied with the manner in which grievances are being handled within the organization. These institutional shifts have exerted pressure on organizations to alter their internal structures, much as changing institutional environments in the 1960s in the United States forced U.S. organizations to alter their internal structures by experimenting with job ladders, employment tests, job descriptions, and the like (Dobbin *et al.* 1993).

The LAC is an institution under the jurisdiction of the Labor Bureau. There is an LAC in each urban district and county. The emergence of the institution of labor arbitration in China is directly related to the issues of economic transition and the emergence of a market economy. As one official who now oversees the Labor Dispute Office in Shanghai's Labor Bureau explained this relationship,

> The need for arbitration in China grew as we moved away from the planned economy. In the planned economy, everything was fixed and decided by the government. No one could be fired from his/her job, and everyone was secure. In the early 1980s we started to move into a market economy. With this came the labor system reform . . . At the same time as we were introducing contracts that allowed factories to only hire workers for a fixed amount of time, we realized that the labor relationship would become much more complicated with this change. We realized we would need a way to settle labor disputes. So also in 1987 we formed the first Labor Arbitration Commission.
>
> (Personal interview)

The emergence of the LAC is grounded in a number of legal and institutional changes of the period of reform. What first defined these changes were the State-Owned Enterprises Labor Dispute Resolution Temporary Rules, which were adopted by the State Council in 1987. While these rules dealt only with dispute resolution in state-owned organizations, the 1993 PRC Labor Dispute Resolution Regulations expanded the rules to include all types of labor relationships. Later, the Labor Law solidified the role of the local LACs as an institution for labor dispute resolution, as Chapter 10 of the law is devoted exclusively to labor disputes and the use of these local institutions. Finally, the Arbitration Law (PRC 1995) established the practice of arbitration as a formally supported legal structure in the governance of labor relations in China's economic transition.[28]

Within the LAC, there are two divisions: the arbitration court and the labor section, which primarily takes care of labor disputes. One group within the labor section is made up of volunteer workers, while the other group is ruled by the presiding official. The volunteer system is dependent upon the participation of workers (they are not paid). Basically, the labor union at each organization submits names of potential individuals to occupy this position, and the LAC chooses from this list of names.[29] Three groups are represented in the labor arbitration process: the government is represented by the Labor Bureau, the organization is represented by the Economic Commission in the Central Economic Administrative Unit, and the worker is represented by the organization's labor union.[30] This governmental unit actually only represents state-owned organizations; if the dispute is with a private company, a separate governmental department represents the organization.

There are basically three types of problems that go through the LAC. The first relates to disagreements over contractual issues surrounding firing or quitting. The second type of dispute relates to salaries, insurance, and benefits. The third type of problem relates to vacation days and work leave. These three kinds of problems are each handled by three different sections within the LAC. The greatest problem area for applications to the LAC is contractual disputes, which comprised over 50 percent of the applications to Shanghai's LACs as of the mid-1990s. Most often, the problem is that people have signed contracts and the work unit is not adhering to the terms of the contract; these cases are usually decided in favor of the workers.[31] The state has created this system, in conjunction with the Labor Law, as an institutional structure to help facilitate due process in the workplace. One official in the Labor Bureau explained the goal of this system, saying, "Our main focus in creating this system is to build a system of legal structures that will make all labor relationships the same. If there is a problem, we want all resolutions to be simple and straightforward" (personal interview).

Thus, among the Labor Law, the LACs, and the institutional changes within the workplace, an infrastructure is now in place to institutionally protect workers from the whim of authoritarian rule. Do these institutional changes matter? That is a more difficult question to answer. However, over the course of the 1990s, cases brought before courts and arbitration boards have been steadily on the rise. By the end of the 1990s, more than 115,000 cases were brought annually before LACs throughout the country. Of these, workers won more than half outright, while only about 13 percent were decided fully in favor of the firm (about one-third of the cases were partially decided in favor of both parties). An increased awareness of workers' rights and the economic downturn caused a dramatic rise in the number of labor disputes in 2009. Interestingly, the percentage of labor disputes won by workers decreased, while partial victories became the largest portion of the disputes won at 49 percent. The percentage won by firms stayed at around 14 percent. Table 7.5 shows the breakdown of these cases from 1999 to 2009 by outcome. In 2004, state-owned enterprises had the highest number of disputes, 50 percent of which were won by laborers. Following in descending order were private firms, collectively owned firms, joint ventures, and government organizations.

Despite the gradual nature of their emergence in Chinese society, these changes mark a radical break from the past. From the national-level

Table 7.5 Labor Disputes by Outcome

	1999	2001	2003	2005	2007	2009
Won by Firm	15,674	31,544	34,272	39,401	49,211	95,470
Won by Laborer	63,030	71,739	109,556	145,352	156,955	255,119
Partial victory	37,549	46,996	79,475	121,274	133,864	339,125
Totals	116,253	150,279	223,503	306,027	340,030	689,714
Percent won by firm	13	21	15	13	14	14
Percent won by workers	54	48	49	47	46	37
Percent partial victory	32	31	36	40	39	49

Source: National Statistical Bureau of China (2000, 750–751; 2002, 794–795; 2004, 876–877; 2006, 890; 2008, 876; 2010, 885)

*Taiwan and Hong Kong owned firms depicted in this category.

institutional changes, Chinese workers have more access to rational institutions and rational law than ever before. As important as the empirical reality of these changes, however, is an understanding of the forces driving this process of change. As mentioned above, if it is true that Chinese workers are experiencing a rationalized economic system, it is an anomaly for developing economies, in general, and for authoritarian societies, in particular. What particular circumstances in the Chinese case have led to the emergence of a rational economy there?

The Dynamics of Change

Market transition in China has been informed by a particular dynamic that amounts to a struggle between a government that wants to stay in power and an international community that wants access to that mythical market of a billion consumers. The Chinese government has resisted rapid economic and political change. The Communist Party made it resoundingly and brutally clear in 1989 that it would not undertake a path of rapid political and economic reform. Instead, the government has maintained political control—at least to the extent that China is still a one-party system—while gradually reforming the economy. Why, then, do proponents of an international economy not simply write China off the way they have Cuba and North Korea? The answer here is that there is simply too much to gain in China; the prospect of access to the internal market there is too enticing to ignore. So the U.S. government and Western capitalists find themselves in a position of wanting to invest in this gradually transforming economy, but, at the same time, they are forced to deal with an authoritarian government that, at least when the economic reforms began, was unpredictable at best. The Chinese government, for its part, recognizes the importance of Western capitalists and international markets on at least two levels.

First, since the economic reforms began, the architects recognized the need for a "modern" rational economy. From Zhao Ziyang to Zhu Rongji, the leaders of this reform have clearly focused on the creation of a rational accountability and the embracing of international standards. Indeed, the "modern enterprise system" and all of the accounting practices that stand behind it are based upon international models and standards of firm management. Second, the government and enterprises themselves recognize the need for foreign capital and technology. The desire to attract foreign investment and technology leads to institutional accommodations that support the role of contracts, rational–legal accountability, and the rule of law within the firm. The rationalization of labor relations is an unintended consequences of this larger dynamic.

As we examine the changes behind the transformation of labor in China, our focus will be on three critical factors. First, contrary to representations of the Chinese government as an unchanging, unresponsive, authoritarian government, China's leaders have aggressively enacted state-level institutional changes that have formed the basis of the rationalized economy emerging in China. Second, pressure from international organizations and Western investors has led to a rationalized economy not only at the state level, but also within firms. Third, changing labor markets and opportunities have transformed the bargaining power of workers in the economy. All these factors have come together to facilitate the emergence of a rule-of-law ethos in China, which has changed the extent to which workers approach the issue of rights. We will explore each of these changes in greater depth here.

Transformation from Above

Economic reform in China has been a state-driven process, as the architects of the reform have aggressively led this transition. Despite the fact that markets have steadily emerged in China, the gradual creation of the new institutions within the market—including the experimentation with these institutions and their measured, steady implementation in the reform-era economy—has been a process that emerged from elite ideologies and reform-minded leaders. At the center of their strategies has been the gradual freeing of firms from reliance on the planned economy, and the implementation of a rational economy. As I discussed earlier, both Zhu Rongji and (before him) Zhao Ziyang have been fundamentally focused on the creation of a rational economy in China, one that operates by independent, transparent accounting systems and respects formal rational laws and contracts. However, where Zhao's goal was to help newly autonomous enterprises survive in the face of economic uncertainty, Zhu's goal has been to create a stable investment environment that will help further integrate China into the global economy. Zhu knows all too well that China's only hope for such integration lies in the creation of an institutional framework that will put corporate investors from advanced capitalist nations at ease; for with these corporate investors comes much-needed technology, and critical technology transfer is now, more than ever, a central part of China's transition plan.

In the early years, the institutional changes were about experimentation with new forms of enterprise management, the creation of a rational economy at the firm level, and the weaning of firms from the purse strings of the state. However, if the 1980s were defined by the creation of a rational economy, the 1990s were defined by the creation of laws that will govern this society for years to come. Since the economic reforms began, the National People's Congress has passed over 700 new laws, and local people's congresses have passed an additional 2,000 to 3,000. An estimated half of these laws is directly tied to the creation of a rational economy. The Company Law, the Bankruptcy Law, and the Joint Venture Law are the most famous among these, but there are many more laws and resolutions that have reshaped the economy in fundamental ways. Several of these laws have had fundamental consequences for labor relations in the economy. The important point here is that despite the depictions of a stolid, unresponsive, and unreformed government in China, the last two decades of reform have, on the contrary, been marked by an activist approach to economic and social reform, one that brought about many new economic practices inside the firm and many new laws to govern the economy in which these firms were embedded.

The Impact of Foreign Investment

While an activist state (transformation from above) has been crucial in setting the institutional framework of changing labor relations in place, equally important are the face-to-face negotiations in the marketplace with the very economic actors the government seeks to attract, as Western investors pressure Chinese firms to take seriously the institutional changes the government has set in place. These negotiations play out differently in the "old" and "new" economies, but they play a central role in the ways these economies are taking shape. The transformation of Chinese factories has been dramatic, and policy makers in debates over trade with China often ignore the radical changes occurring in this sector of the economy. Policy makers focus almost exclusively on issues such as regime type and treatment of political dissidents, but, meanwhile, a "quiet revolution from within" has been occurring in the Chinese workplace.[32] As I have described above, a process of rationalization is occurring in the Chinese workplace, where companies are adopting a number of the rational bureaucratic systems that are most often found in Western organizations, such as grievance-filing procedures, mediation committees, and formal organizational rules and guidelines, among many others. It is striking to see these kinds of changes in Chinese factories, given that this type of legalization within the workplace only occurred in American firms as recently as the 1970s.[33]

Foreign investment and, more important, joint-venture relationships play a crucial role in this process of change. In my own study of Shanghai's industrial economy, I have shown that joint-venture relationships have a statistically significant and consistent effect on the organizational deci-sions and practices of Chinese factories (Guthrie 1999). This relationship amounts to a significant positive effect of foreign joint ventures pushing their partner organizations to adopt stable rational–legal structures and systems. In other words, it is not only joint-venture firms that are different from classical, old-style Chinese factories, but the Chinese parent compa-nies in these relationships are also changing as a result of joint-venture negotiations. While these stable rational–legal systems are adopted more often to attract foreign investors than they are for the good of workers, they nevertheless have radical implications for the structure of authority relations and, therefore, for the lives of individual Chinese citizens.

Chinese factories that have formal relationships with foreign firms are significantly more likely to have formal organizational rules, are almost twenty times more likely to have formal grievance-filing proce-dures, and are more likely to have worker representative committee meet-ings and formal hiring procedures. They pay significantly higher wages (about 50 percent higher), and they are more likely to adopt China's new Company Law, which binds them to the norms of the international community. Those with Western partners are significantly more likely to have arbitration clauses in their joint-venture contracts, which subject them to the authority of international legal institutions, such as the Chinese International Economic Arbitration and Trade Commission. I have had many conversations with managers in which they openly acknowledge that the changes they have set in place have little to do with their own ideas of efficient business practices and much more to do with pressure brought on them by their foreign partners.

Human-rights advocates, as well as others who are knowledgeable about the alliance between capitalists and repressive regimes in developing countries, often remain skeptical of these developments within China. However, the Chinese case is different from that of most circumstances of labor exploitation in the developing world—at least with regard to Western investors, who tend to bring large-scale, high-profile investment projects to China. It is rarely the case that corporations are the leading advocates of civil liberties and labor reform, but they push for these reforms in China for a couple of reasons. Because many foreign investors in China are often more interested in long-term investments to capture market share than they are in cheap labor, they generally seek Chinese partners that are predictable, stable, and knowledgeable about Western-style business practices and negotiations. They want partners who will understand the issues at stake in contractual law and arbitration clauses. In short, they seek partners that have familiarity with Western laws, institutions, and negotiations.

Chinese factories, for their part, want desperately to land these partnerships, and they position themselves as suitable investment partners by adopting a number of the practices that Western partners will recognize as stable, reform-minded business practices. Among the basic reforms they adopt to show their fitness for partnerships with international corporations are labor reforms, as they are often the most visible internal-structure changes Chinese factories can make. Thus, Chinese companies signal a commitment to stable Western-style business practices through making a visible commitment to labor reform. Foreign investors and Chinese firms are not interested in human rights, per se, but the negotiations in the marketplace lead to transformed workplaces, which affect millions of Chinese citizens on a daily basis. As one general manager of a large industrial factory in Shanghai put it,

> [These practices are a] very important part of the economic reforms happening in China . . . It's a way of linking up with the international world. If a foreign company comes to China and wants to invest, who are they going to look for? They are going to look for the organizations with the most progressive and most Western ways of management and organization . . . It's a way of acting the way the foreign companies act, so they will see what kind of organization we are.

> (Personal interview)

The implication here is that Chinese factories are not simply adopting the practices that are most efficient in the market; rather, they are imitating the models of economic practice that are most respected and admired in the marketplace as a way of attracting foreign investment. With joint ventures, the stakes are often very high, so the pressure from foreign investors for a rationalization of economic processes is not surprising. However, the new legal institutions are also touching the piece-rate economy, as Western businesses seek to avoid public relations debacles such as Adidas, the Gap, and Nike have experienced. As one senior manager of an American garments company, who spends much of his time inspecting the labor and human rights situations in the factories he uses, explained to me,

> We're not trying to make [managers of Chinese companies] do anything that they don't already have on the books over here. We just want them to follow the laws that the Chinese government has already set up. The fact is, the Chinese government has set in place a good number of laws and institutions that protect the interests of workers . . . We think we can play a positive role by emphasizing the importance of these laws. If we don't like the way they're running things, we can take our business elsewhere. They need the business, so they're generally pretty cooperative . . . Believe me, we have our own interest in this. The last thing we want is the public relations disaster of allegations that our products are manufactured by a factory that violates human rights. It's just best for everyone that we do these visits.
>
> (Personal interview)

Even within China's emerging new economy, which is much younger and more fluid than the industrial economy, though the players are different, the basic issues are the same. For example, in the industrial economy, where we see powerful industrial giants from the West working to shape Chinese markets in their images, in the new economy, companies like Chinadotcom, Eachnet, and Sina.com have a great deal invested in creating a market that is viable for the virtual economy—one that makes foreign investors feel secure. And where investment banks have played critical roles in helping to finance major projects in the industrial sector— like the initial public offering of shares of Petro-China—in the new economy, the important players are as likely to be the venture capitalists who are setting up incubators to help in the development of a Chinese high-tech economy. Nevertheless, despite the differences in who the players are, the themes of bringing capitalism to China from the players who are most powerful in the international economy are ever present in the emergence of these new Chinese markets.

Foreign investment—specifically in the form of joint venture relationships between foreign firms and their Chinese business partners—has played a crucial role in this process of change. Joint venture relationships have a statistically significant and consistent effect on the rationalization of organizational decisions and practices of Chinese factories. Also, factories and companies that have formal relationships with foreign firms are significantly more likely to have formal organizational rules (Guthrie 1999). They are about seventeen times more likely to have formal grievance-filing procedures, about five times more likely to have worker representative committee meetings, and about twice as likely to have formal hiring procedures. In addition, these companies that have foreign partners are more likely to adopt the laws and regulations the Chinese government has constituted to create a rational–legal economic system—for example, the company law—that binds them to the rules of the international community. This relationship amounts to a significant positive effect of foreign joint ventures pushing their partner organizations to adopt stable rational–legal structures and systems in their organizations. More important, the Chinese partner companies in these joint-venture relationships are also changing as a result of joint-venture negotiations.

While these stable, rational–legal systems are adopted more often to attract foreign investors than they are for the good of workers, they nevertheless have radical implications for the structure of authority relations and, therefore, for the lives of individual Chinese citizens. Compared to the state sector and urban collectives, the average wages in foreign-sector and joint ventures are significantly higher and have increased much faster, especially after 1993. The visible internal-structure changes in Chinese workplaces are affecting millions of Chinese citizens on a daily basis. The workers in those business organizations have greater bargaining power within their own workplaces and now are entitled to numerous human rights (except for the right to independent unionization) guaranteed by the Labor Law (1994). Examples in this realm include the right to file

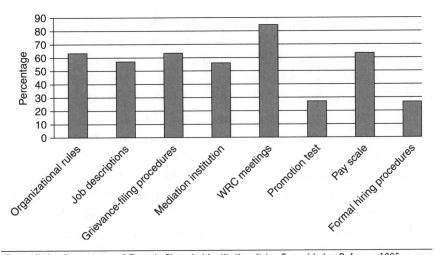

Figure 7.1a Percentages of Firms in Shanghai Institutionalizing Formal Labor Reforms, 1995.

Source: Guthrie (1999, Chapter 3)

Figure 7.1b Percentage of Workplaces in Shanghai's Industrial Economy that have Adopted Various Institutional Changes

Formal organizational rules	64%
Formal job descriptions	57%
Formal grievance-filing procedures	64%
Mediation institution in firm	56%
Institutionalized WRC meetings	85%
Promotion test	28%
Pay scale	64%
Formal hiring procedures	27%

Source: Guthrie (1999, Chapter 3)

---

grievances with Labor Arbitration Commissions (LACs), the right to a fair hearing at the LACs, and the right to a minimum wage. With respect to grievances filed with the LACs, by 2000, workers were winning, on average, about 60 percent of the cases brought before the LACs.

New Labor Markets and New Freedom

Workers in China today are also exposed to changing labor markets and a greater autonomy within these markets than ever before. As I discussed in

Chapter 4, in the planned economy, workers were placed in jobs by the Labor Bureau. This fact, combined with the reality of lifetime employment, meant that there was very little movement in the labor market. Workers had few options for new employment and, therefore, no bargaining power in the labor market. Further, as I discussed in Chapter 3, with the state control over the allocation of jobs, there were significant incentives against dissention with party officials and managers of state enterprises. But over the course of the economic reforms, these incentives keeping workers beholden to the state have withered away. The emergence of true labor markets in China means that individuals have greater bargaining power within their own workplaces. Ultimately, the increasingly autonomous labor markets mean that workers can vote with their feet, as it were, if they do not approve of the way they are being treated in their workplace. In other words, autonomous labor markets mean that laborers are free to exit the firm and find new employment elsewhere. Figures 7.2 and 7.3 show the changes in the labor market for different sectors of the economy. As of 2005, the service sector represented more than 30 percent of the total jobs in China, and there were over 107 million workers working in the private sector. (If you recall our discussion of expansive definitions of state versus private economies in Chapter 4, I have

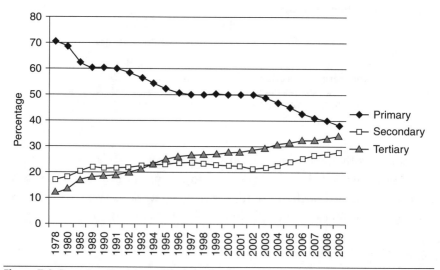

Figure 7.2 Percentage Breakdown of the Labor Force across Key Economic Categories.

Source: National Statistical Bureau of China (2010, 120).

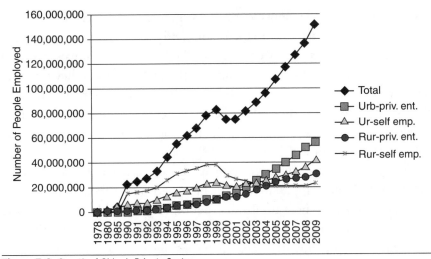

Figure 7.3 Growth of China's Private Sector.

Source: National Statistical Bureau of China (2010, 118–119).

used the conservative definition of the private economy here. By the more broadly conceived private economy, which includes joint stock companies and the like, the number would be much higher than 107 million.) These labor markets provide significant outlets for workers to seek employment beyond the reach of the state. But more important than whether there are jobs in these emerging sectors is the fact that they exist, and that workers are no longer tied to their workplaces with no options elsewhere.

Labor relations are being transformed in fundamental ways in China, and an activist government, self-interested foreign investors, an open labor market, and the emergence of a rule-of-law society in general are all behind these changes. An institutional framework has emerged that allows workers to seek rational–legal protection from capricious authority. The fact that workers can file grievances against employers in an institutional context separate from the firm is a radical departure from the employment relations of the past. Some concerns still exist in this realm. Namely, LACs are institutions of a still-authoritarian government, a fact that may reduce our confidence in the extent to which these institutions are actually set up to protect workers. And, not surprisingly, workers have the least chance of winning cases that are filed against state-owned enterprises and governmental organizations. Yet, across all other organizational types, the majority of cases filed against workplaces are won by laborers. In addition, if their cases are not handled to their liking, citizens like Mr. Bao (described above) can take their employers to court. And finally, individuals in China have greater freedom to move throughout the economy than they have had for fifty years. This is perhaps the greatest leverage that workers have over their workplaces: with the end of the job assignment system and the new freedom that workers have to participate in open labor markets, they can now vote with their feet.

The concerns over abuses of human rights and labor that are inextricably tied to China's reputation in the global economy are significant, and it is not my purpose here to dismiss the importance of the harm that the Chinese government has inflicted on its people. However, it is also the case that gradually implemented reforms have transformed labor relations in China in fundamental ways, and it is important to depict an accurate and empirically grounded picture of those changes. By looking beyond the workplace, we can begin to understand the forces pushing these reforms forward. The programs of reform-minded elites, who are creating the "quiet revolution" occurring within China, are reshaping the institutional terrain within which labor relations occur. Pressure from foreign investors to show commitments to the rational principles of the international economy are reshaping the normative environments in which managers make decisions about labor. Changing labor market dynamics afford the most talented workers to test the boundaries of the rational–legal reforms that are transforming labor. As China continues to evolve under the normative pressures of the international economy, these changes are likely to become even more widespread.

Conclusions

On August 18, 1991, Boris Yeltsin gave a rousing speech from the turret of a tank thwarting the coup attempt against then President of the Soviet Union, Mikhail Gorbachev. In his speech, Yeltsin appealed to the electoral process that we most often associate with the system of democracy: "Your commanders have ordered you to storm the White House and to arrest me. But I as the elected President of Russia give you the order to turn your tanks and not to fight against your own people." The world applauded the turn toward a peaceful democratic transition that ensued, especially given that the images of Tiananmen bloodshed were still so fresh in people's minds. The Russian people—and more importantly the Russian military—had chosen the path of democracy over authoritarianism. And the case of Russia has often been held up as the mirror for the Chinese economic miracle: China may be outperforming Russia on the economic front, but Russia took the high road politically and chose democracy.

But twenty years later, Russia looks a lot more like an autocracy than a democracy. And strongman Vladimir Putin has taken the position that democracy is "nice" but the key thing we are interested in is stability; and stability from the Putin picture comes from strong leadership. The "election" of Putin's handpicked successor, Dmitry Medvedev in 2008 laid bare the weaknesses of Russia's democratic processes; the more recent announcement of Putin's intentions of staying in power for the next decade made it clear just how much closer Russia is to autocracy than democracy. These events have completely overthrown any fantasy of democracy in this budding democratic nation. As the *Washington Post* recently put it:

> Those who defended the White House thought they had changed the course of history, that in standing up so assertively the people had shaken off their Soviet subservience to the state and that the state would begin to serve the people. But today, elections are not fair, courts are not independent, political opposition is not tolerated and the reformers are widely blamed for what has gone wrong . . . Today, Russia works on bribes, and Putin's opponents call his United Russia party the party of crooks and thieves. People can say whatever they want to one another, unlike in Soviet times when they feared the secret police knocking in the middle of the night, but television is controlled and any opposition is publicly invisible.
>
> ("Russia: Once Almost a Democracy," *Washington Post*, 2011)

But elections and political power are only part of the problem. Democratic societies are not built only on election processes; they are also built on the institutions that support these processes. They rely on institutions like the rule of law, an independent court system, organizations that work independent of the state system, and many others (many of which were discussed above). And while free elections are an important feature of democratic societies, they are only part of the story. Take, for example, the issues of freedom of speech and freedom of the press, both cornerstones of

a healthy democratic society. China is often criticized for its lack of progress on these fronts, and rightly so. But are countries, like Russia, that
proclaim the founding of a democracy any better on these fronts? In 2006,
investigative reporter Anna Politkovskaya was found shot dead in her
apartment. If this was an isolated incident, one might not question the
implications for Russia's democratic transition. In 2009, human rights
lawyer, Stanislav Markelov, was shot dead for working on similar issues. In
China, the state is responsible for the curtailing of democratic rights like
free speech; in Russia, which supposedly became a democracy in 1991,
speech around certain topics is still controlled, but it is just not clear who
is curtailing it. This is because the institutions of democracy have not been
built yet. Building a democratic society is a complex process. We often
mistake the words and symbolic acts tied to democracy with the institutions of democracy. But the institutions of democracy take years to build;
not only because they are complex, but also because they take time to gain
traction with the public. There have been many examples of the announcing
of democratic transitions, only to see the cracking of this façade in ensuing
years. Russia is an obvious example here, but let us think also about the
situations of Iraq, which we proclaimed to be a democracy the moment the
statue of Saddam fell. Yet, the weak institutions mean that if the country
is a "democracy" it is in name only.

In the case of China, the government has openly resisted Western
prescriptions about the rapid transition to a democratic system. Yet the
image of an unyielding authoritarian state is not accurate in this case,
either. One cannot deny the path China chose in 1989, but it is also not
accurate to discount the democratic reforms that are occurring there. For
twenty years, the liberal faction of China's Communist Party has been
quietly pushing a reform program that has been building the institutions
that support a democratic system. Hu Jitao, Wen Jiabao, Jiang Zemin, and
Zhu Rongji have spent little time talking openly about a gradual democratic transition, but the gradual building of the institutions of democracy
is clearly part of their agendas.

8

CHINA'S INTEGRATION INTO THE GLOBAL ECONOMY

Since the first missionaries and explorers arrived on China's shores, Westerners have gazed upon East Asia with a mixture of awe, quizzical scrutiny, and even disdain. The West has long held this part of the world as a distant other, where riches and potential abound, but where differences are great enough that the cultural divide always looms in the background, threatening to swallow even the most amicable trade relations. In recent years, as China has emerged from its isolation and entered the global economy, debates over how to view, acknowledge, and accept Asian differences have taken on a pitched tenor, as the realms of economics, politics, military prowess, and human rights have all become intertwined in a discussion of weighty questions. Is democracy a universal ideal to which all nations should aspire? What individual rights should we consider inalienable? To what extent should economic and political relations among nations be intertwined? Will China ultimately be friend and economic partner, or military foe? And to what extent do cultural differences—particularly differences between East and West—play a role in how we address these issues?

The courses of development in East Asia have belied standard assumptions about how we should answer these questions. In different ways, China and the East Asian newly industrialized economies have shown the benefits of a strong state-led development, and the economic success of these development projects has provided concrete evidence against the neoliberal alternative of rapid privatization. If a strong authoritarian state can deliver economic prosperity to its people, do Western democracies have a legitimate position in advocating liberal democracy for these countries when the cost may very well be the economic success the countries have achieved? As the largest remaining communist regime, China is often lambasted by human rights advocates—not to mention the U.S. government—for its record on human rights, and many argue that a country's poor human-rights record should be at the center of any bilateral relationship with an authoritarian government. In addition, China is fast emerging as one of the key geo-political powers that will offset U.S. hegemony as the military force policing the world. Will China's integration pose a threat, as many hawkish members of Congress would have us believe? Or will tensions with the United States and the rest of the Western world rise as China rises? Will the country continue to evolve in the realms of human rights and political reform?

In this book, I have advanced the view that China's transformation has fundamentally been a global project. Reformers have used the country's need to develop economically as a force to push the country down the path of economic and political reform. Even those who have been against the reforms have had to accept that China needed to grow in the economic sphere. From the time of Deng Xiaoping's visit to the United States in January 1979, the orientation has been toward the global economy. In the early years of the reforms, it was about cash and technology. The coastal development strategy helped turn China into an economic juggernaut, one of the most active producing and trading countries in the world, and it has generated a tremendous amount of economic growth in the process. With foreign firms also came the transfer of needed technologies and manage-ment practices. In later years, this integration came to be about more than cash and technology. Reformers like Zhu Rongji used the pressures and standards of the global economy as a means for social reform. The laws that were passed under Zhu's watch were not only helping to create a stable institutional infrastructure for investment in China but were also creating the institutions of social change. In this final chapter, I turn to the issue of what China's integration into the global economy will mean for the rest of the world. Drawing upon the information and arguments of previous chapters, I will discuss China's emerging role in the constellation of powerful nations around the world.

The China Threat

The US economic partnership with China, fragile as it is, is often challenged by our concerns over China as a global threat. Over the last decade, scholars, journalists, and pundits have warned that conflict with China is inevitable. As China's economic power has grown over the last decade, so too has the rhetoric surrounding China's growing military power and the concomitant threat. For example, not long ago an issue of the *Atlantic Monthly* presented a picture of a sinister-looking member of the People's Liberation Army and a jingoistic title, "How We Would Fight China: The Next Cold War." The article within, penned by Robert Kaplan (2005), illustrates the rhetoric often found in the China doomsday scenario:

> The Middle East is just a blip. The American military contest with China in the Pacific will define the twenty-first century. And China will be a more formidable adversary than Russia ever was . . . If not a big war with China, then a series of Cold War-style standoffs that stretch out over years and decades.

More recently, Peter Navarro and Greg Autry published *Death by China: Confronting the Dragon—A Global Call to Action* (2011), in which the authors warn: "Death by China. This is the very real risk we all face as the world's most populous nation and soon-to-be largest economy is rapidly turning into the planet's most efficient assassin." In his book-jacket comments on Navarro and Autry's book, Gordon Chang, author of *The Coming Collapse of China*, writes, "At this moment, Chinese officials are poisoning your medicines, polluting your air and undermining your freedoms. If you're American, Indian, or Japanese, they are planning to wage war on your country." This type of rhetoric is not only common, but it is also not confined to popular reporting. Indeed, just as China was being ushered into the global economy through its accession to the WTO, the ominous Cox Report, issued in 2001, warned,

> The PRC began developing its ballistic missile system in the early 1960s. The first missile, the CSS-2, showed strong Soviet design influences. Launched from mobile launchers, it has a range of up to 1,926 miles. The CSS-3 was the PRC's first intercontinental range missile, but with a range of 3,417 miles it cannot reach the United States. The CSS-4 is the PRC's main ICBM threat against the U.S.

With a range in excess of 7,457 miles, it can hit most of the U.S. During the 1990s, the PRC has deployed approximately 20 CSS-4s in silos, most of which are targeted at the U.S. An improved version of the CSS-4, known as the CSS-4 Mod 2, could allow the PRC to deploy multiple warheads.[1]

Speculation about China's military investment and the threat that it implies has run to the highest levels of government including, when they were in office, former U.S. Secretary of Defense Donald Rumsfeld and former Vice President Dick Cheney. (The Obama Administration has been significantly more measured in its views about a potential "China threat.") And recent reports about China's launching of its new aircraft carrier have only fomented the views of China as the expansionist power. Jingoistic as these accounts are, even more balanced examinations of United States-China relations by authors like Stephen Glain (2011) have predicted an ominous future, a collision course of conflict between China and the United States.

But what is the truth? Does China pose a serious threat to the military order of the world? Has it undertaken a level of activity that is significantly different from that of other powerful nations? One of the key issues that is often pointed to in doomsday scenarios is the rapid rise in military spending that has occurred in China since the economic reforms began. And U.S. Secretary of Defense Donald Rumsfeld (citing no evidence) recently speculated that China's military budget is actually much higher than it officially acknowledges, ominously stating, "Since no nation threatens China, one must wonder: why this growing investment?"[2] As Figure 8.1 illustrates, China's defense spending has indeed increased more than tenfold in the three decades since the economic reforms began. From spending less than $2 billion on national defense in 1978, that commitment has risen to nearly $46 billion by 2006 (according to China's official statistics). One thing we might first ask to contextualize such a figure, however, is whether this spending has outpaced the growth of the economy overall. In other words, has China's commitment to the military grown more rapidly than its overall rise as an economy and society in the reform era? As the second axis in Figure 8.1 illustrates, in fact, since the 1980s, China's spending in this area has remained relatively stable, at about 8 percent of the national budget. A second, and perhaps more important, question we might ask is: Compared to what? How does China's military spending measure up to

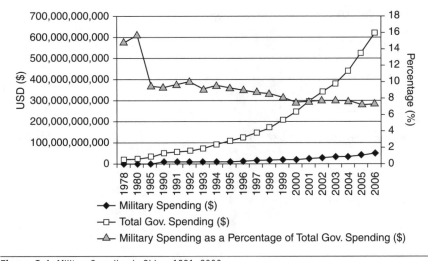

Figure 8.1 Military Spending in China, 1991–2006.

Source: National Statistical Bureau of China (2007, 281).

other countries' spending? On this point, a comparison with the United States reveals an interesting story. As Figure 8.2 shows, in 2009[3] the United States spent over $600 billion on national defense—a figure more than six times larger than what China spent in the same year, and a figure that is greater than the combined military spending of all other countries in the world. (Note here that, in Figure 8.2 I use World Bank estimates, which is probably a more accurate estimate of China's military spending; even with the more aggressive estimate, the United States still outspends China on military by a factor of 6.) And in terms of percentages, the U.S. allocation for national defense is more than twice that of the Chinese (16.4 percent, compared to 7.6 percent in 2009).

China is certainly growing in power, and its strength as a nation will extend well beyond the economic realm into the world of geopolitics. From these figures, it is not obvious that China's expenditures are unreasonable given the size of the nation, the size of the economy, and what other large nations spend on national defense. The real issue behind the concerns over China's military spending is that hawks in the United States want to ensure that China does not emerge as a credible counterbalance to U.S. military hegemony. Or, if you follow the arguments of Stephen Glain, perhaps they *do* want China to emerge as a military power, so that

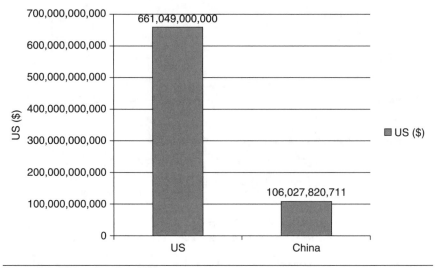

Figure 8.2 Military Spending, 2009.

Source: World Bank http://search.worldbank.org/data?qterm=china%20military%20spending&language=EN Accessed June 23, 2011; *China Military Spending*, World Bank http://search.worldbank.org/data?qterm=united+ statesilitary+spending&language=EN&format= Accessed June 23, 2011; US Military Spending Exchange Rate Calculated at 6.47 www.xe.com June 23, 2011.

there is an argument to feed the military industrial complex in the United States. The bottom line is this: Whether the United States merits, or should strive for, the role of unopposed military power in the world is not the subject of this book; however, it is important to note that China's military activity is not out of step for a country of its size economically and it pales in comparison to the military activity of the United States.

Cybersecurity, Protectionism, and Economic Growth

Another security concern that has worked its way into the public consciousness is issue of cybersecurity and cyber warfare. Whether the issue is "Operation Shady Rat," which has, in some circles, been attributed to China, the hacking into Google email accounts, or the explicit fears about allowing Chinese telecommunications firms invest in or own U.S. telecommunications infrastructure, the concerns over China and cybersecurity are significant. And in some cases they are real; but in some cases they are not. For an analysis of this issue, let us turn to another case study that has been in the news as of late, the case of Huawei telecommunications.

Above, we touched on the issue of protectionism as it relates to currency manipulation and offshore manufacturing. However, there is a second protectionist position the United States has taken over the last couple of years that is equally worrying. In the wake of four decades of offshore manufacturing, the United States has sent a lot of cash overseas to pay for the goods produced in locations like Japan, Taiwan, the Philippines and China. It is through this process that Japan became the No. 1 controller of U.S. cash reserves in the 1980s, as China is the top holder today. Currently, China sits on about $2 trillion in U.S. cash. The best thing for the U.S. economy would be for this money to be reinvested in America in the form of investing in real estate, developing projects or acquiring companies. But the U.S. government seems uninterested in the flow of such resources, at least with respect to China. For example, in 2005, when the Chinese National Offshore Oil Corporation (CNOOC) attempted to buy Unocal, Congress stepped in and declared—in the name of U.S. national interest— that a Chinese state-owned enterprise (SOE) could not own a U.S. energy company. In August 2005, CNOOC, which is a publicly traded company, withdrew its bid to acquire the American company, though it had made a fair tender for the acquisition. A similar signal was sent when the household appliances giant Haier attempted to buy Maytag. In this case, Congress did not step in directly, but it was reported that Haier withdrew its bid out of fear of political repercussions. Huawei has been the target of two of these recent crusades. In 2010 as a result of heavy lobbying by the U.S. government, Sprint rejected Huawei's bid to help the mobile provider modernize its network, despite the fact that the deal would have clearly benefited Sprint. Then in early 2011, the U.S. government scuttled the bid to buy a significant stake in 3Leaf, an American server network firm. The reported reason for the U.S. intervention in both Huawei cases was that the company ownership of a U.S. company could constitute a compromise to American security. The behind-the-scenes word was that certain members of Congress threatened to make this very political issue a topic of the 2012 election and the Obama Administration did not want to handle this political hot potato.

Recently, I talked with Bill Owens, the former CEO of the now-defunct Nortel (whose alliance with Sprint put them in the middle of the Huawei–Sprint deal). Owens has impeccable credentials in both intelligence community (as a retired Admiral) and in the telecommunications sector as former CEO of Nortel and Director of various other telecommunications organizations; and he knows the Huawei people far better than I. In that conversation, the sense of disgust and loss was obvious. As Owens put it:

> The deal was done, and it would have added $1 billion to Sprint's bottom line. But for political reasons, the Administration stepped in . . . So much capital in China is sitting on the sidelines, and we need it desperately. But they just couldn't see it. The whole thing is killing the American telecommunications sector.

There may be a legitimate case for not wanting Chinese SOEs to buy U.S. oil or technology companies. National security should not be ignored when contemplating transactions of import; nor should we dismiss accusations that a Chinese company might have ties to the Chinese military. Thus, we might well understand the U.S. positions against CNOOC or ZTE (another major Chinese telecommunications company, which is state-owned and was also a suitor for Sprint). Haier, on the other hand, seems like an obvious case of congressional activism gone awry. In that case, a privately held Chinese company (Haier was a converted collective, not an SOE) was bidding to buy a struggling U.S. company that makes washing machines. There can be no conceivable reason beyond American pride that a Chinese company be excluded from pursuing a legitimate market offer.

The case of Huawei actually lies much closer to that of Haier than to the cases of CNOOC or ZTE. Huawei has argued convincingly that it is an employee-owned company like any other in China and denies any ties to the military. In some ways, Huawei has been forced to live down its founder's resume—chief executive Ren Zhengfei once served without rank in the People's Liberation Army's (PLA) Engineering Corps—and China's history whenever it seeks to invest overseas. Deputy Chairman of the $28 billion company, Ken Hu, offered a credible defense when those charges surfaced again in early 2011.

> It is a matter of fact that Mr. Ren is just one of the many CEOs around the world who have served in the military, and it is also a matter of fact that Huawei has only offered telecommunications equipment that is in line with civil standards.

Ken wrote in a letter in response to critics of the 3Leaf deal. "It is also factual to say that no one has ever offered any evidence that Huawei has been involved in any military technologies at any time."

Huawei's track record merits much interest. It is one of the few private companies on *Fortune*'s Global 500 and, more impressively, it runs a close second to Ericsson as the largest telecommunications infrastructure company in the world. By the numbers, Huawei is an impressive company: It had $28 billion in revenues in 2010, was awarded *The Economist*'s Innovation Award in 2010 and has more than 17,000 patents in twenty countries. With corporate headquarters in Shenzhen, China, the company does about 50 percent of its business in Asia (about 33 percent in China) with the rest spread through regions throughout the rest of the world. Huawei began international expansion in emerging markets in the late 1990s and has a significant market presence in Europe and Africa, and has been very serious recently about expansion into the United States. In the early 2000s, the company was also renowned for its alleged patent violations with Cisco, which were settled out of court in 2004. More recently (2010), there was another lawsuit with Motorola, which had plaintiff suits running in both directions, and was settled very quickly, with neither side admitting wrongdoing. Huawei's ownership history is both simple and complex. Despite reports to the contrary, Huawei is not and has never been a state-owned company. It has never been favored by the state apparatus, and has never enjoyed special treatment from the Chinese banks (as is often reported). Mr. Zhengfei founded Huawei in 1987 after his relatively short PLA service. He was not part of the Chinese security apparatus, as has often been reported. Privately held companies are under fewer requirements for reporting board structure, ownership share distribution, etc., so there has always been less transparency with the organization than is the case with publicly traded companies that are dealing with public requirements. Today we know exactly who the board members are (as reported in May of 2011 by Huawei at the request of the U.S. government) and we know that the largest shareholder is Mr. Ren, with 1.4 percent of the shares—fairly low as far as ownership concentration goes for a large privately held company. The company has long been considered the model "home-grown multinational." Product lines include: wireless networks, fixed-line networks, optical networks, data communications networks, value-added services, handsets and terminals.

The concerns over Huawei doing business in the United States are these: (1) As a privately held company, Huawei is not nearly as transparent as a publicly listed company is, especially in reporting board structure. (2) Whatever its ownership, it is believed by some that Huawei is an agent of the Chinese state, particularly the military and the state security apparatus. (3) Huawei's role in manufacturing telecommunications infrastructure could open U.S. networks up to cybersecurity threats. My analysis of these frequent critiques of the company is wholly my own and formed based on a review of the company's internal documents and from pointed questions directed at Deputy Chairman Ken Hu and President of Huawei North America Charles Ding. Huawei's complex situation as a Chinese company that is an emerging global powerhouse in the competitive and sensitive sector of telecommunications infrastructure is one that mirrors many of the tensions that have arisen following China's rise in economic power.

First, the transparency issue could easily be assuaged, many journalists and critics have asserted, if Huawei would only undertake a public offering. However, the nuances of Initial Public Offerings (IPO) in China are considerably complex. Huawei actually did attempt an IPO in 1998, but several issues got in the way at that time. For one thing, an international IPO was out of the question at this time, as the Chinese government was working very carefully to prepare the way for PetroChina to be the first international IPO to come out of mainland Chinese in the reform era (2000, NYSE). In addition, even if Huawei were to attempt an IPO on the domestic exchanges (Shanghai or Shenzhen), the central government made it clear it was going to limit the amount of capital Huawei could raise, so that it would not overwhelm the state's favored telecommunication firms, such as China Telecom (ZTE). Given these constraints, Mr. Ren thought it meaningless to embark on an IPO if the company's ability to raise capital was going to be constrained. Today some journalists, such as the *Financial Times'* Kevin Brown, continue to suggest that an IPO would be the simple answer to Huawei's problems, and it is less likely that the Chinese government could stand in the company's way now. And, indeed, many of Huawei's employees would love this to happen, as their shares would all be worth much more than they currently are. As one senior executive put it to me, "We would all like for this to happen, at least those of us who have been with the company a long time. It would be great for us." But the current IPO problem is tied to the ownership structure of the firm—and to peculiarities of Chinese securities regulation. As a private company, Huawei has worked to incentivize as many employees as possible through ownership. Sounds like smart capitalism, right? The only problem is that under China's New Company Law (2006) and the Securities Law (2006), the rule in China is that if a firm is to be publicly listed, no more than 200 employees can own shares. Currently, more than 61,000 of Huawei's 110,000 employees own shares in the company. In order for Huawei to undertake an IPO, it would have to trample on the employee ownership options of about 60,800 current employees. This is quite a dilemma, and it is not surprising that the company's leadership is moving cautiously on this front. From a capitalist perspective, it is a bad law on the Chinese side, but it is not a law of Huawei's making. China insiders will tell you that there are ways around these laws—either through creating a holding company or a subsidiary that meets the less-than-200-shareholders rule and taking that organization public and leaving the rest as an investor in the publicly-traded entity. But both of these approaches bring their own problems, and it is understandable that the company is taking great care in this decision-making process.

Second, with respect to Huawei being an agent of the Chinese state, this argument perhaps dates back to a 2005 Rand Corporation report, which argued, in classic neo-realist logic, that the Chinese government and military would make telecommunications a cornerstone of its next global push toward geopolitical control. The report went on to name Huawei and ZTE as the two key players that would likely be helping the Chinese government in this endeavor. When I asked Ken about this report, he actually spoke quite eloquently about it, saying,

> I actually think this report was extremely intelligent . . . There may be some real merit to what they are predicting. The only problem is that we are not coordinated with the Chinese government or the Chinese military the way they say we are. We are just not in those circles. We do very little business with the Chinese government at this point, and we are not a state-owned firm. But once it was out there, it seemed like everyone took it for granted that it was true.

If anything, according to Ken, the Chinese government has a somewhat cool relationship with Huawei because of Huawei's competitive position vis-à-vis ZTE and because it has been so openly critical of the Chinese company and securities laws. With respect to working with the Chinese government, Huawei bids for this work just like any other company does, and Chinese government contracts (including government grants and PLA contracts) constitute less than 1 percent of Huawei's business at this point. Cisco does a much higher volume of business with the Chinese government than Huawei does. When Huawei is simply lumped in with the likes of ZTE, which *is* an SOE (despite its publicly traded status, which officially makes it a "joint stock" company), it is simply a sloppy characterization of what this firm is about.

The third issue, whether doing business with Huawei opens the U.S. government up to cybersecurity threats, builds in part on the former two propositions. If Huawei has not been transparent enough in terms of ownership structure or in terms of its relationship to the Chinese government or military, the company is working hard to make those issues clear now. But the larger problem with conversations over Huawei's cybersecurity agenda on behalf of the Chinese government is that these allegations often emerge from behind closed doors. They happen with a "trust me" wink and a nod from the American intelligence community, as Kevin Brown recently reported in his account, "Huawei's Opacity a Colourful Issue for U.S.," in the April 19, 2011, *Financial Times*. A concrete example of this strategy to damn Huawei by unsubstantiated intelligence reports is a letter written by five U.S. senators and one U.S. House member—Senators Jon Kyl, Republican, Arizona, Saxby Chambliss, Republican, Georgia, James Inhofe, Republican, Oklahoma, Richard Burr, Republican, North Carolina, and Tom Coburn, Republican, Oklahoma, and Darrell Issa, Republican, California—to President Barack Obama on April 4, 2011:

> We write to you about national security risks associated with the government's recent and proposed investment in broadband technology . . . We are concerned that these initiatives provide an opportunity for the introduction of potentially harmful technology to U.S. broadband infrastructure . . . We are particularly concerned that [companies] such as Huawei and ZTE could benefit from federal investment in broadband technology . . . these companies receive extensive support from the Chinese government . . . American

companies providing broadband access may not be aware of the potential threats that accompany bids from Huawei or ZTE.

Huawei at least deserves to be considered in a different category from ZTE. It is also clear where some of the blatant factual errors exist in this behind-the-scenes document. In addition, no one ever seems to mention that Huawei is the only Chinese vendor to use third-party verification through the well-respected Virginia-based Electronic Warfare Associates (EWA); that it is the only Chinese company to have established a Global Cybersecurity Task Force to work directly with international governments (with great success in Canada and the United Kingdom) to develop ways to mollify the fears of international governments; and that it is the only Chinese vendor to have set up a North American Cybersecurity office (established in 2010). Beyond the misinformation or gaps in the reported facts, even more shocking to me is how little accountability there is for these reports on the U.S. side. I have never seen it detailed, for example, where members of Congress are getting their information or who is supporting their lobbying on this issue. As it turns out, three of the six members of Congress who wrote the letter received campaign funding from Cisco or Motorola, or both. Not that the receipt of campaign funding delegitimizes their concerns, but it does make one wonder about their motivations and about the conversations that are going on behind closed doors.

As Ken reflected on the issue,

> We know that China's reputation in the area of cybersecurity is very bad, but we are not China. We can't change where we were born, just like you can't change who your parents are, but we *can* work very hard with governments around the world to help them understand that we are not part of the problem. In fact, we want to be part of the solution. We want to have the best standards in the world in terms of how we deal with cybersecurity issues.

At one point, Ken described in greater detail the way these negotiations typically go. He detailed specific concerns that were raised by the British and Canadian governments, the process they went through to address the concerns and the key offerings that made the respective governments comfortable. "What about the U.S.?" I pressed. Ken did something between a scoff and a rolling of the eyes. "Of course we want to work with the U.S. It is our biggest potential market. But if the U.S. government simply doesn't want us there, I am not sure how much more we can do."

These days, the hawkish rhetoric over China's military buildup has subsided somewhat (mostly because of the Obama Administration's more moderate stance on the subject), but it has been replaced by an equally loud din of concern over China's impact on the global economy and the corresponding dangers for international business. On July 23, 2007, the cover of *BusinessWeek* gloomily asked "Can China be Fixed?," and spent many pages in the magazine documenting the looming crisis. The article summoned images of Gordon Chang's 2001 screed *The Coming Collapse of China*, which predicted a collapse that never came. The recent press over lead paint in Mattel toy products, poison in dog food, endemic corruption, and the threat to the global environment has made the issues omnipresent in the public consciousnesses. It is an odd juxtaposition: on the one hand we have the most dramatic success of the transition from communism to capitalism; on the other we have visions of the aggressively expansionist military power that is on the verge of collapse due to endemic corruption. The irony, of course, is that China is far more stable (and likely more committed to peaceful global integration) than the nations that have followed U.S. prescriptions and made the rapid transition to a democracy without gradually building institutions to support this system first.

Currency, Trade, and China's Integration into the Global Community

Politics between the United States and China have reached somewhat of a fevered pitch as of late. On the one hand the United States desperately needs China as a trading partner. On the other hand, we have an increasingly complex and suspicious relationship with China and Chinese companies. If we are going to be successful in getting the U.S. economy back on track, foreign direct investment in the United States will be a necessary part of this, and our most important partner in this endeavor will be China. At this point, we need China more than it needs us. Yet, instead of focusing on how to rebuild skilled labor, how to foster competitive business environments, and how to attract capital back to the United States, we obsess over issues like China's currency manipulation as the source of our problems. Meanwhile China sits on some $2 trillion in U.S. currency— money it is looking to invest abroad—and we have become one of the more protectionist economies in the world, especially with respect to China. We do not create business-friendly environments for our own businesses, part of the reason they go abroad, and we do not create business-friendly environments for capital coming back, which we sorely need.

For many in the United States, the common assumption is that greater protectionism is the easiest way to protect the U.S. economy and American jobs. By making imports more expensive, there is less incentive to buy abroad and less incentive for American corporations to take their production facilities overseas. The net effect will be the creation of American jobs. Buy American and, more specifically, buy goods that are produced in America, and the U.S. economy will grow because the wages will stay in the U.S. consumer economy. There is an obvious logic to this view, and if it were possible that greater protectionism would bring all of the jobs that have moved offshore back, this would be great. Unfortunately, the logic of offshore manufacturing is so much more complicated today than it was when the practice was pioneered in the 1960s and 1970s. Today it is not just a matter of finding the cheapest labor; it is also a matter of balancing the access to internal markets, access to skilled labor, balances of trade and internal politics.

Take, for example, the case of Walmart, which is now the single largest exporter from China to the United States. Protectionist policies (or a forced appreciation of the Chinese yuan) are not going to bring Walmart's manufacturing back to the United States. The company is far too committed to and embedded in the Chinese economy—as exampled by its access to China's internal markets—to imagine that higher export prices or trade barriers would bring Walmart's manufacturing processes back to the United States. This part of protectionism is simply a nonstarter. However, there is a second protectionist position the United States has taken over the last couple of years that is equally worrying. In the wake of four decades of offshore manufacturing, the United States has sent a lot of cash overseas to pay for the goods produced in locations like Japan, Taiwan, the Philippines and China. It is through this process that Japan became the No. 1 controller of U.S. cash reserves in the 1980s, as China is the top holder today. The best thing for the U.S. economy would be for this money to be reinvested in America in the form of investing in real estate, developing projects or acquiring companies. But the U.S. government seems disinterested in the flow of such resources, at least with respect to China.

Currency Manipulation

Recently I was asked to come to the office of a U.S. Senator to talk about China and trade. One of his constituents arranged for the meeting, as she thought his China experts should hear my views. What I heard instead was a great deal of well meaning but flawed assumptions about China, its economy and its motives. Conversations about China have grown increasingly frustrating in Washington, but not for the reasons you might suspect. For one thing, Capitol Hill is crawling with twenty-somethings who have visited or lived briefly in China—studying a language and/or teaching English—and who are widely regarded as China experts, though they often lack any economic or social scientific training. With their fluency in Mandarin and a couple of good China "war stories," they have become the closest thing in the room to a China specialist. Moreover, these discussions have become increasingly political, which means election-year politics not reason govern the conversation. Nobody listens to any new facts or ideas, despite the speed of change in today's China. People assume they know what the truth is because their friend, constituent or political advisor told them it was so, regardless of the reality on the ground.

As we have discussed throughout this book, there are a lot of mistaken assumptions and misinformation in the debate over U.S.–China trade relations in Washington, but the ultimate red herrings—and political red flags—are trade imbalance and currency manipulation. The United States had a $252 billion trade deficit with China in 2010. China exported $334 billion to the United States, while only importing $82 billion of U.S. goods and services. The numbers do look unbalanced and unfair if the story ended there. Yet the trade imbalance is much more complicated than this cursory treatment by an ill-informed press or by political leaders with their own agendas. First of all, as discussed in Chapter 4, of the top forty exporters from China, ten are U.S. companies. Multinational corporations like Dell, Motorola and Walmart benefit tremendously from manufacturing in China and exporting to the rest of the world. These benefits result in healthy profits, which boost stock prices and market capitalization for all of these companies. Walmart alone accounts for about $30 billion in exports from China to the United States (a number roughly equal to the U.S. imports from Mexico).

Prior to 1991, under the gross national product (GNP) accounting system, these exports were counted on the U.S. side of the trade ledger because American companies produced the goods. With the shift to the gross domestic product (GDP) in 1991, however, these exports counted on China's side of the export ledger because the goods are produced in China. The accounting slippage works the other way as well: goods produced by U.S. corporations in China and sold domestically do not count as exports from the U.S. to China but simply as Chinese domestic production, despite the fact that U.S. companies are producing the goods. Under GNP, the earnings of multinational corporations were counted according to where a multinational corporation was owned and where the profits returned. Under GDP, the profits are attributed to the site of production, regardless of where the organization is owned or incorporated. Thus, although Walmart is the largest exporter from China to the United States, those imports count as Chinese exports in the balance of trade, and its domestic sales in China do not count as exports from the United States to China. This prompts the broader economic question: Should goods produced by Walmart and for Walmart stores, albeit in China, be counted on our books or China's? Hard to say. Most of those profits are not repatriated, but the cheap prices are passed on to consumers at home. More importantly, the profits affect Walmart's share price, which dictates the capitalization of one of the world's largest companies, and benefits Walmart shareholders. Furthermore, Walmart benefits from being in China not only for its access to cheap labor but also for its access to China's internal markets. The situation of the trade imbalance is murky at best.

With respect to currency manipulation, the impact of currency appreciation is not nearly as unambiguous as it is often portrayed in Washington and in the popular media. The overwhelming consensus in Washington is that if China allows its currency to appreciate, its advantage in the global production supply chain will diminish. As a result, it will be more expensive to produce goods in China. In theory then, U.S. corporations that have moved overseas in search of cheaper labor will be forced to return to the United States and create jobs that were lost to globalization. While this is the political consensus, another scenario is a much more likely outcome. Companies like Walmart are far too embedded in China to simply pick up and return home—and it would be far too expensive for them to do so, regardless of the value of the yuan. Walmart's internal market in China is growing rapidly and will eventually eclipse the value of its exports from the United States to China. The more probable scenario is that Walmart will stay put in China, and will continue to use this as its production base to manufacture less expensive products to benefit consumers in both China and the United States. If this happens, the appreciation of Chinese currency will simply make shopping at Walmart *more* expensive for low-income U.S. consumers, without creating any new jobs, thereby hurting the U.S. economy. This is the most likely outcome.

There is a second possibility. The currency appreciation may force Walmart and other light-industry-goods producers to move to other countries with cheaper labor. While we might be able to hold prices constant, it is extremely unlikely that currency appreciation will create jobs here at home. Indeed, a growing number of intelligent economists have come to similar conclusions. For example, Federal Reserve Bank economists Matthew Higgins and Thomas Klitgaard (2004, 2007) argue that only a strong Chinese economy is going to change the balance of trade between China and the United States. Because U.S.-produced goods are generally more expensive than Chinese goods, it is only through a strengthened Chinese economy, with citizens who can afford to purchase pricier U.S. goods, that the balance of trade will be righted in a healthy way. An appreciated yuan will weaken China's position and thereby weaken the economy, thus creating a situation in which China has less purchasing power vis-à-vis the United States instead of more. Either way, the impact of yuan appreciation is far from clear.

Global Trade

Although there is much hand wringing about the China threat among hawkish writers and politicians and an equal amount of concern from more liberal camps about China's human-rights record, the likely scenario is one of continued integration rather than conflict. The main reason has to do with the fact that economic integration has already occurred to such an extent that it would be simply too costly for any parties to go down the road of conflict. As I described in Chapter 4, since the early 1990s China has become a major recipient of foreign direct investment (FDI), which occupies the major part of total foreign capital (along with foreign loans and other investments) that China has received. In 1993, China received more FDI than any other country, and since then, China had been the second-largest recipient in the world of FDI, behind only the United

States. By early 1999, FDI in joint ventures and wholly foreign-owned companies exceeded U.S.$250 billion, several times larger than cumulative FDI since World War II in Japan, Korea, and Taiwan, combined (Lardy 2002). In 2002, China's total inflow of FDI reached U.S.$400 billion, making it the world's largest recipient of FDI. According to Nicholas Lardy (1995), four factors contributed to the dramatic increases of the FDI China attracted in the early 1990s: (1) the increasing magnitude of aggregate FDI flowing to developing countries in the 1990s; (2) China's political stability in the post-Tiananmen square era, combined with the explosive growth of domestic economy, rebuilt the confidence of foreign firms and investors; (3) after a decade of economic liberalization and the practice of coastal developmental strategies, China's foreign investment regime had been systematically liberalized by then and more sectors had been opened to foreign investors; and (4) Chinese firms disguised their money as "foreign investment" to take advantage of the special policies only provided to foreign-invested enterprises.

It is less widely known that China has also become an increasingly important FDI-exporting country in the reform era. Figure 8.3 shows the growth pace of China's FDI outflow from the late 1970s until 1996. Before the late 1970s, China's outward FDI was minimal, and even in the early

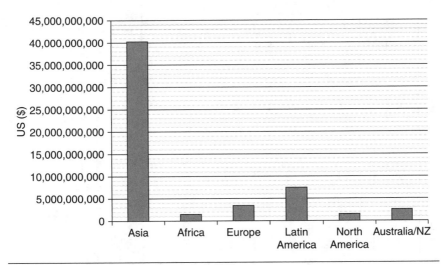

Figure 8.3 China's FDI Outflows (Cumulative), 2009.

Source: National Statistical Bureau of China (2010, 195–200).

Table 8.1 Largest Trading Countries in the World, 2010 (USD, Billions)

Country	1990			2001			2010		
	Total	Imports	Exports	Total	Imports	Exports	Total	Imports	Exports
China	115.5	53.4	62.1	509.8	243.6	266.2	2,813	1,307	1,506
Germany	756.3	346.2	410.1	1,056.8	486.3	570.5	2,457	1,120	1,337
United States	910.6	517.0	393.6	1,911.0	1,180.2	730.8	3,173	1,903	1,270
Japan	523.0	235.4	287.6	752.6	349.1	403.5	1,402	636.8	765.2
France	451.0	234.4	216.6	586.6	292.5	294.1	1,086.4	577.7	508.7
Korea, South	134.9[1]	69.8[1]	65.0[1]	291.5[1]	141.1[1]	150.4[1]	884.2	417.9	466.3
Italy	352.5	182.0	170.5	474.9	236.6[2]	238.3[2]	918.1	459.7	458.4
Netherlands	258.3	126.5	131.8	410.5	194.4	216.1	859.7	408.4	451.3
Canada	250.9	123.3	127.6	487.2	227.3	259.9	813.2	406.4	406.8
United Kingdom	409.7	224.4	185.3	588.3	321.0	267.3	952.1	546.5	405.6
Mexico	84.2	43.5	40.7	341.2	182.7[2]	158.5	609	306	303

Source: National Statistical Bureau of China (2002, 1990–2001 data), *The World Factbook* (2010 Export data, excluding European Union and Hong Kong data) https://www.cia.gov/library/publications/the-world-factbook/rankorder/rawdata_2078.txt Accessed June 30, 2011; *The World Factbook*, 2010 Imports data, Excluding European Union and Hong Kong data. https://www.cia.gov/library/publications/the-world-factbook/rankorder/rawdata_2087.txt Accessed June 30, 2011

[1] *Korea Statistical Yearbook* (2010, p. 575)

[2] Data refers to 2000.

years of the open-door policy, China's outward FDI was insignificant. In 1984, China invested about U.S.$134 million dollars abroad, and in the early years of China's economic reform, most of its investment projects were, to a great extent, motivated by political rather than commercial interests (Cai 1999). Starting in the mid-1980s, China's outward FDI began to develop, and investment projects became more business oriented. In 1985, China's FDI outflows reached $628 million, and five years later this figure was $830 million. In the 1990s, China's outward FDI quickly escalated, and in 1992–1993, the annual FDI outflow surpassed $4 billion before settling back to just over $2 billion. By this time, China had become the largest outward investor among developing countries and the eighth-largest supplier of outward investments among all countries (Lardy 2002).[4] The rapid growth of China's outward FDI in the reform era has been caused not only by the growing economic strength of the nation as a whole but also by the increasing integration of China's economy into the global community, particularly with neighboring countries. Although China's outward FDI flows are still quite small relative to the largest economies in the world, the current trajectory is further evidence of the growing links between China and other nations in the global economy.

Perhaps more important than the trade issues, however, is China's economic support of, and integration with, the U.S. government. Few people understand the extent of the integration of our economies, but suffice it to say that trade is only one part of this equation. For the last several years, China has been the largest purchaser of U.S. Treasury Bonds, making it second only to Japan in its holding of such bonds. It is difficult to get exact numbers on the amount of U.S. securities held by China, but industry insiders place the magnitude at several hundred billion dollars. This is China's trump card. If the country decided to suddenly dump a significant portion of their bond holdings, it could wreak havoc on the U.S. economy, sending ripples throughout the world economy. It is difficult to predict what the true effects would be, but there would certainly be an impact on U.S. stock markets, interest rates, mortgages, and, eventually, consumer spending. Some industry insiders predict that it would undoubtedly lead to a recession. As one bond trader who does significant business with China put it to me, "if they started suddenly dumping bonds, they could turn our economy upside down in a day. It could all come tumbling down if they did that. I don't think people realize what is at stake here.

And it would hurt us a lot more than it would hurt them." One analyst described the potential impact in a similar fashion:

> What would happen if China decided to dump, say, $100 bn of U.S. government bonds on the market all at once? The effects on the U.S.'s financial markets would be immediate, though possibly only short-term. The U.S. stock market would tumble. I would find it easy to believe that a one-day rise in long-term rates of 1 percent could easily trigger a stock market fall of 10 percent. The dollar would also immediately fall. . . . If these changes in asset prices persisted for a period of some weeks, we would then expect there to be noticeable effects on the real economy [as] the sharp jump in U.S. government bond yields would feed through to mortgage and consumer rates.

Another point of economic integration lies in the Chinese purchasing of U.S. corporations. The 2005 bid to purchase Maytag by Haier, the take-over of IBM's computer business by Lenovo, the 2005 bid of the China National Offshore Oil Corporation to purchase Unocal, and Huawei's bids with both Sprint-Nortel and 3Leaf are key examples of the global integration of U.S. and Chinese corporations. Chinese corporations are no longer simply the second-class partners in joint-venture relationships with U.S. multinational corporations; today, they are emerging as the potential owners of these corporations. The largest problem here is that the United States seems to not want these investments from China, as several of them have been blocked by Washington. This is a significant mistake, as China is sitting on about $3 trillion of foreign exchange reserves, the result of three decades of producing goods for the world. The United States should welcome this investment and we need this cash to come back into circulation in our economy.

The U.S. and Chinese economies are, at this point, intimately inter-twined, and the ironies here are many: as the U.S. Treasury blusters about "forcing" China to revalue its currency, it is increasingly China that holds the cards in the stability of our interdependent economies. As the U.S. government has plunged into fiscal irresponsibility over the last seven years, it is China that has softened that decline through its voracious appetite for U.S. bonds. And as U.S. consumers and labor leaders complain about the trade deficit, it is the U.S. consumer who drives that deficit by shopping at Walmart, which is the single-largest contributor to it. Our economies are far too interdependent at this point to talk of coming conflicts with China. We are not even in a situation any longer in which we can dictate the terms of this relationship. Instead, it would behoove all hawks in Congress and in the American media to figure out how we can constructively coexist with China.

The WTO Accession and Membership

After fifteen years of arduous negotiations with the United States and other Western nations, China reached an agreement with the WTO on September 17, 2001, becoming the 143rd member of the WTO on December 11, 2001. By becoming a full member of the WTO, China has made commitments on three levels: (1) a commitment to the objectives of the WTO, such as free trade among all member nations; (2) a commitment to the international rules governing trade for specific sectors, such as agricultural and textile goods or information technology and telecommunications; and (3) a commitment to bilateral agreements that China signed with its major trading partners, without whose support China's accession to the WTO would have been impossible. The protocol of China's accession to the WTO provides for "additional liberalization of China's trade regime and further opening up of opportunities for foreign direct investment" (Lardy 2002, 65). Around these provisions are two broad categories of issues: market access and evolution of the institutions that govern the market within China.

The issues around market access are substantial. For agricultural products, China pledged to reduce tariffs from an average level of 31.5 percent to about 15 percent. It pledged to eliminate export subsidies and rapidly increase the volumes of tariff-rate quotas on most imports. For industrial products, China pledged to phase out restrictions and cut the average tariff from 24.6 percent to 9.4 percent by 2005. China also agreed to sign the WTO Information Technology Agreement, which will eventually result in the elimination of all tariffs on telecommunications equipment, semiconductors, computers and computer equipment, and other information technology products. The most far-reaching change, however, is expected to take place in the service sector, which has largely been closed to foreign competition. China promised to open important service markets, including those of telecommunications, banking, insurance, securities, and many other professional services, to foreign service providers. Foreign firms will eventually be granted trading and distribution rights, and thus they can engage in wholesale and retail trade, transportation, service, and maintenance, as well as import and export. Besides these commitments in the area of market access, China pledged to comply with almost all provisions set forth in the WTO agreement, with the aim of increasing transparency in China's trade and investment regimes. The country agreed to eliminate all prohibited subsidies (including those to state-owned enterprises), liberalize trading rights, and standardize the operations of state trading companies. Perhaps the most significant commitment within the WTO agreement is that China consented to accept the provisions of trade-related aspects of intellectual property rights, among the thorniest of issues in U.S.–Chinese trade relations in the last two decades.

The depth of China's WTO commitments compare favorably with those of other WTO nations (Lardy 2002). Both market access and rule-based commitments far surpass those made by founding members of the WTO and also go beyond those made by countries that have joined the WTO since 1995. What, then, was the incentive behind China's pursuit of WTO membership in the 1990s? First, as a result of China's WTO accession, the United States granted China permanent, normal trade-relations status, ending the decade-long annual conflict over considering China's trade status under the Jackson–Vanick Amendment.[5] Second, several of China's trading partners had to lift most of their restrictions against China on a range of products. According to the Agreement on Textiles and Clothing, for example, all quotas on China's textiles and clothing were to be phased out. Other quotas will also be phased out in accordance with negotiated schedules. This is actually an important point in understanding the politics behind the United States blocking China's entry into GATT and the WTO since 1989. To wit: every year, the late U.S. Senator Jesse Helms, from North Carolina, was one of the loudest proponents of blocking China's bid for Most Favored Nation (and later, Normal Trade Relations) status on the grounds that the United States should not be doing business with an authoritarian government that brought on such human-rights abuses as China did in Tiananmen Square in 1989. However, the jingoistic Helms could hardly claim a long-standing position of advocating for human rights around the world. What was behind this? Economic interests, plain and simple. North Carolina is one of the largest producers of textiles in the United States, and the phasing out of the "multi-fiber" agreement meant that North Carolina was going to be hurt most by growing competition from China. The other sector that would be threatened by China's entry into the WTO would be tobacco, also a mainstay of the North Carolina economy.

There is little doubt that WTO accession benefited Chinese consumers and led to greater economic efficiency, even though some heavily protected sectors suffered as trade barriers fell. For China's labor force, increasing unemployment was unavoidable in a few state sectors, but the opening of the service sector generated some employment in the near term. Finally, with WTO membership, China can now resort to the WTO dispute settlement mechanism to protect its own trade interests, as well as participate in multilateral negotiations on trade rules and future trade liberalization. Another potential benefit of WTO membership was the opportunity for China to play a role in shaping the rules of the international trading system over time. Probably the most important motivation behind China's joining the WTO was rooted in the realization among liberal reformers that the country needed greater external impetus to overcome domestic obstacles to further reform. During the past three decades, China has experienced dramatic institutional change in almost every field. The country has come a long way in liberalizing and opening up its economy, but some of the most difficult structural adjustments still lie ahead, especially in the highly protected industries. WTO membership will inevitably exert increasing pressure on the measures China will take shortly in the areas of institution building and in continuing to reform the state sectors. There is little doubt that China's WTO membership will further push the nation toward broader and deeper integration into the global economy.

The implications stemming from China's accession to the WTO and, thus, greater integration into the international community lie on three levels. First, on the level of the international economy, the implications of China's membership in the WTO are immense. China's emergence as one of the largest players in the global economy inevitably led to shifts in world production, trade, investment, and employment. China's economy and foreign trade are so large that the growth of global trade and the pace of expansion of global output will undoubtedly be affected. Not surprisingly, concerns have been raised in some developing countries that global demand for their exports will shrink and their FDI inflow will fall due to

China's vast market and great potential in the production of labor-intensive exports. Advanced industrialized nations have worried that China's exports would flood their domestic markets. The reality, however, has been that the way in which China's WTO accession and relative openness affect other countries is a much more complex issue than simple FDI and exports statistics reveal. China's accession to the WTO definitely strengthened trade and investment ties with its Asian neighbors and, thus, provided them with a more stable external environment. The newly industrialized economies of Asia benefited the most from China's WTO accession, given their heavy investment in China in the 1980s and 1990s. China's WTO membership also brought many opportunities and challenges for the United States and other advanced industrial economies. Over time, the opening up of China's services sector offered these countries large trade and investment opportunities. Most advanced industrial nations are expected to increase their exports of capital and technology-intensive manufactures to China. In addition, as the only major trading nation that was not an advanced industrial economy, China brought "a distinct perspective to the negotiations" and will "be influential in future rounds of WTO trade negotiations" (Lardy 2002, 134), and will thus be able to exert greater influence over the multilateral trading system.

Second, with respect to China's macroeconomic policy, it is likely that China will continue to dismantle its remaining central planning mechanisms, formulate more laws and policies consistent with its WTO commitments, and enforce uniform rules through the country. In the past three decades, foreign capital and global corporations that have moved to China have exerted considerable pressure on China's economic reforms, mainly concentrating on driving economic organizations within China to adapt to the rules of the global market. Starting in the early 1990s, the government has made greater strides in creating a rational–legal economic system, based on which Chinese firms could "get onto the international track" as quickly as possible. Among the important strides is the construction of numerous laws and regulations directly tied to the building of a rational economy, such as the Joint Venture Law (1979), the Enterprise Bankruptcy Law (1986), the Company Law (1994), the Labor Law (1994), and the Securities Law (1998). At the beginning of this century, China's entry into the WTO brought more intensive pressure in this ongoing institution-building process.

Third, influences from foreign investors and global trade partners are also evident in the organizational changes at the firm level that are affecting millions of Chinese citizens on a daily basis. With China's increasing involvement with international organizations and Western investors, a process of rationalization has been occurring in the workplace, where Chinese companies are adopting a number of the rational bureaucratic systems that are most often found in Western organizations. China's accession to the WTO has accelerated the rationalization of the country's economic system both at the state level and within firms. While stable rational–legal systems are adopted more often to attract foreign investors or comply with the universal rules than they are for the good of workers, they nevertheless have radical implications for the structure of authority relations and, therefore, for the lives of individual Chinese citizens.

The Human Rights Debate

Another issue that has troubled many constituents about the United States' close relationship with China lies in the area of human rights. What does it mean for a country that purports to hold democratic values and a respect for individual civil liberties above all else to have such close and supportive economic relations with an authoritarian government that does not have the same respect for human rights?

In the Fall of 1978, it was unclear whether China would follow the legacy of Mao Zedong—stick to Soviet style economic principles, deepen the Communist Revolution, hold the Western capitalist world at arms length—or follow Deng Xiaoping down the road of "economic opening" [*jingji kaifang*] and general economic and political reform. As part of the political struggle occurring at the uppermost reaches of Chinese political leadership, individual citizens—many of them former Red Guards who spent a decade in the countryside hung their views on Beijing's Democracy Wall agitating for change. In some ways, Deng Xiaoping rode this wave of sentiment to power in December of 1978. However, the tenor of the Democracy Wall Movement (also known as Beijing Spring) changed on December 5, when the famous dissident, Wei Jingsheng, hung a poster called "The Fifth Modernization," calling for democratic reform. In February of 1979, Wei was arrested on trumped up charges of selling state secrets. He would spend the next fifteen years in jail. A decade later, China would turn its military might on its own citizens, many of whom saw themselves as carrying on the tradition of Wei Jingsheng.

China is much freer today than it was thirty years ago. However, there is no denying the human rights abuses occur there on a regular basis still. Whether it is the case of Ai Weiwei's detention or the changing laws, which allow dissidents to be detained for any "threat" they might pose to the state. The question is, what direction is the freedom-versus-austerity pendulum swinging? Are human rights and individual civil liberties more respected in China today than they were thirty years ago? And what is the best way to continue to encourage change in this area?

Starting in 1986, China actively campaigned to resume its status in the General Agreement on Tariffs and Trade (GATT), the predecessor of the World Trade Organization (WTO), which was established in 1995. However, following the Tiananmen Square massacre in 1989, the logic of the Jackson–Vanick Amendment guided U.S.–Chinese relations for more than a decade. The basic position was that the United States would agree only to have "favored" trade relations with China on an annual basis, depending on an annual review of the country's record on human rights. At the time, following the language of Jackson–Vanick, this was referred to as Most Favored Nation status (MFN), and then later as Normal Trade Relations. Each spring, a group of politicians, pundits, and lobbyists would converge on Washington to debate the merits of engaging in trade relations with China. Behind the annual debate was a set of issues that are intimately tied to larger theoretical questions about the relationship between economic and social reforms. On one side of the divide sat the proponents of engagement, who argued that social change would follow from economic engagement. The view among many in this group was that liberal markets create a kind of freedom that transforms authoritarian systems from within. As U.S. president Bill Clinton, who was a proponent of this view, once put it,

> In the new century, liberty will spread by cell phone and cable modem ... We know how much the Internet has changed America, and we are already an open society. Imagine how much it could change China. Now, there's no question China has been trying to crack down on the Internet—good luck. That's sort of like trying to nail Jello to the wall.[6]

Scholars like Michael Santoro (1999) have argued that American firms were really playing a significant role in changing China from within. On the other side of the divide sat opponents of engagement. Individuals in this camp believed that engaging with an authoritarian regime (1) rewards the very systems they believe should change; (2) actually strengthens the regime in question; and (3) gives away the one bargaining chip we have to force social and political change in the world today. Opponents of engagement also remained very committed to the view that, while the reforms have clearly transformed the economy in fundamental ways, little has changed in social and political realms in China and it is still the same despotic and corrupt place it was twenty years ago. On this side of the debate sat a diverse political alliance, which included labor and liberal politicians like Nancy Pelosi and the late Paul Wellstone and hawkish politicians like the late Jesse Helms and Christopher Cox.

Opponents of engagement misunderstand the situation in China today. First, while change has been gradual, over the course of three decades of reform, we have seen radical changes that make China a fundamentally different society from what it was before the reforms began. Statutes like the National Compensation Law, which allows Chinese citizens to sue the government for past wrongs, and the Prison Reform Law—which, according to most extensive research on the topic, has fundamentally altered the treatment of prisoners—have radically reshaped the reality of human rights in China. (Indeed, it was with the National Compensation Law that the relatives of the deceased of the Tiananmen massacre were able to sue the government for wrongful deaths.) In the area of legal institutions and labor, the Labor Law and the Labor Arbitration Commissions are radical steps toward a rational, rights-based workplace and society. These changes amount to nothing less than radical social change. Reform in China has been a gradual process, and in our desire to see something dramatic like the fall of the Berlin Wall, we have imperiously ignored and arrogantly dismissed the radical changes that have evolved over the course of more than two decades of reform.

Second, as was discussed in Chapter 7, it is on the factory floor where the emergence of a rights-based workplace is the most apparent, and it is here that we can see the direct impact of foreign (particularly Western) investment. Those who blithely state that foreign direct investment has resulted in no increased protections for human rights in China simply have no idea of what is going on there. In my own research, I have visited hundreds of factories, spent hundreds of hours interviewing hundreds of managers and workers, and systematically studied the impact of foreign investment on the transformation of labor relations. I watched these factories transform over the course of the 1990s. The emergence of rights-based labor practices is easily apparent to anyone who cares to look, but it is the Chinese firms that are engaged in relationships with Western investors who are leading the way in these changes. The findings of this body of research speak to the real issues before us—the impact of foreign investment on the transformation of Chinese society.

Formal relationships with foreign firms have a significant impact on the ways in which enterprises are changing in China's urban industrial economy. As I described in Chapter 7, Chinese factories that have formal relations with Western MNCs are significantly more likely to have formal grievance-filing procedures and a variety of other intra-organizational structures that protect workers' rights. They pay significantly higher wages, and they are more likely to have adopted institutions that put them on track with other firms in the global economy. Managers trace these rapidly changing practices to their relations with foreign firms, arguing that, although they are primarily motivated by the prospect of attracting foreign investment with these changes, the changes may, at the same time, be radically altering the lives of workers in their firms. Partnerships with foreign multinational corporations are fundamentally altering the lives of citizens in the Chinese economy.

Foreign investment—and therefore engagement—has influenced this process of change in China in fundamental ways. Corporations are rarely the leading advocates of civil liberties, human rights, or labor reform. However, the Chinese case is special for a couple of reasons. Because many MNCs in China are as interested in long-term investments as they are in cheap labor, they most often seek Chinese partners that understand the needs, goals, and desires of MNCs investing in China. They seek long-term partners that have embraced a rational–legal approach to doing business—partners that are predictable, stable, and knowledgeable about Western-style business practices and negotiations. These partnerships are important to Chinese factories—with them come an infusion of capital, access to international markets, and often technology transfers—and they want desperately to land these partnerships. They position themselves as suitable investment partners by adopting a number of the practices that Western partners will recognize as stable, reform-minded business practices. Among the basic reforms they adopt to show their fitness for "linking up" with the international community are labor reforms, and the adoption of these reforms has fundamentally changed the lives of workers and citizens throughout China today. Thus, commitments to stable Western-style business practices and to labor reform have led to key changes in the labor relations in the Chinese workplace. These changes have had radical consequences for human rights across China.

There is also a good deal of evidence that the sanction-and-isolation position does not work in any except the most extreme circumstances. What did the 50-year-old embargo of Cuba and the ten-year embargo of Iraq (before the war) tell us about the usefulness of isolation in toppling despotic regimes? Has isolation done anything to transform North Korea? If anything is clear, it is that the citizens of these countries suffer while the resolve of their leaders is strengthened. The only case in which a successful international coalition has brought a country to its knees for social change is South Africa, and this case is so different from that of China that the comparison does not even merit discussion. (There will, quite simply, never be an international coalition united to isolate China the way there was in the case of South Africa.)

Though it is not really a live debate any longer—we are too economically intertwined with China to really consider isolationist positions—there are still some who think we should not be in business with countries that trample human rights. However, those who advocate isolation (in the name of human rights) should look closely at whom they are aligning themselves with in China: the true despots of Chinese society are the ones who would like to roll the clocks back on the economic, legal, and political reforms in China—and they would welcome the isolation position, because they know that the WTO will further erode their dictatorial power in China. In the 1980s, Zhao Ziyang was focused on reform and the opening up of China, and he knew that the further integration of China into the international community would bring this about. Jiang Zemin and Zhu Rongji followed Zhao, focusing on further integrating China into the international community. (Where Jiang and Zhu diverged from Zhao's path was in being open about any goals of political change.) These leaders have been changing China from within, and they have been using the arguments about stability and global integration to do so. China's current President, Hu Jintao, has adopted an even more complicated balancing act, on the one hand striking the pose of the strong authoritarian, while on the other pushing forward very progressive institutional reform. Pushing forward institutional changes like the new rights for independent union- ization and the new property rights reforms is clearly a progressive agenda about institutional change. However, unlike his predecessors, Hu has not been silent on the issue of democratization, vowing to expand democratic rights and processes in his 17th Party Congress speech in October of 2007. Skeptics dismissed his speech (which mentioned democracy over sixty times) as empty words; Hu's own track record on institutional change belies this view.

As a final note on integration, it is important to briefly address the area that often causes the greatest concern as a potential catalyst for a pending conflict between China and Taiwan and Tibet. But even here, it increas- ingly looks like integration is largely being guided by economic integra- tion. In the early 1990s, an important shift in Mainland China–Taiwan relations occurred (Hsing 1998). After 1989, many countries in the Organization for Economic Cooperation and Development pulled out of China; foreign investment dropped from U.S.$2 billion in the fourth quarter of 1988 to $900 million in the first quarter of 1990. In order to win back foreign capital, China appealed to Chinese investors from Hong Kong, Macau, and Taiwan by offering favorable investment conditions.[7] Among these were several industrial zones in Fujian Province, the ances- tral birthplace of many Taiwanese citizens that were designated for Taiwanese investors. As a result, direct Taiwanese investment in China increased by 75 percent in 1990. Taiwanese linguistic and cultural affinity with Mainland China made it relatively easy for small- and medium-sized investors to cross the straits. And in 1990, under pressure from Taiwan's business communities and industrial organizations, the Taiwan govern- ment finally allowed Taiwanese firms to conduct indirect investment in China. Taiwanese investments in China have been small in terms of the size of the project (average investments are less than U.S.$1 million); however, by 1992, Taiwan had become the second-largest investor in Mainland China, behind Hong Kong. This economic interdependence, combined with the weakening of the Taiwanese economy over the last decade, has rendered the economic viability of an independence bid feeble.

Before the Asian financial crisis of 1997, Taiwan might have been in a position to push the issue of Taiwanese independence, but not today. Even politicians like Chen Shuibian, who was once bullish on the issue in years past, backed away from explicit conversations about independence as soon as he was elected. And immediately after winning the election in March of 2008, President-elect Ma Ying-Jeou pledged to forge closer ties with Beijing. Taiwan's economic fate is now heavily dependent on good relations with Mainland China, and it is likely that both countries will simply continue to move down the path toward integration.

This discussion would be incomplete if we did not touch on the issue of Tibet, a topic that has become the focus of China's human rights abuses by a number of public figures in the United States. There is no doubt that China has exercised abusive control in annexing and subduing Tibet since 1951. However, it is important to put this into some of the historical and comparative context that we put Taiwan in above. First, a little history: the first invasion of Tibet by China came in the year 1720 under the leadership of Emperor Kangxi (1661–1722). China continued to expand its reach during the Qing Dynasty under the reign of Emperors Yongzheng (1723–1735) and Qianlong (1736–1799). Even as the Qing Dynasty was in decline in the first decade of the twentieth century, the regime had successful campaigns to reestablish its authority in Tibet. However, with China descending into chaos (following the fall of the Qing Dynasty, and the uncertain future of the Nationalist Revolution), in 1913, Britain took advantage of this weakness and sought to ensure Tibet's independence. As the colonial power of the region, Britain's main motivation seemed to be the establishment of an independent buffer between China and India. By 1938, with the Japanese occupation of China, the Chinese Empire that had been united under the Qing fragmented with Xinjiang, Taiwan, and Tibet all asserting independence. Tibet was reoccupied in October of 1950 by the Communists, who claimed they were occupying Tibet to "liberate" it from foreign imperialism, though there was no foreign presence in Tibet at the time. The UN did nothing to stop the occupation. In addition, the only country that had been active in asserting Tibetan independence was Britain, and because of Indian Independence in 1947, Britain no longer had need of Tibet as a buffer between India and China. The Chinese occupied key points in the country within a year and pressured the Dalai Lama's advisors into general acceptance of China's sovereignty over the region. In March of

1959, after a decade of occupation by the Chinese government, a surge of protests against the Chinese occupation turned into armed rebellion. Many Tibetans were killed by Chinese troops in bitter fighting, and some of the most beautiful monasteries were destroyed by the Chinese. The Tibetans' spiritual leader, the Dalai Lama, fled to India where he was given sanctuary despite Chinese protests. Eventually, in the 1980s, Beijing would impose martial law in Lhasa to control the region, as well as a news embargo (no foreign journalists were allowed to enter the region). Chinese citizens have been indoctrinated to believe that they are carrying out patriotic duty by migrating to Tibet to help "develop" the region.

Although Beijing has worked hard at economic integration, it has not been as successful as the dependence that has been created with Taiwan. However, in assessing Tibet (and Taiwan's) claims of independence and China's claim of sovereignty, it is important to acknowledge that these are complicated matters, and we should be careful in thinking about parallels in our own history before being too judgmental of Beijing on its claim to sovereignty over Tibet. The annexation of Hawaii in 1898, which began with the forcible surrender of Queen Liliuokalani in 1893, is not as different from the situation in Tibet as we might like to think. And of course, after the Jackson Amendment was signed into law in 1830, the acquisition of all land west of the Mississippi amounted to an illegal annexation of land (according to the Jackson Amendment) on a much grander scale than that of Hawaii or Tibet. The point here is not to justify China's actions with the citation of past wrongs by other nations like the United States. However, it is important to keep perspective on the complexities of state sovereignty and the strategic claims to land. In the end, China has embarked on a path of economic integration with Tibet, much like its plan for dealing with the tensions over Taiwan, though the process is at a much earlier stage in Tibet. However, global integration is also in play here: the international media, Beijing's concerns over potential Olympic protests, and Gordon Brown's ability to weigh in on the issues with Premier Wen Jiabao are all issues that speak to China's relative openness compared to a decade ago.

Conclusions

It is no longer controversial to state that China will play a pivotal role in the political and economic structure of the world in the twenty-first century; the question that remains is what that role will be. China's reform process has been an inherently global one and all indications are that China's growth will continue to integrate the country into the global economy. The reforms of the last three decades have radically transformed China's economy and society. From the agricultural policies that transformed rural China and the transformation of the state sector to the institutional changes that have transformed social life in China, the changes have been radical and deep. This is not a story about the ways that markets lead to liberal policies. Rather, it is about the ways in which reform-minded elites have engineered a gradual reform process, slowly liberalizing economic, political, and social realms. In this book, I have emphasized four key points about the economic reforms in China. First, changes in China are much more radical than is often understood by outside observers.

Second, the enacting of China's reforms has fundamentally been a state-led process. For decades, we have been skeptical about the possibility of a successful transition to capitalism in which the state plays a key role. China's reforms not only show that states can be effective in this process, they suggest that state-led development may be far superior to letting the market work its magic. The reasons for this, I argue, are stability and experimentation. New economic and political systems take time to learn, and it is important for states to provide stability as societies make the transition between the two. These processes of change are driven by state-led initiatives that have gradually transformed the rules of society across the board. Experimentation has emphasized getting the institutions right rather than blindly assuming that one path of institutional change—rapid privatization—will necessarily lead to the successful development of a market economy. The state begins this process of gradual experimentation that is then codified in broad-based institutional changes (in the form of laws and policies). As the state gradually implements these new policies, Chinese citizens adapt to these new rules, and the social worlds that they live in are transformed as well.

Third, economic reform in China will lead to democratization, but not because of what some neoliberals argue is the fundamental connection between liberal economic and political systems. Rather, China will become a democracy because that is the agenda some of the key powerful leaders in China have had over the course of the economic reforms. They have used the economic reforms to bring this change about. They have not talked about it openly, because, since 1989, they have lived in the shadow of Zhao Ziyang's fate. But both Zhao Ziyang and Zhu Rongji were clearly pushing radical reform agendas; and now Hu Jintao is following in the footsteps of his predecessors. Markets do not, in and of themselves, breed liberalism; liberal-minded leaders do. This process of change in China has been a fundamentally global one. Chinese leaders have leveraged the process of global integration to transform China from within. China's role in the global economy will continue to grow and transform, and that role will also continue to transform China from within.

Finally, it is important to note the extent to which China's rise signals a shift in the balance of power not only among nations but also in terms of models of capitalism and global corporations. The sub-prime credit crisis of 2007–2009 (and subsequent write-downs, near bankruptcies, and bail-outs) of storied American banks like Lehman Brothers, Merrill Lynch, Citigroup, and Bear Stearns was yet another example of the fact that the self-regulating notion of a market discipline is a flawed concept. As we learned with the Savings and Loan Crisis of the late 1980s and the accounting scandals of the early 2000s, minimally-regulated market actors will push the boundaries of ethical (and sensible) behavior as far as they can, especially when they believe that, as global corporations, they often act beyond the reach of the law (and when they believe that the U.S. government will bail them out). These scandals have left a serious black eye on the face of American capitalism, and they have had a significant impact on the American and Chinese consumer alike. However, it is also interesting to note that in the decade that brought us the accounting and sub-prime credit, we have also seen Chinese hybrid state-owned companies emerge as forces in the global economy. We have seen Lenovo's growth from a small-scale privately-owned high tech company to a global player in the PC industry that would eventually purchase IBM's laptop division; we would see Hiaer's growth to a global brand that would build a $40 million science park in North Carolina and eventually make a bid to buy Maytag; we would see CNOOC's bid for Unocal. We have seen Huawei's bids for alliances with two different U.S. companies. We have seen Chinese MNCs emerge as the largest IPO in history (Chinese International Monetary Bank) and (briefly) as the largest company in the world in terms of market capitalization (PetroChina, valued at over $1 trillion). The performance of these companies has been impressive. But this is not just a

story of Chinese economic growth and a few large state-owned corporations; it is also a story of superior economic management and the fact that
model of state ownership was not quite as clear-cut as we believed it to be
in the 1980s and 1990s. Since the 1980s, it has widely been assumed that
the problem with SOEs was that they could never be efficient. The Chinese
process of change has proved this story incomplete; in fact, it is highly
possible to get the incentives aligned so that state officials can actually run
corporations that are much more efficient than the classic state-owned
firms of command economies around the world.

However, the issues also extend beyond efficiency to the question of the
stakeholders that corporations serve. In the U.S. system, multi-national
corporations often operate beyond the reach of the U.S. law and they rarely
serve any national interests beyond the narrowly defined interests of their
shareholders. But China's hybrid-form corporations are a different breed.
They are increasingly efficient in ways that other MNCs are, but they are
also directed toward a much broader set of stakeholders. They are also
constrained in a way that might just be healthy from an economic perspective. In the decade that has given us the economic debacles of Enron and
Bear Stearns, it seems increasingly difficult to make the case that the
unfettered capitalist model is truly superior. As China's influence grows
over the course of this century, it will be interesting to see just how powerful
and prominent Chinese corporations become.

Yet, the year 2011 has been a mixed period for Beijing as well. On the
one hand, the years since 2008 have been shown Beijing flexing its muscle
as a (relatively) strong economy in the midst of a global recession. China's
open questioning of the Federal Reserve and the U.S. dollar more generally demonstrates a shift in the balance of power between Beijing and
Washington. This is uncharted territory for both governments. However,
the same stretch has seen as humbling scandals like the high-speed rail
crash, which left thirty-five people dead, and the report from the Bank of
China that since 1990, some 18,000 corrupt officials have fled China with
assets on the order of 800 billion yuan. We have seen scandalous recalls of
poorly manufactured toys and poisonous dog food; the world has focused
a significant amount of attention on Beijing's handling of Tibet; we have
seen poorly made schools tragically crumble in the earthquake of May
2008. With China's rapid growth, many corners have been cut in the
process, and China's growing macroeconomic strength and influence in

the global economy will continue to be balanced against its growing tensions internally.

Regardless of China's strengths and weaknesses, one thing is clear: The Chinese economy and Chinese firms will increasingly be central players in the global economic system. As the Chinese economy continues to expand and grow, it will reshape global politics and also our core assumptions about how firms work within the global political economy. The question for the United States is whether we will choose the path of an ally or an adversary. From an economic standpoint, the choice is obvious. However, it still remains to be seen what view the U.S. government will take on this global economic and political powerhouse.

NOTES

Chapter 1

1 A country's GDP represents all of the income the country generates within its borders. GDP is generally used as a measure of national wealth. The countries with the top GDP in the world are, in order, the United States, Japan, and Germany. One problem with the GDP statistic is that it does not account for the cost of goods in a given country. For example, if a bushel of rice costs half as much in China as in the United States, then a unit of currency is twice as valuable there. As a solution to this problem, GDP statistics will, when appropriate, be adjusted for purchasing power parity (PPP), a statistic that adjusts for cost-of-living differences by replacing exchange rates with relative measures of local purchasing power. In terms of PPP, China is second only to the United States. PPP was introduced into the international accounting system by the International Monetary Fund in 1993.

2 In the mid-1990s, world grain exports totaled about 250 million tons per year. China currently produces and consumes about 330 million tons of grain per year. However, if trends of declining productivity in grain yields within China follow trends from the 1990s, China's grain production will fall to about 270 million tons by 2030; this despite a continuously growing population that is projected to reach 1.5 billion people by 2017. For further discussion, see Brown (1995).

3 For discussion of China's Internet usage, see Galloway and Guthrie (2011). For discussion of China's oil consumption, see *Time Asia*, October 18, 2004.

4 Gordon Chang (2001); "Contrarian Investor Sees Economic Crash in China" by David Barboza, *The New York Times*, January 7, 2010.

5 Sachs and Woo (1997). To be fair to Sachs, he has significantly changed his tune about the importance of understanding institutions, social inequality, and even culture. However, in the years that he was among the most influential economists in the world, shaping processes of economic reform in developing nations, he saw little beyond a deep-seated trust in the magic of the market.

6 Also implicit in Sachs and Woo's (1994a, 1997) argument is the a priori assumption that private ownership will always outperform state ownership. This is a stance that is reflected in the privatization school in general. See especially Woo (1999) and Sachs (1992, 1993, 1995b).

7 Essentialism is the notion that a group of people is defined by a few key traits or some sort of essence.

8 For discussions of these cases, see, for example Michael J. Enright, "Successful Multinationals in China," Asia Case Research Center, the University of Hong Kong (HKU 360), 2005.

9 "Manager" [*jingli*] is the term that is used for upper-level executives in industrial organizations that have made the transition to being companies [*gongsi*] through adoption of the 1994 Company Law (Guthrie 1999). For industrial organizations that have not made this transition—they are still referred to as factories [*gongchang*]—the top positions are referred to as factory director [*changzhang*] and vice director [*fu changzhang*]. In both organizational types, I spoke with the top- or second-ranked individual in the organization. For the sake of simplicity, I refer to these positions as managerial or executive positions throughout the book.

Chapter 2

1 For discussion of the structure of Chinese society under Mao, see, for example, Schurmann 1968; Parish and Whyte 1978; Whyte and Parish 1984; and Walder 1986a. For discussion of the process of economic reforms in China, see, for example, Field 1984; Wong 1991; Field 1992; Wong 1992; Rawski 1994; Naughton 1995; and Walder 1995a. Unless otherwise noted, the basic historical details in this section draw upon Hsu 1999 and Spence 1999.

2 Today, there are actually four municipalities that hold provincial-level administrative status—Chongqing being the recent addition to the group of Beijing, Shanghai, and Tianjin.

3 Bian 1994, 9. See also Walder 1992a and 1995a and Guthrie 1999. Walder 1992a and Bian 1994a refer to this administrative structure as the "budgetary rank" of a given work unit, placing emphasis on the variable access to resources that organizations had in this system. I use the more general term nested hierarchy to emphasize the fact that this administrative hierarchy had many purposes of governmental control over work units, with budgetary control being only one of these areas.

4 Note that these last two issues were not problems in their own right in the era of the planned economy. In the pre-reform era, the Chinese socioeconomic system—the so-called iron rice bowl—was a redistributive system, so factories were never meant to cover their own costs in terms of the social welfare of their employees. Revenues flowed up the hierarchy and were redistributed by the government to cover the costs of the factories under their jurisdictions. The social welfare burden for factories in the command economy would become a major challenge in the reform era, as budget constraints were gradually hardened from factories.

5 There was an additional critical moment in this narrative, which played a central role in Mao's decision to "deepen" the revolution. In the spring of 1956, Mao spoke of the need to help relationships between party members and non-party members. Mao was encouraging people to speak out about their experiences in, and grievances with, the party. He called this the movement of letting "one hundred flowers bloom"; in other words, he was calling for all of the differing opinions within the party to be put on the table. Mao spent a good deal of political capital to make this movement happen—overcoming resistance from Liu Xiaoqi and many others in the party—and by April 1957, intellectuals were encouraged to speak out against such abuses and vices of the party as bureaucratism, sectarianism, and subjectivism. The criticism became much stronger than Mao anticipated it would, quickly spreading beyond the party-defined agenda of the "reform" to more difficult issues of democracy, totalitarianism, human rights, and freedom. In response to this, Mao launched his "anti-rightist campaign," turning on intellectuals as if his plan all along had been to root out the intellectuals who did not support the party. By the end of 1957, over 300,000 intellectuals had been branded "rightists" and "enemies of the party."

6 Although the economic architects of the planned economy did not acknowledge "unemployment" as a problem, they did acknowledge a growing category of individuals who were "waiting for employment" in the job assignment system.

7 A number of scholars have used the term quiet revolution to describe China's reforms. See, for example, Goodman and Hooper 1994; Walder 1995c; and Guthrie 2003.

8 See, for example, Sachs (1995a) and Sachs and Woo (1997). There are many other scholars who have made this argument; Sachs is the most famous voice among this line of scholarship from the 1990s.

9 For discussion of the "attenuation of property rights" and the local control over enterprises, see Walder 1994a and Walder 1995a.

10 The "One-China" policy actually dates back to the Shanghai Communiqué, which was signed by both Mao Zedong and U.S. president Richard M. Nixon on February 28, 1972. As the communiqué stated, the Taiwan question is the crucial question obstructing the normalization of relations between China and the United States; the government of the PRC is the sole legal government of China; Taiwan is a province of China which has long been returned to the motherland; the liberation of Taiwan is China's internal affair in which no other country has the right to interfere; and all U.S. forces and military installations must be withdrawn from Taiwan. The Chinese Government firmly opposes any activities, which aim at the creation of "one China, one Taiwan," "One China, two governments," "an independent Taiwan" or advocate that "the status of Taiwan remains to be determined." As a result of this agreement, any country wanting to form diplomatic relations with China had to end its formal diplomatic relations with Taiwan.

11 As a result of the Carter–Deng Normalization Agreement, in April 1979 the U.S. Congress passed the Taiwan Relations Act, which reflected the worries of pro-Taiwan forces by reaffirming the U.S. commitment to Taiwan and especially by underlining that the United States intended to provide Taiwan with arms of a defensive character and pledged to resist any coercion that would jeopardize the security or the social or economic system of the people of Taiwan.

12 Debora Spar, "China (A): The Great Awakening." Harvard Business School Case 9-794-019.

13 See Wong 1991; see also Oi 1992; Wong 1992; Walder 1995a; and Guthrie 1999.

14 This was first discussed at a working conference of the Central Committee in April 1979; it was officially adopted on November 26, 1981.

15 Naughton (1995) puts forth a broad analysis of the institutions that defined China's command economy, the new institutions that emerged in the market reforms, and the process of transition between the systems. Naughton's explanation of this process is one of the most comprehensive and insightful accounts published to date. He limits his study to the industrial economy because, as industry is so closely tied to state investment and saving—and therefore to governmental fiscal policy—reforming the industrial economy becomes the central task of economic transitions from planned to market-based systems. Naughton's work is also important because of what it says about the economic reform debate. Observing the early years of transforming command economies in Europe, China's reform experience and, more recently, the aggressive reform programs in Czechoslovakia and Russia have given researchers the rare opportunity to comparatively assess various strategies of economic reform. The central debate that has emerged over the utility of different reform strategies pits the gradualist, incremental approach to reforms against an approach that emphasizes rapid privatization—the so-called big bang or shock therapy models of economic reform. Advocates of the former argue that there are clear benefits to a gradual approach to economic reforms, while proponents of shock therapy argue that rapid and complete destruction of the command system is the only possible approach to creating a market-based system. Naughton takes a strong and convincing position in this debate, arguing that the China case shows that gradual reform is not only feasible but also preferable to the radical transformation of shock therapy.

16 While many accounts focus on the performance of the non-state sector, Naughton's focus is on the fact that this sector was an essential link to the creation of a competitive marketplace, which changed the behavior of firms in the state and non-state sectors alike.

17 *Statistical Yearbook of China* (National Statistical Bureau of China 1999). See also the discussions in Oi and Walder 1999.

18 For example, according to Li's (1997) study of state enterprises in the 1980s, those enter-
    prises supervised by local governments were more likely to reduce workers' wages based on
    "poor performance" than those supervised by the central state. Li's study also indicates the
    enterprise's hardening budget constraints in local governments' supervision of state
    enterprises.
19 In many ways, firms at this level of the industrial hierarchy are proving to be much more
    successful in reform than those at other levels of the urban industrial economy. For example,
    previous research suggests that firms under municipal companies have not only adopted the
    most extensive changes in intraorganizational structure but have also been the most produc-
    tive in Shanghai's urban industrial economy (Guthrie 1999, 2001).
20 For a discussion of the 1984 Reform Declaration, see Naughton (1995, 248); for a discussion
    of the "price reformers" and "enterprise reformers" see Naughton (1995, 188–196); for a
    discussion of a lack of reform by the end of 1984, see Naughton (1995, 136).
21 As a document from the State Council put it in 1983, "The current system of employment
    in China, under which the majority are permanent workers, in practice operates as a kind of
    unconditional system of life tenure" (People's Republic of China 1983; for a full translation,
    see Josephs 1989, Appendix A). The Great Leap Forward (1958–1960) actually provides a
    caveat to this system, as approximately 16 million workers were laid off and sent down to the
    countryside during that campaign. This is the only period, however, where layoffs were not
    accompanied by reassignment (Walder 1986a).
22 The main reason for the difference is that the Japanese law on foreign investment, which
    dates to 1950, was extremely restrictive.
23 The term rational-legal refers to Max Weber's notion of rational–legal authority, one of the
    three ideal types of authority that characterize modern states. According to Weber, rational–
    legal authority is characterized by bureaucracy and a reliance on the rule of law.
24 Officially, revenue extraction was replaced by taxation in the Decision of the Standing
    Committee of the National People's Congress on Authorizing the State Council to Reform
    the System of Industrial and Commercial Taxes and Issue Relevant Draft Tax Regulations
    for Trial Application, adopted September 18, 1984, at the Seventh Meeting of the Standing
    Committee of the Sixth National People's Congress and later codified in the State-
    Owned Enterprise Second Phase Profits to Taxes Reform of 1985 (*Statistical Yearbook of
    China* 1994, 226); for other discussions, see Institutional Economic Yearbook of
    Shanghai 1994. The first of these documents states that the Standing Committee and State
    Council recommend "introducing the practice according to which state enterprises pay
    taxes instead of turning over their profit to the state and in the course reforming the system
    of industrial and commercial taxes" (People's Republic of China 1984a). However, in
    practice, revenue extraction (and management and oversight fees) lasted for many more
    years, declining gradually over time. See Naughton 1995 for a further discussion of tax
    reform.
25 See "The Practical Applications and Experimental Methods of 'The Separation of Taxes
    and Profits, Fees After Taxes, and Residuals After Taxes' for State-Owned Enterprises,"
    pp. 64–66 in the *Shanghai Institutional Economic Yearbook*, 1989–1993 (1994).
26 For other estimates of the number of cases brought before court, see *New York Times*,
    April 27, 1998. For discussion of the percentage rise in suits against the government, see Pei
    (1995 and 1997).

Chapter 3

1 Names depicted in this anecdote have been changed.
2 See, for example, Calhoun (2002).
3 The notion of a "world of total institutions" is an allusion to Erving Goffman's work on the
   ways that certain societies create institutional environments that engulf the individuals who
   reside within them.

4 Some scholars, like Vivienne Shue (1988), have argued that the "honeycomb"-like village structure that emerged in Mao's China actually protected individuals from "the reach of the state." However, her point of comparison is the era of economic reform, where, she argues, the state is actually more able to penetrate down to the level of individuals. Regardless, it is unquestionably true that the state was a greater force of social control in Mao's era than it was in the era prior to the Communist Revolution.

5 When individuals were sent to the countryside for "reeducation," it meant essentially that they needed to engage in manual labor in the agricultural or industrial sectors (usually the former) in order to better understand the class issues confronted by the Communist Revolution.

6 Information on population-growth trends in the People's Republic of China is drawn largely from Spence (1999).

7 The Great Leap Forward was a major project of social reorganization in order to "deepen" the revolution. In 1957–1958 this meant setting up the people's communes; by the end of 1958, 740,000 cooperatives had been merged into 26,000 communes; these comprised 120 million rural households—99 percent of the rural population. One of the central problems with production was that grain was not being produced at a high-enough rate. Grain was a necessary part of industrial growth, because it was the primary product China could export to the Soviet Union. In 1957, the Chinese Communist Party began organizing people into huge workforces for irrigation, construction projects, and the like. The year 1958 also saw the creation of over 1 million backyard steel furnaces. The result was a huge famine from 1959 to 1962 in which 20 million people died of starvation.

8 See, for example, Wolff et al. (1995) and Wong (2004).

9 "China's Missing Girls," *Shanghai Star*, October 24, 2002.

10 This information comes from the Xinhua News Agency. Note that these figures are officially reported figures and likely under-represent the problem.

11 If non-party members are elected in village-level elections to leadership positions in the village, they are required to join the party.

12 Other members of the Politburo Standing Committee of the Chinese Communist Party occupy such leadership positions: Huang Ju is vice premier of the State Council of China; Jia Qinglin is chairman of the People's Political Consultative Conference; Li Changchun has no formal position but is known to many as "propaganda chief"; Luo Gan is a state councilor and secretary of the Political and Legislative Affairs Committee; Wu Guanzheng is secretary of the Central Commission for Discipline Inspection; and Zeng Qinghong is vice president of the People's Republic of China.

13 "Grassroots Democracy is Flourishing in China," *China Daily*, October 18, 2002.

14 Where Oberschall (1996) presents the party-state and work units as distinct institutions, the situation was actually a little more complicated than this, as the exercise of political control from the party-state operated largely through the dependence that was created through the work-unit system; see Walder 1986a.

15 A large volume of literature exists on this phenomenon. Typical studies in this approach include, for example, Ho and Tsou (1969), Solomon (1971), Hsu (1999), Rozman (1981), Fairbanks (1983), Pye (1988), Pye (1992), and Chen and Deng (1995).

16 See the results from Transparency International's Corruption index; http://www.transparency. org/policy_research/surveys_indices/cpi/2010.

17 For further discussion, see Gold et al. (2002).

Chapter 4

1 For further discussion, see Yang (1990, 1991) and Vogel (1989).

2 This lack of control was viewed by conservatives as partially responsible for the Tiananmen Square uprising.

3 Primary goods refers to food and live animals chiefly used for food; beverages and tobacco; non-edible raw materials; mineral fuels, lubricants, and related materials; and animal and

vegetable oils, fats, and wax. Manufactured goods refers to chemicals and related products; light and textile industrial products; rubber products; minerals and metallurgical products; machinery and transport equipment; miscellaneous products; and products not otherwise classified.

4　In the case of Taiwan, this trend gained momentum after 1989, when many countries of the Organization for Economic Cooperation and Development pulled out of China in response to the Tiananmen Square massacre; foreign investment dropped from U.S.$2 billion in the fourth quarter of 1988 to U.S.$900 million in the first quarter of 1990. In order to win back foreign capital, China appealed to Chinese investors from Hong Kong, Macau, and Taiwan by offering favorable investment conditions. Among these were several industrial zones in Fujian Province, the ancestral birthplace of many Taiwanese citizens, which were designated for Taiwanese investors. As a direct result, Taiwanese investment in China increased by 75 percent in 1990 (Hsing 1998).

5　*BusinessWeek*, October 13, 2003.

6　Under GNP, the earnings of multinational corporations were counted according to where a multinational corporation was owned and where the profits were eventually returned. Under GDP, the profits are attributed to where the site of production is located, regardless of where the organization is owned or incorporated.

7　James Flanigan, *Los Angeles Times*, April 17, 2005.

8　See Guthrie (1998b, 1999, 2002b). Although labor contracts officially afforded SOEs the opportunity to end lifetime employment, the practice continued for many years, though it has been declining steadily since these formal changes in 1986.

9　As with all reforms adopted over the course of China's transition, these formal laws and regulations that governed enterprise behavior were first experimented with in many venues over significant periods of time before becoming officially codified in formal laws and regulations.

10　See *The Decision on Several Issues for Establishing a Socialist Market Economy System*, passed in the Third Plenary Session of the Fourteenth National Congress of the Chinese Communist Party in 1993.

11　For further discussion, see Wong (2002).

12　For example, a city government divided the land for one foreign project into several small lots and granted land-use permission individually, in order to satisfy the standard of the smaller size of land that this level of government had the authority to grant (see Hsing 1998). Similar strategies have been used more widely for foreign investment arrangements in regions throughout southern China.

13　In the simplest terms, classical definitions of business organizations would posit that they are (1) comprised of relationships between owners and workers and (2) established for the purpose of pursuing profits in exchange for the provision of goods and/or services (see Sparling 1906). For example, Noble (1927, 232) defines business organizations as an

> association expressed in a variety of relationships—joint owners, joint operators, agent and principal, trustee and beneficiary, employer and employee. The history of efforts of these individuals or groups of individuals within the business unit to accomplish that purpose for which the business unit was formed, namely, the making of profit, is recorded in the accounts of the enterprise.
>
> (Howard 1917, 107)

places the concept squarely in the realm of property rights, positing the right that owners have as residual claimants on revenues generated by the services: business organizations are "cooperative arrangements of men for the purpose of acquiring . . . property rights (quantitatively measured by the unit of value, the dollar) by producing some product or service exchangeable for some form of property, usually a right to money, which may be distributed as income to individuals." According to these terms, only private enterprises and some foreign-funded enterprises in China would fall under the category of business organizations.

14 The data here come from the *Statistical Yearbook of China*, 2006. The figure includes "all the state-owned and non-state-owned industrial enterprises."

15 There are obvious and famous exceptions here; state-owned enterprises like Baoshan Steel were still closely monitored and supported by the state (Steinfeld 1998). However, while these organizations are often viewed as the markers of what is occurring in the Chinese reform process, this view is mistaken. While important to the economy, these largest state-owned organizations are not representative of the economy as a whole. Thus, while many scholars view these organizations as measures of the progress of China's reforms, they are more accurately the exceptions that prove the rule.

16 It is important to note the interdependence of these sectors here: as state-owned enterprises were placed on the dual-track system, private firms were allowed to emerge in the economy, becoming a force that essentially forced the state sector to compete (Naughton 1995). Similarly, the foreign sector has been a key factor in the teaching of management practices (Guthrie 1999) as well as in the transfer of technology.

17 Here again, we are speaking of joint-venture partnerships as opposed to other types of foreign investment.

18 Details of this venture are taken from Smith 2001.

19 Most of the large joint-venture deals come in at just under U.S.$30 million, as this is the level at which approvals need not go beyond the municipal government. A joint-venture deal the size of Time Warner and Legend's must be approved directly by the State Council.

20 The Third Annual Meeting of the Advisory Council of International Business Leaders was held on May 9–10, 2001, in Beijing.

21 Arbitration clauses are particular cases in which the government gives away control over joint ventures. If a joint-venture contract specifies nothing about how a dispute will be resolved, disputes that arise will be handled by the Chinese courts. This is the best-case scenario for the Chinese government in terms of sovereignty, because the courts, at this point, are still an arm of the authoritarian government. However, if a joint-venture agreement specifies that disputes will be settled through arbitration, there are two possible venues for this. The first is the Chinese International Economic Trade and Arbitration Commission (CIETAC), an institution of arbitration in Beijing (with branches in Shanghai and Shenzhen). The significant fact about CIETAC, in terms of arbitration, is that one-third of the arbitrators who sit on any case are from other countries. Thus, once cases go to CIETAC, the Chinese government no longer has control over their outcome. A second possibility is that a joint-venture agreement can specify third-country arbitration, in which the dispute will be settled in the arbitration institution of some specified third country. The Chinese government has even less control—if any at all—over the outcome of these cases (Guthrie 1999, Chapter 7).

22 Although the Patent Law (People's Republic of China 1984b), which was put into effect on April 1, 1985, may have been relevant for this dispute, the more pertinent question is which Chinese body (e.g., the Chinese courts or the Chinese International Economic Trade and Arbitration Commission—CIETAC) was hearing this dispute and to what extent that body chose to seriously consider DuPont's claims. In the DuPont case, the joint-venture contact presumably did not specify CIETAC arbitration, as disputes over contracts that do not specify arbitration (CIETAC or third-country) go automatically to the courts, which was the case with DuPont's dispute.

23 With respect to the former, there are other types of contractual relations between foreign and Chinese firms that are not commitments over time. For example, the piece-rate production agreements that prevail in the garment and shoe industries tend to be per project and are renegotiated and shopped in a competitive production market in each round of production. Thus, the commitment of a company like Liz Claiborne or Gap to an individual factory is marginal, as they are always shopping for cheaper production prices. This is fundamentally different from a licensing agreement or a joint venture, as these commitments are long-term agreements.

24 Geely Corporate Website (http://www.geeley.com/english/index.html).

25 *Taiwan Economic Journal*, *"TEJ Company Profile—Geely* Automobile Holdings Ltd."
26 The comparison here is not between state/collective on the one hand and foreign firms on the other; rather, it is between those state- and collectively-owned firms that have received some kind of foreign involvement through joint-venture deals, licensing agreements, and other types of "cooperative" agreements, and those who have not. Note also that a common misconception with the "collective" sector is that these organizations are somehow hybrid or mixed-property-rights organizations. Collectively owned organizations are fundamentally state organizations; the variation is in the level of government control over property rights and the period of the founding of such organizations (Walder 1995e; Guthrie 1999).
27 For econometric analyses of these effects, see Guthrie 2005.
28 In a few places, such as Xinjiang and Tibet, foreign-funded firms consistently perform worse across economic indicators like productivity (the same holds true for ratios of profits to cost and output to assets). However, for those economic indicators listed in Table 4.1, no fewer than twenty-eight (out of thirty-one) administrative areas show better performance among foreign-funded firms than state-owned firms that have no such relationships with foreign corporations.

Chapter 5

1 Jim Yardley, "As China Roars, Pollution Reaches Deadly Extremes," *New York Times*, August 26, 2007.
2 Andrew Jacobs, "In China, Pollution Worsens Despite Efforts," *New York Times*, July 28, 2010.
3 Joseph Khan and Jim Yardley, "As China Roars, Pollution Reaches Deadly Extremes," *New York Times*, August 26, 2007; Kevin Holden Platt, Chinese Air Pollution Deadliest in the World, Report Says, *The National Geographic*, July 9, 2007.
4 Jonathan Ansfield and Keith Bradsfield, "China Report Shows More Pollution in Waterways," *New York Times*, February 9, 2010.
5 Statement by John Doerr, Partner Kliner Perkins Caufield and Byers, Thursday, July 16, 2009, Submitted to U.S. Senate Committee on Environment and Public Works, Hearing Regarding "Ensuring and Enhancing U.S. Competitiveness while Moving toward a Clean Energy Economy."
6 "China Winning Green Race—U.S. Venture Capitalist," Reuters, March 4, 2010.
7 "Hard Choices: Evergreen Solar's China Move—CEO Michael El-Hillow on why he closed his U.S. plant, fired 800 workers, and is moving his company to China as told to Diane Brady," *Bloomberg Businessweek*, January 27, 2011.
8 Based on conversation with former Chairman and CEO of DuPont, Chad Holliday. Mr. Holliday was head of the company during the time that Dupont built its most recent photovoltaic plant in Guangdong Province.
9 Dan Bobkoff, "Ohio's Burning River in Better Health 40 Years Later," *National Public Radio*, June 22, 2009, http://www.npr.org/templates/story/story.php?storyId=105750930.

Chapter 6

1 The details of these men's lives are taken from Roberts (1999).
2 Beijing and Tsinghua Universities (widely regarded as the top two universities in China) received an additional 1.8 billion yuan, spread over three years (1999–2001), while Nanjing and Fudan (widely regarded as the third, and fourth, best universities, respectively) received an additional 1.2 billion yuan.
3 United Nations Development Programme, 2001.
4 See Figure 2.1 for an example of the nested hierarchy of state administration.
5 For a sense of scale, note that this population of migrant laborers is equal to the entire population of Northern Europe or about one-third of the total U.S. population.

Chapter 7

1 For discussions of the "quiet revolution" within China, see Walder (1995c), Goodman and Hooper (1994), and Guthrie (2003).

2 I refer to this movement throughout my discussion as the 1989 Chinese movement, rather than the 1989 student movement, as it is commonly called, because the widespread participation of "ordinary citizens" (Strand 1990) is part of what distinguishes this movement from its predecessors (Guthrie 1995; Walder 1989a).

3 Extensive discussions of this movement can be found in Calhoun (1989), Walder (1989b), Shen (1990), Calhoun (1991), Esherick and Wasserstrom (1992), Perry and Wasserstrom (1991), Calhoun (1995), Guthrie (1995), Deng (1997), and Zhao (1997).

4 This description of events is taken primarily from Shen Tong's *Almost a Revolution* (1990), which, along with Craig Calhoun's *Neither Gods Nor Emperors* (1995), is the best firsthand account of the movement available.

5 Though not central to my discussion here, workers were actually an important part of this movement, and declining party power operated in workplaces and universities in similar ways. Walder and Gong (1991) and Calhoun (1995) all examine the importance of workers in the movement.

6 Here again, we come back to fundamental institutional changes of the reform era: the loosening of the household passport laws in 1983 (and the fact that political dossiers do not follow individuals around the way they did when the Labor Bureau was allocating jobs) changed the extent to which students could leave their pasts behind. Under the old system, individuals could not simply pick up and move to a new city or province. In China today, there are no such restrictions on social mobility.

7 This was the case with Motorola in 1996. Up until that time, Motorola had only a wholly owned foreign enterprise in China and a licensing agreement with a variety of factories, including the Hangzhou Telecommunications Factory, to produce their handsets. Motorola made a great deal of money through this arrangement, which allowed them to produce and sell phones without transferring any technology in the process. Then, in 1995, they began negotiating a joint venture with the Hangzhou Telecommunications Factory. In a personal interview with one of the insiders on this deal, I inquired as to what had led to the change of heart. The American manager said, "Let's just say that the [Chinese] government decided it was time for us to share the wealth. And if we were going to keep doing what we are doing in China, we were going to have to set up a joint venture deal with someone."

8 With China's recent entry into the World Trade Organization, changes in the state's control of this sector are imminent, as the agreement China and the United States reached in the negotiations over China's entry mandates that foreign firms will be able to own minority stakes in the telecommunications industry.

9 It is very likely that the strife between the former chief executive officer, Wang Zhidong, and the board of directors is most likely the result of the complex business structure that was required in establishing Sina.com's initial public offering of stock, which was a result of Beijing's prohibitions against foreign ownership in this sector. When Sina.com went public, the company had to give up its control over the Internet within China. Sina.com, which is an Internet portal company in China, actually can only provide "technical assistance" to the Chinese-based Sina Internet Information Service Company, Ltd., which has an Internet content provider license, of which Wang also owns a majority stake. Thus, we have an American listed company, with an American board of directors, that is purportedly an Internet content provider but does not have an Internet content license in China and has to rely solely on a Chinese-based company for access to the Internet.

10 *China Daily*, June 26, 2001.

11 Industry experts have put China's Internet usage at 450 million in 2010—larger than the online populations of the United States, Japan, the UK, and France combined (which together have an online population of 401 million). By 2015, it is predicted that the online

population in China will reach about 750 million (the United States, Japan, the United Kingdom and France combined will be about 447 million). See Galloway and Guthrie (2011).

12 As was discussed in Chapter 3, decollectivization reversed the main economic policy through which farmers in China have been organized since the 1950s. Namely, in 1952, the new government of the People's Republic of China began organizing Chinese farmers into cooperative units of anywhere from thirty to 300 households (communes), where production was monitored and controlled by the government (Spence 1999).

13 This change is not so different from the "dual track" system that industrial work units were placed on in the 1980s and 1990s, as they were gradually weaned off the planned economy (Naughton 1995). The important difference here is that, inasmuch as the market and economic autonomy teach citizens about the fundamental changes occurring in China's economic and political system, Chinese citizens were exposed to this autonomy at the household level, while only managers of industrial work units were exposed to this change in the transformation of the industrial work unit in urban areas.

14 It is important to note that while the changes occurring in urban China are much more conspicuous and therefore much clearer throughout the world, only about 50 percent of the Chinese population resides in urban China. The other 50 percent resides in the township and village areas of rural China.

15 See, for example, Pearson (1994), Unger and Chan (1995 and 1996), Foster (2002), and Kang (2002).

16 The Chinese Academy of Social Sciences recently released a report on social stratification of contemporary China in 2004 that suggested China's "middle class" accounted for 19 percent of the country's 1.3 billion population by 2003. According to the academy's standard in their report, families with assets valued from 150,000 yuan (U.S.$18,137) to 300,000 yuan (U.S.$36,275) can be classified as middle class.

17 See, for example, Sik (1994), Boisot and Child (1996), Shao (1998), Lu (2000), and Sik (2000). This is not to say there are not proponents of the view that a rational-legal system is gradually emerging. For example, Pei (1994), Naughton (1995), and Guthrie (1999) have all taken the view that the emergence of a rational-legal economy in China is significant and real. However, the overwhelming tenor of scholarship on China's transition is that despite the success of the reforms, corporatism, corruption, crony-capitalism, and a still-authoritarian government are all impeding the development of a rational–legal economy in China.

18 For further discussion, see Guthrie (1999, esp. Chapters 3, 7, and 9).

19 The facts of this case are presented in Lo and Tian (2005).

20 Relying on internal documents, public sources, and personal interviews with former prisoners, Seymour and Anderson put together a comprehensive comparative study of the *laogai* in three provinces in Northwest China—Gansu, Qinghai, and Xinjiang—the heart of the *laogai* system. The comparison of the labor reform system in these provinces allows the authors to explore variations across geographic boundaries, and the differences across the cases reveal a fact that is well known to China scholars but often lost in the political rhetoric over the Chinese government and its policies: despite the Chinese government's interest in having a unified set of policies, the reality is one of a decentralized and fragmented system, with often divergent structures and outcomes. The comparative framework allows for variation in levels of economic development and ethnic composition, as well as a comparison of one case that is often viewed as representative of the Chinese system (that of Gansu) with two that are often viewed as unique within this system.

21 As Walder (1986a, 11) puts it,

> The discretion of supervisors, relatively unrestrained by enforceable regulations and contracts, [was] quite broad ... [supervisors had] considerable ability to influence the promotions, raises, and, more importantly, the degree to which a worker and his or her family may enjoy the many nonwage benefits and advantages potentially supplied by the enterprise.

22 As a document from the State Council put it in 1983, "The current system of employment in China, under which the majority are permanent workers, in practice operates as a kind of unconditional system of life tenure" (People's Republic of China 1983); See also Guthrie 1998a and Josephs 1989 for further discussion.

23 The Great Leap Forward (1958–1960) provided a caveat to this system, as approximately 16 million workers were laid off and sent down to the countryside during that campaign. This is the only period, however, where layoffs were not accompanied by reassignment (Walder 1986a). For further discussion of "waiting for employment," see Gold (1989a).

24 See People's Republic of China (1986a, 1986b). See also Zhongguo tongji nianjian (*Statistical Yearbook of China* 1994, 131); and Josephs (1989). These documents explicitly define three types of contracts: the fixed limited-term contract [*guding qixian laodong hetong*], the nonfixed limited-term contract [*wuguding qixian laodong hetong*], and the per-project work limited-term contract [*yixiang gongzuo wei qixian laodong hetong*]. My interviews with managers indicate that, of these three, the fixed limited-term contract is the most stable in that it guarantees employment at an organization for the duration of the time period defined in the contract. It is also the type of contract that workers in industrial factories are signing. The nonfixed limited-term contract and the per-project work limited-term contract are typically used in more project-oriented sectors, such as construction. Accordingly, I focus here on the fixed limited-term contract.

25 See Naughton (1995, 210–212).

26 While the official Provisional Regulations document (see People's Republic of China 1986a and 1986b) was promulgated in 1986, local governments began experimenting with contracts as early as 1983, by order of the Trial Implementation Notice of the State Council promulgated that year; see People's Republic of China (1983). Typically, this is the way broad institutional changes are set in motion in China: an institutional change begins with a policy idea that emerges as a "notice" from the State Council and is then experimented with in different localities and different sectors of the economy. When the kinks have been worked out to some degree, the institutional change is legitimized through an official law, rule, regulation, or decree from the State Council.

27 As with most other indicators, there is significant variation across the administrative regions of China: Shanghai, for example, has a considerably higher proportion of its laborers on labor contracts (49.9 percent). The less-developed areas of Tibet and Anhui Province are among the lowest, with 10.5 percent and 12.5 percent of the labor force on contracts, respectively. However, it is also clear that the implementation of the labor contract is not only a function of industrial development, as Tianjin—one of the major industrial municipalities in China—is also among the lowest, with 13.8 percent of the labor force on contracts.

28 Some officials and managers hold the view that these legal frameworks have a direct impact on the use of outside arbitration. As one government official explained,

> We believe that the Labor Law will have a huge impact on the labor arbitration situation. We think this is already beginning to happen. Over the last few years there has been a steady increase of applications to the Labor Arbitration Commission. But this year we expect a huge increase because of the Labor Law. Because of the Labor Law, everyone will start to know what kind of personal power they have. The Labor Law is changing peoples' understanding of their rights ... We are hoping that the combination of the Labor Law and the Labor Arbitration Commission will force all types of organizations to focus on the laws more and more. Now that we are developing a market economy, changes are happening so quickly, and it's very important that everyone is protected by the laws.
>
> (Personal interview, Shanghai, 1995, originally reported in Guthrie 1999)

29 Individuals can also apply to serve in this group, but few do, because it is not a paid position. Of the people that do apply as volunteers, most are lawyers working at universities who want to get some experience with the legal changes that are happening in China. According to

officials, there are really not enough individuals working in this capacity, and, as a result, many cases are simply heard by the presiding governmental official.

30 The representation of workers in dispute resolution and more generally overseeing the implementation of the Labor Law have become the primary functions of labor unions in China. As of 1999, labor unions had set up more than 140,000 agencies to oversee the implementation of the Labor Law in local workplaces.

31 Although there is a separate section for disputes relating to benefits and pay in the LAC, individuals generally rely on labor unions to solve such problems.

32 For discussions of the "quiet revolution" within China, see Walder (1995c), Goodman and Hooper (1994), and Guthrie (2003).

33 For discussion of the adoption of these systems in U.S. workplaces, see Dobbin *et al.* (1993) and Sutton *et al.* (1994). These scholars have shown that U.S. firms responded to federal mandates that were not directly aimed at labor reform by rationalizing labor processes, which has parallels in U.S. labor history as well. For example, U.S. firms rapidly adopted rational labor processes in the late 1960s and early 1970s in response to the civil rights legislation of the 1960s.

Chapter 8

1 Cox Report (United States Congress 2001).

2 Newman (2005); Newman, Richard (2005) "The Rise of a New Power." *U.S. News and World Report*, June 20.

3 I use 2001 as the comparison point here, because this was before the rapidly escalating expenditures of the recent Iraq War began to have effect.

4 China was one of the twenty-three original signatory nations of the General Agreement on Tariffs and Trade (GATT) in 1948. After the Communist Revolution, two things happened. First, the nationalist government of Taiwan announced that it, not the Beijing Regime, would be the participant in the GATT. Second, the People's Republic of China became extremely isolationist in the decades following its founding, so there was little follow-up to the Taiwan announcement until 1986.

5 Adopted by Congress in 1974, the Jackson–Vanick Amendment was established to limit trade with the Soviet Union in response to its poor record in the area of human rights, particularly in the area of emigration. It became more general policy and was applied to countries like China to address the question of whether the country deserved "most favored nation" trade status.

6 President Bill Clinton, quoted in Drake *et al.* 2000.

7 Hong Kong and Macau accounted for more than 60 percent of China's total outward foreign direct investment from 1979 until the mid-1990s. North America accounted for 15 percent during this time period.

REFERENCES

Andrews, Steven Q., 2009. "Seeing Through the Smog: Understanding the Limits of Chinese Air Pollution Reporting." *China Environment Series* 10: 5–29. Washington, DC, Woodrow Wilson International Center for Scholars. http://www.wilsoncenter.org/sites/default/files/andrews_feature_ces10.pdf

Aunan, Kristin, Terje Koren Bernsten, and Hans Martin Seip. 2000. "Surface Ozone in China and Its Possible Impact on Agricultural Crop Yields." *Ambio* 29(6): 294–301.

Barro, Robert and Xavier Sala-i-Martin. 1995. *Economic Growth*. Boston, MA: McGraw Hill.

Beamish, P.W. and A. Delios. 2005. "Selling China: Looking Back and Looking Forward." *Management and Organization Review* 1(2): 309–313.

Bian, Yanjie. 1994a. *Work and Inequality in Urban China*. Albany: State University of New York Press.

——. 1994b. "Guanxi and the Allocation of Urban Jobs in China." *China Quarterly* 140: 971–999.

——. 1997. "Bringing Strong Ties Back In: Indirect Ties, Network Bridges, and Job Searches in China." *American Sociological Review* 62: 366–385.

Bian, Yanjie and S. Ang. 1997. "Guanxi Networks and Job Mobility in China and Singapore." *Social Forces* 75(3): 981–1005.

Bian, Yanjie and John R. Logan. 1996. "Market Transition and the Persistence of Power: The Changing Stratification System in Urban China." *American Sociological Review* 61: 739–758.

Bian, Yanjie, John Logan, and X. Shu. 2000. "Wage and Job Inequalities in the Working Career of Men and Women in Tianjin." In *Re-Drawing Boundaries: Work, Household, and Gender in China*, ed. Barbara Entwisle and Gail Henderson. Berkeley and Los Angeles: University of California Press.

Biello, David. 2011. "China Syndrome: Going Nuclear to Cut Down on Coal Burning." ScientificAmerican.http://www.scientificamerican.com/article.cfm?id=china-goes-nuclear-to-avoid-coal-burning

Blanchard, Ben. 2011. "China Gives Bleak Assessment of Its Battered Environment." Reuters. www.reuters.com

Blanchard, Oliver, Maxin Boycho, Marek Dabrowski, Rudiger Dorubusch, Richard Layard, and Andrei Shleifer. 1993. *Post Communist Reform: Pain and Progress*. Cambridge, MA: MIT Press.

Boisot, Max and John Child. 1996. "From Fiefs to Clans and Network Capitalism: Explaining China's Emerging Economic Order." *Administrative Science Quarterly* 41: 600–628.

——. 1999. "Organizations as Adaptive Systems in Complex Environments: The Case of China." *Organization Science* 10(3): 237–252.

Borton, James. 2002. "Motorola University Scores High Grades in China." *Asia Times Online* (June 4).

Brinton, Mary C., Yean-Ju Lee, and William L. Parish. 1995. "Married Women's Employment in Rapidly Industrializing Societies: Examples from East Asia." *American Journal of Sociology* 100: 1099–1130.

British Petroleum, 2011. *Statistical Review of World Energy 2011.* London: British Petroleum. http://www.bp.com/statisticalreview

Brown, Lester. 1995. *Who Will Feed China?* New York: W. W. Norton.

Burawoy, Michael. 1985. *Politics of Production: Factory Regimes under Capitalism and Socialism.* London: Verso.

Burawoy, Michael and Pavel Krutov. 1992. "The Soviet Transition from Socialism to Capitalism: Worker Control and Economic Bargaining in the Wood Industry." *American Sociological Review* 57: 16–38.

Burawoy, Michael and János Lukacs. 1985. "Mythologies of Work: A Comparison of Firms in State Socialism and Advanced Capitalism." *American Sociological Review* 50: 723–737.

Bureau of Economic Analysis. 2011. *National Economic Accounts.* Washington, DC: U.S. Department of Commerce. http://www.bea.gov/national/index.htm#gdp

Busenitz, Lowell and Jay B. Barney. 1997. "Differences between Entrepreneurs and Managers in Large Organizations: Biases and Heuristics in Strategic Decision-Making." *Journal of Business Venturing* 12: 9–30.

Cai, Kevin G. 1999. "Outward Foreign Direct Investment: A Novel Dimension of China's Integration into the Regional and Global Economy." *China Quarterly* 160: 856–880.

Cao, Mingde and Yixiang Xu. 2010. "Climate Protection and Motor Vehicle Regulations: Evaluation of Motor Vehicle Regulations in China in the Context of Greenhouse Gas Management." *Natural Resources Forum: A United Nations Sustainable Development Journal* 34(4): 266–274.

Calhoun, Craig. 1989. "Protest in Beijing: The Conditions and Importance of the Chinese Student Movement of 1989." *Partisan Review* 4: 563–580.

——. 1991. "The Problem of Identity in Collective Action." In *Macro-Micro Linkages in Sociology*, ed. J. Huber. Beverly Hills, CA: Sage, pp. 51–75.

——. 1995. *Neither Gods Nor Emperors: Students and the Struggle for Democracy in China.* Berkeley and Los Angeles: University of California Press.

——, ed. 2002. *Dictionary of the Social Sciences.* New York: Oxford University Press.

Central Intelligence Agency. 2011. *The World Factbook.* https://www.cia.gov/library/publications/the-world-factbook/rankorder/rawdata_2087.txt

Chai, Joseph C. H. 1992. "Consumption and Living Standards in China." *China Quarterly* 131: 721–749.

Chan, Kam Wing and Li Zhang. 1999. "The Hukou System and Rural–Urban Migration in China: Processes and Changes." *China Quarterly* 160: 818–855.

Chang, Gordon. 2001. *The Coming Collapse of China.* New York: Random House.

Chang, Jesse T. H., and Charles J. Conroy. 1987. "Trademark Law in the People's Republic of China." In *Foreign Trade, Investment, and the Law in the People's Republic of China*, ed. Michael J. Moser. New York: Oxford University Press, pp. 427–452.

Chen, Gang. 2009. *Politics of China's Environmental Protection.* Singapore: World Scientific Publishing Co. Pte. Ltd.

Chen, Jie and Peng Deng. 1995. *China Since the Cultural Revolution: From Totalitarianism to Authoritarianism.* Westport, CT: Praeger.

Chen, Kuan, Wang Hongchang, Zheng Yuxin, Gary H. Jefferson, and Thomas G. Rawski. 1988. "Productivity Change in Chinese Industry: 1953–1985." *Journal of Comparative Economics* 12: 570–591.

Cheng, Lucie and Arthur Rosett. 1991. "Contract with a Chinese Face: Socially Embedded Factors in the Transformation from Hierarchy to Market, 1978–1989." *Journal of Chinese Law* 5: 143–244.

Child, J. 2001. "Learning through Strategic Alliances." In *Handbook of Organizational Learning and Knowledge*, ed. M. Dierkes, A. B. Antal, J. Child and I. Nonaka. Oxford: Oxford University Press, pp. 657–680.

China Daily. 2011. "A review of the 11th Five-Year Plan." *China Daily*. www.chinadaily.com.cn

China Environment Yearbook. Vol. 4, Dongping Yang. Leiden, The Netherlands: Koninklijke Brill NV.

China International Economic and Trade Arbitration Commission. 1994. *Arbitration Rules*. Beijing: People's Republic of China.

China Online. 2000. "China to become Asia-Pacific Region's Second-Largest IT Market, Study Says." *China Online*, June 22. www.chinaonline.com.

Chinese Directory of Organizations and Institutions Publishing Committee. 1993. Zhongguo qi shi ye ming lu quan shu [Chinese Directory of Organizations and Institutions]. Beijing: People's Republic of China.

Christiansen, Flemming. 1992. "Market Transition in China: The Case of the Jiangsu Labor Market, 1978–1990." *Modern China* 18: 72–93.

Clarke, Donald C. 1991. "Dispute Resolution in China." *Journal of Chinese Law* 5: 245–296.

Cohen, Wesley M. and Daniel A. Levinthal. 1990. "Absorptive Capacity: A New Perspective on Learning and Innovation." *Administrative Science Quarterly* 35(1): 128–152.

Cooper, Caroline. 2000. "Look at India; It's Where China Wants to Be." *China Online*, June 22, www.chinaonline.com.

Cramer, John. 2011. "Enforce Environmental Laws." *Vermont Law School*, South Royalton, VT. http://www.vermontlaw.edu/x12877.xml

Cui, Ning. 2001. "Technology a Growth Engine to Economy." *China Daily*, June 18.

Davis, Deborah and Steven Harrell. 1993. "Introduction: The Impact of Post-Mao Reforms on Family Life." In *Chinese Families in the Post-Mao Era*, ed. Deborah Davis and Steven Harrell. Berkeley and Los Angeles: University of California Press, pp 1–22.

Dean, Earl Howard. 1917. "Economics and the Science of Business." *Journal of Political Economy* 25(1): 106–110.

Demsetz, Harold. 1967. "Toward a Theory of Property Rights." In *Ownership, Control, and the Firm: The Organization of Economic Activity*, Vol. 1. Oxford: Blackwell.

Deng, Shasha. 2011. "Key targets of China's 12th five-year plan." *Xinhua News Agency*. www.english.news.cn

Deng, Zhenglai. 1997. *Guojia yu shehui [The State and the Society]*. China: Sichuan People's Press.

Deng, Zhenglai, and Jing Yuejin. 1992. "Constructing China's Civil Society." *Chinese Social Sciences Quarterly*, September.

Dickson, Bruce. 2003. *Red Capitalists in China: The Party, Private Entrepreneurs, and Prospects for Political Change*. New York: Cambridge University Press.

DiMaggio, Paul. 1988. "Interest and Agency in Institutional Theory." In *Institutional Patterns and Organizations: Culture and Environment*, ed. Lynne Zucker. Cambridge, MA: Ballinger, pp. 3–22.

DiMaggio, Paul and Walter Powell. 1983. "The Iron Cage Revisited: Institutional Isomorphism and Collective Rationality in Organizational Fields." *American Sociological Review* 48: 147–161.

Dobbin, Frank and John Sutton. 1998. "The Strength of a Weak State: The Rights Revolution and the Rise of Human Resources Management Divisions." *American Journal of Sociology* 104: 441–476.

Dobbin, Frank, John R. Sutton, John W. Meyer, and W. Richard Scott. 1993. "Equal Opportunity Law and the Construction of Internal Labor Markets." *American Journal of Sociology* 99: 396–427.

Drake, William J., Shanthi Kalathil, and Taylor C. Boas. 2000. "Dictatorships in the Digital Age: Some Considerations on the Internet in China and Cuba." *Information Impacts*, October.

Dyck, Alexander and Yasheng Huang. 2004. "PetroChina." Harvard Business School Case #9-701-040. Cambridge, MA: Harvard Business School Case.

Economy, Elizabeth. 2004. *The River Runs Black: The Environmental Challenge of China's Future.* Ithaca, NY: Cornell University Press.

———. 2007. "The Great Leap Backward?" *Foreign Affairs* September/October.

Edelman, Lauren B. 1990. "Legal Environments and Organizational Governance: The Expansion of Due Process in the American Workplace." *American Journal of Sociology* 95: 1401–1440.

———. 1992. "Legal Ambiguity and Symbolic Structures: Organizational Mediation of Civil Rights Law." *American Journal of Sociology* 97: 1531–1576.

Energy Information Administration. 2010. *Country Analysis Briefs: China.* Washington, D.C.: Energy Information Administration.

Entwisle, Barbara and Gail Henderson, eds. 2000. *Re-Drawing Boundaries: Work, Household, and Gender in China.* Berkeley and Los Angeles: University of California Press.

Entwisle, Barbara, Gail E. Henderson, G. E. Short, J. E. Bouma, and F. Y. Zhai. 1995. "Gender and Family Business in Rural China." *American Sociological Review* 60: 36–57.

Environmental Protection Agency. 2010. "Six Common Air Pollutants." Washington, DC: Environmental Protection Agency. http://epa.gov/airquality/urbanair/

Ericson, Richard E. 1991. "The Classical Soviet-Type Economy: Nature of the System and Implications for Reform." *Journal of Economic Perspectives* 5(4): 11–27.

Esherick, Joseph W. and Jeffery N. Wasserstrom. 1992. "Acting Out Democracy: Political Theater in Modern China." In *Popular Protest and Political Culture in Modern China: Learning from 1989*, ed. Elizabeth Perry and Jeffery Wasserstrom. Boulder, CO: Westview, pp. 28–66.

Fabel, Oliver. 1990. *Insurance and Incentives in Labor Contracts: A Study in the Theory of Implicit Contracts.* Frankfurt: Anton Hain.

Fairbanks, John King. 1983. *The United States and China.* Cambridge, MA: Harvard University Press.

———. 1992. *China: A New History.* Cambridge, MA: Belknap Press of Harvard University Press.

Fan, Cindy. 2006. "China's Eleventh Five-Year Plan (2006–2010): From 'Getting Rich First' to Common Prosperity." *Eurasian Geography and Economics* 47(6): 708–723.

Fang, Yiping, Yong Zeng, and Shiming Li. 2008. "Technological Influences and Abatement Strategies for Industrial Sulfur Dioxide in China." *International Journal of Sustainable Development and World Ecology* 15: 122–131.

Farh, Jiing-Lih, Anne Tsui, Katherine Xin, Bor-Shiuan Cheng. 1998. "The Influence of Relational Demography and Guanxi: The Chinese Case." *Organization Science* 9(4): 471–488.

Fei, Xiaotong. 1946. "Peasantry and Gentry: An Interpretation of Chinese Social Structure and Its Change." *American Journal of Sociology* 52: 1–17.

———. 1992. *From the Soil: The Foundations of Chinese Society.* Berkeley and Los Angeles, CA: University of California Press.

Feng, Liu, Yongguan Zhu, and Ying Zhao. 2008. "Contribution of Motor Vehicle Emissions to Surface Ozone in Urban Areas: A Case Study in Beijing." *International Journal of Sustainable Development and World Ecology* 15: 345–349.

Fewsmith, Joseph. 1999. "Elite Politics." In *The Paradox of China's Post-Mao Reforms*, ed, Merle Goldman and Roderick MacFarquhar. Cambridge, MA: Harvard University Press, pp. 47–75.

Field, Robert M. 1984. "Changes in Chinese Industry since 1978." *China Quarterly* 100: 742–761.

———. 1992. "China's Industrial Performance Since 1978." *China Quarterly* 131: 577–607.

Fields, Karl J. 1995. *Enterprise and State in Korea and Taiwan*. Ithaca, NY: Cornell University Press.

Fischer, Stanley. 1992. "Privatization in Eastern European Transformation." In *The Emergence of Market Economies in Eastern Europe*, ed. Christopher Clague and Gordon C. Rausser. Cambridge, MA: Blackwell, pp. 227–243.

Fischer, S. and A. Gelb 1991. "The Process of Socialist Economic Transformation." *Journal of Economic Perspectives*, 4: 91–106.

Fishman, Ted. 2004. "The Chinese Century." *New York Times Magazine*, July 4.

Fitzgerald, C. P. 1964. *The Birth of Communist China*. Harmondsworth, England: Penguin.

Fligstein, Neil. 1990. *The Transformation of Corporate Control*. Cambridge, MA: Harvard University Press.

———. 1996. "Markets as Politics: A Sociological View of Market Institutions." *American Sociological Review* 61: 656–673.

Fortes, Meyer. 1969. *Kinship and the Social Order*. Chicago: Aldine.

Foster, Kenneth W. 2002. "Embedded with State Agencies: Business Associations in Yantai." *China Journal* 47: 41–65.

Fruin, W. Mark and Penelope Prime. 1999. "Competing Strategies of FDI and Technology Transfer to China: American and Japanese Firms." William Davidson Institute Working Paper Series No. 218. Ann Arbor: University of Michigan School of Business.

Fu, Jun. 2000. *Institutions and Investments: Foreign Direct Investment in China During an Era of Reform*. Ann Arbor, MI: University of Michigan Press.

Furubotn, Eirik and Svetozar Pejovich, eds. 1974. *The Economics of Property Rights*. Cambridge, MA: Ballinger.

Gallagher, Kelly. 2010. "The Challenge for Environment, Development, and Sustainability in China." *Environment, Development, and Sustainability—Perspectives and Cases from Around The world*, 1st edition. ed. Gordon Wilson, Pamela Furniss, and Richard Kimbowa. Oxford: Oxford University Press, pp. 14–23.

Galloway, Scott and Doug Guthrie. 2011. "L2 Prestige 100: China Digital IQ." New York: L2 Thinktank. http://l2thinktank.com/research/china-iq-2011/

Gao, Sheldon. 2002. "China Stock Market in a Global Perspective." Research Report. New York: Dow Jones.

Gates, Hill, 1993. "Cultural Support of Birth Limitation among Urban Capital-Owning Women." In *Chinese Families in the Post-Mao Era*, ed. Deborah Davis and Steven Harrell. Berkeley and Los Angeles: University of California Press, pp. 251–274.

Gelatt, Timothy A. and Richard D. Pomp. 1987. "China's Tax System: An Overview and Transactional Analysis." In *Foreign Trade, Investment, and the Law in the People's Republic of China*, ed. Michael J. Moser. New York: Oxford University Press, pp. 42–89.

Gerber, Theodore P. and Michael Hout. 1995. "Educational Stratification in Russia During the Soviet Period." *American Journal of Sociology* 101: 611–660.

Gerlach, Michael L. 1992. *Alliance Capitalism: The Social Organization of Japanese Business*. Berkeley and Los Angeles: University of California Press.

Glain, Stephen. 2011. *State vs. Defense: The Battle to Define America's Empire*. Crown.

Gold, Thomas B. 1980. "Back to the City: The Return of Shanghai's Educated Youth." *China Quarterly* 84: 55–70.

———. 1985. "After Comradeship: Personal Relations in China since the Cultural Revolution." *China Quarterly* 104: 657–675.

———. 1989a. "Guerilla Interviews among the Getihu." In *Popular Culture and Thought in the People's Republic*, ed. Perry Link, Richard Madsen, and Paul Pickowicz. Boulder, CO: Westview, pp. 175–192.

———. 1989b. "Urban Private Business in China." *Studies in Comparative Communism* 22(2–3): 187–201.

———. 1990. "Urban Private Business and Social Change." In *Chinese Society on the Eve of Tiananmen: The Impact of Reform*, ed. Deborah Davis and Ezra F. Vogel. Cambridge, MA: Harvard University Press, pp. 157–178.

——. 1991. "Urban Private Business and China's Reforms." In *Reform and Reaction in Post-Mao China: The Road to Tiananmen*, ed. Richard Baum. New York: Routledge, pp. 84–103.

Gold, Thomas, Doug Guthrie, and David Wank, eds. 2002. *Social Connections in China: Institutions, Culture, and the Changing Nature of Guanxi*. New York: Cambridge University Press.

Gong, Ting. 1994. *The Politics of Corruption in Contemporary China: An Analysis of Policy Outcomes*. Westport, CT: Praeger.

Goodman, David. 1999. "The New Middle Class." In *The Paradox of China's Post-Mao Reforms*, ed. Merle Goldman and Roderick MacFarquhar. Cambridge, MA: Harvard University Press.

Goodman, David and Beverley Hooper, eds. 1994. *China's Quiet Revolution*. Melbourne: Longman Cheshire.

Granick, David. 1990. *Chinese State Enterprises: A Regional Property Rights Analysis*. Chicago: University of Chicago Press.

Granovetter, Mark. 1985. "Economic Action and Social Structure: The Problem of Embeddedness." *American Journal of Sociology* 91: 481–510.

Groves, Theodore, Yongmiao Hong, John McMillan, and Barry Naughton. 1994. "Autonomy and Incentives in Chinese State Enterprises." *Quarterly Journal of Economics* 109(1): 193–209.

——. 1995. "China's Evolving Managerial Labor Market." *Journal of Political Economy* 103: 873–892.

Guo, Jiann-Jong. 1992. *Price Reform in China, 1979–86*. Basingstoke, UK: St. Martin's.

Guthrie, Doug. 1995. "Political Theater and Student Organizations in the 1989 Chinese Movement: A Multivariate Analysis of Tiananmen." *Sociological Forum* 10: 419–454.

——. 1996. "Organizational Action and Institutional Reforms in China's Economic Transition: A Comparison of Two Industries." *Research in the Sociology of Organizations* 14: 181–222.

——. 1997. "Between Markets and Politics: Organizational Responses to Reform in China." *American Journal of Sociology* 102: 1258–1303.

——. 1998a. "Organizational Uncertainty and the End of Lifetime Employment in China." *Sociological Forum* 13(3): 457–494.

——. 1998b. "The Declining Significance of Guanxi in China's Economic Transition." *China Quarterly* 154: 254–282.

——. 1999. *Dragon in a Three-Piece Suit: The Emergence of Capitalism in China*. Princeton, NJ: Princeton University Press.

——. 2001. "The Emergence of Market Practices in China's Economic Transition: Price Setting in Shanghai's Industrial Firms." In *Managing Organizational Change in Transition Economies*, edited by Daniel Denison. Mahwah, NJ: Lawrence Erlbaum.

——. 2002a. "Information Asymmetries and the Problem of Perception: The Significance of Structural Position in Assessing the Importance of Guanxi in China." In *Social Connections in China: Institutions, Culture, and the Changing Nature of Guanxi*, ed. Thomas Gold, Doug Guthrie, and David Wank. New York: Cambridge University Press.

——. 2002b. "The Transformation of Labor Relations in China's Emerging Market Economy." *Research in Social Stratification and Mobility* 19: 137–168.

——. 2002c. "Entrepreneurial Action in the State Sector: The Economic Decisions of Chinese Managers." In *The New Entrepreneurs of Europe and Asia: Patterns of Business Development in Russia, Eastern Europe and China*, ed. Vicki Bonnell and Thomas Gold. Boulder, CO: M. E. Sharpe, pp. 159–190.

——. 2003. "The Quiet Revolution: The Emergence of Capitalism in China." *Harvard International Review* 25(2): 48–53.

——. 2004. "Information Technology, Sovereignty, and Democratization in China." In *Digital Formations: Cooperation and Conflict in a Connected World*, ed. Robert Latham and Saskia Sassen. Princeton, NJ: Princeton University Press.

——. 2005. "Organizational Learning and Productivity: State Structure and Foreign Investment in the Rise of the Chinese Corporation." *Management and Organization Review* 1(2): 165–195.

Guthrie, Doug and Junmin Wang. 2007. "Business Organizations in China." In *Handbook of Asian Business*, ed. Henry Yeung. London: Edward Elgar Publishing, pp. 99–121.

Guthrie, Doug, Zhixing Xiao, and Junmin Wang. 2007. "Aligning the Interests of Multiple Principals: Ownership Concentration and Profitability in China's Publicly Traded Companies." Stern School of Business, Department of Economics, Working Paper Series.

——. 2009 "Work and Productivity in Reform-Era China." *Research in the Sociology of Work* 19: 35–73.

Hamilton, Gary G. 1991. *Business Networks and Economic Development in East and Southeast Asia.* Centre for East Asian Studies, Hong Kong: University of Hong Kong Press.

——. 1996. "The Theoretical Significance of Asian Business Networks." In *Asian Business Networks*, ed. Gary Hamilton, Berlin: Walter de Gruyter, pp. 283–298.

Hamilton, Gary and Robert Feenstra. 1994. "Varieties of Hierarchies and Markets: An Introduction." Paper presented at the annual meeting of the American Sociological Association, August 5–9, Los Angeles.

Hamilton, Gary and Nicole Woolsey Biggart. 1988. "Market, Culture, and Authority: A Comparative Analysis of Management and Organization in the Far East." *American Journal of Sociology* 94: S52–S94.

Hannum, Emily and Yu Xie. 1994. "Trends in Educational and Gender and Inequality." *Research in Social Stratification and Mobility* 13: 73–98.

Harner, Stephen. 2000. "Shanghai's New Five-Year Plan: The Pearl Starts to Shine." *China Online*, December 18, www.chinaonline.com.

Hertz, Ellen. 1998. *The Trading Crowd: An Ethnography of the Shanghai Stock Market.* New York: Cambridge University Press.

Hessler, Peter. 1999. "Tibet through Chinese Eyes." *Atlantic Monthly*, February.

Hiebert, M. and T. Saywell. 2000. "Market Morality." *Far Eastern Economic Review* 163: 56–58.

Hill, David and Krishna Sen. 2000. "The Internet in Indonesia's New Democracy." *Democratization*, Spring.

Higgins, Matthew and Thomas Kiltgaard. 2004. "Reserve Accumulation: Implications for Global Capital Flows in Financial Markets." *Current Issues in Economics and Finance* 10 (10, September/October): 1–8. New York: Federal Reserve Bank of New York.

——. 2007. "Financial Globalization and the U.S. Current Account Deficit." 13(11, December): 1–7. New York: Federal Reserve Bank of New York.

Ho, Ping-ti, and Tang Tsou, eds. 1969. *China in Crisis.* Chicago: University of Chicago Press.

Hoff, Karla and Joseph E. Stiglitz. 1990. "Introduction: Imperfect Information and Rural Credit Markets—Puzzles and Policy Perspectives." *World Bank Economic Review* 4(3): 235–250.

Hohfeld, Wesley. 1913. "Some Fundamental Legal Conceptions as Applied to Judicial Reasoning." *Yale Law Journal* 23(1): 16–59.

Holt, Thomas Ford. 1969. *Dictionary of Modern Sociology.* Lanham, MD: Littlefield Adams.

Honig, Emily and Gail Hershatter. 1988. *Personal Voices.* Stanford, CA: Stanford University Press.

Howard, Earl Dean. 1917. "Economics and the Science of Business." *Journal of Political Economy* 25 (1 January, 1917): 106–110.

Hsing, You-Tien. 1998. *Making Capitalism in China: The Taiwan Connection.* New York: Oxford University Press.

Hsu, Immanuel C. Y. 1999. *The Rise of Modern China.* New York: Oxford University Press.

Hsueh, Roselyn. 2011. *China's Regulatory State: A New Strategy for Globalization.* Ithaca, NY: Cornell University Press.

Huang, Ruicai and Xiaowen Cong. 1994. *Xiandai qiye caichan guanli* [*Managing Property in the Modern Enterprise*]. Jinan: Jinan University Press.

Huang, Laiji, and Zhou Jingen, eds. 1994. *Gongsifa huiyi yu zujian gongsifa jingyan* [*Answers to Questions Regarding the Company Law and the Experience of Constructing the Company Law*]. Beijing: Shijie tuanti chuban gongsi.

Huang, Yasheng. 1990. "Web of Interests and Patterns of Behaviour of Chinese Local Economic Bureaucracies and Enterprises During Reform." *China Quarterly* 123: 431–458.

——. 1995a. "Administrative Monitoring in China." *China Quarterly* 143: 828–843.

——. 1995b. "Why China will not Collapse." *Foreign Policy* 99: 54–68.

——. 2003. *Selling China: Foreign Direct Investment during the Reform Era*. New York: Cambridge University Press.

Hui, C. and G. Graen. 1997. "Guanxi and Professional Leadership in Contemporary Sino-American Joint Ventures in Mainland China." *Leadership Quarterly* 8(4): 451–465.

International Energy Agency. 2009. *Cleaner Coal in China*. Paris: International Energy Agency.

Jakobson, Linda. 1998. *A Million Truths: A Decade in China*. New York: M. Evans Publishing.

Jefferson, Gary H., and Wenyi Xu. 1991. "The Impact of Reform on Socialist Enterprises in Transition: Structure, Conduct, and Performance in Chinese Industry." *Journal of Comparative Economics* 15: 45–64.

Jin, Hao. 2006. "How Do Foreign Auto Suppliers Need to Compete Differently in China Market?" MS Thesis in Engineering and Management, MIT.

Johnson, Chalmers. 1987. "Political Institutions and Economic Performance: The Government-Business Relationship in Japan, South Korea, and Taiwan." In *The Political Economy of the New Asian Industrialism*, ed. Frederic C. Deyo. Ithaca, NY: Cornell University Press, pp. 136–164.

Josephs, Hilary K. 1989. *Labor Law in China: Choice and Responsibility*. Sevenoaks, UK: Butterworth Legal Publishers.

Kamm, John. 1989. "Reforming Foreign Trade." In *One Step Ahead in China: Guangdong under Reform*. Cambridge, MA: Harvard University Press, pp. 338–392.

Kang, Xiaoguang. 2002. "A Study of China's Political Stability in the 1990s." *Twenty-First Century* 72: 33.

Kaplan, Robert. 2005. "How We Would Fight China." *Atlantic Monthly Magazine* (June).

Keister, Lisa A. 2000. *Chinese Business Groups: The Structure and Impact of Interfirm Relations during Economic Development*. New York: Cambridge University Press.

——. 2002. "Guanxi in Business Groups: Social Ties and the Formation of Economic Relations." In *Social Connections in China: Institutions, Culture, and the Changing Nature of Guanxi*, ed. Thomas Gold, Doug Guthrie, and David Wank. New York: Cambridge University Press.

Kennedy, Michael D. and Pauline Gianoplus. 1994. "Entrepreneurs and Expertise: A Cultural Encounter in the Making of Post-Communist Capitalism in Poland." *East European Politics and Societies* 8(1): 58–93.

King, Ambrose Y. C. 1985. "The Individual and Group in Confucianism: A Relational Perspective." In *Individualism and Holism: Studies in Confucian and Taoist Values*, ed. Donald J. Munro. Ann Arbor: Center for Chinese Studies, University of Michigan, pp. 57–70.

Kipnis, Andrew. 1997. *Producing Guanxi: Sentiment, Self, and Subculture in a North China Village*. Durham, NC: Duke University Press.

Kirby, William C. 1995. "China Unincorporated: Company Law and Business Enterprise in Twentieth-Century China." *Journal of Asian Studies* 54: 43–63.

Kornai, János. 1980. *The Shortage Economy*. Amsterdam: North-Holland.

——. 1990. *The Road to a Free Economy*. New York: W. W. Norton.

Kristof, Nicholas, and Sheryl WuDunn. 2001. *Thunder from the East*. New York: Vintage.

Krug, Barbara. 1994. "Review of Price Reform in China, 1979–86, by Jiann–Jong Guo," *China Quarterly* 138: 528–530.

Kwong, Julia. 1997. *The Political Economy of Corruption in China*. Armonk, NY: M. E. Sharpe.

LaFraniere, Sharon. 2011. "Leading Poisoning in China: The Hidden Scourge." *New York Times*. www.nytimes.com

Lardy, Nicholas R. 1984. "Consumption and Living Standards in China, 1978–83." *China Quarterly* 100: 849–865.

——. 1992. *Foreign Trade and Economic Reform in China, 1978–1990*. New York: Cambridge University Press.

———. 1994. *China in the World Economy: Issues, Recommendations, Results*. Washington, DC: Peterson Institute.

———. 1995. "The Role of Foreign Trade and Investment in China's Economic Transformation." *China Quarterly* 144: 1065–1082.

———. 1996. "The Role of Foreign Trade and Investment in China's Economic Transition." In *China's Transitional Economy*, ed. Andrew Walder. New York: Oxford University Press.

———. 2002. *Integrating China into Global Economy*. Washington, DC: Brookings Institution Press.

Lawrence, Susan. 1994. "Democracy, Chinese Style." *Australian Journal of Chinese Affairs* 32: 61–68.

Lee, Ching-Kwan. 1995. "Engendering the Worlds of Labor: Women Workers, Labor Markets, and Production Politics in the South China Economic Miracle." *American Sociological Review* 60: 378–397.

Lee, Hong Yung. 1991. *From Revolutionary Cadres to Party Technocrats in Socialist China*. Berkeley: University of California Press.

Lee, Michael Y. 2003. "Changing Dynamics of Chinese Automotive Industry: The Impact of Foreign Direct Investment, Technology Transfer, and WTO Membership." MS Thesis, Sloan School of Management, MIT.

Levitt, Barbara and James G. March. 1988. "Organizational Learning." *Annual Review of Sociology* 14: 319–340.

Li, Cetao. 1993. *Gufen zhi lilun yu qiye gai zhi zao zuo [The System and Theory of Stocks and Enterprise Reform]*. Shanghai: Fudan University Press.

Li, Dun. 2010. "We are All Victims of Pollution and Responsible for Our Planet." *The China Environment Yearbook*. Vol. 4, Dongping Yang. Leiden, The Netherlands: Koninklijke Brill NV.

Li, Jing and Yining Peng. 2011. "A Hard Rain is Falling as Acid Erodes Beauty." *China Daily*.

Li, Lianjiang and Kevin O'Brien. 1999. "The Struggle Over Village Elections." In *The Paradox of China's Post-Mao Reforms*, ed. Merle Goldman and Roderick MacFarquhar. Cambridge, MA: Harvard University Press, pp. 129–144.

Li, Linda Chelan. 1997. "Provincial Discretion and National Power: Investment Policy in Guangdong and Shanghai, 1978–93." *China Quarterly* 152: 778–804.

Li, Peilin and Zhang Yi. 2000. "Consumption Stratification in China: An Important Tool in Stirring up Economy." *Zhongguoshehuikexi [Chinese Social Science]*, *Development and Society* 29(2, December): 55–72.

Li, Yushan. 1992. *Shehui zhuyi guojia jingji: gaige yu fazhan gongcheng [Socialism and National Development: Reform and Development]*. Dalian, China: Ligong University Press.

Lieberthal, Kenneth. 1995. *Governing China: From Revolution through Reform*. New York: W. W. Norton.

Lin, Nan, 1995. "Local Market Socialism: Local Corporatism in Action in Rural China." *Theory and Society* 24: 301–354.

Lin, Nan and Bian Yanjie. 1991. "Getting Ahead in Urban China." *American Journal of Sociology* 97: 657–688.

Liu, Feng, Yoongguan Zhu, and Ying Zhao. 2008. "Contribution of Motor Vehicle Emissions to Surface Ozone in Urban Areas: A Case Study in Beijing." *International Journal of Sustainable Development and World Ecology* 15: 345–349.

Liu, Pak-Wai, Xin Meng, and Junsen Zhang. 2000. "Sectoral Gender Wage Differentials and Discrimination in the Transitional Chinese Economy." *Journal of Population Economics* 13: 331–352.

Lo, Vai Io and Xiaowen Tian. 2005. *Law and Investment in China: The Legal and Business Environments after China's WTO Accession*. London: RoutledgeCurzon.

Luo, Jianxi. 2005a. "The Growth of Independent Chinese Automotive Companies." Working paper, MIT International Motor Vehicle Program, Cambridge MA, USA.

Lovett, Steve, Lee Simmons, and Raja Kali. 1999. "Guanxi Versus the Market: Ethics and Efficiency." *Journal of International Business Studies* 30(2): 231–247.

Lu, Xiaobo, 2000. *Cadres and Corruption: The Organizational Involution of the Chinese Communist Party*. Stanford, CA: Stanford University Press.

Lu, Xiaobo and Elizabeth Perry, eds. 1997. *Danwei: The Changing Chinese Workplace in Historical and Comparative Perspective*. Armonk, NY: M. E. Sharpe.

Lubman, Stanley. 1986. *China's Economy Looks Toward the Year 2000, Vol. 1: The Four Modernizations. Joint Economic Committee*. Washington, DC: Government Printing Office.

——. 1987. "Technology Transfer in China: Policies, Law, and Practice." In *Foreign Trade, Investment, and the Law in the People's Republic of China*, ed. Michael J. Moser. New York: Oxford University Press, pp. 170–198.

——. 1995. "Introduction: The Future of Chinese Law." *China Quarterly* 141: 1–21.

Lubman, Stanley B. and Gregory C. Wajnowski. 1993. "International Commercial Dispute Resolution in China: A Practical Assessment." *American Review of International Arbitration* 4: 107–178.

Luffman, George A. and Richard Reed. 1984. *The Strategy and Performance of British Industry, 1970–80*. New York: St. Martin's.

Luo, Jianxi. 2005. "The Growth of Independent Chinese Automotive Companies." Working paper, MIT International Motor Vehicle Program, Cambridge MA, USA.

Luo, Xiaopeng. 1990. "Ownership and Status Stratification." In *China's Rural Industry: Structure, Development, and Reform*, ed. William A. Byrd and Lin Qingsong. New York: Oxford University Press, pp. 134–171.

Luo, Yadong. 1997. "Partner Selection and Venturing Success: The Case of Joint Venturing Firms in the People's Republic of China." *Organization Science* 8(6): 648–662.

——. 1998. "Timing of Investment and International Expansion Performance in China." *Journal of International Business* 29(2): 391–407.

——. 2001a. "Toward a Cooperative View of MNC-Host Government Relations: Building Blocks and Performance Implication." *Journal of International Business Studies* 32(3): 401–419.

——. 2001b. "Antecedents and Consequences of Personal Attachment in Cross-Cultural Cooperative Ventures." *Administrative Science Quarterly* 46(2): 177–201.

Luo, Yadong and Mike Peng. 1999. "Learning to Compete in a Transition Economy: Experience, Environment, and Performance." *Journal of International Business Studies* 30(2): 269–295.

Luo, Yadong, Oded Shenkar, and Mee-Kau Nyaw. 2001. "A Dual Perspective on Control and Performance in International Joint Ventures: Lessons from a Developing Economy." *Journal of International Business* 32(1): 41–58.

Ma, Jiantang. 2011. "Press Release on Major Figures in of the 2010 National Population." National Bureau of Statistics. http://www.stats.gov.cn/english/newsandcomingevents/t20110428_402722237.htm

McKinnon, Ronald. 1992. "Taxation, Money, and Credit in a Liberalizing Socialist Economy." In *The Emergence of Market Economies in Eastern Europe*, ed. Christopher Clague and Gordon C. Rausser. Cambridge, MA: Blackwell, pp. 109–127.

March, James. 1981. "Footnotes to Organizational Change." *Administrative Science Quarterly* 26(2): 563–577.

——. 1991. "Explorations and Exploitation in Organizational Learning." *Organization Science* 2(1): 71–87.

Matthews, R. and Victor Nee. 2000. "Gender Inequality and Economic Growth in Rural China." *Social Science Research* 29: 2–32.

Meyer, John W. and Brian Rowan. 1977. "Institutionalized Organizations: Formal Structure as Myth and Ceremony." *American Journal of Sociology* 83: 340–363.

Meyer, Marshall. 2005. "Is China for Sale?" *Management and Organization Review* 1(2): 303–307.

Min, Anchee. 2000. *Becoming Madame Mao*. New York: Houghton Mifflin.

Ministry of Environmental Protection of the People's Republic of China, 2010. *Report on the State of the Environment in 2009*. Beijing: Ministry of Environmental Protection of the People's Republic of China. http://english.mep.gov.cn/standards_reports/soe/soe2009/201104/t20110411_208979.htm

Mizruchi, Mark and Lisa Fein. 1999. "The Social Construction of Organizational Knowledge: A Study of the Uses of Coercive, Mimetic, and Normative Isomorphism." *Administrative Science Quarterly* 44: 653–683.

Moody, Marcy Nicks. 2010. "Too Much of a Good Thing? Phosphorus Flows and Water Eutrophication." *The China Environment Series*, Issue 11. Washington, DC: Woodrow Wilson International Center for Scholars, pp. 222–225.

Moser, Michael J. 1987. "Foreign Investment in China: The Legal Framework." In *Trade, Investment, and the Law in the People's Republic of China*, ed. Michael J. Moser. New York: Oxford University Press, pp. 90–169.

Mote, Frederick. 1989. *Intellectual Foundations of China*. New York: Alfred A. Knopf.

Mueller, D. 1997. "First-Mover Advantages and Path Dependence." *International Journal of Industrial Organization* 15(6): 827–850.

Murphy, Michael. 1993. "Competition under the Laws Governing Soviet Producer Cooperatives during Peristroika." In *Capitalist Goals, Socialist Past: The Rise of the Private Sector in Command Economies*, ed. Perry L. Patterson. Boulder, CO: Westview, pp. 147–167.

Murrell, Peter. 1990. *The Nature of Socialist Economies: Lessons from Eastern Europe Foreign Trade*. Princeton, NJ: Princeton University Press.

——. 1992. "Evolution in Economics and in the Economic Reform of the Centrally Planned Economies." In *The Emergence of Market Economies in Eastern Europe*, ed. Christopher Clague and Gordon C. Rausser,. Cambridge, MA: Blackwell, pp. 35–53.

National Statistical Bureau of China. 1989. 1994. 1996. 1999. 2000. 2002. 2003. 2004. 2005. 2006. 2007. 2008. 2010. *Statistical Yearbook of China*. Beijing: National Statistical Bureau of China Press.

Naughton, Barry. 1992. "Hierarchy and the Bargaining Economy: Government and Enterprise in the Reform Process." In *Bureaucracy, Politics, and Decision Making in Post-Mao China*, ed. Kenneth G. Lieberthal and David M. Lampton. Canberra: Contemporary China Center, Australian National University, pp. 245–279.

——. 1993. "Deng Xiaoping: The Economist." *China Quarterly* 135: 491–512.

——. 1994. "What is Distinctive about China's Economic Transition? State Enterprise Reform and Overall System Transformation." *Journal of Comparative Economics* 18: 470–490.

——. 1995. *Growing Out of the Plan: Chinese Economic Reform 1978–1993*. New York: Cambridge University Press.

——. 2007. *The Chinese Economy: Transitions and Growth*. Cambridge, MA: MIT Press.

Nee, Victor. 1985. "Peasant Household Individualism." In *Chinese Rural Development: The Great Transformation*, ed. William Parish. Armonk, NY: M. E. Sharpe, pp. 164–190.

——. 1989a. "A Theory of Market Transition: From Redistribution to Markets in State Socialism." *American Sociological Review* 54: 663–681.

——. 1989b. "Peasant Entrepreneurship and the Politics of Regulation." In *Remaking the Economic Institutions of Socialism: China and Eastern Europe*, ed. Victor Nee and David Stark. Stanford, CA: Stanford University Press, pp. 169–207.

——. 1991. "Social Inequalities in Reforming State Socialism: Between Redistribution and Markets in China." *American Sociological Review* 56: 267–282.

——. 1992. "Organizational Dynamics of Market Transition: Hybrid Forms, Property Rights, and Mixed Economy in China." *Administrative Science Quarterly* 37: 1–27.

——. 1996. "The Emergence of a Market Society: Changing Mechanisms of Stratification in China." *American Journal of Sociology* 101: 908–949.

Nee, Victor and Yang Cao. 1999. "Path Dependent Societal Transformation: Stratification in Mixed Economies." *Theory and Society* 28: 799–834.

Nee, Victor and Rebecca Matthews. 1996. "Market Transition and Societal Transformation in Reforming State Socialism." *Annual Review of Sociology* 22: 401–435.

Newman, Richard. 2005. "The Rise of a New Power." *U.S. News and World Report*, June 20.

Noble, Howard S. 1927. "The Relation of Business Organization to Accounting." *Accounting Review* 2(3): 232–236.

Nolan, Peter. 2004. *Transforming China: Globalization, Transition and Development*. London: Anthem Press.

North, Douglass C. 1990. *Institutions, Institutional Change and Economic Performance*. New York: Cambridge University Press.

O'Brien, Kevin. 1990. "Is China's National People's Congress a 'Conservative' Legislature?" *Asian Survey* 30(8): 782–794.

Oberschall, Anthony. 1996. "The Great Transition: China, Hungary, and Sociology Exit Socialism into the Market." *American Journal of Sociology* 101: 1028–1041.

Ogden, Suzanne, ed. 2004. *Global Studies: China*. New York: Dushkin/McGraw-Hill.

Ohe, Takeru, Shuji Honjo, and Ian MacMillan. 1990. "Japanese Entrepreneurs and Corporate Managers: A Comparison." *Journal of Business Venturing* 5: 163–176.

Oi, Jean C., 1989. *State and Peasant in Contemporary China: The Political Economy of Village and Government*. Berkeley and Los Angeles: University of California Press.

———. 1992. "Fiscal Reform and the Economic Foundations of Local State Corporatism." *World Politics* 45: 99–126.

———. 1995. "The Role of the Local State in China's Transitional Economy." *China Quarterly* 144: 1132–1149.

Oi, Jean C. and Andrew Walder, eds. 1999. *Property Rights and Economic Reform in China*. Stanford, CA: Stanford University Press.

Orrù, Marco, Nicole Woolsey Biggart, and Gary G. Hamilton. 1991. "Organizational Isomorphism in East Asia." In *The New Institutionalism in Organizational Analysis*, ed. Walter W. Powell and Paul DiMaggio. Chicago: University of Chicago Press, pp. 361–389.

Oshita, Stephanie B. and Lynn K. Price. 2010. "Lessons For Industrial Energy Efficiency Cooperation With China." *The China Environment Series*, Issue 11. Washington, DC: Woodrow Wilson International Center for Scholars, pp. 49–88.

Palmer, Michael. "The Re-Emergence of Family Law in Post-Mao China: Marriage, Divorce, and Reproduction." *China Quarterly* 141: 110–134.

Pan, Wenjing. 2010. "Eco-Farming: A Long-Term Strategy for Dealing with Climate Change." *China Environment Series*. Issue 11. Washington, DC: Woodrow Wilson International Center for Scholars, pp. 219–221.

Parish, William L. and Ethan Michelson. 1996. "Politics and Markets: Dual Transformations." *American Journal of Sociology* 4: 1042–1059.

Parish, William and Martin King Whyte. 1978. *Village Life in Contemporary China*. Chicago: University of Chicago Press.

Parris, Kristen. 1999. "The Rise of Private Business Interests." In *The Paradox of China's Post-Mao Reforms*, ed. Merle Goldman and Roderick MacFarquhar. Cambridge, MA: Harvard University Press, pp. 262–282.

Pearson, Margaret. 1994. "The Janus Face of Business Associations in China: Socialist Corporatism in Foreign Enterprises." *Austrian Journal of Chinese Affairs* 31: 25–46.

———. 1997. *China's New Business Elite: The Political Consequences of Economic Reform*. Berkeley and Los Angeles: University of California Press.

Pei, Minxin. 1994. *From Reform to Revolution: The Demise of Communism in China and the Soviet Union*. Cambridge, MA: Harvard University Press.

———. 1995. "Creeping Democratization in China." *Journal of Democracy* 6(4): 65–79.

———. 1997. "Citizens v. Mandarins: Administrative Litigation in China." *China Quarterly* 152: 832–862.

———. 1998. "Is China Democratizing?" *Foreign Affairs* 68–82.

Peng, Mike and Peggy Sue Heath. 1996. "The Growth of the Firm in Planned Economies in Transition: Institutions, Organizations, and Strategic Choice." *Academy of Management Review* 21(2): 492–528.

Peng, Mike and Anne Ilinitch. 1998. "Export Intermediary Firms: A Note on Export Development Research." *Journal of International Business Studies* 29(3): 609–620.

Peng, Mike and Yadong Luo. 2000. "Managerial Ties and Firm Performance in a Transitional Economy: The Nature of a Micro-Macro Link." *Academy of Management Review* 43(3): 486–501.

Peng, Mike and Anne York. 2001. "Behind Intermediary Performance in Export Trade: Transactions, Agents, and Resources." *Journal of International Business Studies* 32(2): 327–346.

Peng, Yusheng. 1992. "Wage Determination in Rural and Urban China: A Comparison of Public and Private Industrial Sectors." *American Sociological Review* 57: 198–213.

People's Republic of China [Zhonghua renmin gongheguo] (PRC). 1979. Law of the People's Republic of China on Chinese-Equity Joint Ventures. Adopted on July 1, 1979, at the Second Session of the Fifth National People's Congress.

——. 1981. Economic Contract Law of the People's Republic of China. Adopted on December 13, 1981, at the Fourth Session of the Fifth National People's Congress.

——. 1983. Laodong renshi bu guanyu jiji shixing laodong hetong zhide tongzhi [Notice of the Ministry of Labor and Personnel on Active Trial Implementation of the Contract Employment System]. *Sixth State Council Gazette* 213.

——. 1984a. "Decision of the Standing Committee of the National People's Congress on Authorizing the State Council to Reform the System of Industrial and Commercial Taxes and Issue Relevant Draft Tax Regulations for Trial Application." Adopted on September 18, 1984 at the Seventh Meeting of the Standing Committee of the Sixth National People's Congress.

——. 1984b. Patent Law of the People's Republic of China. Adopted at the 4th Session of the Standing Committee of the Sixth National People's Congress on March 12, 1984.

——. 1986a. Guoying qiye shixing laodong hetong zhanxing guiding [Provisional Regulations on the Implementation of the Contract Employment System in State Enterprises]. Promulgated by the State Council on July 12, 1986; Effective October 1, 1986.

——. 1986b. Guoying qiye citui weiji zhigong zanxing guiding [Provisional Regulations on the Dismissal of Workers and Staff for Work Violations in State Enterprises]. Promulgated by the State Council on July 12, 1986; Effective October October 1, 1986.

——. 1986c. Guoying qiye zhaoyong gongren zhanxing guiding [Provisional Regulations on the Hiring of Workers in State Enterprises]. Promulgated by the State Council on July 12, 1986, Effective October 1, 1986.

——. 1988. Law of the People's Republic of China on Chinese–Foreign Contractual Joint Ventures. Adopted at the First Session of the Seventh National People's Congress and promulgated by Order No. 4 of the President of the People's Republic of China on April 13, 1988.

——. 1993. The Company Law of the People's Republic of China. Adopted at the Fifth Meeting of the Standing Committee of the Eighth National People's Congress on December 12, 1993; effective July 1, 1994.

——. 1994. The Labor Law of the People's Republic of China. Adopted at the Eighth Meeting of the Standing Committee of the National People's Congress on July 5, 1994; effective January 1, 1995.

——. 1995. The National Compensation Law of the People's Republic of China. Adopted at the Seventh Meeting of the Standing Committee of the Eighth National People's Congress on May 5, 1994; effective January 1, 1995.

——. 1999. Securities Law of the People's Republic of China. Adopted at the 6th Meeting of the Standing Committee of the 9th National People's Congress on December 29, 1998.

——. 2001. The Tentative Measures for Decreasing State Shareholding. National People's Congress.

Perry, Elizabeth and Jeffery Wasserstrom. 1991. *Popular Protest and Political Culture in Modern China: Learning from 1989*. Boulder, CO: Westview.

Pew Charitable Trusts. 2010. "Who's Winning the Clean Energy Race? Growth, Competition and Opportunity in the World's Largest Economies." Washington, DC: Pew Charitable Trusts.

Pocket World in Figures 2004. 2005. 2008. 2010. London: Profile.

——. 2011. London: Economists Books.

Polanyi, Karl. 1957. *The Great Transformation: The Political and Economic Origins of Our Time.* Boston: Beacon.

Potter, Pitman B. 1988. *The Mandarin and the Cadre.* Ann Arbor: University of Michigan Center for Chinese Studies.

——. 1994. "Riding the Tiger: Legitimacy and Legal Culture in Post-Mao China." *China Quarterly* 138: 325–358.

Price, Lynn, Xuejun Wang, and Jiang Yun. 2010. "The Challenge of Reducing Energy Consumption of the Top-1000 Largest Industrial Enterprises in China." *Energy Policy*, 38(11). http://china.lbl.gov/sites/china.lbl.gov/files/Top-1000.Energy_Policy_November 2010.pdf

Pye, Lucian. 1988. *The Mandarin and the Cadre: China's Political Cultures.* Ann Arbor: University of Michigan Press.

——. 1992. *The Spirit of Chinese Politics.* Cambridge, MA: MIT Press.

——. 1995. "Factions and the Politics of Guanxi: Paradoxes in Chinese Administrative and Political Behavior." *China Journal* 34: 35–53.

Rawski, Thomas G. 1994. "Progress without Privatization: The Reform of China's State Industries." In *Changing Political Economies: Privatization in Post-Communist and Reforming Communist States,* ed. Vedat Milor. Boulder, CO: Lynn Reinner, pp. 27–52.

——. 1995. "Implications of China's Reform Experience." *China Quarterly* 144: 1150–1173.

——. 1999. "Reforming China's Economy: What Have We Learned?" *China Journal* 41: 139–156.

Redding, Gordon S. 1990. *The Spirit of Chinese Capitalism.* Berlin: Walter de Gruyter.

Reynolds, Bruce L., ed. 1987. *Reform in China: Challenges and Choices.* Armonk, NY: M. E. Sharpe.

Riedel, James, Jing Jin, and Jian Guo. 2007. *How China Grows: Investment, Finance and Reform.* Princeton, NJ: Princeton University Press.

Roberts, Dexter. 1999. "A Tale of Two Families: How China's Transformation to a Market Economy is Having Jarringly Different Effects on Ordinary Citizens." *BusinessWeek* 3635: 48–53.

Róna-Tas, Ákos. 1994. "The First Shall Be Last? Entrepreneurship and Communist Cadres in the Transition from Socialism." *American Journal of Sociology* 100: 40–69.

Rowe, W.G. 2006. *Restructuring CNPC and the Proposed Listing of PetroChina.* Ontario, Canada: Ivey Management Services.

Rosenthal, Elisabeth. 1998. "A Day in Court, and Justice, Sometimes, for the Chinese." *New York Times,* April 27, A1.

Rozman, Gilbert, ed. 1981. *The Modernization of China,* New York: Free Press.

Ruttan, V. 1997. "Induced Innovation, Evolutionary Theory and Path Dependence: Sources of Technical Change." *Economic Journal* 107(444): 1520–1529.

Sachs, Jeffrey D. 1992. "Privatization in Russia: Some Lessons from Eastern Europe." *American Economic Review* 80: 43–48.

——. 1993. *Poland's Jump to the Market Economy.* Cambridge, MA: MIT Press.

——. 1995a. "Consolidating Capitalism." *Foreign Policy* 98: 50–64.

——. 1995b. "Reforms in Eastern Europe and the Former Soviet Union in Light of the East Asian Experience." *Journal of the Japanese and International Economies* 9: 454–485.

Sachs, Jeffrey D. and Wing Thye Woo. 1994a. "Experiences in the Transition to a Market Economy." *Journal of Comparative Economics* 18(3): 271–275.

——. 1994b. "Structural Factors in the Economic Reforms of China, Eastern Europe, and the Former Soviet Union." *Economic Policy* 9(18): 101–131.

——. 1997. "Understanding China's Economic Performance." Working Paper #5935, National Bureau of Economic Research, Inc. Working Paper Series.

Sachs, Jeffrey D. and Lipton David. 1990. "Poland's Economic Reform." *Foreign Affairs* 69: 47–66.

Santoro, Michael. 1999. *Profits and Principles*. Ithaca, NY: Cornell University Press.

Schumpeter, Joseph A. 1934. *The Theory of Economic Development*. Cambridge, MA: Harvard University Press.

——. 1949. "Economic Theory and Entrepreneurial History." In *Essays on Entrepreneurs, Innovation, Business Cycles, and the Evolution of Capitalism*, ed. Richard Clemence. Wokingham, UK: Addison-Wesley.

Schurmann, Franz. 1968. *Ideology and Organization in Communist China*, 2nd edition. Berkeley and Los Angeles: University of California Press.

Segal, Adam. 2003. *Digital Dragon: High-Technology Enterprises in China*. Ithaca, NY: Cornell University Press.

Seymour, James D. and Richard Anderson. 1998. *New Ghosts, Old Ghosts: Prisons and Labor Reform Camps in China*. New York: M. E. Sharpe.

Shanghai Academy of Social Sciences. 1986. *Shanghai shehui kexue yuan lunwen xuen* [*Shanghai Academy of Social Sciences Papers*]. Shanghai: Shanghai Academy of Social Sciences Press.

——. 1988. *Shanghai shehui kexue yuan lunwen xuen* [*Shanghai Academy of Social Sciences Papers*]. Shanghai: Shanghai Academy of Social Sciences Press.

——. 1990. *Shanghai shehui kexue yuan lunwen xuen* [*Shanghai Academy of Social Sciences Papers*]. Shanghai: Shanghai Academy of Social Sciences Press.

——. 1992. *Shanghai shehui kexue yuan lunwen xuen* [*Shanghai Academy of Social Sciences Papers*]. Shanghai: Shanghai Academy of Social Sciences Press.

——. 1994a. *Shanghai shehui kexue yuan lunwen xuen* [*Shanghai Academy of Social Sciences Papers*]. Shanghai: Shanghai Academy of Social Sciences Press.

——. 1994b. *Shanghai jingji nianjian 1994* [*Economic Yearbook of Shanghai 1994*]. Shanghai: Shanghai Economic Yearbook Department.

——. 1994c. *Xiangzhen qiye yunxing jizhi yanjiu* [*The Institutional Structure of TVEs*]. Shanghai: Shanghai Academy of Social Sciences Press.

——. 1994d. *Chengshi jinbu, qiye fazhan he zhongguo xiandaihua* [*Urban Progress, Business Development, and China's Modernization*]. Shanghai: Shanghai Academy of Social Sciences Press.

——. 1995. *Shanghai kaifang shiwu nian* [*Fifteen Years of Economic Development in Shanghai*]. Shanghai: Shanghai Academy of Social Sciences Press.

Shanghai Foreign Investment Commission. 1995. *Guide to Foreign Investment in China*. Shanghai: Shanghai Foreign Investment Commission.

Shanghai Municipal Statistical Bureau. 1990. *Shanghai tongji nianjian 1990* [*Statistical Yearbook of Shanghai 1990*]. Shanghai: Chinese Statistics Publishing House of the Shanghai Municipal Statistical Bureau.

——. 1991. *Shanghai tongji nianjian 1991* [*Statistical Yearbook of Shanghai 1991*]. Shanghai: Chinese Statistics Publishing House of the Shanghai Municipal Statistical Bureau.

——. 1993. *Shanghai tongji nianjian 1993* [*Statistical Yearbook of Shanghai 1993*]. Shanghai: Chinese Statistics Publishing House of the Shanghai Municipal Statistical Bureau.

——. 1994. *Shanghai tongji nianjian 1994* [*Statistical Yearbook of Shanghai 1994*]. Shanghai: Chinese Statistics Publishing House of the Shanghai Municipal Statistical Bureau.

Shanghai Reform Collections Office. 1994. *Shanghai jingji tizhi gaige 1989–1993* [*Shanghai Economic Institutional Reform Yearbook 1989–1993*]. Shanghai: Shanghai Reform Collections Office.

Shanghai Stock Exchange (SSEa). 2005. *Shanghai Stock Exchange Factbook*, 2004. Shanghai, China.

Shao, Chongzhu, ed. 1998. *Zhong gong fan tan da an zhong an* [*Big Cases and Serious Cases in the Chinese Communists' Fight against Corruption*]. Hong Kong: Xiafeier.

Shao, Min, XiaoyanTang, Yuanhuang Zhang, and Wen Li. 2006. "City Clusters in China: Air and Surface Water Pollution." *Frontiers in Ecology and the Environment* 4(7): 353–361.

Shen, Tong. 1990. *Almost a Revolution*. Boston, MA: Houghton Mifflin.

Shenzhen Stock Exchange (SSEb). 2005. *Shenzhen Stock Exchange Factbook*. Shenzhen, China.

Shi, Tianjin. 1997. *Political Participation in Beijing*. Cambridge, MA: Harvard University Press.

Shi, Yizheng. 1998. *Chinese Firms and Technology in the Reform Era*. London: Routledge.

Shih, Victor C. 2008. *Factions and Finance in China: Elite Conflict and Inflation*. New York: Cambridge University Press.

Shue, Vivienne. 1988. *The Reach of the State: Sketches of the Chinese Body Politic*. Stanford, CA: Stanford University Press.

Sik, Endre. 1994. "Network Capital in Capitalist, Communist, and Post-Communist Societies." *International Contributions to Labor Studies* 4: 73–70.

——. 2000. "The Bad, the Worse and the Worst: Guesstimating the Level of Corruption." Paper presented to the Princeton University–CEU Joint Conference on Corruption, Budapest, April.

Silva, Beverlee, Sarah Babcock, and Trudy Caraballo. 2011. "China: Environmental Compliance Abroad: the China Conundrum." Alston & Bird LLP.

Singer, Joseph. 1982. "The Legal Rights Debate in Analytical Jurisprudence from Bentham to Hohfeld." *Wisconsin Law Review*: 980–1059.

——. 1988. "The Reliance Interest in Property." *Stanford Law Review* 40(3): 611–751.

Siu, Helen. 1989. "Socialist Peddlers and Princes in a Chinese Market Town." *American Ethnologist* 16(2): 196–212.

Smith, Adam. 1789. *An Inquiry into the Nature and Causes of the Wealth of Nations*, reprint. New York: Random House, 1994.

Smith, Craig. 2001. "AOL Joins Chinese Venture, Gaining a Crucial Foothold: A Deal to Develop Services for the Internet." *New York Times*, June 12.

Smyth, R. L., Zhai, Q., Hu, W. 2001. "Restructuring China's Large-Scale State-Owned Enterprises: A Case Study of the Fushun Petrochemical Company." *Post-Communist Economies* 13(2): 243–261.

Solinger, Dorothy. 1999a. "Chinese Floating Population." In *The Paradox of China's Post-Mao Reforms*, ed. Merle Goldman and Roderick MacFarquhar. Cambridge, MA: Harvard University Press.

——. 1999b. *Contesting Citizenship in Urban China: Peasant Migrants, the State, and the Logic of the Market*. Berkeley and Los Angeles: University of California Press.

Solomon, Richard. 1971. *Mao's Revolution and Chinese Political Culture*. Berkeley and Los Angeles: University of California Press.

—— 1999. *Chinese Negotiating Behavior: Pursuing Interests through "Old Friends."* Washington, DC: United States Institute of Peace Press.

Sorensen, Aage B. 1994. "Firms, Wages, and Incentives." In *Handbook of Economic Sociology*, ed. Neil J. Smelser and Richard Swedberg. Princeton, NJ: Princeton University Press, pp. 504–528.

Spar, Debora. 1993. "China (A): The Great Awakening." *Harvard Business School Case* 9-794-019.

Sparling, Samuel E. 1906. *Introduction to Business Organization*. New York: Macmillan.

Spence, Jonathan. 1999. *The Search for Modern China*. New York: W.W. Norton.

Stanway, David. 2011. "China Says Environment Still Suffering Growth Pains." Reuters. www.reuters.com

Stark, David. 1992. "Path Dependence and Privatization Strategies in Eastern Europe." *Eastern European Politics and Societies* 6: 17–54.

——. 1996. "Recombinant Property in East European Capitalism." *American Journal of Sociology* 101: 993–1027.

Stark, David and Victor Nee. 1989. *Remaking the Economic Institutions of Socialism*. Stanford, CA: Stanford University Press.

State Statistical Bureau (SSB). 1994. *Zhongguo tongji nianjian, 1994* [*Statistical Yearbook of China, 1994*]. Beijing: Statistical Publishing House of China.

State Statistical Bureau's City Social Survey Team. 1990. *Zhongguo chengshi tongji nianjian* [*Statistical Yearbook of Chinese Cities 1990*]. Beijing: Chinese Statistical Publishing House.

Steinfeld, Edward. 1998. *Forging Industrial Reform in China: The Fate of State-Owned Industry*. New York: Cambridge University Press.

Stiglitz, Joseph E. 1992. "The Design of Financial Systems for the Newly Emerging Democracies of Eastern Europe." In *The Emergence of Market Economies in Eastern Europe*, ed. Christopher Clague and Gordon C. Rausser. Cambridge, MA: Blackwell, pp. 161–184.

Stiglitz, Joseph E. and A. Weiss. 1981. "Credit Rationing in Markets with Imperfect Information." *American Economic Review* 71(3): 393–410.

Strand, David. 1990). "Protest in Beijing: Civil Society and Public Sphere in China," *Problems of Communism* 34: 1–19.

Su, Si-jin. 1994. "Hybrid Organizational Forms in South China: 'One Firm, Two Systems.'" In *The Economic Transformation of South China: Reform and Development in the Post-Mao Era*, ed. Thomas P. Lyons and Victor Nee. Ithaca, NY: Cornell University East Asia Program, pp. 199–213.

Sutton, John R., Frank Dobbin, John W. Meyer, and W. Richard Scott. 1994. "The Legalization of the Workplace." *American Journal of Sociology* 99: 944–971.

Szelényi, Iván. 1978. "Social Inequalities in State Socialist Redistributive Economies." *International Journal of Comparative Sociology* 19: 63–87.

———. 1983. *Urban Inequalities under State Socialism*. Oxford: Oxford University Press.

———. 1988. *Socialist Entrepreneurs: Embourgeoisement in Rural Hungary*. Madison: University of Wisconsin Press.

———. 1989. "Eastern Europe in Transition." In *Remaking the Economic Institutions of Socialism: China and Eastern Europe*, ed. Victor Nee and David Stark. Stanford, CA: Stanford University Press, pp. 208–232.

Taizhou Property Rights Reform Leadership Group. 1994. *Chanquan Gaige [Property Rights Reform]*. Taizhou, China: Taizhou Economic Reforms Commission.

Tanner, Murray Scot. 1994. "The Erosion of Communist Party Control over Lawmaking in China." *China Quarterly* 138: 381–403.

———. 1995. "How a Bill Becomes a Law in China: Stages and Processes in Lawmaking." *China Quarterly* 141: 39–64.

———. 1999. "The National People's Congress." In *The Paradox of China's Post-Mao Reforms*, ed. Goldman and MacFarquhar. Cambridge, MA: Harvard University Press.

Torbert, Preston M. 1987. "Contract Law in the People's Republic of China." In *Foreign Trade, Investment, and the Law in the People's Republic of China*, ed. Michael J. Moser. New York: Oxford University Press, pp. 321–342.

———. 1994. "Broadening the Scope of Investment." *China Business Review* 21(3): 48–55.

Tsang, Mun C. 1996. "The Financial Reform of Basic Education in China." *Economics of Education Review* 15(4): 429.

———. 2000. "Education and National Development in China since 1949: Oscillating Policies and Enduring Dilemmas." *China Review*.

Tsai, Kellee S. 2007. *Capitalism Without Democracy: The Private Sector in Contemporary China*. Ithaca, NY: Cornell University Press.

Tsui, Anne S. and Jing-lih Larry Farh. 1997. "Where Guanxi Matters: Relational Demography and Guanxi in the Chinese Context." *Work and Occupations* 24(1): 56–79.

Unger, Jonathan. 1996. "Bridges: Private Business, the Chinese Government, and the Rise of New Associations." *China Quarterly* 147: 795–819.

Unger, Jonathan and Anita Chan. 1995. "China, Corporatism, and the East Asian Model." *Australian Journal of Chinese Affairs* 33: 29–53.

———. 1996. "Corporatism in China: A Developmental State in an East Asian Context." In *China after Socialism: In the Footsteps of Eastern Europe or East Asia*, ed. Jonathan Unger. Armonk, NY: M. E. Sharpe.

United Nations Development Programme (UNDP). (2001) *United Nations Development Programme*. New York: United Nations.

United States Congress. 2001. *The Report of the Select Committee on U.S. National Security and Military/Commercial Concerns with the People's Republic of China*. United States Congress, Christopher Cox. Washington, DC.

Vogel, Ezra. 1989. *One Step Ahead in China*. Cambridge, MA: Harvard University Press.

Wakeman, Frederic, Jr. 1975. *The Fall of Imperial China*. New York: Free Press.

Walder, Andrew. 1986a. *Communist Neo-Traditionalism: Work and Authority in Chinese Industry*. Berkeley and Los Angeles: University of California Press.

———. 1986b. "The Informal Dimension of Enterprise Financial Reforms." In *China's Economy Looks Toward the Year 2000, Vol. 1: The Four Modernizations*, ed. Joint Economic Committee. Washington, DC: Government Printing Office, pp. 630–645.

———. 1989a. "Factory and Manager in an Era of Reform." *China Quarterly* 118: 242–264.

———. 1989b. "The Political Sociology of the Beijing Upheaval of 1989." *Problems of Communism* 38: 30–40.

———. 1991. "Workers, Managers, and the State: The Reform Era and the Political Crisis of 1989." *China Quarterly* 127: 467–492.

———. 1992a. "Property Rights and Stratification in Socialist Redistributive Economies." *American Sociological Review* 57: 524–539.

———. 1992b. "Local Bargaining Relationships and Urban Industrial Finance." In *Bureaucracy, Politics, and Decision-Making in Post-Mao China*, ed. Kenneth G. Lieberthal and David M. Lampton. Berkeley and Los Angeles: University of California Press, pp. 308–333.

———. 1994a. "Corporate Organization and Local Government Property Rights in China." In *Changing Political Economies: Privatization in Post-Communist and Reforming Communist States*, ed. Vedat Milor. Boulder, CO: Lynn Reinner, pp. 53–66.

———. 1994b. "The Decline of Communist Power: Elements of a Theory of Institutional Change." *Theory and Society* 23: 297–323.

———. 1995a. "Local Governments as Industrial Firms: An Organizational Analysis of China's Transitional Economy." *American Journal of Sociology* 101: 263–301.

———. 1995b. "Career Mobility and the Communist Political Order." *American Sociological Review* 60: 309–328.

———. 1995c. "The Quiet Revolution from Within: Economic Reform as a Source of Political Decline." In *The Waning of the Communist State*, ed. Andrew Walder. Berkeley and Los Angeles: University of California Press, pp. 1–24.

———. 1995d. "China's Transition Economy: Interpreting Its Significance." *China Quarterly* 144: 963–979.

———. ed. 1995e. *The Waning of the Communist State: Economic Origins of Political Decline in China and Hungary*. Berkeley and Los Angeles: University of California Press.

———. 1996. "Markets and Inequality in Transitional Economies: Toward Testable Theories." *American Journal of Sociology* 4: 1060–1073.

———. 2004. "The Party Elite and China's Trajectory of Change." *China: An International Journal* 2(2): 189–209.

Walder, Andrew and Xiaoxia Gong. 1991. "Workers in the Tiananmen Protests: The Politics of the Beijing Workers' Autonomous Federation." *Australian Journal of Chinese Affairs* 29: 1–29.

Walder, Andrew, Zhou Lu, Peter M. Blau, Danching Ruan, and Zhang Yuchun. 1989. "The 1986 Survey of Work and Social Life in Tianjin, China: Aims, Methods, and Documentation." *Working Paper Series*. Cambridge, MA: Harvard University Department of Sociology, Center for Research on Politics and Social Organization.

Wang, Junmin, Doug Guthrie, and Zhixing Xiao. 2012. "Multiple Principals, Ownership Concentration and Profitability in China's Publicly Traded Companies."

Wang, Shaoguang. 1995. "The Rise of the Regions: Fiscal Reform and the Decline of Central State Capacity in China." In *The Waning of the Communist State: Economic Origins of Political Decline in China and Hungary*, ed. Andrew Walder. Berkeley and Los Angeles: University of California Press.

Wang, Shaoguang and Hu Angang. 2001. *The Chinese Economy in Crisis: State Capacity and Tax Reform*. Armonk, NY: M. E. Sharpe.

Wang, Wallace Wen-Yeu. 1992. "Reforming State Enterprises in China: The Case for Redefining Enterprise Operating Rights." *Journal of Chinese Law* 6: 89–136.

Wank, David. 1995a. "Civil Society in Communist China? Private Business and Political Alliance, 1989." In *Civil Society: Theory, History, Comparison*, ed. John A. Hall. Cambridge: Polity Press, pp. 56–73.

——. 1995b. "Bureaucratic Patronage and Private Business: Changing Networks of Power in Urban China." In *The Waning of the Communist State: Economic Origins of Political Decline in China and Hungary*, ed. Andrew Walder. Berkeley and Los Angeles: University of California Press, pp. 153–183.

——. 1996. "The Institutional Process of Market Clientelism: Guanxi and Private Business in a South China City." *China Quarterly* 147: 820–838.

——. 1999. *Commodifying Communism: Business, Trust, and Politics in a Chinese City*. New York: Cambridge University Press.

——. 2002. "Business-State Clientelism in China: Decline or Evolution?" In *Social Connections in China: Institutions, Culture, and the Changing Nature of Guanxi*, edited by Thomas Gold, Doug Guthrie, and David Wank. New York: Cambridge University Press.

Watts, Jonathan. 2010. "China resorts to blackouts in pursuit of energy efficiency." The Guardian. www.guardian.co.uk

——. 2011. "Greenpeace report links western firms to Chinese river polluters." The Guardian. www.guardian.co.uk

Weber, Max. 1968. *The Religion of China: Confucianism and Taoism*, transl. and ed. Hans H. Gerth. New York: Free Press.

——. 1976. *The Protestant Ethic and the Spirit of Capitalism*, transl. Talcott Parsons with an introduction by Anthony Giddens. New York: Charles Scribner's Sons.

Weiss, Warner and Franz Mauthner. 2011. *Solar Heat Worldwide: Markets and Contribution to the Energy Supply 2009*. Paris: International Energy Agency.

Wen, X. and S. Ming. 2009. China's execs sweating over stock options: After nine years and billions of yuan in cash-ins, China is reviewing stock options for state-owned company chiefs. Available at Caijing.com.cn.

Westney, D. Eleanor. 1987. *The Transfer of Western Organizational Patterns to Meiji Japan*. Cambridge, MA: Harvard University Press.

White, Gordon. 1996. "The Dynamics of Civil Society in Post-Mao China." In *The Individual and the State in China*, ed. Brian Hook. Oxford: Clarendon Press.

White, Gordon, Jude A. Howell, and Shang Xiaoyuan. 1996. In *Search of Civil Society: Market Reform and Social Change in Contemporary China*. Oxford: Clarendon Press.

White, Harrison C. 1981. "Where do Markets Come From?" *American Journal of Sociology* 87: 517–547.

Whitley, Richard. 1990. "East Asian Enterprise Structures and the Comparative Analysis of Business Organizations." *Organization Studies* 8: 125–147.

——. 1992a. *Business Systems in East Asia: Firms, Markets, and Societies*. London: Sage.

Whitley, Richard, ed. 1992b. *European Business Systems: Firms and Markets in Their National Context*. London: Sage.

——. 1992. "Urban China: A Civil Society in the Making?" In *State and Society in China: The Consequences of Reform*, ed. Arthur Lewis Rosenbaum. Boulder, CO: Westview.

Whitley, R., J. Henderson, L. Czaben, and G. Langgel. 1996. "Trust and Contractual Relations in an Emerging Capitalist Economy: The Changing Trading Relationships of Ten Large Hungarian Enterprises." *Organization Studies* 17(3): 397–420.

Whyte, Martin K. 1993. "Deng Xiaoping: The Social Reformer." *China Quarterly* 135: 513–533.

Whyte, Martin K. and William L. Parish. 1984. *Urban Life in Contemporary China*. Chicago: University of Chicago Press.

Wiemer, Calla. 1992. "Price Reform and Structural Change: Distributional Impediments to Allocative Gains." *Modern China* 18: 171–196.

Wijnberger, Sweder van. 1992. "Intertemperol Speculation, Shortages and the Political Economy of Price Reform." *Economic Journal* 102: 1396–1406.

Williams, Ian. 2004. "China-U.S.: Double Bubbles in Danger of Colliding." *Asia Times*, January 23.

Wilson, Scott. 1997. "The Cash Nexus and Social Networks: Mutual Aid and Gifts in Contemporary Shanghai Villages." *China Journal* 37: 91–112.

Wolf, Alexander, David Fleming, and Jeff Lilley. 1995. "The China Syndrome: Chinese Athletes are Increasingly Subject to the Ills and Temptations that Afflict Sports in the West." *Sports Illustrated*, October 16.

Wong, Christine. 1991. "Central–Local Relations in an Era of Fiscal Decline: The Paradox of Fiscal Decentralization in Post-Mao China." *China Quarterly* 128: 691–715.

——. 1992. "Fiscal Reform and Local Industrialization: The Problematic Sequencing of Reform in Post-Mao China." *Modern China* 18: 197–227.

——. 1997. *Financing Local Government in the People's Republic of China*. New York: Oxford University Press.

——. 2002. "China's Provincial Public Expenditure Review." Paper presented at the World Bank Workshop on Decentralization and Intergovernmental Fiscal Reform, Washington DC, May 13–15, 2002.

Wong, Christine, Christopher Heady, and Wing Thye Woo. 1995. *Fiscal Management and Economic Reform in the People's Republic of China*. Oxford: Oxford University Press.

Wong, Desmond. 2004. "It's High Noon in China: Do You Know Where Your Customers and Competitors Are?" Global Automotive Center, Ernst and Young, LLP. SCORE Retrieval File No. QQ419, CSG No. 03090463870.

Wong, John and William T. Liu. 1999. *The Mystery of China's Falun Gong: Its Rise and Its Sociological Implications*. Singapore: World Scientific Publishing and Singapore University Press.

Wong, Kar-Yiu. 1992. "Inflation, Corruption, and Income Distribution: The Recent Price Reform in China." *Journal of Macroeconomics* 14: 105–123.

Woo, Wing Thye. 1997. "Improving the Performance of Enterprises in Transition Economies." in *Economies in Transition: Comparing Asia and Eastern Europe*, ed/ Wing Thye Woo, Stephen Parker, and Jeffrey Sachs. Cambridge, MA: MIT Press, pp. 299–324

——. "The Real Reasons for China's Growth." *China Journal* 41: 115–137.

Woo, Wing Thye, Stephen Parker, and Jeffrey Sachs. 1997. *Economies in Transition: Comparing Asia and Eastern Europe*. Cambridge, MA: MIT Press.

Woo, Wing Thye, Wen Hai, Yibiao Jin, and Gang Fan. 1993. "How Successful Has Chinese Enterprise Reform Been? Pitfalls in Opposite Biases and Focus." *Journal of Comparative Economics* 18: 410–437.

World Bank. 1997. *China 2020: Sharing Rising Incomes: Disparities in China*. Washington, DC: World Bank.

——. 2006 *Water Quality Management—Policy and Institutional Considerations*. Washington, DC: The World Bank.

——. 2010. *China Military Spending*. Washington, DC, The World Bank. http://search.world-bank.org/data?qterm=china%20military%20spending&language=EN

——. 2010. *US Military Spending*. Washington, DC, The World Bank. http://search.worldbank.org/data?qterm=united+states+military+spending&language=EN&format=

World Bank and SEPA. 2007. *Cost of Pollution in China—Economic Estimates of Physical Damages*. Washington, DC: The World Bank.

World Health Organization. 2005. "Air Quality Guidelines for Particulate Matter, Ozone, Nitrogen Dioxide and Sulfur Dioxide." Geneva: Geneva: World Health Organization.

——. 2008. *Air Quality and Health*. Geneva: World Health Organization. http://www.who.int/mediacentre/factsheets/fs313/en/index.html

——. 2010. "Exposure to Air Pollution: A Major Public Health Concern." Geneva: World Health Organization. http://www.who.int/ipcs/features/air_pollution.pdf

World in Figures. 1999. New York: John Wiley and Sons.

World in Figures. 2010. New York: John Wiley and Sons.

Wu, M. 2002. *A Restructuring of the Chinese Petroleum Sector*. Cambridge, MA: Massachusetts Institute of Technology.

Xie, Yu and Emily Hannum. 1996. "Regional Variation in Earnings Inequality in Reform-Era Urban China." *American Journal of Sociology* 101: 950–992.

Xin, K. and J. Pearce. 1996. "Guanxi: Connections as Substitutes for Formal Institutional Support." *Academy of Management Journal* 39(6): 1641–1658.

Yan, Yunxiang. 1996. *The Flow of Gifts: Reciprocity and Social Networks in a Chinese Village*. Palo Alto, CA: Stanford University Press.

Yang, Ailun, Rashid Kang, Xingmin Zhao, Xu Huang, Hanhua Zhou, Miaochan Su, Hongyuan Tang, and Fei Li. 2010. "The True Cost of Coal—An investigation into Coal Ash in China." Greenpeace.

Yang, C. K. 1959. *Chinese Communist Society: The Family and the Village*, Cambridge, MA: MIT Press.

Yang, Dali. 1990. "Patterns of China's Regional Development Strategy." *China Quarterly* 230–257.

——. 1991. "China Adjusts to the World Economy: The Political Economy of China's Coastal Development Strategy," *Public Affairs* 42–64.

Yang, Mayfair Mei-hui. 1989. "Between State and Society: The Construction of Corporateness in a Chinese Socialist Factory." *Australian Journal of Chinese Affairs* 22: 31–60.

——. 1994. *Gifts, Favors, and Banquets: The Art of Social Relationships in China*. Ithaca, NY: Cornell University Press.

——. 2002. "The Resilience of Guanxi and Its New Deployments." *China Quarterly* 170: 459–476.

Yeh, K. C. 1992. "Macroeconomic Issues in China in the 1990s." *China Quarterly* 131: 501–544.

Yeung, Henry Wai-Chung. 1997. "Business Networks and Transnational Corporations: A Study of Hong Kong Firms in the ASEAN Region." *Economic Geography* 73(1): 1–25.

Yeung, I. and R. Tung. 1996. "Achieving Business Success in Confucian Societies: The Importance of Guanxi (Connections)." *Organizational Dynamics* 25(2): 54–65.

Zhang Wenxiang and Zhen Fazhi. 1991. *Zengqing qiye huoli: baijai zhengming ji [Building Enterprise Participation: Letting One Hundred Flowers Bloom]*. Shanghai: Shanghai Academy of Social Sciences Press.

Zhang, XingYing, Peng Zhang, Yan Zhang, XiaoJing Li, and Hong Qiu. 2007. "The Trend, Season Cycle, and Sources of Tropospheric NO_2 over China During 1997–2006 Based on Satellite Measurement." *Science in China Series D: Earth Sciences* 50(12): 1877–1884.

Zhao, Chunsheng, Xuexi Tie, Geli Wang, Yu Qin, and Beicai Yang. 2006. "Analysis of Air Quality in Eastern China and Its Interaction with Other Regions of the World." *Journal of Atmospheric Chemistry* 55: 189–204.

Zhao, Dingxin. 1997. "Decline of Political Control in Chinese Universities and the Rise of the 1989 Chinese Student Movement." *Sociological Perspectives* 40: 159–182.

Zhou, Xueguang, 1993a. "Unorganized Interests and Collective Action in Communist China." *American Sociological Review* 58 (1): 54–73.

——. 1993b. "The Dynamics of Organizational Rules." *American Journal of Sociology* 98: 1134–1166.

Zhou, Xueguang, Nancy Brandon Tuma, and Phyllis Moen. 1997. "Institutional Change and Job-Shift Patterns in Urban China, 1949 to 1994." *American Sociological Review* 62: 339–365.

Zhu, Enjoyce. 2001. "China's Silicon Valley Ready to Take OFF." *Beijing Business*, June.

Zhu, F. D., X. M. Wang, D. J. Bennett, and K. G. Vaidya. 1995. "Technology Transfer under China's Economic Reforms: Business Environment and Success Factors." *Technology Management* 2(1): 2–17.

Zissis, Carin and Jayshee Bajoria. 2008. "China's Environmental Crisis." Council on Foreign Relations.

INDEX